ALL FALL
DOWN

by Donald Goddard

Also by Donald Goddard

JOEY
LAST DAYS OF DIETRICH BONHOEFFER
EASY MONEY

ALL FALL
One Man
DOWN
Against the Waterfront Mob

NYT **Times** BOOKS

364.106

N. Y. Times [c1980]

Published by TIMES BOOKS, a division of
Quadrangle/The New York Times Book Co., Inc.
Three Park Avenue, New York, N.Y. 10016

Published simultaneously in Canada by
Fitzhenry & Whiteside, Ltd., Toronto

Copyright © 1980 by Donald Goddard

All rights reserved. No part of this book may
be reproduced in any form or by any electronic
or mechanical means including information storage
and retrieval systems without permission in writing
from the publisher, except by a reviewer who may
quote brief passages in a review.

Library of Congress Cataloging in Publication Data

Goddard, Donald.
  All fall down.

  Includes index.
  1. Racketeering—Florida—Miami. 2. Teitelbaum,
Joe. 3. International Longshoremen's Association.
I. Title.
HD6490.R3G62 1980   364.1'067 [B]   80-5146
ISBN 0-8129-0938-0

Manufactured in the United States of America

To Natalie

Contents

ALL FALL DOWN

*"Go into the street and give one man
a lecture on morality, and another a
shilling, and see which will respect
you most."*
—SAMUEL JOHNSON

Ring-a ring-a roses,
A pocket full of posies,
A-tishoo, a-tishoo,
All Fall Down.
—SEVENTEENTH-CENTURY CHILDREN'S PLAGUE SONG

Prologue

HEROES are out of style. America loves a winner.

Heroes reproach with higher standards of behavior. Winners excite with higher standards of performance. Heroes go against self-interest. Winners never do. Winners are cost-effective.

Joe Teitelbaum is a hero.

In the home of the smart and land of the worldly-wise, heroes can still get away with it if they look like Robert Redford and mind their own business, but not if they are short, Jewish, and their business is the shipping business. Then, according to conscience or complicity, they are patronized, belittled, dismissed as suitable subjects for psychoanalysis, or just ignored.

Joe Teitelbaum is short, Jewish, and in the shipping business.

But he is also a winner, which may make a difference in the end. Defying self-interest, he took on the entrenched bureaucracy of America's oldest and toughest criminal enterprise, and he won.

It was a most unlikely victory, and they may have to kill him for it.

For 65 years, the International Longshoremen's Association has controlled the business of the Atlantic and Gulf coast ports as a front for organized crime. For most of that time, the racket bosses of the waterfront have collected a private tax on the nation's import/export trade of up to 5 percent of its wholesale value. Say, fifteen thousand million dollars a year added to the cost of doing business on the docks and passed along to the consumer. Or, to put it another way, a contribution of $75 a year by every man, woman, and child in the United States toward the upkeep of the mob.

For 65 years, nobody did much about it. A handful of old-timers were ceremonially sacrificed on the altars of reform in the 1950's (without it hurting them much), but behind the scenes, the march of crime continued on to Miami and Joe Teitelbaum, who was already a winner and could

3

then have made it bigger still. He could have become the richest man in shipping, an American Onassis.

Instead, in secret, and in constant danger of his life, he led the Federal government through the ILA's defenses, and for more than a year, worked undercover with its agents to undermine the whole crooked edifice from inside.

Some of it has toppled already—George Barone's organization in Miami, and Anthony Scotto's in New York. When (or, perhaps, *if*) the rest of it falls, the tremors will be felt in the White House, the United States Senate, the House of Representatives, the federal judiciary, sundry Governors' mansions, in the legislatures and judiciaries of all the maritime states from Maine to Texas, and in the boardrooms of American business, finance, and industry.

This has not made Joe Teitelbaum popular.

It has not even made him well-known, although if Americans truly resent paying taxes, they should be raising statues to him in public squares from Concord to Sausalito. Rather, it has led people to find fault with his character, and certainly, if a blameless life and purity of heart are added to the looks of Robert Redford, then Joe Teitelbaum may have trouble qualifying as a folk hero.

But nobody's perfect, and the smart and worldly-wise will do well not to invoke standards of judgment that could be turned against them. America's principles have become very accommodating lately. As is said to be the case with government, a country probably gets the heroes it deserves—although it is not yet clear that America deserves Joe Teitelbaum, for it has not treated him well, and may yet permit him to be killed.

This is his story, as he remembers it, and as federal case files, unpublished wiretap transcripts, intelligence data, grand jury testimony, and various eyewitnesses bear him out. . . .

1
Territorial Demands

By midday, it was hot enough in the ship's forward hold to bake bread. She was a 1,500-ton freighter in the Central American trade. Bound for Miami with a badly stowed cargo of lumber, cowhides, and fishmeal, she had been hit by a squall in the Yucatan Channel. When the hatch covers came off, it looked as though a bomb had exploded below decks. Two hours later, they could smell her in the Everglades.

Working on the apron of the Eagle Shipping terminal, Joe Teitelbaum had got wind of her coming as soon as she steamed in through Government Cut. So had the port director. With 10,000 cruise passengers expected over the weekend, he had asked Eagle, as the ship's agent and stevedore, to do him a favor and get that shit-bucket out of there before the rush started. Put on his mettle, Joe had spent all night in the hold with a gang of longshoremen, trying to clear out the mess.

It was the heat that bothered him now, not the stench. On deck for a breather, he sat propped against the rail, upwind from the open hatch, drinking Coke from a can and fanning himself with his hard hat. Normally dark as stained wood from working in the sun, he was purple as a plum. When his brother-in-law, Ben Mussary, found him there, he bent to see if he was all right, but straightened up quickly, pulling a face.

"Boy," he said, coming around to Joe's windward side. "How can you stand yourself?"

Joe scythed at him with his hat, and Ben hopped out of range.

"Gus says to remind you about the union meeting."

"Okay." Joe had promised his father he would cover it for him. He held out a hand and Ben pulled him to his feet.

"You got two gangs working now?"

"Yeah. We cleaned out most of the crap. They should finish this off in four, five hours." Joe grinned wearily. "Unless you fuck up as usual."

Not needing to evade the hugely inaccurate kick Ben aimed at the seat of his shorts, he waved to the bridge, clumped down the gangway, and, like a small-town mayor greeting his constituents, strutted the length of the dock to his car, swapping cheerful obscenities with the longshoremen and forklift drivers who pretended to recoil or swoon, holding their noses, as he passed.

They all knew Joe. He always made them smile. Barely five foot five, jaunty, muscled like a bantam but thickening in the middle, he was the port's resident celebrity, and, for most people's money, the best damn stevedore in the South, even if he *was* a Jew.

Two hours later, smelling only of Brut, and wondering what Fat Freddy wanted *this* time, he arrived at the Caribbean Hotel, Miami Beach, for what was supposed to be the opening session of a new round of bargaining talks with the union on the question of gang sizes. But Fred R. Field, Jr., general organizer of the International Longshoremen's Association, was not in a bargaining mood. He had flown down with a delegation from ILA headquarters in New York to install a new labor boss in place of Judge Henderson, former president of Local 1416, Miami.

At the coffee break, Fat Freddy invited Joe to join him.

"It's time you and me talked a little business," he said, trying to wedge himself in a chair too small for him. Squeezed upwards, the rolls of flesh pushed his arms out from his sides.

"Business?" said Joe. "I'll be lucky if I *got* a business after you guys get through."

"Bullshit. So labor's gonna cost a little more. Figure it into your rates and pass it on. Fucking owners'll pay."

"Uh-uh. I can't charge New York prices, Fred. I'll lose business. We're hurting already."

"Bullshit. I seen the figures. You're getting rich down here." He squirmed ponderously. "They musta made these chairs for fucking midgets."

"Fred, this is Florida. It's not the same."

"Yeah? I didn't know that. You mean, they have smaller fucking chairs?"

"I mean, in New York, you got the shipping lines by the balls. You can hit 'em all you want, and they gotta pay. But not here. You push up the rates in Miami, and you'll push out the work."

"You trying to tell *me* about the shipping business?" Settled at last, Fat Freddy looked around, his eyes hooded with boredom. "There's gonna be some changes in this fucking port."

"Fred, all I'm trying to tell you is, it's a right-to-work state, and we got a lot of one-boat, island lines down here. You squeeze 'em too hard, and they're all gonna move to non-union ports."

"Fine," said Field. "Let 'em. We'll take care of that later. Right now, we're gonna need the space for the new business we got coming in."

"Yeah?" Joe looked at him curiously. "That what you wanna talk to me about?"

Field stared, unsmiling, at a trio of Joe's fellow shipping executives, who seemed intent on joining them. They sheered off as though the thought had never crossed their minds.

"I hear you're pretty good," he said.

"The best," Joe agreed.

"And pretty big. For Miami."

"I got about half the stevedoring in the port, yeah. And some agency." He was ready to take offense. "Three hundred on the payroll. That's pretty big."

"You been lucky, then. No labor troubles or nothing."

"No," said Joe. "Not lucky." He wasn't sure what Field was getting at, but whatever it was, he didn't like it. "I got nothing I didn't work for. Nothing lucky about it. I work my *ass* off. *And* I treat the men right. Ask 'em. The union's got no beef with me."

"Did I say that?" Fat Freddy appealed to some invisible referee. "Did I? You're not hurting, right? That's all I'm saying."

"No, I'm not hurting. Not yet."

"Right. You got something to protect, then. And that's why we got to get together. We got the fucking future to consider." He rubbed his chin reflectively. "Is there someplace we can talk?"

"We're talking now."

Field nodded, humoring him. "Someplace private. I don't want a lot of fucking gossip. You know what I mean?"

Joe didn't know. But Field was a top man in the union, and there was no point inviting more trouble than he sensed on the way already.

"You wanna go fishing?"

Fat Freddy shrugged, pushing out his lip. "Sure."

"Okay. Friend of mine owns a charter boat. When do you want to do it?"

"Thursday." He rocked vainly back and forth, trying to get up. "You wanna pull this fucking chair off my ass?"

At thirty-four, Joe Teitelbaum had spent enough years on the waterfront to know the score. Transportation is to business what circulation is to the body. A powerful union like the Teamsters or the Longshoremen has only to apply its thumbs to a pressure point and sooner or later, the firms affected must give in or die. A manufacturer can, if he chooses, build up his inventory against a showdown with labor and make a fight of it, but a stevedore has nothing to sell once his men walk off the pier.

Unlike some employers on the Miami waterfront, Joe had seen the changes coming and decided he could live with them. Fat Freddy was right. In the end, the shipowners would have to pay. He might lose a few small accounts to unorganized firms on the Miami River, but the city's new Dodge Island seaport was already bringing in bigger steamship lines and larger vessels. For his part, Joe had no objection to higher wage scales provided every employer had to pay them. If that was all the New York union bosses had in mind, he foresaw no particular problem. But driving over the Causeway Thursday morning to pick up Fat Freddy, he had a feeling there was something else, and it did not go away when he reached the hotel. Waiting with Field in the lobby were William Murphy, a vice president of the International, his brother Francis Murphy, and Benny Astorino from Brooklyn, who was dressed to go fishing in a business suit.

They made an oddly assorted group, boarding Shelley Spiegel's *Playmate* at the Fifth Street pier: Joe, perky as a fighting cock; Astorino, neat as a ferret; Fat Freddy, already pink and sweating with exertion; and the Murphys, as grossly built as Field, but harder, like rhinos next to a hippo. Except for Joe, who liked to get up early, it was also a silent group.

About an hour out, Shelley hauled his own considerable bulk up to the flying bridge, and Joe went back to see how his guests were getting along. Fat Freddy was sitting in the right-hand trolling chair, next to Francis Murphy, who had obviously been fishing before. His brother Willy sat hunched at his feet, chomping on a wet cigar. Joe perched on the transom, across from Astorino.

"Couldn't have picked a better day for it," he said cheerfully, squinting out across the blinding glitter to a stained glass-blue horizon. They were making just enough breeze to be comfortable, but the rail was too hot to touch. "You guys want a beer or something? We got plenty of stuff in the locker."

Astorino nodded, blotting his forehead carefully with a folded handkerchief.

"Why don't you take your coat off?" Joe suggested, signaling Phil the mate to bring drinks. "You'll be more comfortable."

Astorino stared, and Willy Murphy made a noise at the back of his throat that might have been a laugh. Each chose a can from the picnic ice chest that Phil brought up for them.

"Listen, tell the guy to go upstairs with the captain," said Astorino.

Joe hesitated, never good at taking orders. Then he smiled up at the mate, shading his eyes from the sun.

"Okay, Phil?" he said. "We're gonna talk business."

"Yeah," said Francis Murphy. "There's no fucking fish out here anyway. Tell him, find us some fucking fish."

"Hey, Shelley's the best there is," Joe said sharply. He raked through the ice for a can of soda, muttering to himself.

"You know, that's what they say about *you,* Joe." Astorino was so insincere it was insulting. "We hear a lotta good things. About Eagle. And your old man, Gus. And about your uncles and everything. A lotta good things. You really made a name for yourself, Joe."

"Yeah, we built a pretty good business, me and my family."

"That's what we heard. And it's growing, right? With Dodge Island opening up now, who knows how big you're gonna get? With the right kind of help."

"Help?"

"Yeah. Help. With the business."

Joe didn't know what he was talking about. "We're doing all right, Benny. We about doubled our size in five years."

"See?" said Astorino, as though Joe had just proved his point. "It's a whole new ballgame. This port's really gonna grow now. And if you wanna grow too, you're gonna need help. Stands to reason. You're gonna need new accounts. You're gonna need good labor. You know what you're gonna need? You're gonna need *muscle.*"

Joe looked at Fat Freddy, who seemed not to be listening. "I'm not sure I know what you mean," he said. "You just get me good labor, and I'll get the business. Don't worry about it."

"Look." Astorino smiled patiently. "You're an independent, right? That's good and that's bad. It's good because you got the personal touch, and you get to keep the money. It's bad because look what you're gonna be up against. You're gonna be up against the big guys now. The big stevedores who work in *all* the ports, okay? New York. Boston. Philly. New Orleans. Already they're working for these big steamship lines that are coming in here. They already got their business relationship, right? So who's gonna handle their ships in Miami? Ask yourself. You're a smart man. I don't have to draw you a picture. You're gonna need some help with a problem like that."

"I'm not worried." Joe took a leisurely pull at his Coke. "I'll whip their ass on price and service."

"It don't work that way, Joe. Not with the big guys."

"Listen, Benny. Miami's a clean port. The only muscle I'm gonna need is for handling cargo. *I'll* take care of the rest."

Astorino shook his head. "Well, you could have a problem there," he said sadly.

"Yeah?" Joe put down his can. "What kind of a problem?"

"Well, look what happened. There's a lot of unrest about. The men see guys on the New York waterfront getting a better break . . . You know how it is. You want labor peace down here, you're gonna have to work real close with the union. And I mean *close.*"

"Never had trouble before," Joe said. "My only beef with Judge Henderson was when he tried to tell me how many men I need. I'll pay the scale, but nobody's gonna tell me how to run my business."

"All right. It's up to you. Trouble with Henderson, his head got too big for his hat, but that don't mean he was wrong. Not about gang sizes."

"Well, we'll see." Joe was getting tired of this fencing. "Since Henderson left, they got nobody over there you can talk to anyway."

"We took care of that," said Willy Murphy unexpectedly. "We put a new nigger in."

"Right." Astorino waited with elaborate courtesy to see if Murphy had anything more to say, but that seemed to be all. "Like Willy says, these days we gotta give our black brothers a helping hand. So local boy makes good. Name of Cleveland Turner."

"Cleve Turner? *He's* your new president?"

"Yeah. You know him?"

"He used to drive a winch for me."

"Yeah? No trouble there, then. Not if you treat him right."

Joe slapped hands on knees and stood up. "Benny, if you got something to say to me, either come right out and say it, or I'm gonna show you guys how to catch fish."

Astorino shaded his eyes. "I just think it's nice when everything's friendly. I like it when everybody cooperates. You gotta show a little good faith in this world, Joe. We're gonna start a checkers' local down here. Local 1922? You musta heard about that."

"I heard." He sat down again, and stared out across the water. The breeze had freshened a little. Flecks of spray were blowing back and drying the moment they splashed the deck. "Won't affect us," he said. "We check all the cargo ourselves."

"You *do?*" Astorino could not have been more aghast if Joe had confessed to selling secrets to the Russians. "The men are not gonna like *that.*"

"Benny, what the fuck are you talking about? What's not to like all of a sudden? We always did it."

And as far as Joe was concerned, they always *would* do it. Checkers ran the port. No cargo could be received or released unless they signed it in or out, and no ship could be loaded or unloaded without a checker on the dock. For a stevedore, to surrender control of the checking was to surrender control of his pierside operations. A slow or dishonest checker could raise his costs out of sight or rob him blind.

"You're not listening to me, Joe. It's a new ballgame. I keep telling you. You wanna do business with 1416, you're gonna have to do business with 1922." Astorino smiled at him gently. "I mean, it's all ILA, right? We're all brothers. And we gotta look out for each other in this cruel world."

"Now *you're* not listening," said Joe, puzzled. "You wanna organize the checkers, be my guest. We don't employ any. I told you. Me and my relatives do all the checking."

"Then I guess we'll have to sign *you* up, won't we?" He looked at the others and shrugged slightly. "Look, I'm gonna have you meet George Barone, okay? George is a big man in the union. Real upper echelon. And he's come down here from New York to be the president of the checkers, so maybe *he* can show you how it's gonna be. Face it, Joe. You can't keep it all to yourself no more. The port's getting big, and we're coming in to stay."

Joe glanced at Field, who seemed to be asleep, and caught Willy Murphy's eye.

"He's right," Murphy said. He plucked the cigar from his mouth, inspected the sodden butt, and tossed it over the side. "You gotta share the wealth, Joe."

"No, I don't. And I don't have to agree we're going union with the checking. What's he gonna do if I don't?"

"Barone?" Murphy spat out bits of tobacco. "He takes 'em."

"I don't understand."

"What are you, stupid? The checkers. He just takes 'em. We put in our own."

They might have come from Mars for all the sense Joe could make of it. Then Francis Murphy hooked something, and as Joe glanced up at the bridge, Shelley cut the engines and the *Playmate* settled gently in the water.

Joe began preparing a line for himself. "Look, Benny," he said, "just lay it out for me, will you? What is it you guys really want?"

Astorino edged into the shade as the boat drifted around a point or two in the wind. Field was facing their way, but still showed no sign he was listening.

"Well, Joe, it's like I said. There's some big stuff coming in here. You got a good name, and you got no ties. If you come in with us now, we can make you the biggest."

"I *am* the biggest."

"I mean, on the whole Atlantic coast, Joe. You can have it all. The Gulf as well, maybe. Fred can get you all the accounts you want, and you'll have no trouble with labor. That I guarantee."

Joe eyed him, then went on baiting his hook. "And what do *I* have to do?"

"Show a little good faith," said Astorino, exasperated. "Do the right thing. Fred's got a big customer all lined up, ready to come in. Could be a million-dollar account. And it's all yours if you want it. Right, Fred?"

Field was watching Murphy try to gaff his fish, but might have nodded.

"See?" Astorino rested his case. "We can help *you,* if *you* work with us. All it takes is a little good faith."

"How little?"

"Well, I dunno. What would *you* say, Willy? Three thousand? Yeah. That'd show good faith. Give Freddy three aces, and he'll become your silent partner, more or less. All right? You understand what I'm talking about?"

"You're talking about three thousand dollars."

"That's it. For good faith."

Joe trailed out his line. They were all looking at him, except Field. "Well, I don't know," he said. "I'll have to think about it."

"Think about it? What kinda fuck answer is that? Three grand? That's nothing to you. You kidding me? You won't even feel it."

"Maybe not. But there's my old man to consider. He likes his cards dealt from the top."

"Well, don't tell him, for Chrissake." Astorino threw his beer can furiously over the side. "I mean, what the fuck *is* this? Here's a new account worth maybe a million dollars, and you're bitching about a stinking three thousand? Shit. Maybe we picked the wrong guy."

"Maybe we ought to talk to his old man," said Willy Murphy.

"No, I wouldn't do that," Joe said. "I told you. I'll think it over."

"Yeah, well . . ." Astorino subsided into the shade again, patting his face with his handkerchief. "Okay. Only you're not gonna turn us down, are you, Joe? Not after we put our cards on the table and everything."

"I'll think about it," he said, "and I'll let you know."

Willy Murphy muttered something to Field, who shrugged indifferently, and looked out to sea.

"Hey," said Murphy to his brother. "Get the fuck out of that chair. We wasted enough fucking time already."

With that, the four of them started kidding around as though Joe had ceased to exist. They also started to hook snapper. Before long, the intervals between cast and strike were so short that the fish might have been lining up to surrender—to everyone but Fat Freddy. After about an hour, he tangled his line with Willy Murphy's for the third time, unstrapped himself from the chair, and waddled unsteadily into the shade.

"Fuck it," he said.

"Fred's had enough," Astorino announced, his face the color of oiled bone. "He wants to go back."

Shelley Spiegel, who had come down from the bridge to join in the slaughter, looked at Joe inquiringly. They were both unwilling to leave before their luck ran out.

"Okay, Shelley," he sighed. "Take her in. Before they start climbing aboard and sink us."

Fat Freddy and the others were still ignoring him, but that was nothing. So they were looking to cover their expenses . . . No harm in that. And if they *did* have accounts in their pocket, they could talk about it when the time came.

Joe kept himself busy until minutes from the pier, helping Phil ice the fish and stow away the tackle. When the mate went forward to stand by the bow line, Astorino came over to Joe, buttoning his jacket.

"We'll grab a cab," he said. "I'll call you when I got it set up."

"Got what set up?"

"The meet with Barone. And don't forget what I told you. We're coming in to stay, so do yourself a favor. Be nice." He rubbed his fingers together, crinkling imaginary greenbacks.

"I'll let you know."

He watched them scramble onto the dock, and waved when they stopped to look back.

"What do you want me to do with the fish?"

"Stick 'em up your ass," said Willy Murphy. It was mid-afternoon before Joe realized that Benny Astorino had probably kept his coat on because he was packing a gun.

2

Open City

"Do I look naive to you?"

Mel Kessler surveyed him critically. "Yeah. You do a bit."

"I wasn't even nervous. Can you beat that? I didn't know enough to be nervous. I'm out there alone in the middle of the ocean with these fucking gangsters, and I'm telling Field to get lost."

"Well, you weren't exactly *alone,*" said Kessler, who was Joe's attorney as well as his oldest friend. "There was Shelley and the mate."

"You think that'd make any difference to guys like that? If they wanted to do something? Let me tell you about the Murphys. I remembered who they were after we got back. *After,* right? They killed some union guy in Hoboken in front of witnesses, and then they beat the rap. That's what Astorino meant by muscle. And I'm just dumb enough to go fishing with 'em."

Kessler smiled. "Listen, with Field there, it was probably the safest place in Miami. They were just feeling you out, that's all."

"Okay. But why? What do they want? I'll tell you something about Field. United Brands—companies like that—pay that guy a tax on every fucking banana they ship to this country. He's a heavyweight. People get in his way, and you don't hear about them anymore."

Kessler had long ago learned to allow for Joe's colorful approach to life. He had a tendency, sometimes, to overstate the case in his urgency to convey the truth as he saw it, but the truth was always there. For years after they left high school, Kessler had listened to Joe's stories about his million-dollar corporation, picturing a calm, orderly, modern office run by serious-minded executives. On his first visit to Eagle's headquarters, Kessler had been shown into a grubby room with salamis hanging from the ceiling. Such furniture as there was had disappeared under a blizzard of unfiled business papers and greasy paper plates. And when Joe's Uncle

Mutzie rose to greet him from behind a desk littered with a week's worth of abandoned coffee containers, he wiped his mustardy fingers on his shirt before shaking hands. Nevertheless, Eagle had grossed over a million dollars that year, and since then, Kessler had been inclined to take Joe most seriously when Joe seemed most inclined to exaggerate.

"You're not in anybody's way," he said. "And if there's any rough stuff, Field'll be in Washington when it happens, addressing a joint session of Congress. He's not going to leave his fingerprints on anything. Besides, you know how these stories get around on the waterfront. You should hear what they say about *you.*"

"Okay. Fine. I'm no angel. And Dodge Island isn't paradise. If you wanna do business, you gotta maneuver a little. You gotta look after people. They expect that. But this is a clean port. And these guys, they give me a bad feeling. They weren't *asking* me if I wanna play along. They were telling me I *got* to. And I was just too dumb to understand that."

"Maybe it wasn't so dumb," said Kessler. "You told 'em you'd think about it. If you'd come on like a hero, they might have thought you were going to holler cop or something. Then you *could* have had a little trouble. Maybe."

Kessler was right. Joe's faintly comical guests on the *Playmate* were advance men for a confederation of illegal business interests controlling the movement of goods in and out of the continental United States by sea. They represented a vast criminal bureaucracy so long established as to be part of the structure of maritime trade, and so powerful as to rival the federal government as the final authority on the waterfront.

Joe's failure to understand that he was its first choice as an instrument for corrupting the new Port of Miami on Dodge Island quite possibly *did* save his life. Though short in stature, he was long on pugnacity, with a habit of reacting explosively to situations that threatened his independence, or offended his sense of what was right. Had he declared himself as a threat, he could have expected no more consideration from the ILA's New York bosses than they had previously shown toward others who stood in their way.

Nothing in Joe's life had encouraged the idea of compromise, least of all when defending his interests. Born in Chicago on April 20, 1932, he was the first child and only son of Hyman "Gus" Teitelbaum, a Polish immigrant, and Fern Teitelbaum, née Kratish, the daughter of an immigrant family which had settled there around the turn of the century. Their marriage had been a love match, but it had also sealed a merger between Gus's tire business—he sold recaps, cast in his own molds—and the junk business founded by his father-in-law, Morris Kratish. As there were more Kratishes than Teitelbaums, several of Morris's sons soon found themselves handling tires, and after Joe was born, the family ties grew still closer, for old Moe and his wife, Rose, doted on their grandson. From the time he could walk, they virtually took over his upbringing, so that when Gus decided to move his tire business to Miami in 1939, there was never any doubt that the whole tribe would go, too.

The seven-year-old Joe took to his new home on Meridien Avenue, Miami Beach, an unswerving devotion to the Chicago White Sox, a reputation for rebelliousness, and a two-year record of indifferent scholarship from a South Side grade school. Nothing changed. A White Sox fan to this day, he much preferred the kind of education he was getting from his grandfather, who promptly started up again as a junkman, to that offered by the local school system. And while Joe played hookey with old Moe, his father and uncles built up the tire business to the point where, in 1945, they expanded almost by accident into shipping.

Among Eagle's best customers were two Cubans, who not only met any price that Gus asked for used military surplus tires, but also agreed to extortionate freight charges in getting them back to Cuba. In fact, there was so much money to be made from shipping tires that Gus and Joe's late Uncle Julius went out and bought a minesweeper. Converted as a freighter for the Cuban run, Eagle's flagship plied very profitably for several years between Havana and the Miami River terminal of Eagle Docks and Warehouses, Inc.

Joe, meanwhile, was becoming fluent in Yiddish. At seventeen, he was out with his grandfather, who spoke little English, as often as he was in Miami Beach High School. The uncles had bought the old man a truck, with a painted sign reading "Moe and Joe," and unless Joe drove it for him, Moe stayed home, making life unbearable for everyone.

"Grandpa, I have to go to school today," he would tell him.

And just as often, Moe would say, "No, you don't have to go to school. Today, we got to pick up a load of old batteries."

And off they would go to pick up a load of old batteries, with Joe driving, and Moe holding the money.

On one such mission, Joe received his first practical object lesson in business ethics. Though well-muscled from hauling junk, he was small for his age and lightly built, which probably misled a fellow scrap merchant into thinking the old man and the kid were easy marks. At any rate, he gave them a fast count on a heap of batteries, and when Moe protested, raised a fist to him.

Before his wits caught up with his hand, Joe was showing the man a tire iron.

"You lay a finger on my grandfather," he said, "and I'll bust your fucking head open."

Though half as big again as Joe, the dealer blinked, shuffled his feet and backed off.

Moe nodded approvingly. "See?" he said. "Learn from that. If you know you're right, stick up for it. Only first make sure you got a tire iron."

Their partnership lasted well into Joe's first year at the University of

Miami, but by then, Joe had already decided to cut short his college career. His grandfather rarely allowed him enough time for it; his grades were not the best, and the draft board was lying in wait for him anyway. A hitch in the service, he thought, would give him a chance to measure himself against something broader and more challenging than his family background, and perhaps to see more clearly where his future lay.

He soon saw it did not lie with the Army, and so did the Army. After training at Fort Bliss, Texas, he was posted to Kansas City, where the combination of a bitterly cold winter and a warm woolen uniform brought on a severe attack of psoriasis. After less than a year, he was mustered out with a medical discharge, and an even stronger distaste for following orders than he had taken in. It was a crucial piece of luck. In the interval, two things had happened to make his prospects in Miami look more attractive.

The first was Ann, a pretty little blonde from a nice Jewish family. They had met at a freshman party on her first day at the University of Miami in September 1952. As it was almost his *last* day, he had not been able to do much about it, but she had written to him regularly, encouraging the hope that their acquaintance might grow into something else when he returned.

The other big factor in his change of heart was Eagle Shipping. Partly at Joe's urging, Gus had decided to diversify the family's stevedoring interests, reducing its dependence on the banana trade and expanding into general cargo. As there was no room for this at the river terminal, he had taken the big step, in Joe's absence, of leasing space on Pier 3, off Biscayne Boulevard, in what was then the main downtown seaport of Miami. He had also tendered to do the stevedoring for Three Bays Line, and to his mixed excitement and alarm, looked like winning the contract. Now he really *needed* Joe, who, in turn, now saw a more stimulating future in the family business than humping bananas or old car batteries.

He and Ann were married on July 11, 1954. They moved into a little house on Southwest 16th Terrace. There, ten months later, their daughter Marilyn was born. Joe had $50 in his pocket that day—nearly all the money they had in the world. He spent $48.50 on a watch as a present for Ann, bought a dollar's worth of gasoline to get to work, and blew the odd 50 cents on his dinner.

Not that he saw very much of his wife and daughter in those days. Three Bays owned five freighters and operated three more under charter, which meant that Eagle almost always had a ship to unload and load. Joe would often go to work on Monday and return home Friday or Saturday, sometimes working two or three days around the clock without stopping. When he could stay awake no longer, he would catch a nap in the warehouse on a pallet of lumber or a sack of sugar.

Apart from the weekends, the only time he spent at home was when he was sick or injured. Stevedoring is a dangerous business, and the worst accident he ever had was in those early years. While unloading a banana boat, he lost his footing and fell through the hatch into the hold, breaking an arm so badly that it later needed a skin graft, and so damaging the cartilage in both knees that it took nine operations over a period of seven years to put matters right.

But in spite of the grinding labor and cruel hours, he loved every minute he spent around ships. He loved the hustle, the noise, the smells, the raw confusion of life on the waterfront. He loved every rusty old scow that tied up at Pier 3. He loved the daily emergencies, snatching up his hard hat as he charged onto the dock from his poky office, dodging forklift drivers like a matador, strutting his way to the ship between the stacked-up pallets, crates, and bales to bellow orders at his sweating gangs. He loved the tough talk, the jokes, the foul-mouthed camaraderie.

It all delighted him: the snarl and clank of winches, the loaded slings plummeting precisely through open hatches, the stench of bilge and Diesel smoke, the lazy swing of lattice booms against a forest of masts and rigging. It felt like the hub of the world, and he was always reluctant to leave it, even after his son Mark was born in August 1958. Though the days of having to break his back around the clock were long gone, he would still work all night on the pier if he felt he had to baby a boatload of shrimp or a badly stowed shipment of Haitian pineapples. And even when he did go home, he would dream of ships heading in over the dark sea.

Ann understood this, up to a point, but saw less reason why the family should have to settle for an absentee husband and father now that Eagle was well established. Joe sometimes felt guilty about his preoccupation with the business, but it had no lasting effect. The pull of the waterfront was irresistible. It was the natural place for him to be, and with his instinct for the maritime trade, he sensed a new era coming that only bound him closer to it.

There were already plans for a new seaport on Dodge Island, the salt-white flat skirted by freighters and cruise ships as they steamed in from the Atlantic through Government Cut, passing Fisher and Watson Islands, to tie up at the crumbling piers just east of Biscayne Boulevard.

But Joe had no patience with those who saw Dodge Island merely as a means of relieving the congestion. Nor was he much impressed with the acumen of the port's planners when the official dedication ceremony was held on the wrong island in November 1960. The omen was not encouraging. In all the haggling and bickering that had attended the birth of the project, Joe had heard very little to match his own vision of its future. There were two factors, in his estimation, that were working not just to boost the volume of trade but also to change its nature. One was the economic growth of Central America and the islands. The other was the revolution he saw coming in shipping technology.

No point in the Caribbean was more than three and a half days' steaming from Miami, which made it the logical center for both the cruise trade *and* the export of American goods. As tourism and industry developed in the Central American region, so Miami's maritime trade was bound to grow with it. Conversely, Miami was also ideally placed to become the region's principal *import* center. Sitting on shipping lanes to and from the Pacific via the Panama Canal, its new deep-water harbor also lay on direct, open-sea routes from Europe, the Middle East, and Africa.

Sprawled out with his boots on the desk at the end of the day, Joe could see the future as plainly as if it were printed on the map of the world that hung on his office wall. Big ships, 10,000 tons or more, bringing goods from Europe and Asia for the developing markets of the Caribbean and the southern United States could never make the direct route pay if they had to stop at a dozen small ports and unload part of their cargo in each. They needed one strategically sited deep-sea port where they could discharge everything they carried at one time: a port served by feeder lines to carry separate consignments on to their final destinations; a port where return cargoes could be assembled for them. In short, they needed Dodge Island and Joe Teitelbaum.

And that was where the new technology came in, the second factor that had to be taken into account if the new port was to play the role he foresaw for it. For five thousand years, every freighter that sailed had operated on the "break-bulk" principle. Its cargo, brought together on the dock from various sources, had been loaded aboard as a single shipment and then broken down again into separate consignments on arriving at its destination. Ships were simply self-propelled containers that stevedores stuffed as tidily as possible with crates, sacks, boxes, and bales. And for as long as the world's trade could be conveniently handled in this fashion, and the cost of waterfront labor remained conveniently low, there was no particular reason to question traditional methods.

Neither condition applied, however, by the mid-fifties. International trade was booming, and longshoremen had begun to earn a living wage, which naturally set employers to worrying about their overhead. By the end of the decade, the industry came up with the final solution. Instead of using the vessel itself as a packing container for assorted items of general cargo, shipping lines would have everything prepacked in steel boxes, up to 40 feet in length and holding 20 tons or more, and then fit them into purpose-built ships as neatly as safe-deposit boxes in a vault.

Freighters earn their keep only when at sea, but with the break-bulk system, they spend up to two-thirds of their time in port. With the new system, heavy-lift dockside cranes could remove 600 containers of inbound cargo from a big ocean-going transport and replace them with the same number already packed with outward bound freight in 36 to 48 hours, as compared with a turnaround time for a conventional ship with the same cargo tonnage of seven to eight *days.*

The capital investment required for the new system was prodigious, but looking at the map on his office wall, Joe Teitelbaum saw the future and knew that it would work. By 1960, he was ready for the big leagues.

For Ann and the children, it meant they would have to go on with a part-time husband and father. It also meant he had to carry the rest of the Teitelbaum/Kratish clan with him, and there were now a round dozen of them in the firm. (There had been 13, but to Joe's great sorrow, old Moe Kratish, honorary president of Eagle, and his former partner in the junk business, had died that year.) Gus's vote was the one that counted, however, and Joe put it to him straight.

"We built a good little business here," he said. "We got some nice accounts. We got a dock and warehouse. We got a decent bunch of people working for us, and twenty-five forklifts. All we need now is a crane. A big one. Big enough to handle containers."

"No crane," said Gus. "We use Moe Harrison's crane. As long as he's alive and in the crane business, Moe Harrison gets the work. I gave him my solemn word."

"Okay. No crane. But we're still a *little* business, and look what's happening here. Dodge Island's on the way, and the big lines are coming in. Like Holland–America. And who's got that? Shaw Brothers. Who's got Mitsui? Eller and Company. Who's got Hamburg–America? Albery. And what have *we* got? Jealousy pangs."

"So, what do you want to do?"

"I want to get Zim–Israel Navigation in here," Joe said. They were both strong supporters of Israel.

"So, who's holding you back?" asked Gus.

Joe caught the dinner flight to New York, and in the morning, found himself waiting in the Brooklyn office of Mordechai Chovers, operations chief for Zim in the United States. He had arrived without an appointment, and Chovers never saw anybody without an appointment. His secretary explained this to Joe several times that day, but he waited just the same, and after six hours, Chovers agreed to see him.

"You're a very persistent young man," he said.

"No good having a general agent and stevedore in Miami who isn't persistent," Joe replied.

"We don't *go* to Miami."

"No, but you will. And that's what I've come to see you about."

Joe then described his vision of Miami's future, based on its commanding position on the world's shipping routes, and on what he personally guaranteed would be the finest freight and passenger terminal in the South.

"Never mind all that," said Chovers. "Be practical. Before I can send a ship in there, I've got to have a minimum freight revenue of five thousand dollars. Guaranteed. Just to pay the port charges."

"Okay. You got it." Joe heard himself say this, and winced. Nobody had said he could offer guarantees.

"What do you mean? Got what?"

"I mean that if the freight's any less than five thousand dollars, we'll pay you the difference."

Chovers pushed a box of cigars across the table.

"One sailing's no good," he said. "We'd have to schedule two at least, just to show you mean business."

"Right," said Joe, selecting a cigar to cover his agitation. "Let's make it one a month."

"Okay. Now you're talking about a ten thousand-dollar guarantee."

"I know that. I also know Miami, and what I can do for you. So I guess I'll shoot craps for ten thousand. I'm not worried."

Chovers looked again at Joe's business card, shaking his head doubtfully. "We're trying to build a major national shipping line, Joe. I have to deal in certainties when I commit the prestige of Israel. We're not running a crap game."

"Neither am I, Mr. Chovers." This was it, make or break. "I'm as serious as you are. We're Jewish. We support Israel, and there's a great opportunity opening up for Zim in Miami. I'm so sure of that I'm willing to pay you, if I have to, to show the flag down there. But I don't think I'll have to. I think . . . in fact I *know* . . . I can find enough business tomorrow to cover those guarantees. More than enough. From people in the Jewish community who'll be glad of the chance to get behind the flag of Israel and bring in their goods in Israeli ships. Believe me, I can do that."

Chovers considered him for a moment. Then he shrugged. "Okay. It's heads I win, tails you lose. If everything checks out, two sailings. After that, we'll see."

Joe flew back to Miami that night with a letter of intent in his pocket. Gus wrinkled his nose when he came to the part about the $10,000 guarantee, but said nothing.

"What do you think?" asked Joe.

"You know Nathan Lee?" said his father. "Miami Tile and Terrazzo?"

"I know who you mean."

"Then ask him about all that tile he's bringing in from Italy."

So Joe went to see Nathan Lee. They were both Jewish, he said, and Zim–Israel needed their support. Lee saw his point, and paid $6,000 for freight on the first of the two scheduled sailings.

With other odds and ends of cargo he picked up, plus the revenue from the stevedoring, Joe was well-pleased with his first venture as a shipping agent. And so was Mordechai Chovers when freight revenues from the second sailing reached $15,000. After that, Eagle brought a Zim–Israel ship into Miami at least once a month for the next 17 years. And in November 1961, just 10 months after the service began, Zim honored his achievement by sending its new flagship, the passenger liner S.S. *Jerusalem,* into Miami on its maiden voyage.

It was a big day for the Teitelbaum/Kratish clan, and for Joe's sister Eileen in particular. In the best traditions of shipboard romance, she fell madly in love with the handsome young second mate in his dazzling white uniform. His name was Ben Mussary, and they were married within a month.

Always an event in Miami, the arrival of a new cruise liner put Eagle on the map. From then on, the newspapers adopted Joe as their spokesman for the shipping industry. His direct, often pungent response to questions meant he was usually good for a quote, and there was plenty to ask him about. Just as he had predicted, the old Port of Miami was finally bursting its seams.

When the *Miami Herald* interviewed Joe in 1964 about conditions on the waterfront, its reporter found him "bone-tired, with dark circles around his eyes" from working all night to save a perishable cargo from spoiling.

"Miami's potential is fantastic," Joe told him, still harping on his favorite theme, "but this port is too small. And by the time Dodge Island is ready next year, *it* will be too small."

It was partly his own fault. In an average month that summer, Eagle worked 42 ships.

Joe was bringing home the business with a combination of dauntless globe-trotting—he would fly anywhere in the world on an hour's notice to meet a prospective client—and the same hair-trigger, promise-now-and-work-it-out-later gall that had won him the Zim account.

"You know, in the high school yearbook, how they put everybody's ambition?" he said to the *Herald* reporter. "Well, my ambition at Miami Beach High School was to be the number one stevedore in the State of Florida, and I'm getting close."

Of all the people Joe met while foraging for business around this time, none had a more telling effect on his life than John Anthony Caputo. Joe had set his sights on Mamenic, the national steamship line of Nicaragua, which, in those days, belonged to the Somoza family—like most of that country's assets. It was represented in the United States, along with several other Central and South American shipping lines, by American Hemisphere Marine Agencies, a New York firm, whose president, Marion Dudak, had awarded Eagle the stevedoring contract for American Star Line some years earlier. When he heard what Joe wanted, he referred him to John Caputo, who was then managing the Mamenic account.

They took to each other on sight, though the two could hardly have been less alike. In his sleek Italian suit, Caputo stood head and shoulders taller than Joe in his J.C. Penney wash 'n' wears; fair-haired yet olive-skinned against Joe's black crew cut and laborer's tan. Insider and outsider, they were equally contrasted in manner: Caputo, smooth and watchful, the perfect front man; Joe brash and electric, making waves. All they really had in common was their feeling for the shipping business, and here, each saw interesting possibilities in the other. As he was already filling his ships in New York, Caputo was looking for big freight guarantees if Mamenic were to call regularly at Miami, but Joe reckoned he could meet them, and Caputo promised to think it over.

A few weeks later, he called Joe early in the morning. One of Mamenic's ships, in trouble at sea with a fuel line, was putting into Miami with open cargo space. He thought Joe might be interested. Joe was. He made a couple of calls to local freight forwarders, and when the ship eventually sailed from Miami after repairs, she was fully loaded.

"I like your style, Joe," Caputo said. "I guess we're gonna have to send her in there every month from now on."

And so he did. He also sent in Flomerca, the national line of Guatemala, appointing Eagle to act as its Miami agent and stevedore.

By now, Ann Teitelbaum was resigned to her husband's ways. It had not been easy to accept that she and the children held the lesser place in his life, though Joe always denied this vehemently. There was no denying his scale of priorities, however. Trouble with a ship in Curacao or Kingston would always outweigh trouble with a wife in South Miami, where they were now living in a fine new house on Southwest 143rd Street.

Joe loved his family, she knew that. No one else in the world meant anything next to them. And he did try. Guiltily, he would drive himself every so often to spend more time with the children, even volunteering as a Little League coach at one point to see more of Mark. It was certainly no hardship. He enjoyed every moment he spent with them, but sooner or later, some new crisis or business prospect would call him away, and life would go on as before. Separately. Joe belonged on the waterfront.

On January 11, 1965, however, the ILA began the longest walk-out in its history. It was the start of an enforced 54-day vacation for Joe Teitelbaum, who spent more time with his family than he had in years, taking trips, catching up with odd jobs around the house, and working on his huge stamp collection, which he had started when he was five. But even with the port closed, he still had to think and live ships. Having graduated from stevedore to shipping agent, the next step, and the only firm foundation for the maritime empire he had set his heart on, was to own his own shipping line. And having recently met Sir Roland Symonette, then Prime Minister of the Bahamas, he had a shrewd idea of how to go about getting one.

Meanwhile, the ILA bosses had agreed on contract terms everywhere except in Miami, where Judge Henderson was still holding out for a fixed minimum gang size. This meant that no longshoremen could go back to work anywhere, for the one irreducible principle of the ILA had always been, "One port down, *all* ports down."

The Northern employers, however, were concerned with quite another principle. Though they had settled with the union in *their* ports, they were still strike-bound because of a dispute in the South to which they were not a party. They therefore applied to the courts, and on February 12, Thomas W. "Teddy" Gleason, president of the ILA was forced to break the union's closed ranks by ordering the Northern Locals back to work. With his general organizer, Fred R. Field, Jr., he then descended on Miami like the wrath of God.

On March 6, Henderson gave way, and released his men for work. As usual on such occasions, the *Miami Herald* carried a picture of Joe Teitelbaum on the pier, this time supervising the loading of his first ship in nearly eight weeks, but the dockworkers were in an ugly mood. Before the day was over, they had walked off the job again in protest. Encouraged, it was said, by Henderson, they stayed out for another week before finally ratifying the contract and returning to work in earnest.

That was enough for Gleason. Though a vice president of the International, Henderson was suspended from office, and Local 1416 passed into trusteeship by order of the executive council of the ILA, which later in the year appointed William Murphy and four others to a Judge Henderson Trial Committee. After a three-day hearing, Murphy and company found Henderson guilty of "instigating a strike in violation of a duly negotiated collective bargaining agreement," and kicked him out of the union.

The secretary of the Trial Committee was Anthony M. Scotto, president of Local 1814, Brooklyn, New York. Announcing the verdict against Henderson, he said: "This may appear to be an unpleasant action to take, but in the broad and better interest of unity, it was necessary. When we go to the bargaining table two years from now to negotiate a new contract, we have to go as a team that will command management's respect . . ."

Judge Henderson died not long after, and Joe Teitelbaum, like most employers in the port, was sorry to see him go. He had cost them dear, but not nearly as much as the new regime now threatened to do. With Scotto, Field, Barone, and the Murphys, the ILA had all the muscle it needed to "command management's respect."

3

Annexation

"THREE *thousand?*" Gus Teitelbaum wouldn't hear of it. "Don't give 'em a quarter. You give those guys money, they'll hit us every time they wanna go to the races. No way. You tell 'em, kiss my ass."

Uncle Mutzie concurred. So did Uncle Sam Kratish.

"Okay," said Joe. "That's it, then. I was pretty sure you'd say that, but I just wanted to put you in the picture."

"I'm in the picture. We don't want no part of it. Not if they got an account for us. Not if they give us the whole port of Miami."

"Well, that's what they say they wanna do."

"Good. Fine. When it's theirs to give, then maybe we'll talk. You get in their clutches, you never get out. I know these kind of people. I seen it happen."

"Okay," said Joe. "I'm with you. Fuck 'em. But there's gonna be trouble."

"So what else is new?"

It was Friday, the day after the voyage of the *Playmate* and Joe's talk with Mel Kessler. On Monday, Benny Astorino called.

"So what's the good word?" he asked. "You talk to your old man? What did he say?"

"Yeah, I talked to him," said Joe. "And he's, you know, one of the old school. It's no go, Benny. I'm sorry. We're just not interested."

There was a short silence.

"That's too bad," said Astorino. "They're not gonna like that. We could have put a pretty nice deal together for you. Now I don't know."

"Well, that's the way it goes, Benny. I guess we'll just have to try and make it on our own."

"It's not smart, Joe, turning the boys down like this. That's really not too swift, you know?"

"I know, Benny. What can I tell you? They didn't go much for this checkers' deal either."

"Well, that's what I mean. That's just stupid. You coming to the meeting today? There's somebody here wants to talk to you."

"You mean Barone?"

"You coming or not?"

"What's he gonna do? Sign me up for the union?"

"Why the fuck don't you get your ass over here and find out?" suggested Astorino, and he hung up.

Joe decided not to go. He drove out to the ship they were working, but Ben Mussary was already there and needed no help. So now Joe decided he would go after all, remembering what Mel Kessler had said. There was no sense losing his temper and antagonizing these guys for no reason. Eagle had too many mouths to feed.

Then Fat Freddy kept him waiting for 20 minutes in the lobby of the Caribbean Hotel while he talked to Cleve Turner and another man, and Joe lost his temper anyway. They were not a very intimidating sight. Field was again immobilized by his chair; Turner he had known too long to take seriously, and if the third member of the group was Barone, he was not much bigger than Joe himself.

"Hey, Fred," he said, breaking into their conversation. "I gotta get back. I got a ship working. Hi, Cleve."

Field looked up at him impassively.

"Benny said this guy Barone wants to see me," Joe went on.

"I'm Barone," said the third man.

Up close, he was a little more daunting; short but barrel-chested, with a fleshy, heavy featured face, and small, slightly vacant brown eyes that seemed to focus a little behind whatever he was looking at. He wore a hearing aid.

"You Teitelbaum?" he asked.

"Yeah. Can you make it quick? I gotta go."

Barone took a piece of paper from his pocket, and studied it deliberately. "That's Eagle, right?"

"Yeah, right. You wanna do this some other time? When I'm not so busy?"

"Teddy Gleason—you know who that is? That's the president of the whole ILA, the International, okay? He sent me down here. I got a charter from him to organize the checkers in this port. They're all gonna join a new Local. Local 1922. And I'm president."

"Yeah, I heard."

"Okay. So that's what I'm doing. With Fred here. And your checkers are gonna join."

"No, we do the checking ourselves. The family does it. I told Fred that."

Barone stared, then consulted his piece of paper. "I hear different. You got a couple of guys doing it for you. Maybe more."

"No, no," said Joe impatiently. "There's a couple of kids we use sometimes when we're real busy, but they're not regular checkers. They just come and help us out when we're short, that's all."

"If they check cargo, they're checkers. And if they're checkers, they're gonna have to join the union."

"Well, that's up to them, isn't it? That's their business."

"Right. If they wanna work on the dock, they'll join. And then they can't work for you no more until you sign a contract with the union."

"Hey, I told you." Joe began to get hot. "They're just kids. I was doing 'em a favor, letting 'em earn a few bucks for themselves. I don't need 'em. And I don't have to sign anything."

"You don't have to stay in business either," said Field, looking bored. "I don't know what I have to do to get through to you fucking people."

"Just sign the contract," Barone said. "Then all you gotta do is call for what you need, just like you do with Cleve here. Now what's wrong with that?"

"Nothing. Except, like I said, we do our own checking. And I really got to go now."

"Just a minute." Field's pale eyes sank deep in the folds of his frown. "Don't say no. I know you're fucking ignorant, but don't say no, we do it ourselves. You'll do like we fucking tell you, all right? You'll sign the fucking contract."

"Sign it?" said Joe. "I wouldn't wipe my ass on it."

"This is an ILA port," said Barone. "You think Cleve's boys are gonna work with non-union checkers?"

Turner shook his head solemnly. "No way. Listen to the man, Joey. We done had enough trouble in this port already. We get a checkers' Local in here, we gonna help 'em all we can."

"Cleve, with you I *got* a contract," Joe said. "You mess with my labor, and you'll find yourself explaining why to a federal court judge."

Field chewed his lip. "And I thought you were smart," he said. "Okay. Now I'm gonna have to teach you something. Too bad it's gotta be the hard way, but I'm gonna have to hurt you a little bit so you can learn. No hard feelings, okay?"

"Fred," said Joe uneasily. "Fuck off, will you? Just leave me and my family alone."

He went to look for Gus.

"So what do you think they'll do?"

His father shrugged. "Maybe nothing."

"Don't make book on it. These guys are heavy. Barone didn't get kicked out of New York for doing nothing."

"No, I heard that," said Gus. "But what's he gonna do? Kill somebody? Make a big noise and get kicked out of Miami, too? I don't think so."

"It's Fat Freddy that worries me. He likes to play pussycat, but that's a bad man. With a lot of power."

"Listen, what's done is done. I say we sit back and watch and see what happens. Maybe they'll leave us alone now."

Next morning, the gangs Ben Mussary had ordered overnight from Local 1416 showed up on time and worked a full day, with no unusual delays or mishaps. When the following day also passed off normally, Joe began to lower his guard. Maybe Gus was right. This was not New York.

Field and his guys were just getting started. They wouldn't want trouble right off the bat.

On the evening of the third day, he arrived home around six with the idea of taking Ann out to a movie. She came to the truck to meet him, looking stricken. His first thought was that something had happened to one of the kids.

"My God," he said. "What is it?"

He tried to take hold of her, but she fended him off, shaking her head.

"What happened?" He caught her by the arm. "Ann, I want to know what happened."

"Nothing, nothing," she said, twisting free. "A man . . . Some man called, that's all."

"Who? You mean, someone came *out* here?"

"No, no. On the phone." She took a deep breath to steady herself. "I don't know who it was."

"Well, what did he say? I'll kill him. I'll kick his fucking head in for him. Tell me what he said."

She frowned. "Joe, I wish you wouldn't use that kind of language."

"Ann, just tell me what the guy said, all right?"

"You're not on the pier now, you know."

"I wanna know what he said to scare you. Did he talk dirty, or what?"

"No, no. Nothing like that. It was something about the union. He said you're making trouble for them."

He started to shake, and leaned against the side of the truck.

"Is that true, Joe? Something about the checkers? You won't sign their contract?"

He was so angry, he thought he might choke. "Go on. What else? Did he threaten you?"

"I don't know. I guess he did." She laughed uncertainly. "He said I was a nice lady. 'You have nice kids.' That's what he said. He said, 'Tell your husband to get some knowledge. Tell him he better sign.' "

"Is that all?"

"Well, it was the *way* he said it. In this thick, scary voice. It just gave me the shivers."

"When was this?" He pulled himself together. "How long ago?"

"Few minutes. Just before you came. They wouldn't do anything to hurt us, would they, Joe? Not to the children?"

"I'll kill that fat son of a bitch."

He grabbed the door handle of the truck, but Ann got in his way.

"You'll do no such thing," she said sharply. "You'll come in the house and take a shower before we eat."

Joe rarely discussed business with Ann. By the time he got home, he was generally too tired to start explaining everything, and he had a suspicion it bored her anyway. But he had no difficulty holding her attention on this particular evening while he told her as much as he thought sensible about Fat Freddy, trying to pass off the telephone call as just a stray shot in New York's takeover of the local union. More than willing to be convinced that her family was in no danger, she seemed calm again by the time they went to bed.

Joe, however, was not. He lay awake most of the night, his insides churning over, and was out of the house by 6 A.M. with blood in his eye. His sense of outrage at the thought of some hoodlum trying to get at him through his family was so extreme that, if he had owned a gun, he would have shot Fred Field that day, if Field had been in town. Joe hunted for him until the banks opened, but then had to return to the office for his usual morning juggling act with Eagle's cash balances to cover the day's payroll. After that, he called the union office and learned that Field had returned to New York with his delegation the previous evening.

"You think I ought to tell the cops?"

"Tell 'em what?" Kessler asked. "That some guy told your wife she had nice kids?"

"But he frightened her, for Chrissake."

"*Who* did?"

Joe swallowed. "You mean, he's gonna get away with this? No way, man. I'll kill the son of a bitch."

"There you go again. Running around, threatening to chop people's legs off. Can't we just take a quiet look at this without strewing the place with bodies?"

"That fat fuck. He better not mess with *my* family."

"Well, now, who says he did? What makes you think Field had anything to do with it?"

"Oh, come on. One minute he says he's gonna hurt me. Next minute, Ann gets a phone call. I mean, what do you want?"

"A lot more than that, if we're going to plead justifiable homicide. You tell Field you won't sign. And he says, 'Okay, then I'm going to teach you a lesson.' Right?"

"He says, 'I'm gonna have to hurt you a little bit.'"

"All right. Now what I think he meant was, hurt the business."

"You guarantee that?"

"No. But I don't think they want to stir up that kind of heat. There's no need for it."

"Well, *somebody* called her, Mel. She didn't make it up."

"No. But I don't think it was Field. I think it was maybe one of his boys putting in his two cents' worth. They're heading back up to New York, so one of 'em figures it's worth a quarter to let you know that *they* know where you live."

"Then what are you saying? I should let it pass?"

Kessler played with a pencil. "You *could* sign the contract," he said mildly.

"Oh, fine. After that, I could give 'em the deed to the house, and then they'd have everything."

"You sure you're not just being stubborn?"

"Yeah, I'm being stubborn. They're thieves. If I let Barone's guys into the business, they'll steal it out from under us."

"What does Gus say?"

"He agrees. Gus, Mutzie, Sam, Manny, Ben, me . . . we all say the same thing."

"Well, that's an historic moment right there."

"You wanna help or make jokes?"

Kessler turned up his hands. "Sounds like you made up your mind already," he said. "If you're not going to sign, there's at least two things you ought to do. *Three* things. First, stay away from Field and Barone. Second, go talk to your clients. Make sure they're in solid. And third, have a quiet word with Bob Richardson."

Joe had already thought of that. Richardson was a detective in Dade County's Public Safety Department; they had both known him since high school. But it had not crossed Joe's mind that his accounts might be in danger; he had been looking for trouble with his labor. Next day, he flew up to New York to inspect Eagle's fences, after making Kessler and Richardson promise to keep an eye on Ann.

John Caputo for one was delighted to see him.

"You saved me a trip," he said over lunch. "I was gonna set up a meet for next week."

"Yeah?"

"Yeah. We gotta talk, Joe. This whole fucking business is busting wide open."

"How do you mean?"

"Well, you've seen it. New people. New money. We got a whole new ballgame here. And for somebody who knows shipping, like you do, plus somebody with the right connections, like I got . . . I tell you, Joe, in two, three years, we could all be fucking millionaires."

"Hey, I'm willing."

"You only gotta look at what's happening. Container ships. Trailer ships. New routes. New ports. More traffic. It's all there, Joe . . . for those that can see it. Anybody who gets ready now for what's gonna happen five years from now, he's gotta wind up controlling the whole fucking industry. I mean it."

"Right, right. It's like I'm hearing myself, listening to you. I keep telling Gus and Mutzie, 'Now's the time. Don't wait till we gotta fight for the crumbs. Get in early.' "

"Yeah, well . . . I don't wanna say anything against your family, Joe, but they're nuts. You know that. You're gonna have to do something about them."

"I know. They drive me fucking crazy. But what can you do with family? You can't fire 'em."

"No, but you can *leave* 'em. Go out on your own. Or better still, come in with us."

"With *Dudak?*"

"No, not with Dudak." The idea amused him. "With these new people I'm telling you about. In five years, they'll have control. Maybe less. They'll have the whole fucking industry laid out the way they want it. And you can have a piece, Joe. A *big* piece. If you come in with us now."

Joe knew better than to ask Caputo who "they" were. When Caputo wanted him to know, he would tell him. He also knew better than to doubt what he said.

"Hey, John. Can you see me telling Gus? 'Listen, I'm leaving. It's all on you now. And by the way, I'm not just leaving. I'm taking the accounts and setting up against you.'" He laughed. "Shit. He'd kill me."

Caputo smiled only faintly. "Doesn't have to be that way. I'm not just talking Miami. I'm talking Charleston and Savannah and Jacksonville. I'm talking Mobile and Houston and maybe New Orleans as well. This is big, Joe. No limit to it."

"I like to work ships," Joe said. He was impressed, but not tempted. "That sounds like a desk job."

"If you got it all, you can do what you want."

He shook his head doubtfully. "I don't think I'm your boy," he said. It was the second time he had heard this, or something like it, in a week. "If Gus didn't get me, Ann sure as hell would. I drive her crazy already with all the running around I do. And Miami's my home. I like it there."

"So you'll operate out of Miami. No problem. And we'll find something for Gus. He's pretty close to retiring anyway, right? Must be. But look at you. You got your whole life ahead of you. How do you think he'd feel if he thought he was standing in your way?"

"Probably wouldn't give a shit."

They both laughed. With Gus, business was business.

"Okay. But he can't go on for ever. Then what? If you already missed the fucking boat? Come in with us now, Joe. Bring him in with you. Ben, too. That way, Gus can give up any time he wants to, and no money worries. You'll be doing him a favor."

Joe scratched his head. "I don't think he'd see it that way, John. He's like me. He likes to make up his *own* mind. I couldn't do it to him. Mutzie, yes. My cousins? Sure. They'd do it to me, if they could. But Gus? No. When he's ready to retire, he'll let me know."

"It'll be too late then."

"Too late for what? To tell you the truth, John, I'm not sure I go for it anyway. I mean, hey, it's a great opportunity and everything . . . I can see that. And I take it very kindly that you thought of me, I really do. But I'm not a good team player. You're my friend, so you know that. I gotta do everything myself, right? That's not gonna change."

"You'll have a free hand, Joe. You can run things any way you want."

"Yeah, John, sure. But for somebody else, and that's not my scene. I did all right so far, even *with* the family, so I guess I'll get by."

"Don't turn me down, Joe." Caputo looked very serious now. "Not before you thought about it. I'm asking you as a friend."

"What's to think about?" Joe could not make him out. "There's plenty of good men know agency and stevedoring. If your people got the money and the ships, John, you'll have to beat 'em off with a stick. You don't need *me.*"

"You're not listening, Joe," Caputo said in a harder tone. "If you wanna control shipping, what do you need? Money and ships comes after."

Then Joe understood, and he was disappointed. "You mean labor? You're talking union?"

"Hey, I didn't say anything, okay? You figured that out for yourself."

"Yeah. Sure."

"But you got it. That's the key, Joe."

"Yeah, I know. They're turning it on me already, your people. You know Fred Field?"

"Right church, wrong pew. Different family, okay? And bad news."

"You're telling me. I got 'em on my back."

"Oh, boy. That's *very* bad news."

Just *how* bad soon became clear. Though all had seemed secure in New York, Captain Zeno Adelstein of Zim–Israel Navigation telephoned Joe the day after he got back to Miami.

"What the hell's going on down there?" he demanded.

"Here? Nothing. What are you talking about?"

"I'm talking about these labor problems you got. Fred Field called me. He says you're giving him all kinds of trouble."

"I'm giving *him* trouble? That son of a bitch. I'll kick his fat ass."

"Now just a minute. He says things are so bad he can't guarantee labor for the next ship. Something about a checkers' contract? What are you doing, Joe?"

"Nothing." He had such a bad premonition that it hurt his chest. "Field brought a bunch of New York hoodlums down here to start a new local, only nobody's buying it."

"That's not what *he* says. You know a guy named Harrington?"

"*Neal* Harrington?"

"Yeah. *He* signed. And Field says the rest are getting on line. So you better do the same."

"Listen, Field's a fucking crook," said Joe, heating up. "You know what he's doing down here? You want me to spell it out?"

"No, you don't have to spell it out." Adelstein was silent for a moment. "All right. But I can't have my ships tied up while you slug this out with them, you understand? It's not just Miami I got to worry about. It's New York, and Boston, and Philly . . . You know what I'm talking about, Joe. I don't have to tell you."

"Right. You're telling me to sign."

"I'm not telling you anything, Joe. You're a good agent. You get paid for using your judgment. And I'm looking at the schedule. We don't have another boat in there for, what? Thirty days?"

"Just about."

"Okay. That should give you enough time to sort out this mess."

Joe could see his point. As a prospective shipowner himself, he could even sympathize. To have a vessel stand idle, earning no revenue but costing thousands of dollars a day in crew's wages, interest charges, port fees, and so on, would be a body blow for any steamship line. Multiplied by the number of Zim ships serving American ports, it was a prescription for bankruptcy.

What puzzled him was how Neal Harrington fitted into the picture. Joe knew him slightly as a former clerk and agency representative with Eller & Company. An ambitious young man, whose previous claim to fame had been as Miami's first March of Dimes poster boy back in 1936, he had suddenly blossomed out a few months before this with an agency and stevedoring business of his own. He had plenty of dock and warehouse space, but nothing much to do with it, as far as Joe could see, so that if Harrington was the only employer Field had so far "persuaded" to sign the checkers' contract, it was nothing much to boast about.

Gus agreed. A lot could happen in 30 days, he said.

The following morning, Joe took a call from Marion Dudak, John Caputo's boss at American Hemisphere Marine Agencies.

"I hear you got yourself in trouble down there," he said. "With the checkers?"

"Who told you that, Mr. Dudak? Fred Field?"

"Just take care of it, Joe. Don't make *your* problems *my* problems. We can't afford friction with labor. You know how things are."

"I'm learning, Mr. Dudak. I'm learning."

The next to call was Julio Delvalier, of Coordinated Caribbean Transport, a division of U.S. Freight.

"Bad news, Joe. I'm sorry."

"Don't tell me. Fat Freddy called. Well, don't worry. I'm taking care of it. We never let you down yet."

"I know you didn't, Joe. That's what makes it hard. We're moving the account."

"You're *what?* What are you talking about?"

"I mean we're giving it to Harrington. I'm sorry. It came from upstairs, you know?"

"Harrington?"

"Yeah. He set up on his own. You didn't know?"

"Yeah, I knew. Listen, Julio. Did Field tell you to go with him?"

"Hey, come on. Don't ask things like that."

"Okay, Julio. I got the message."

There was more to come. Next morning, Captain Roy Collins of Caribbean Shipping Limited, another major account, announced that he, too, was transferring his business to Harrington & Company, much as he regretted it.

"I don't know, Joey," said Gus, who seemed older suddenly. "Looks like they got us by the balls."

"Yeah, we're hurting. What do you want me to do?"

"What you should have done up front," said Mutzie. "Sign the fucking contract."

"Sign?"

Ben Mussary choked on his coffee, splashing his shirt, and Joe took the container from him as he groped blindly for somewhere to put it down.

"I getta gun first," he wheezed, trying to speak, cough, breathe, and wipe his eyes at the same time.

"He could be right," Joe said. "We could be giving up too easy. We still got a helluva big business here. We got Zim."

"For thirty days. Maybe less."

"We got American Star Line and Mamenic."

"Not unless we sign," Mutzie said. "You know Dudak."

"No." Ben shook his head vehemently, to make up for the faintness of his whisper. "Fight. We lose? Okay. We lost anyway."

"How about it?" said Joe. "At least we get to keep our self-respect."

"Fine," said Mutzie. "See how much *that* buys in the supermarket."

They all looked at Gus, who sighed. Then he shook his head, not looking at any of them.

"Okay." Joe owed his father that much. "Field's out of town. When he gets back, I'll see him. He's made his point. Maybe now he'll make a deal."

"Just sign the fucking contract," said Mutzie. "Before they wipe us out."

Joe wished afterwards he had taken his uncle's advice. Before he could speak to Field, Marion Dudak called again from New York, this time to say that in view of the continuing uncertainty, he felt compelled to switch American Star Line and Mamenic to Harrington & Company. In the space of a week, the business Joe and his father had built up over the years with so much labor and devotion had half melted away, and Neal Harrington had jumped to the top of the heap. It took no great feat of deduction to identify Field and Barone as the heels in his spring.

Then Fred Field called.

"Listen," he said. "Have you got a change of heart in reference to the three aces?"

"Well, no, Fred," said Joe calmly, determined to deny him any satisfaction. "It's like I told your man Astorino. We're kind of old-fashioned that way."

Field grunted. "Then I hope you like living on Social Security."

"And another thing. I don't appreciate the heat you're putting on my customers."

"Heat? They're sensible people, that's all. I tried to tell you. There's an easy way, and there's a hard way, and you chose wrong. So you had to learn. You had to have a little demonstration. When we ask people nice, they don't tell us no."

"You been talking nice to Harrington?"

"We been talking nice to everybody. And they're all in. Eller. Shaw Brothers. Albery. Strachan Shipping. Everybody. We always talk nice. You're the only one that give us any trouble, but I'm even talking nice to you. I want you to come on over here now and sign the contract like a good boy."

"Well, fuck you, Fred," he said. "We're not done yet. We still got a couple of cards to play."

"You mean Zim?" He laughed. "You know where Zim makes its money? New York. And who controls Zim's labor? Local 856. And who controls Local 856? *I* do. So just you get your little ass over here quick, like I tell you. And you say thank you to me because nobody dropped nothing heavy on your head."

Joe licked his lips. "Uh, yeah. Well . . . Maybe we can work out some kind of a deal on that."

"Listen, prick," said Field, losing interest. "You'll sign the fucking contract and like it. No deals. I know you fucking Jews stick together, but I got a direct wire to Israel, all right? I can turn 'em on, and I can turn 'em off. You hearing me now? You got that? Or have I gotta put you out of business altogether?"

Joe unclenched his jaw. "I hear you," he said.

On May 23, 1966, in the presence of Fred R. Field, Jr., general organizer of the ILA, George Barone, organizer and assistant to the president of the ILA, and Cleveland Turner, president of Local 1416, ILA, Joe Teitelbaum signed a labor contract between Checkers Local 1922, Miami, and Eagle, Inc.

On May 24, he told Ben Mussary to take over, and flew to Nassau to see the Prime Minister of the Bahamas.

4

Mob Rule

EVEN then, Joe had no clear idea of who he was up against, or how close he had come to an "accident"

Thirteen years earlier, Governor Thomas E. Dewey of New York had described the International Longshoremen's Association as "a racket, not a union." Commenting on the work of the State Crime Commission, which spent most of 1952 examining the ILA's activities, he said: "A clear picture emerges of a ruthless mob attempting to preserve by force unlicensed power which it gained by force."

The New York Times went further. "The ILA," it concluded, "is controlled by labor gangsters who direct kickbacks, extortion, thievery, usury and other rackets on the piers, and intimidate the longshoremen.

"The mobsters could not run the waterfront without the consent of the stevedore and shipping companies. These companies cooperate with the ILA in hiring criminals and bribing union officials because the thugs keep the dockers in line.

"Neither the ILA nor the companies could perpetuate the system without at least the tacit consent of [elected] officials . . . Many of these officials accept campaign contributions from ILA racketeers and stevedore executives, give them political jobs, keep up social contacts with them."

The Crime Commission, in short, had proved the existence of a vast criminal enterprise controlling the Port of New York, which then accounted for about half the dollar value of the nation's maritime trade. Using the ILA as a weapon and a front, the mob had for years been levying the equivalent of a 5 percent tax on all general cargo moving in and out of the harbor.

The evidence for this was so overwhelming, and public outrage so acute, that when the Commission reported on its work, the legislatures of New York and New Jersey set up a bi-state Waterfront Commission to police the piers, taking unusual care to protect its powers from criminal subversion.

At the same time, and for the same reasons, the American Federation of Labor also cleaned house. On September 22, 1953, its new president, George Meany, publicly reviewed the Crime Commission's findings before the AFL convention in St. Louis, and, finding in the ILA's record "nothing that resembled legitimate trade union activity," asked the delegates to revoke the ILA's charter, which they did at once by a vote of 72,362 to 765. Two months later, "King Joe" Ryan, president of the first

AFL member union to be kicked out for corruption since the Federation's formation in 1881, was indicted for stealing ILA funds.

In his 26-year reign, King Joe had shaped the union into the most effective machine for extortion, coercion, intimidation, and general commercial piracy ever placed at the disposal of organized crime. At the working level, it was a very blunt instrument, for the issue was always starkly simple on the waterfront: Pay out or stay out. But at the political level, Ryan used it with often surprising finesse, muffling the ILA's lawlessness for so long and so effectively that when the Crime Commission began its hearings, many people saw them as a Communist plot against a pillar of the American system. Indeed, Ryan's skill in managing a huge criminal conspiracy while appearing to act in the public interest seems to have been the most durable part of his legacy to subsequent ILA leaders.

Among his more respectable friends were Mayors Jimmy Walker and William O'Dwyer of New York; Mayors Frank Hague and John V. Kenny of Jersey City; Grover Whalen, William J. McCormack ("Mr. Big"), the multimillionaire dock tycoon and former New York State Boxing Commissioner, and Robert F. Wagner, Jr., a future Mayor of New York, who as late as 1952, was organizing testimonial dinners for Ryan and his mobster employers.

For sterner measures, he had another circle of friends. These included Albert Anastasia, Lord High Executioner of Murder, Inc., who ran six ILA Locals in Brooklyn during the thirties; Eddie McGrath, a notorious protection racketeer and numbers banker with a record that featured a five-year stretch in Sing Sing and arrests for assault and homicide, whom Ryan appointed an ILA organizer, and the Mickey Bowers Gang, bank robbers and extortionists, to whom Ryan awarded Local 824, the so-called "Pistol Local," in 1940 after they had murdered one of its officials.

For similar services on the Jersey side, he could call on Albert Ackalitis, the machine-gun artist who, when not serving time, eked out his income as pier boss by running the murderous Arsenal Mob, or Eddie Florio, bootlegger, loan shark, and ex-con, whose power across the Hudson River was so unmistakable that Ryan made him ILA organizer for the area. Called upon by the Crime Commission to explain some of these appointments, Ryan rode the elevator to the hearing room in New York's County Courthouse, singing "When Irish Eyes Are Smiling," and publicly denied all knowledge of his friends' criminal pasts.

The ILA machine ran on fear and greed. With his gangster colleagues, Ryan made the employers pay for "labor peace," but the true victims were his own members, the longshoremen themselves.

They did not complain, however—at least, not out loud. "Talkers" were usually beaten, maimed, or killed. More quelling even than that, there were about 22,000 regular longshore jobs in the harbor, and some 48,000 men available to fill them. At base rates of pay, only one man in four managed to earn between $2,000 and $4,000 a year, while the rest had to support themselves and their families on casual earnings of $8.50 or so for an occasional four-hour shift.

Their leaders managed a little better. King Joe had been averaging $50,000 a year in salary and expenses for some time, and probably twice as much again in illegal payments from employers. (He was also buying his silk shirts and Cadillacs with money taken from what the ILA's executive council described as "a confidential anti-Communist fund set up by our International for use by our International president in combating Communist activity.")

Dissent was ruthlessly suppressed. The last significant reform movement, coalescing in 1939 around a Brooklyn longshoreman named Peter Panto, came to nothing when he was strangled and buried in a lime pit by Albert Anastasia. The District Attorney in Brooklyn was then William O'Dwyer. Pressed to investigate the Panto killing more vigorously, he denounced his critics as "Communists," a charge echoed by ILA counsel Louis Waldman when the matter came up again at the Crime Commission hearings. The greatest problem on the waterfront, he said, was "the long and bitter civil war" that the "visible and invisible forces of the Kremlin" were waging to seize control of American ports.

Joe Stalin had met his match in Joe Ryan, however. ILA men like the Murphy brothers, William, Francis, and Michael, ran the piers as tightly as any commissar. With George Barone, hiring boss on Pier 58, North River, and Fred R. Field, Jr., heir-apparent to mobster Michael Clemente in Local 856, they represented the rising generation of labor racketeers, in their twenties and thirties, but they had learned their business from experts of the old school.

In 1951, Michael Murphy was bumped from his job as hiring boss on Pier 3 by Nuncio Aluotto, a protégé of the Bowers Gang. The brothers were distinctly upset. A few days before starting work, Aluotto called at the office of ILA Local 867, opposite Pier 3, and the Murphys followed him there to remonstrate. In the middle of their animated discussion, Aluotto was shot dead.

The Murphys then left. In fact, they disappeared. William surrendered three weeks later, and was let out on bail, but it was another 22 months before the FBI finally ran Francis and Michael to earth in a tourist cottage at Madeira Beach, Florida. Brought to trial in Jersey City, William was acquitted of murder in February 1954, while his brothers received directed verdicts of not guilty on the grounds that the state had failed to make out a case for them to answer.

Though the Waterfront Commission later barred the Murphys from the piers because their presence would "constitute a danger to the public," the Aluotto killing did little harm to their careers. Michael Murphy, the least successful of the three, held a variety of well-paid posts in various ILA Locals before retiring into private practice to make use of his union heft as a "container coordinator" in Jersey City. Francis Murphy became business agent of ILA Clerks and Checkers Local 1 and his brother William's number one enforcer, while William himself went on to the post of business agent and president of ILA Local 2.

Using this as a power base, he and Francis Murphy eventually pacified the Jersey side of the harbor, and as a reward, William was elected a vice president of the International at its 1963 convention.

George Barone's career, meanwhile, had taken a different turn. He first came to public notice in 1954 after a particularly brutal assault on a Chelsea dockworker, but at 30, he was already a favorite son of the mobsters who ran Local 1804, and who had installed him as hiring boss for Pier 58 on New York's lower West Side. In this capacity, Barone had found it necessary to "discipline" a maintenance man named William Torres by denying him work on two consecutive days, but when, on the afternoon of the third day, a Saturday, he bumped into him on 15th Street, Torres still seemed unrepentant.

"What are you doing?" demanded Barone, who had two of his goon squad with him. "Looking for trouble?"

Though accompanied by a friend, Torres read the signs correctly, and ran for his life.

Cornered in the hallway of an apartment building on West 14th Street, he was punched, kicked, beaten with an 18-inch iron bar, and finally left insensible in the stairwell, but they had not bent his neck. After St. Vincent's Hospital stitched him up, Torres went back on the streets with a patrolman to look for Barone, and had him arrested for felonious assault; in the circumstances, an act of the purest heroism.

With a little string-pulling by his ILA masters, Barone contrived to wriggle out of serious trouble by pleading guilty to a charge of disorderly conduct, but the conviction was enough to cost him his job as a hiring boss. Not that the union cared: Its executives went on to make him an organizer for the International and gave him three Locals to play with. But the Waterfront Commission now had grounds enough to bar him from the piers.

The bi-state Commission had taken over the supervision of the Port of New York and New Jersey on December 1, 1953. From then on, anyone found guilty of criminal or shady practices in the harbor was liable to have his license suspended or revoked, a power the Commission promptly exercised in cases like Barone's "disorderly conduct."

But to be struck off the register was not necessarily the same thing as being kicked off the waterfront. The statutes from which the Commission derived its powers had been framed in such a hurry, passing through the legislatures of New York and New Jersey in a mere 16 days, that holes were left in the net, and Barone was among a shoal of bigger fish who swam through, out of the Commission's reach. With the mob's backing, he took over "Chenango" Local 1826, which represented the men who worked New York's railroad lighters and harbor craft, a vital link between the port and its railheads on the Jersey side.

It was not until 1960, when the Commission persuaded the Governors of both states to endorse further legislation extending its reach to other areas of dock-related employment, that the mobsters began to worry.

The union's immediate reaction was to sponsor a Port Council of Greater New York under the presidency of Anthony M. Scotto, fast rising to prominence under the aegis of his father-in-law, Anthony "Tough Tony" Anastasio, boss of Brooklyn Local 1814. Claiming to represent 175,000 trade unionists connected with the waterfront, the Council managed to stall the new law until January 1962, but by March, the Chenangoes were registering with the Waterfront Commission, and Barone had at last retreated to Florida under a hail of subpoenas. Dropping discreetly out of sight for a while, he surfaced again in 1966 with several old cronies from Local 1826 to build a new empire in the South with Fat Freddy Field.

Field was the politician of the group, despite his foul mouth, his coarseness of manner, and a police record for burglary and car theft going back to 1935. When faced with a problem, he reached for a solution rather than a lead pipe, a policy encouraged by his tutor in the rackets, Michael Clemente, secretary-business agent of Locals 856 and 856-1, a negotiator by temperament, and boss of the downtown Manhattan waterfront from the East River piers to the United Fruit Lines terminal on the lower West Side. In 1952, however, Clemente failed to negotiate a satisfactory deal with the federal government in connection with his income tax, and Fred R. Field, Jr. moved up to fill the vacancy thus created.

Unlike most of the old guard, Field understood what was happening. Under Joe Ryan, the ILA had exploited its members and squeezed their employers. Kept in line by the mob, dockworkers had not dared to complain, and the industry had not cared to, as long as it could pass the cost along to its customers. But that era had ended with the Waterfront Commission. By driving the goon squads off the piers, it had given the longshoremen a chance to assert the democratic rights which had always been theirs in theory but always withheld in practice. Only the employers (and the public) were now available for victimization, and to exert the necessary pressure, Field and his racketeering colleagues needed the men behind them. Voluntarily.

Hard though it was for the old guard to grasp, if the ILA was going to survive as a money-maker, it now had to behave like a trade union. If the support of its members could no longer be exacted by force, it would have to be bought with contract benefits.

This meant Ryan had to go. He and his fellow members of the wage-scale committee had been taking money for years to settle for five-and-dime contracts, and the dockworkers knew it.

He was replaced as International president by Captain William V. Bradley, the fat, amiable, constantly sweating president of the ILA's tugboat division, and one of the few International vice presidents to emerge from the Crime Commission hearings without being charged with complicity in the rackets. Gullible, vacillating, a devout Catholic and family man, Bradley was an ideal puppet for Teddy Gleason, who now, as International organizer, became the real power in the union.

These changes suited Field very well. He was on good terms with Gleason, who shared his views about mending fences with the membership, and who was looking to buttress his control behind the scenes by placing friends in strategic positions. On May 26, 1955, he made Field president of the New York District Council, with the responsibility for coordinating the activities of 38 ILA Locals in New York and New Jersey. It was just the power base Field had always wanted. He could now "negotiate" on equal terms with any employer in the port—except in Brooklyn, which belonged to "Tough Tony" Anastasio. And except that the container shipping revolution was about to alter the rules of the game by doing away with two-thirds of the waterfront's labor force.

Yielding to the inevitable, the ILA agreed, in 1960, to handle container ships in return for a cargo royalty payment of up to $1 a ton, a deal that was clearly going to net the union tens of millions of dollars a year as the industry continued to automate itself, but which also amounted to a closure notice for Manhattan's piers. Short of razing the Wall Street area, there was simply no room on the island for the huge upland storage areas needed for the operation of container ships, and consequently no future for Local 856, from which Field ultimately derived his position. The International union was now a more suitable vehicle for his talents.

In 1963, Teddy Gleason dropped his puppet president Bradley, and took over the office himself. Field moved up to general organizer, which, in theory, made him number three in the union hierarchy, but a new power had emerged in the back rooms in the person of Anthony Scotto.

Though only a few months had passed since the death of Tony Anastasio, Scotto played the role of kingmaker as though born to it. Field was left in no doubt that he owed his election to Scotto's bloc of 111 votes —nearly half the New York total—rather than to Gleason, who controlled only 41.

The point was not lost on Field, whose Manhattan Local had been losing out to Scotto's Brooklyn Local for years. No longer in a position to "negotiate" with New York's employers as profitably as in the past, he now adopted a Southern strategy, aiming to build a position in the sunbelt ports comparable to Scotto's in the North.

As president of the International Banana Handlers' Council, through his "Banana Local" 856-1, he already had a foot in the door. With Barone and his Chenango colleagues moving South, he had just the muscle he needed to push it open, and walk right over Joe Teitelbaum.

Ten days after Field's election, as though to speed him on his way, a federal grand jury in Manhattan indicted Fat Freddy on 11 counts of embezzling union funds.

5

Phony Peace

CHARACTERISTICALLY, Joe Teitelbaum went into business with the Prime Minister of the Bahamas after threatening to sue him. Sir Roland Symonette had chartered one of his ships to a company that hired Eagle as its stevedore in Miami but failed to pay its bill. Although the sum involved was only about $1,500, Joe cared about the principle.

"It's your ship," he said, when Sir Roland came to see him about it. "Either you pay me or I'll slap a lien on her the next time she puts in here."

"My dear fellow," said Sir Roland mildly. "These people owe me a hundred times more than they owe you. We're both in the same boat, so to speak."

"Yes, but it's *your* boat."

"Well, certainly it is. But how can you possibly hold me responsible for someone else's bad debts? If they owe you money, that's *your* problem."

"Yes, but it's *your* ship."

Sir Roland tried a Prime Ministerial frown. When that failed, he laughed. "Tell you what. I'll meet you half way. I'll pay you fifty cents on the dollar."

Joe gave in ruefully. "No wonder you're a rich man," he said.

"And no wonder you've got this port by the tail." Sir Roland drummed his fingers on the desk. "Look here, I've just built a new ship. Roll-on, roll-off. Twelve trailers. Any idea what we could do with her?"

Joe settled back in his chair. "Funny you should ask me that," he said. "I've got some spare trailers. And I've been thinking about Jamaica."

"Have you really? So have I. How about a spot of lunch?"

"Only if you're paying," said Joe.

He left for Jamaica next morning.

Thirty days later, the M/V *Common Entrance,* flagship of the new Narwhal Line, duly sailed from Miami on her maiden voyage to Kingston, Jamaica with $5,300-worth of freight. As she cost about $1,000 a day to run, the partners stood to make about $150 apiece.

Within six months, however, the ship was running 12 full trailers each way every 10 days, with cargo backed up in the warehouses at both ends.

Joe went to see his partner about it in Nassau.

"Sir Roland," he said, "we need a bigger ship."

"Won't be easy, Joe. You know what the charter market's like. There's not much around."

"No, I want to build one. I've been working on the design."

"Build one? You can't be serious."

"Why not? I know exactly what I want. I want a warehouse that floats, with an engine big enough to get it to Jamaica in two days or less. I made a few drawings. You wanna see?"

"Now hold on a minute, Joe. Not so fast. You're talking serious dollars now."

"Well, we're *making* serious dollars. And with the right kind of ship, we can do even better. Now look at this."

Sir Roland put his hand over the drawings. "Joe," he said patiently, "you're talking a million dollars at least."

"Sure." Joe was surprised. "Maybe more."

Sir Roland sighed. "And it's not just the money, Joe. You've got to find the right yard to build it. You can't rush into a thing like this."

"I know. I got a friend in New York who's a ship broker. He says the German yards are probably best for the kind of ship I got in mind. His associate in Stockholm has had a lot of experience with 'em."

"Well, that's better. We have to study this carefully."

On his next visit to Nassau, Joe brought Uncle Mutzie with him and plans for the *Jamaican Provider,* a 300-foot, 1,500-ton motor vessel to be built to his own specifications by J.J. Seites of Hamburg.

"Look at that," he said proudly. "Nearly all aluminum. Saves weight. Saves fuel. And look at the trailer deck. No columns. No casings. That's all usable space. Big hydraulic ramp. I can roll thirty, forty trailers in and out of there in half a day, easy. No sweat at all. And look at the main deck. See that? That's a full one hundred feet for deck cargo. Unobstructed. Carry anything. More boxes. Cars. Transformers. Anything. Isn't she great?"

"Never saw anything like it."

"That's what they said at the yard. Nothing else in the world like her. So what do you think?"

Sir Roland sat back helplessly. "Well, I don't know, Joe. It *sounds* all right. Funny looking thing, though."

"Funny looking?" Joe was hurt. He pulled the drawings around to see for himself. "I don't think so. That's pure functional design. A floating money machine. Nothing funny about that."

Sir Roland smiled. "How much?"

"Seventeen-knot design speed. That's not funny either. That's Miami–

Kingston in a day and a half. We could even run her from Jacksonville, with a stop in Miami, and still keep on schedule in and out of Kingston. I don't call *that* funny."

"How *much,* Joe?"

"Million and a quarter. Twenty-five percent down."

Uncle Mutzie cleared his throat. "We'll put up thirty-seven and a half percent," he said.

And so it was agreed. Contracts were signed, a quarter of the purchase price was deposited with J.J. Seites against a completion date in December 1967, and Sir Roland Symonette formally invited Ann Teitelbaum to launch the ship when the time came, thereby fending off still another domestic crisis over her husband's chronic absenteeism. Much of his time was now taken up just keeping Eagle afloat. Only a shadow of itself after Field's mauling, the stevedoring business had suffered a further blow when Alvin P. Chester, boss of Chester, Blackburn and Roder, and his assistant, Jeremy Chester (no relation) withdrew the Pan–American Line account.

Joe was alone in his office one afternoon, catching up with his paperwork when James Vanderwyde came to see him. A short, stocky, gray-haired man in his late forties, Vanderwyde was "office manager" of Local 1922 and Barone's hatchet man, a job of sufficient importance to have merited a vice presidency in Chenango Local 1826, and to have earned him a police record that included gun charges, assault, robbery, and a five-year stretch in Sing Sing for grand larceny. His brother William had enjoyed a similar career until his execution in 1948 for the murder of a hiring boss.

Starting in the morning, he said, Eagle would have to hire union checkers.

"Why don't you get off my back?" Joe said. "We signed the contract. We pay our goddamn dues. What more do you want?"

"You're out of the union."

"We're *what?*"

"You're management. You're out."

Joe blinked. "Great. First you tell me I got to be in. Now you tell me I'm out. Okay. So what?"

"So this is a union port. You gotta use union checkers."

Joe ground the base of his spine in his chair. "When I need labor, I'll order it," he said.

"Okay. How many you gonna need? I'll send 'em over."

"You can send 'em to the moon for all I care. When I need thieves, I'll hire my own."

Vanderwyde watched him impassively. "You don't learn, do you? Looks like we're gonna have to teach you again."

He turned to go, and Joe bounced to his feet. These were the first people he had met who offered not the slightest room for give and take.

"Just who the hell do you think you're talking to?" he bawled. "Coming in here, telling me what to do."

"I'm talking to a Jew prick who don't learn."

It was said without heat, but with such naked ill will that Joe flinched in spite of himself.

"*They* don't come, *nobody* comes."

And nobody did. Not one longshoreman reported for work next morning.

"We can't take this, Joey," said Gus. "They're killing us. I gotta call Barone."

Joe had had a pain in his chest all day. "They're killing us anyway," he said. "Who *needs* this?"

"We got mouths to feed. They go to Zim with this . . ." He pulled a face.

"I know, I know." Joe pumped at his cigar and swatted away the smoke. "Bastards. I could kill that son of a bitch."

"Sure. You could kill one a day for a month and we'd still be in trouble. I think we should go with SACAL into Jacksonville. Let things quiet down a little."

The South American & Caribbean Line account had become more important to Eagle after its recent reverses. Indeed, with Zim and Seawind Line, it was all the business the firm had left, apart from Narwhal. But after making good money on the stevedoring, Eagle was now showing practically no profit from the account at all. Under pressure itself from the ILA, the line had chopped prices, cut off Eagle's warehousing income, refused to pay for overtime, and generally pared its margins to the bone.

"You're out of your mind," said Joe. "Those people are gonna bankrupt this corporation."

"Then they better hurry while they got the chance. What else can happen to us? SACAL's going into Jacksonville, and we can have the business. Go play with your boat."

Eagle hired Barone's checkers; Gus and Uncle Mutzie went ahead with the Jacksonville terminal, and Joe took Ann to Hamburg on December 16, 1967, to launch the *Jamaican Provider*. After completing her sea trials, she sailed from Hamburg at the end of March 1968, crossed the Atlantic at an average speed of 17 knots, and was met on her arrival at Dodge Island by a reception committee of Jamaican notables, Miami civic leaders, and shipping experts drawn from all over the world by her revolutionary design. It was a proud moment for Joe. Here was a ship he had conjured into existence with drive, imagination, and nerve. She was *his* ship, and his peers had come to learn from her.

One of them learned that his days as a cargo carrier to Jamaica were probably numbered unless he acted quickly. After less than six months of scheduled service, in which the *Provider* vindicated all his hopes, Joe

received a call from Sir Roland. He was selling out to Court Lines, he said
—Narwhal's main competitor on the Kingston run. And he was not to be
moved, not by Joe's insistence on the contract between them, nor yet by
appeals to his sense of fair play.

Incensed, Joe slapped a lien on the *Jamaican Provider* as soon as she
sailed into port. Sir Roland promptly bonded her out again, but Joe was
already off on another tack. Turning the case over to his father to fight,
he flew to England to confer with a British yard about *two* new ships of
similar design. He had been nursing this project along to expand the
Narwhal fleet. Now he thought he might run them to Venezuela in partnership with Eagle, but his bad luck continued. At the very last moment,
just as the contracts were being drawn up, he learned that the ships were
to be financed with Kuwaiti oil money. This killed the deal instantly.
Already blacklisted by the Arab boycott office in Damascus, had he wished
to proceed, he would have had to renounce his connection with Zim–
Israel Navigation, and that was unthinkable. He flew back empty handed
to Miami, only to find that, in his absence, his father had settled out of
court with Sir Roland Symonette.

"What in hell did you want to go and do a thing like that for?" he yelled,
exasperated beyond measure. "My God, we were gonna *win*. Didn't you
know that? *He* did. *I* did. Why in the world would you wanna settle for
less?"

"Take it easy," said Gus. "You'll give yourself a heart attack. You like
fighting more than you like winning. The guy wasn't gonna give up."

"Neither was I."

"So? You like making lawyers rich? Appeals. Appeals against appeals.
This could go on for years."

"So what? In the end, we'd have won."

"So what, he says. In the end, winning would cost us money, that's so
what. This way is better. We get our money back. We even make a little.
Us." He hammered his chest. "Not the lawyers."

Joe went for a walk along the dock. When he cooled off, he returned
to the office, where Gus was still waiting patiently.

"All right," said Joe, knowing he had no choice. "We'll do it your way.
I'll take the money and build my *own* ship."

His father scratched his head. "Well," he said doubtfully. "We could
use it in Jacksonville, but I guess you got the right."

Joe went home for a change of laundry, and caught the next plane out
to Madrid, where he conferred with the naval architect who had designed
the *Jamaican Provider* and a Spanish broker, who introduced him to a
shipyard in Vigo. Together, they worked up plans for a bigger, roll-on,
roll-off trailer vessel of some 3,000 tons displacement to compete directly
with Court on the Kingston run. The final price was $1.8 million, with a
20 percent down payment to be made in four installments, the first falling
due on signing the contract.

With some reluctance, because Eagle had meanwhile gone public with an offer of over-the-counter stock to raise money for the Jacksonville terminal, Gus Teitelbaum persuaded Uncles Sam and Mutzie Kratish to go along with the deal. The first $90,000 was duly deposited with the yard, and Joe set about financing the rest.

The Symonette affair had given him an idea of how he might do it. The *Jamaican Provider* had fetched far more than she had cost. Every maritime country in the world was scrambling to build or buy container ships. With their value rising, and with inflation weakening most European currencies against the dollar, to have such a vessel under construction on a fixed-price contract in Spain was better than money in the bank. Three months after making the first payment, and having talked the idea through with Mel Kessler, Joe sat down again with Gus.

"I wanna build another ship," he said.

"Oi." Gus laced his fingers over his head. "Go home. Call the doctor."

"I already told the yard, and we're damn lucky they can do it. Their order book's full now."

"That's lucky? You know how much we're gonna owe? You're acting crazy, Joe. We ain't got that kind of money."

"We will," Joe said. "Don't worry about it. I told 'em we wanna run the second ship to Panama."

"To Panama." Gus nodded, humoring him. " 'Don't worry about it.' My God, Joe. I worry about *you*. Where the hell are you gonna get $720,000 from for a down payment on *two* ships? What are you trying to do? Make admiral?"

"Listen." But he was wasting his breath.

Gus paced back and forth in front of him, waving his arms. "We got a million dollars tied up in Jacksonville," he wailed. "We got Barone and these sons of bitches killing us down here. We got every kind of problem with the business and the family, and what does my son want to do? He wants to buy ships. A million eight each, and he wants to buy ships." He collapsed dramatically into his chair. "Stay in bed tomorrow. *I'll* call 'em. Say you had a breakdown or something."

"And throw away a million dollars? Maybe two?"

Gus stared.

"Look at Symonette," said Joe. "People are lining up to buy this kind of ship. Two years from now, who knows? Maybe we'll sell one to pay for the other."

He watched the play of expressions on his father's face.

"What a load to carry, Joe," Gus said slowly. "I don't know. Looks like we're in over our head already up there."

"Didn't I tell you? Didn't I say you shouldn't build on SACAL? Maybe next time you'll listen."

"Yeah, yeah. Next time. Right now is when we got the problem."

"Okay. Here's what I'll do. You take care of Sam and Mutzie on this, and I'll get you a new account for Jacksonville. I want that second ship."

He got the second ship.

After talking to his father, Joe called John Caputo in New York, and Eagle's business in Jacksonville was duly augmented by the Lloyd–Brasileiro and Dover Line accounts, although the terminal proved too small for their bigger vessels. That was Gus's problem, however. Having kept his side of the bargain, Joe set off with Mel Kessler to see about financing his ships.

But on their return to Miami, Joe found he wouldn't need it. In almost daily touch with Mordechai Chovers, Zim's chief of operations in New York, Joe had made no secret of his Spanish ship-building program, so that he was not really surprised when Chovers called him for a progress report.

Though Zim's fleet was already overstretched, the line had contracted to operate a roll-on, roll-off service between Haifa and Trieste, hoping to scrape through while the additional ships it needed were under construction. But delivery dates for new vessels had now lengthened beyond the point where Zim could still expect to improvise, and its only hope, Chovers explained, lay in taking over an existing contract. As a true supporter of Israel, would Joe consider selling to Zim the two trailer ships he had building in Vigo?

Joe was not sure. He was ready to sell one. He had counted on doing so. But selling both meant starting all over again for the third time. He told Chovers he would think about it. On the deal Zim proposed, he stood to make a profit of about half a million dollars, but it was a ship he wanted, not the money.

Then, one afternoon in the spring of 1971, not long after his thirty-ninth birthday, Joe wanted the money.

He was cleaning up his desk before going home when Gus shuffled in, lowered himself into a chair and sat there without speaking. Joe looked at him with some alarm.

"Hey, you all right?"

Gus shrugged.

Joe sorted through the possibilities.

"Okay. Let me guess. Momma ran off with the newsboy."

Gus avoided his eye. "We're busted."

"Busted? What do you mean, *busted?*"

"What's the matter?" He flared up irritably. "That's not English? I mean, busted, okay? I mean, we lost all our money." Then he subsided. "You wanna say I told you so, now's the time."

"SACAL?" asked Joe.

Gus nodded "They're pulling out of Jacksonville."

"Oh, man."

Joe was appalled. He had not been paying much attention to the new terminal, but he knew Eagle had been running at a loss up there for almost a year.

"How much are we in for?"

"A million? Million and a quarter?"

Joe grimaced, and Gus bowed his head.

"We're wiped out, Joey," he said tremulously. "I don't know what your mother is gonna say. How am I gonna find *that* kind of money?"

"What does Mutzie say?"

His father brushed this aside, chin on chest.

"Go home, Gus," Joe said. "I'll take a look at it."

"Looking won't change nothing. We're busted."

"It might. Go home now. You look terrible. Get some rest."

"Rest? How can I rest? I tell you we're bankrupt, and you say to me, 'Go home and rest'? I got to spell it out to you? We're finished. It's over."

"Not for me, poppa. Not yet."

Gus didn't hear him. "First those crooks. Now this. Wiped us out. And don't shake your head. What's the matter with you? You don't believe me? You wanna see the books?"

"Yes, I do. And I want you to go home, eat a little something light, and go to bed. We'll talk again tomorrow."

They looked at each other.

"You retiring me, Joey?"

"If I'm gonna do anything, poppa, I need a free hand."

Gus thought for a while, and then nodded.

"Mutzie's got to understand that, too," Joe said. "I don't want him on my back either."

His father hung his head again. "Sure. Okay. I'll tell him. Maybe Sam should be chairman."

He pulled himself up to go, and Joe knew better than to help.

"Drive safely, poppa."

Gus nodded. "I got a good name, Joe," he said, turning at the door. Joe got up and hugged him.

"It's my name, too," he said. "We'll pay back every nickel."

A week later, his father had a heart attack, and very nearly died; Uncle Sam Kratish moved up to board chairman, and Joe formed Pierside Terminal Operators, Inc., to take over the group's stevedoring interests.

His job now was to extricate Eagle as gracefully as possible from Jacksonville, and coax some compensating growth out of their Miami business, but even as he scoured Europe and the Caribbean for new accounts, he knew he would never find a better client than himself.

After selling his two trailer-ship contracts to Zim–Israel, Joe had changed his mind about Jamaica. Honduras now looked a better bet, particularly after he met an official of BCIE, the Central American investment bank, in Tegucigalpa, the capital. The bank had a lot of development capital at its disposal, mainly from World Bank and American aid sources, and had shown a marked preference for port improvement and shipping schemes. The snags were that the money was available only to Central American corporations, and then for no more than 60 percent of the cost of any given project.

Neither difficulty detained Joe for very long. The bank official's brother-in-law, Oscar Martinez, was willing, even anxious, to help when he heard what Joe had in mind, and so were his associates, Virgilio Guzman, and Guillermo Medina Santos. As for the 60 percent rule, Joe soon found a way around *that.*

"Mel," he said. "This is a masterpiece."

"I don't think I want to hear about it," said Kessler.

"These guys are willing to come in as partners with me in a Honduran corporation, right? They own two percent, Eagle owns the rest. That takes care of the first problem."

"Maybe. What do you know about these people?"

"Not much. But what can they do with two percent? Okay. So now we need about one point eight million to build the ship."

"Which you don't have."

"Which I don't have."

"In fact, you don't even have forty percent of one point eight million dollars. And you'll need to put up that much before the bank'll lend you the rest."

"Right. But let's say the project costs three million dollars, not one point eight million. Sixty percent of three million is about what we need." Joe mentally checked his figures. "Sure. If we put in for sixty percent of three million dollars, the loan will just about cover the cost of the ship."

Kessler felt his forehead tenderly. "Joe," he said. "Go home. If you don't have forty percent of a million eight, you sure as hell don't have forty percent of three million. Please go home."

"Ships gotta have containers, right?" Joe shook his head at such obtuseness. "We'll need trailers, tractors, forklifts . . . all kinds of expensive equipment. That could put the price up to three million dollars, couldn't it?"

Kessler sighed. "I knew I should never have listened to this. Are you telling me you want to pledge Eagle's equipment into this new corporation?"

"There you go." Joe beamed. "Paint it up a little, and I figure I can get it appraised at a million, million and a quarter, easy. Add on the ship, and we got ourselves a three million-dollar project. Didn't I say it was a masterpiece?"

"What makes you think they'll buy a deal like that?"

"Because I asked them, and they said yes. In principle. And why not? What's wrong with it? They'll pass the loan in a minute. And here's something else. I'm gonna name the ship *Morazan.* Francisco Morazan is like the George Washington of Honduras, okay? When they heard that, this guy at the bank, he damn near had an orgasm."

Kessler nodded philosophically. "Where are you going to build this thing? You told me the yards are all full."

"Yeah. But remember that broker in Madrid? Ferrer? He found us a spot in Gijon. Design work's done. All we gotta do is make the first payment."

"Uh-huh. Pretty pleased with yourself, right? Got yourself a two million-dollar ship for free."

"Hell, no. She's already cost me ten grand in travel expenses."

6

Paying Tribute

Now they needed a crane.

Moe Harrison had died, releasing Joe from his promise not to buy one while the old man lived, and Harrison's son was refusing to work for Pierside Terminal Operators until Joe paid a disputed bill for $30,000. Meanwhile, there were ships to unload.

"We should get our own crane," said Ben Mussary, who had taken charge of operations.

"Right," said Joe. "I got one spotted."

"Yeah?" Ben sat up eagerly. "What kind? I wanna see it."

"Big mother," said Joe. "Ninety-ton lift. American made. Got about a hundred hours on it. And no, you can't see it, because the son of a bitch is in St. Croix."

"Great," said his cousin Manny Levy, who had come in full time to run the office. "Sounds like a couple of hundred grand at least."

"No. *Three* hundred. And worth every nickel. But the price to us is a hundred and twenty-five. *If* I can get it up here."

He awaited their expressions of pleasure and amazement, but Manny just sighed.

"Joe, we got Jacksonville," he said. "We got a law suit on our hands with Harrison. Everybody's taking us to the cleaners and you want to buy a crane?"

"Who's this talking?" Joe was not very pleased. "Mutzie?"

"I just want to know what you're planning to use for money, that's all."

"Yeah, well, that's *my* business. *I'll* buy the crane, and you can lease it from me. I'm gonna see Mel."

Melvyn Kessler had spent the day in court, and was not at his most receptive.

"What are you planning to use for money?"

"Hey, I can pay it off over four years. It's a fantastic buy. What's the matter with you people?"

"Nothing. Except that you owe a million dollars already. Now why don't you just file a Chapter 11 bankruptcy, like I told you, and start off fresh?"

"Because I promised Gus I wouldn't. And anyway, *I'm* gonna buy this crane personally. And at that price, it's like stealing. This is a ninety-ton Lima we're talking about."

"What's that? Some kind of huge bean? You're crazy."

"Mel, I want that crane."

"Okay." Kessler saw he had to take him seriously, and put his feet on the desk. "What's the catch?"

"No catch," Joe said. "It's a repossession. Isbrandtsen was running a couple of little ships out of New York to the Virgins. They bought the crane on some kind of a lease–purchase deal last summer, used it a couple of months before the strike hit, and never started up again. So this big Lima's been sitting down there on the dock for seven months doing nothing. She's almost brand-new."

"Is that Lima, Peru, or Lima, Ohio?"

"That's Lima, Ohio. So I called Hoffman Crane, who own it, and the guy tells me a hundred and seventy-five thousand dollars. He says he's got a hundred and twenty-five thousand tied up in it, and has to get that back to break even."

"So that's what you offered him, right?"

"Right. But then he says, 'Well, I need the extra money to pay off the port authority in St. Croix. They're claiming for seven months' dockage and wharfage and God knows what. And then I'll have to ship it up,' he says, 'so I'm still not gonna make anything on this.' So I told him, I said, 'Well, in that case, I'll make you a better deal. I'll buy the crane for a hundred and twenty-five thousand financed over four years at six percent —let's say a twenty-five percent add-on. That brings the total price to a hundred fifty-six thousand two hundred and fifty dollars, and the monthly payments to three thousand two hundred fifty-six dollars and twenty cents. I'll give you the first and last installments as security, and it'll be *my* job to bring the crane up. I'm buying as is, where is.' "

Kessler shook his head helplessly. Joe's deals had amused and impressed him since high school. "So what did *he* say?"

"He's coming down next week to draw up the contract."

"Now wait a minute. So you can maybe get by with the three thousand a month if you lease it to Eagle. What about the charges down in St. Croix? How much is that?"

"I don't know." Joe shrugged. "Didn't ask."

"You didn't *ask?*"

"No." He looked surprised. "I don't care. Nothing to do with me. *I'm* not going to pay. *I* didn't leave it there."

Kessler hesitated. "I don't think I want to hear this next part," he said. "How are you going to get the crane if you don't pay the charges?"

"Well, I'll get a trailer ship in there one night, and . . ."

"Never mind," he said. "I'll take care of the contract, but after that you're on your own. Is there anything else I should know?"

"Yeah. I gotta put the house up as collateral."

Kessler rubbed his eyes. "Okay," he said. "And after we draw up the contract, we'll step across the street and get you certified insane."

The coveted Lima was a black-and-yellow mobile crane about 100 feet high and weighing an equally noticeable 110,000 pounds. To smuggle it out of St. Croix under the nose of the port authority would take friends and organization. After signing the contract, Joe flew down to size up the situation. His best hope was Tug Haraldson, a Swedish seaman who had settled on the island with a black girl and now supported their four kids by occasionally representing American shipping interests. He rose to the bait as though breaking a hunger strike.

"Oh, man," he breathed, "that's dynamite. We get all kinds here. Guys who wanna move dope or booze and cigarettes. We got guys running guns and moving crates of cash around. There's illegal immigrants, stolen boats, hijacked airplanes, but I never heard about a hot crane before. I love it."

"Hey," said Joe. "It ain't hot. I got title to it."

"Never mind, man. I don't care. Count me in."

"Listen, if anybody's liable to go to jail, I'd rather pay the money, okay?"

"And spoil my fun? Man, you just bring that ship in here, and I'll get a few guys together to load her on. No sweat." But he looked thoughtful.

"That simple, huh?"

"Well . . . Almost. Biggest problem we got is a couple of port authority guys we gotta take care of. Miserable, mean bastards. No sense of humor at all. Once they're off the dock, the rest is easy."

"What's it gonna take?" Joe rustled invisible dollar bills between thumb and forefinger.

Haraldson shook his head. "You wanna go to jail, that's the way to get there. You're gonna have to spread a little bread around, but not with them." He stared into his beer for inspiration. "One's a drunk, so that's no problem. I'll find another one to keep him company that night, so long as *you* pick up the tab."

"My pleasure," Joe said. "How about the other one?"

"Harder. That's his boss. Hates to go home. So would you if you had *his* old lady." He smiled suddenly. "And he's no problem either. We'll get him Puerto Rican Red."

"What's that? Marijuana?"

"No. That's a well-known piece of ass. He likes redheads. Soon as you know what night you want to do this, we can fly her in from San Juan." He looked at Joe inquiringly. "It's getting a little expensive now."

"No, I like it. I like it. We could slug him in the head for nothing, but then he'd tell the cops, and the cops would want to know what happened to the crane. This way, what's he gonna do when he sees it's gone? Complain about getting laid?"

"Not if I know Puerto Rican Red," said Haraldson. "Goddamn. I love it."

"Right. We'll move her next week."

Back in Miami, Joe went to see an agent friend of his who ran a roll-on, roll-off ship once a week to St. Thomas. For $2,000, plus a bonus for the captain, he booked space on the return leg of his next trip, and arranged for the vessel to make an unscheduled stop at St. Croix, arriving at 11 P.M. precisely on Saturday night. She was to enter and leave the harbor on her riding lights alone, and get the hell out as soon as the cargo was loaded.

Like the few others he had to confide in, the agent immediately took a personal interest in his scheme, curious to see if he could really pull it off. And the money had nothing to do with it now. Joe was not going to save much anyway, by the time he had finished flying whores around and getting people drunk, but he was enjoying himself hugely. He had fallen in love with a beautiful crane, and the idea of carrying her off in a midnight abduction was beyond considerations of profit. It was now a matter of self-expression.

He flew down early on the Saturday to go over the details with Haraldson and his hand-picked crew of five longshoremen. The crane had been standing idle for months on a deep-water pier not much used by other shipping, and to avoid any last-minute embarrassment, Haraldson had already been out there with a fresh battery and a couple of cans of fuel to check her over and start the motor. He had not been able to do more than that for fear of attracting official attention, which meant they had several hours work ahead of them before the ship put in.

The sun slid into the sea, and as the dark came on behind it, the seven went singly to the dock to meet by the pair of forklift trucks that Haraldson had parked out of sight behind the shed. He was the last to arrive, having waited in town to make sure that his drinking buddy and Puerto Rican Red had closed with the enemy. They then worked flat out in the dark for three hours, cursing softly as they banged up their hands, and stopping every now and then to consult Joe's drawings by flashlight. It was almost 10:30 before they finished, dropping on the dock in sweaty heaps, but the crane's boom and gantry were down, stacked in sections ready for the forklifts to load them. There were bright lights and ships and a few men still working on the piers of the inner port, but no one had come near.

"I got her listed on the manifest as stevedoring equipment," Joe said. His voice sounded very loud in the stillness, and he dropped it a tone or two. "Returned American goods. Think Customs'll buy that?"

"Here, you mean?" asked Haraldson. "Or in Miami?"

"Oh, Miami's no problem. I got the invoice and everything."

"Well, there's no problem here, man. This time of night? With those two bums out of the way? Man, they'll clear her right off the bat, I guarantee you."

"Well, that's good. Because here she comes."

Looking out to sea some minutes earlier, he had spotted the riding lights of a biggish ship just outside the harbor. Now she was coming in toward them, her lights drifting almost imperceptibly through the velvet black.

"Oh, *shit.*"

They were worried about the tide. Though rising fast, and more than deep enough for the ship to berth, the water was still too low to get the right angle on the ship's ramp for the crane to be driven across. The moment had to be judged with extreme care, which was why Joe, after consulting the tide tables, had specified 11 P.M. With the water level too low, the crane would have to negotiate too steep a descent into the ship; too high, and it faced a climb. Designed to run on a level dock, the machine was going to be difficult enough to drive on board in any case, especially in semi-darkness.

There was another, and worse, hazard. A row of mooring bollards along the pier meant that the ramp could not be properly supported along its length. Only a few feet at the end would rest on the dock, forming a bridge between ship and shore over which the crane would have to pass. One slip, and the 50-ton machine would be sitting on the bottom under 30 feet of black water. And so would its driver.

The ship nosed in cautiously. At the last moment, Haraldson switched on the dock lights, but as soon as the lines were secured, the pier stepped back, lamp by lamp, into darkness. Then the ramp eased down like a drawbridge, opening up the ship's gullet, and a soft, diffused light from its trailer deck spilled out on the dock. It was just enough to see by.

Joe and Haraldson looked down at the water, heaving and glinting uneasily between the ship and the pier.

"What do you think?"

Haraldson shrugged. "I don't know. Twenty minutes. Half an hour, maybe?

"Okay." Joe glanced toward the town. "I'll go talk to the skipper. No reason he can't get her cleared while we're waiting. The minute she comes up flush, we'll run her across and haul ass."

The delay undermined them all. There had never been a way of hiding the arrival and departure of the ship from Customs and the port authority, but every unnecessary minute she spent in the harbor increased the risk of someone wondering what business she had at that particular pier. Her presence also increased the risk of a routine visit from the port security patrol, which so far had obviously seen no cause to venture out.

As the ship inched upward on the tide, and the minutes stretched out, the worst affected by the suspense seemed to be Haraldson's driver. Muttering to himself and shaking his head, he prowled back and forth between the crane and the water's edge, twice turning toward Joe and Haraldson as though to say something, then changing his mind.

"He's chickening out," said Joe. The ramp was almost horizontal with the dock.

"No." Haraldson eyed him doubtfully. "It's the waiting got to him, that's all. I'll tell him to start her up."

He walked over to the crane, signaling to the driver to join him, and the two exchanged a few heated whispers in its shadow. Then, still muttering, the man swung himself up into the cab, the starter cranked and cranked, the motor coughed, caught, exploding a jet of smoke up into the nimbus of light from the ship's hold, and settled into a steady pounding that boomed and rolled around the silent harbor.

Joe winced, and went back again to the edge to check the angle on the ramp. Haraldson joined him there for a last look, and as he turned to wave the driver across, Joe caught his arm.

"Not yet," he shouted. "That's a lot of weight. When she hits the ramp, that ship's gonna tilt, and there's no damn top clearance there. If he panics out, he'll be over the side."

Haraldson scratched his jaw. "So what do you want?"

"I wanna ten-degree angle on it, so she tilts flush. Go tell him to shut her down till I give you the signal. Goddamn thing's gonna wake up the whole fucking island."

The silence, driven off by the hammer of the crane's motor, came back and smothered them. The ship hummed, the water slapped, and away off from the town, its night noises came at them again across the harbor. Haraldson sent a man down to the end of the pier to keep watch for the security patrol, although what Joe would say or do if they came was something he had yet to figure out.

The ship eased higher. The ramp came level with the dock, and began to slant perceptibly upwards. The captain and most of his crew leaned on the rail to watch.

Joe waved to Haraldson, who banged on the side of the cab. The starter cranked, and when the motor fired, Joe walked onto the ramp. He could feel it stirring under his feet with the easy movement of the ship as she rose gently on the tide. Turning to face the crane, he beckoned it on with both hands, bracing himself against the expected tilt. The driver gunned the motor, forcing a snarling plume of smoke skyward, but the machine did not budge. Impatiently, Joe repeated his signal, and the motor dropped back to idling speed. Now furious, he started forward to see what was wrong, but before he was off the ramp, the driver jumped down from the cab, shouting angrily at Haraldson, and walked away, hands sawing at the air as though washing them of the whole affair.

"Son of a bitch chickened out," said Haraldson savagely. *"I'll* take her."

"The hell you will," said Joe. "Get on the ramp and guide me over."

"No, that ain't right, man. It's my job."

"Yeah, but it's my crane. And I don't have time to argue."

Joe hauled himself up into the cab and took a good look around to steady himself. From this vantage point, the crane and its massive wheels looked very wide, and the ramp much narrower than before. It was also a long way down to the humpy, restless water winking and gleaming between the ship and the dock.

Haraldson, walking backwards, motioned him to follow. Joe put her in gear, released the brake, and before he was really ready, the front wheels were bumping over the end of the ramp. He gunned the motor against the gradient and felt it give way, flattening out as the ship pitched toward him under the weight.

Haraldson staggered and Joe slowed down, wiping his mouth with the back of his hand as the other regained his balance and skipped backwards out of harm's way, still beckoning him on.

The ship then began a slow tilt back. With visions of the ramp lifting off the end of the pier if she went too far, Joe speeded up a little, trying to time his entry into the hold for the moment of maximum clearance, but Haraldson and several waiting members of the crew were suddenly yelling and waving their arms wildly for him to stop.

Heart pounding, he braked hard, and waited for the ship to dump him in the harbor. He could feel her every motion, as though the crane itself were afloat.

"Man, she's gonna foul on top," Haraldson shouted in his ear. "We got to drop the muffler and exhaust pipe."

Joe let out his breath. "Not here we don't. She'll break the fucking ramp."

He looked back over his shoulder, and guessing what he had in mind, Haraldson jumped down and ran ahead to guide him off. Cursing continuously under his breath, Joe selected reverse and gunned the crane straight back toward the dock. Driving into his own shadow, he had no idea where he was going, but as soon as he felt the wheels on solid ground, he stopped, drenched in sweat, and cut the motor. Three men clambered up on the housing and attacked the muffler with wrenches as though it were their mortal enemy.

"Okay," said Haraldson. "Come on down, man. It's my turn."

Joe shook his head. He wasn't ready to trust his legs. "You get those damn forklifts loaded," he said. "I want them over there right after me."

"You bet. Now just . . ."

"And don't get in my way this time. The angle that ramp's sticking up, I'm gonna have to take a run at it."

"Okay." Haraldson looked critically at the ship. "If she tilts too fast for you, let her come back again before you tuck in under the rail. You need all the height you can get."

Joe grunted. "What the hell are those guys doing?"

"Pipe's hot, man. They're trying their best."

He clambered out on the housing in his safety boots, pulled one of the men aside and aimed a series of heavy kicks at the loosened muffler joint. Joe felt the damage like a physical pain, but with the water still rising, there was no help for it. The joint parted suddenly, and the muffler and tail pipe clattered onto the dock. As the men jumped clear, Joe restarted the motor.

Without the muffler, the noise ripped the night to shreds, like a gigantic chain saw, a bewildering, battering onslaught that hurt Joe's ears, echoing back across the water in brittle, staccato fragments. The trailer deck was now well above the level of the dock. Not allowing himself to think, he slammed the crane into gear and set it at the ramp.

With so short a run before meeting the gradient, the machine slowed right down as soon as it left the pier. For one choking moment, he thought it might stall or slide back, but then the ship started to pitch, and his next problem was to hold the crane back on a downward slope into the hold, knowing that it must foul the hull at such an angle, and most probably bounce back over the side.

The ramp groaned—a distinct, drawn-out protest of overstressed metal—and Joe almost jumped for it. But there was no point in hitting the water first if 50 tons of crane fell on top of him a split-second later.

The ship righted herself, and the ramp straightened. Letting off the brake, he rolled into the hold, ducking involuntarily as the cab passed through with just inches to spare. He then parked, with the help of a grinning member of the crew, and switched off. After sitting still for a moment, he climbed down stiffly, ears singing, to meet the two forklifts as they clattered off the ramp with the first of the boom sections.

Scarcely five minutes later, her ramp up, the ship was standing off from the dock. Joe sat on a bollard watching until she cleared the harbor and her riding lights passed from view.

"Think anybody heard us?" he asked slyly.

"Jesus, man." Haraldson caught himself as he realized that Joe wasn't serious. "I'm ready to buy a drink for any son of a bitch who didn't. It'd cost me about two dollars."

The watchman on the gate waved as they went through.

After taking a shower, Joe sat up for the rest of the night in his hotel room drinking coffee and tomato juice while Haraldson toasted himself into insensibility. At 5:45, Joe put $2,000 on his chest and left him sleeping. He caught the Carib Airways "goose" to Puerto Rico, and was home in time for Sunday brunch with Ann. He tried to explain about the crane, but she was not very interested.

Wherever he happened to be in the world after that, Joe made a habit of telephoning Manny or Ben every day. When he spoke to Ben, he would generally ask after the health of his crane, which was now in service on the dock, and when he talked to Manny, it was usually about money. But after a few weeks, the Lima became the main topic of conversation with both of them. Somebody was tampering with it.

Starting up one morning, the driver found a punctured hydraulic line. It took three hours to repair, while a full gang of longshoremen sat around and watched at a cost of over $200 an hour. Some days later, two hydraulic lines were found with holes punched in them, and a whole morning's work was lost. A few days after that, the same thing happened again.

Joe flew home to keep watch on the crane that night, but saw nothing, and nor did Ben, who stood guard after work on the following day. This served a double purpose, for the firm was suffering also from a plague of cargo thefts, but Joe now had to fly back to New York. When he called next day, Ben was full of self-reproach. Two of the Lima's massive tires were flat. During the night, someone had stripped the valves.

Apart from the anguish Joe felt for his crane, he simply could not afford to have it out of action. Another crane company seemed the likeliest saboteur, but the port watchmen had seen nothing, and the Metro police, while sympathetic, had no men to spare for crane-watching on Dodge Island. Though Ben insisted he was ready to sleep in the driver's cab every night, the only practical solution seemed to be the hiring of a private security guard.

Then Joe had a call from Sebastian "Benny" Cotrone.

They were on nodding terms. About a year previously, Cotrone had moved down from New York, where he was well-known on the waterfront, and bought from Neal Harrington a firm called Portside Repair & Service, which he then relaunched as United Container & Ship Repair, Inc. Joe had given him some of PTO's repair work, although he was doing most of his own in those days, and when Cotrone called, assumed that he wanted more, but Cotrone evidently had something else in mind. He had to see Joe privately, he said—not in the office. It was important, by which he clearly meant important to Joe.

Knowing something of Cotrone's New York connections, Joe asked him over to the house on Sunday morning, and suggested that Ann should take a ride with the kids. He didn't want his family getting mixed up with these people, he told her. Bad enough that *he* had to. She was not pleased, but as he went outside to see them off, a green Cadillac drew up across the street, and she seemed happy enough then to leave him to it.

Cotrone walked over, smiling and holding out his hand. At his heels was another man, unsmiling, with his hands in his pockets. Joe took them into the kitchen for a cup of coffee.

"Nice home you got, Joe."

The tone was pleasant enough, but just having them there made him uncomfortable, as though he had given them some sort of leverage.

"What do you want, Benny?"

"Well . . ." He was not at all put out by Joe's inhospitable tone. "It's this problem you got with the union," he said. "We gotta settle that. It's making things bad for everybody."

"Benny, I got no problems with the union. I signed the contract. I hire his checkers. And anyway, it's none of your business."

"It gets 'em nervous, you see, when you don't work with 'em. They don't know what's going on."

"Neither do I." Joe was in two minds now. "Bunch of fucking thieves. You know how much cargo I'm losing? You wouldn't believe it. Even if it *was* any of your business."

Cotrone looked at his friend. "Don't get hot, Joe," he said. "Get smart. Let's look at it nice and calm. You been fighting George for years, and who got hurt? You did. Port's growing all the time, and who's getting the business? Not you, Joe. You gotta maneuver a little bit, you know what I mean? Okay. You're making a living. But look where you were five, six years ago. The biggest, right? What I'm trying to tell you . . . Enough's enough, all right? It's time to make your peace."

Joe considered them both for a moment. "That's up to Barone," he said. "And Benny, I still don't see what this has got to do with you. Unless he sent you?"

Cotrone sipped his coffee. "I've known George for years," he said comfortably. "I know him from New York in the old days. And he's a reasonable man, Joe. He's not greedy. He knows we all gotta live. We all gotta right to a piece of the action, he knows that. But he don't like people rocking the boat. He don't like a lot of fighting and arguments, because then you get all kinds of snoops poking around. You understand? He likes things nice and quiet. All in the family."

It was beginning to sound like an ultimatum. "I hear you, Benny, but I don't know what you're saying."

"I gotta spell it out?" He gave Joe a pitying look. "I'm saying you're in or you're nowhere. Okay? I'm saying share the wealth or you won't have no wealth to share. That's all. Simple as that. I been around a long time, Joe. You listen to me."

"I hear there's gonna be a grand jury," Joe said casually. "This got something to do with that?"

Cotrone eyed him. "Get smart," he said. "You're making George nervous with all the running around and suing people. Make your peace. Show a little good faith. Let us in for a little of what *you* got, and we'll give you some of what *we* got. We'll help each other."

Joe laughed. "He damn near killed my business, Benny. Him and Fat Freddy. Left us on the balls of our ass. Now you're telling me give him a piece of what's left? How's that gonna help me?"

"It's gonna show the right spirit. Live and let live."

"Benny, what do they want?"

Cotrone looked again at his silent partner. "We want all the container repairs," he said, "and a piece of the action of the crane."

Joe watched them steadily. "That may not be worth much, the trouble we've been having with it."

"Well, maybe we can help you with that."

He nodded. "And with all this stealing that's going on, business is pretty bad. Half the fucking cargo's walking out the door."

"I know," said Cotrone. "It's a problem. Maybe George can have a word with those guys. Before it gets worse."

"Yeah, Benny."

"And fifteen bucks an hour on the crane ain't gonna hurt you," he went on. "Not with the extra work you're gonna get."

"Extra work? Tell me about it, Benny."

"Well, you go see George Wagner over at Marine Terminals, and he'll put the crane to work for you."

Joe shook his head. "Marine Terminals is Al Chester," he said. "He's not gonna do *me* any favors."

"Did I say see Al? See Wagner. He's head checker over there. Big man in the union. He'll take care of it for you."

"And then I take care of Barone, right?"

"Just see Wagner," Cotrone said. "He knows what to do."

"I'll bet. And if I don't go along with this? What happens then?"

Cotrone inspected his fingernails. "Don't talk like that, Joe," he said. "You got everybody all upset as it is. You're either in or you're out, that's all. You know what they can do. They showed you."

Joe knew.

"You got a nice home, and a nice family. That's a big responsibility these days. You gotta think about these things."

Joe thought about them.

He had paid commissions before, given presents, but never anything like this. He thought of going to Bob Richardson, but there was no proof, and if the police moved in, Field would surely finish him off. Besides, he was frightened for his family.

Monday morning, he talked things over with Manny Levy, who relieved him of the problem by going over himself to see George Wagner. And every week after that, as soon as he had figured out the hourly total from the time sheets, Levy would go to see Wagner with the $15-an-hour payoff. In cash. In a brown paper bag.

It cost Joe nothing. He just charged $15 an hour extra, and Marine Terminals paid. There were no more punctured hydraulic hoses either, but Joe no longer felt the same about his crane. Nor did Ben Mussary when he found out what was going on. He was ready to throw Cotrone, Barone, and Wagner in Biscayne Bay, along with anyone who tried to stop him, until Joe talked him down.

Listening to himself, Joe did not admire what he heard. Gus had warned him. Having given into them once, he knew they'd be back, and it didn't take long.

Barone's chief bagman was William Boyle, secretary-treasurer of Local 1922. A lively, sharp-featured man, full of treacherous, mock-Irish bonhomie, he had worked as a longshoreman in New York, among other things, until 1965, when he moved to Miami and met George Barone, who hired him for his new union.

Joe knew him as he knew Vanderwyde, Doug Rago, and the other racketeers on Dodge Island; their offices were in the adjoining building, and they lunched most days in the Red Coach Grill or Howard Johnson's or the Everglades Hotel, along with the rest of the shipping community. After Cotrone's visit, he was surprised, and yet not surprised, therefore, when Boyle called in at the office one day, radiating goodwill, and suggested he should go see Jack Sylvia, of Coordinated Caribbean Transport, about the crane. When Joe asked why, Boyle laughed, and rubbed his thumb and forefinger together in a gesture now widely recognized as the ILA salute.

"You know the rate?" Joe asked Sylvia.

"You know the terms?" Sylvia asked Joe.

From then on, whenever CCT rented Joe's crane, he billed them at $65 an hour, and when the invoice was paid, kicked back $15 an hour to Sylvia for Barone.

A month or so later, Boyle called on Joe again to cement their new relationship.

"You're doing real well with the crane," he said, leaving it uncertain as to whether he was admiring Joe's good fortune or complimenting him on the regularity of his payoffs. "Maybe you can help us out with your Cousin Bobby."

It appeared that Uncle Mutzie and his son, Bobby Kratish, had fallen foul of the union in their management of Eagle Trucking.

Formed originally to service the ill-fated SACAL account, and to find something for Cousin Bobby to do, this division of the company had also been "organized" by Barone, and was thus obliged not only to deduct union dues from its employees but also to pay so much a head into the ILA's health and welfare fund. According to Boyle, Eagle Trucking was now $2,000 in arrears, but Kratish insisted that the contract covered only some of his drivers, and that Boyle was demanding dues for all of them. And he wasn't going to pay. Cousin Bobby didn't care what anybody said —Boyle could whistle for it.

Joe had quite a lot to say, not only about this, but about the general mismanagement of Eagle, and the impossibility of finding top executive jobs for *all* his cousins and in-laws. He was sick of having to clean up after his relatives, he said, and sick of finding his own neck on the block for their incompetence. If Cousin Bobby wouldn't pay, then *he* would—not for Cousin Bobby's sake, but to protect Eagle from the damage they all knew Barone could inflict. He arranged with Boyle to pay off the arrears in weekly installments.

He resented every cent of it, just as he begrudged every cent of the $15 an hour he had to pay to protect the crane. They were making money, but he felt soiled and diminished. So did Ben Mussary, who never stopped bitching about it. And Joe knew they would never let go. When he handed over a check for the last installment, Boyle said "the little guy" wanted to see him.

That was never good news.

The office of Local 1922 was on the second floor of Dodge Island's 1001 Building. Joe found Vanderwyde barricaded in a corner of the room behind a desk, listening to someone on the telephone. Now in his fifties, he looked like a Yankee hobgoblin, with his disgruntled red face, white hair, and glassy blue eyes.

He hung up abruptly, without saying a word, and began to write on his pad.

"You done a good job," he said, "paying off your cousin's debt. Don't let it stop there."

"What are you talking about?"

Vanderwyde looked up sharply, his irritation turning to contempt when he saw that Joe truly had no idea what he meant.

"What are you . . . stupid?" He stuck out his hand, palm upward. "I'm talking about *control,*" he said, his lips drawing back. "You understand? We're gonna have control of this fucking port, right *here.*" And he closed his stubby fingers slowly, like the jaws of a trap. It frightened Joe.

Vanderwyde was the only man who had ever done that. There was nothing in him to appeal to. He had a kind of mindless quality that ruled out compromise. With Vanderwyde, nothing seemed negotiable.

Without taking his eyes from Joe's face, he reached over and pulled out the drawer of his card index, which was not unlike a safe-deposit box in shape. He then unclenched his fingers over it, pretending to empty his fist inside, and slowly closed the drawer again.

"All right, Jay." Joe nodded, shaking himself into motion. "I understand."

That afternoon, Boyle stopped by to reap what Vanderwyde had sown.

"How'd you make out with Jay?" he asked cheerfully. "Big talker, right?"

"Yeah. Right."

"Well, I'll tell you something. His bite is worse than his bark. He even makes *me* nervous."

Joe smiled politely. "Then tell me something else. Just what does it take to keep you guys happy? Blood?"

"No, no. You can keep your blood. But a couple of hundred a week wouldn't hurt. To start."

"And how am I supposed to get *that?*" he asked, still smiling. "Off the books, I mean. You're making fifteen bucks an hour on the crane already."

"That don't cost you nothing," said Boyle reproachfully. "We got you the work, didn't we? *You* make money, *we* make money. That's fair, right? Same with this. You're gonna get new business."

Joe hesitated. "I been talking to Mike Zonis," he said. "Carnivale Cruise Lines. I wanna passenger boat for PTO."

"You mean, the *Mardi Gras?*" Boyle thought for a moment, pulling at his nose. "All right. I'll talk to the boys about it."

The boys took care of it. The stevedoring contract for the S.S. *Mardi Gras,* sailing every Saturday from Dodge Island for a week-long cruise of the Caribbean, was awarded to Pierside Terminal Operators in the absence of a lower bid.

On the Monday after she sailed on her maiden cruise, Boyle came to see Joe again.

"The boys did a nice thing for you," he said. "I think you ought to show your appreciation."

"Yeah?"

"Yeah. Like a couple of big ones. Plus a free trip now and again."

"Two thousand dollars?"

"Sure. Not all at once. Like I said, two hundred a week. You can afford it."

"Sure," said Joe. "My pleasure."

He could certainly afford it—the account was worth $1,000 to $1,500 a week net profit—but it was no pleasure. He was short-tempered, sleeping badly, and so estranged from family life that he finally agreed with Ann to get some marriage counseling, just to keep the peace.

Mike Zonis, on the other hand, was not sure *he* could afford it. His agreement with PTO was on the basis of cost plus 15 percent, the cost being largely determined by the number of longshoremen porters specified in the ILA labor contract.

"You gotta get me an edge on the porters," Zonis said after the first two cruises. "You're making more out of this fucking boat than *I* am."

"I gotta get Zonis an edge on the porters," said Joe to Boyle. "You're making more out of this fucking boat than *he* is."

Boyle, who obviously saw nothing wrong with that in principle, told him to take it up with Cleveland Turner.

The contract with Local 1416, the longshoremen's union, specified 10 porters for the first 300 passengers, plus one more for every additional 50 passengers, bringing the total to 18 for the 700-berth *Mardi Gras.* But to handle the job efficiently, Joe actually needed only 12 or 13, as he proceeded to explain in Turner's sympathetic ear.

"You like money. I like money. We all like money," he said. "I gotta have an edge on the porters."

Though still under Barone's thumb, "The Prez" had evolved a style of his own, befitting his 6-foot 5-inch, 230-pound stature. Most days he would make a ceremonial progress along the dock to show himself to his members, to hear complaints and dispense justice.

"This is *my* port," he was often heard to say. "I am The Man on this dock. I can turn it on, and I can turn it off."

When Joe asked him to turn off five or six of his porters, Turner was glad to do it—and for only $50 a boat.

"If Bill say it, you got it," he said. "We all friends together."

Joe went home and took a bath. Ben Mussary went home and took a week to forgive him. The only person who had a worse problem than theirs with the payments was PTO's bookkeeper.

"How do you want this classified?" she asked Joe one day. "Two hundred a week, plus the crane . . . It's too much for petty cash or general dockage. I don't know how to lose it anymore."

"Put it through as payoffs to union delegates," he told her.

"I can't do *that,*" she said, scandalized.

"You do like I tell you," he said. "Some day, there's gonna be an investigation."

7

Power Struggle

THERE had been one already, and another was under way.

Federal, state, and local law-enforcement agencies had known what to expect from the day Barone moved to Miami with his Chenango union colleagues. Before Local 1922 was even chartered, FBI agents had interviewed him about a stock fraud, and generally made the point that his presence had been noted.

But knowing what to expect was a long way from proving him responsible when it happened, particularly as this plain hint of federal interest reinforced a native caution already bordering on paranoia. As Field's executive officer, Barone moved with extreme care and patience, hardly ever discussing business outside his own inner circle of associates, and never with anybody on the telephone, in hotel rooms, or on ground not of his own choosing.

Denied hard evidence, the government was impotent. In 1971, a federal grand jury in Miami succeeded only in confirming what the Strike Force already knew: that the Port of Miami was being plundered as systematically as the Port of New York and New Jersey. There was not enough proof to indict anybody for anything, and subsequent leaks of grand jury testimony wiped out whatever slim chance there might have been of persuading witnesses to come forward of their own accord to testify against the racketeers. The only possible way to break the case was to get somebody on the inside to work with them, but where was the incentive?

In the fifties, the New York Crime Commission had been able to draw on the testimony of rebel longshoremen and businessmen with nothing left to lose. Twenty years later, the ILA still carried a big stick, but in its other hand was a big carrot. Its corrupt officials could still enforce silence as a last resort, but buying it had proved more efficient. By making their victims prosperous, racketeers like Barone also made them accomplices, with as much, and sometimes more, to lose. In 1972, the government needed a witness, who, for no material advantage, was willing to gamble not only with his life and the safety of his family, but also with his property and income.

"We need your help, Joe," said Doug MacMillan, then chief of the Federal Strike Force in Miami.

"You don't know what you're asking."

"I think we do," said Special Agent John Hexter. "Unless you help us, you'll have 'em on your back for life. We know these guys."

"Well, if you know, you know I can't help you."

"You paying off, Joe?" MacMillan asked.

"I'd rather not answer that question right now."

"We could subpoena your records," Hexter said. "Would you rather tell a grand jury?"

"If that's supposed to be a threat, these other guys are better at it."

"It's not a threat, Joe," said MacMillan. "And you won't be subpoenaed. I just want to be sure you'll tell us if there's anything you think we can use. Any information, any lead you can give us . . . anything at all."

"Sure. I wish I could help you. I really do."

"Well, okay. I wanted to know where you stand. If they ask why we came, tell 'em it's about the cargo they're stealing."

But thievery was only a fringe benefit. The real money was being made from carving up the cargo traffic among the port's stevedores and "taxing" them on their shares. Having unified the labor force, Barone had tuned it like a musical instrument to strike the right note for every occasion—working to rule here, cutting corners there, and sometimes not working at all, as in the "Italian strike," when everybody seems very busy but nothing gets accomplished. By 1972, shipowners, agents, stevedores, truckers, contractors, and service companies south of Norfolk, Virginia, were caught in a web of corrupt practices from which few even wanted to escape. They had only to pay their "rent" in order to enrich themselves with guaranteed profits.

North of Norfolk, the waterfront belonged to Anthony Scotto. Still only thirty-seven, he not only wielded the largest bloc of votes in the ILA, but had also emerged as a significant force in New York State and national politics. Though Teddy Gleason was reelected unanimously in July 1971, to his third four-year term as International president, Scotto had been openly rounding up delegates at the convention to back him as heir apparent.

"I think I could run this union better than anyone around," he told them, within earshot of reporters.

Scotto had never seen eye to eye with Gleason, who, at seventy, had learned the business under the Ryan school of management. In the thirties, with Ryan's blessing, Gleason had begun his rise from obscurity by forming a committee to "organize" New York's checkers. Chartered as Local 2150, its founder members included mob chieftain Eddie McGrath; Cornelius "Connie" Noonan, who managed McGrath's interests in the numbers racket, and John "Cockeye" Dunn, McGrath's brother-in-law, who was later executed for murdering a longshoreman.

Investigators for the Crime Commission also reported that Gleason owned a piece of several prizefighters, and an interest in Brown's Hotel at Greenwood Lake, New Jersey. Before it burned down in mysterious circumstances, Brown's was summer camp for Ackalitis and the Arsenal Mob, whose sponsorship of Gleason, or vice versa, had been suspected ever since Gleason "recommended" Ackalitis to the Jarka Corporation as a pier boss. (According to the Crime Commission, Jarka was one of several port employers from whom Gleason accepted money for various unspecified favors.)

Though "dismissed" on this evidence from his post as ILA organizer for Manhattan, Gleason was too close to the top to be denied. After Ryan's enforced resignation in 1953, it was simply a matter of waiting for the fuss to die down before publicly assuming the mantle of national labor leader, elder statesman, and White House confidante.

Near the knuckle business arrangements, coupled with blind resistance to change and crude appeals to reactionary sentiment, were the hallmarks of the Ryan/Gleason school of union management. Any benefits accruing to the membership were contingent upon, and usually incidental to, some greater benefit accruing to its officers. The Anastasio/Scotto style, though rooted in the same experience, was somewhat different.

Born in Tropea, Calabria, in 1907, Anthony "Tough Tony" Anastasio was one of five brothers who shipped out as deckhands and entered the United States illegally during the twenties. The first to arrive was Albert, who preferred to spell the family name Anastasia, and who prospered greatly as a parter of Joe Adonis and Abe Reles in Murder, Inc. during the thirties, setting himself up as overlord of the Brooklyn waterfront from the Bridge to 20th Street.

It was an ideal situation for Tony to get into the stevedore and strike-breaking business, but in 1948, he had a sudden change of heart. Though he continued to associate with Albert and other leading mobsters, he gave up the stevedoring business and identified himself completely with the interests of Brooklyn's longshoremen. It was 1955 before he managed to reorganize some of the Brooklyn ILA Locals into one new union, Local 1814, and to command an ILA vice-presidency, but within a year, he had placed himself at the head of almost half the longshoremen employed in New York harbor.

Among the unions he controlled was Local 1827, whose treasurer was John Scotto, father of Anthony Scotto, the young and ambitious recording secretary of Local 1814, who was dating Anastasio's daughter Marion.

Starting out as a longshoreman in a gang bossed by *his* father, Antonio Scotto, a hard-working immigrant from Naples, John Scotto had picked up a routine police record during the Depression as well as an interest in union work that later led to his suspension from New York's Sanitation Department, to which he turned for steadier employment after his marriage. It was perhaps inevitable, therefore, that his son Anthony, born on Henry Street in the Red Hook section of Brooklyn on May 10, 1934, and growing up on the waterfront, should gravitate toward the ILA in choosing a career. After attending St. Francis Preparatory High School, he took a pre-law course at Brooklyn College, but dropped out in his second year, after meeting Marion Anastasio, to work for her father in one of the unions soon to be merged into Local 1814.

She was a slim, pretty blonde; he was tall, dark, and handsome. The marriage of Anthony Scotto to Marion Anastasio in 1957 brought a list of notables to their reception at the Plaza Hotel, Manhattan, that included Carlo Gambino, Albert Anastasia, Joe Profaci, Carmine Lombardozzi, John "Bath Beach" Oddo, and many others who hid their faces in their hats when the photographs were taken. Gambino at the time was under-boss to Albert Anastasia. Before the year was out, he arranged for Anastasia's assassination in the barbershop of the Park-Sheraton Hotel, and took over the "family."

The death of his brother deeply affected Tough Tony, but the loss of his protection, always implicit rather than openly demonstrated, made no difference at all. Anastasio's strength lay in the loyalty of his longshoremen, which had not been impaired by the opening that year of Local 1814's new $2 million medical center. If anything, Anastasio now took an even tougher line.

In 1959, he attacked Bradley/Gleason for flirting with James Hoffa and the Teamsters; publicly criticized their conduct of the ILA's financial affairs; integrated Local 968, the only all-black Local in New York, into 1814; and ensured the ILA's readmission to the AFL–CIO by voting his men in favor of it.

At fifty-six, Anastasio looked more like "a prosperous grocer" to *The New York Times* than "Czar of Brooklyn." Short, gray-haired, and always conservatively dressed, he had lived with the Scottos and his three grandchildren since the death of his wife, rising early to be on the piers by 7 A.M., and usually in bed by 9 P.M. A heavy gambler in his youth, he now enjoyed a Saturday morning game of pinochle at the social club and liked to relax quietly with his cronies in restaurants where he could be sure of getting a good steak. Despite these temperate habits, however, he suffered a serious heart attack early in 1963, and died soon afterwards, on March 1, in Long Island Hospital.

As a labor leader, Anastasio had rarely been moved by theory, nor was he much worried about nepotism or conflicts of interest. He had run his union in the same way as his brother Albert had run his "family"—like a minor princeling who enjoyed the politics and exercise of power, who honored his word, punished disloyalty, and fiercely protected his people against all comers. The crucial difference, of course, was that Tony's people were the dockworkers of Brooklyn, while his brother's were hoodlums and killers, but Tony passed no moral judgments nor hesitated to use his brother's methods when they seemed appropriate. In that sense, he was no better than any of the racketeers with whom he vied or coexisted in the ILA, but whereas they used the longshoremen to further their interests, Anastasio's interests *were* the longshoremen.

He was succeeded by his son-in-law without challenge or argument. Within two weeks of his death, the executive council of the ILA—relieved, prematurely, at the substitution of young Tony for Tough Tony—had ratified Anthony Scotto's accession by installing him in the vacant vice-presidential chair of the International. But if Bradley/Gleason had counted on an easier ride with the new boss of Brooklyn, still some weeks short of his twenty-ninth birthday, they were speedily disabused of the notion.

Though smoother in style and less volatile than Anastasio, he was cut from the same obdurate stuff. Ten years of on-the-job training had given him his father-in-law's sureness of touch with the men, the same pragmatic attitude toward the jungle of conflicting interests on the waterfront, and an essentially progressive response to change. He had learned how to get things done, uninhibited by principle or prejudice.

To this, Scotto had added a subtler, broader-ranging intelligence and a more adventurous political sense, a third-generation readiness to push out into wider reaches of society. As organizational director of Local 1814 since 1959, and president of the Maritime Port Council, he had tried to give legislative effect to the union's implacable hostility toward the Waterfront Commission, building on the ILA's traditional links with machine Democrats, and in particular, with Meade Esposito, the Brooklyn Democratic leader, and Congressman (later Governor) Hugh Carey.

Gleason's Manhattan group soon discovered it was dealing with a change in method rather than in aim; with intrigue instead of confrontation. Within six weeks of taking over, Scotto had won a 10-year fight to bar Manhattan dockers from Brooklyn piers by trading off his support for the Gleason ticket at the 1963 convention against a change in the port-wide seniority agreement. In this way, he "found" another 700 jobs for his members, to reinforce their confidence in him, and at the same time, established himself as kingmaker at his first convention as union leader. Thirty years younger than Gleason, he could afford to bide his time.

As part of the same deal, he also encouraged Fat Freddy Field to look southward by achieving another of Anastasio's unrealized ambitions: breaking Manhattan's domination of the New York District Council. A new formula gave Local 1814 25 votes instead of 10, and Scotto a powerful voice in coordinating ILA activities in the port. With a bill he had sponsored to abolish the Waterfront Commission also doing well in the legislatures of New York and New Jersey, it was an auspicious start to his reign. To celebrate his thirtieth birthday and his first year in office, he went to Harvard University to lecture on business administration.

With the membership now more than half black, he was strong on civil rights, favoring complete racial integration in every port, although, he said, "the sticky truth is that . . . the Negro especially fears that integration will only mean that he will be stuck handling hides, bananas, and reefer cargo, while his white counterparts will be running the winches and forklifts and checking the cargo." He was just as "sound" on the issues of redundancy. There was no stopping progress, but the "ILA wants, not compensation for lost work, but preservation of the work itself." Speaking out of both sides of his mouth, he was playing one faction off against another so successfully that the only cloud apparent on the Scotto horizon in 1967 was the Waterfront Commission's denial of a license to Court Carpentry and Marine Contractors, Inc., an employer of ILA labor, on the grounds that Marion Scotto was "a de facto stockholder" in the company.

The largest company of its kind on the New York waterfront, it was run by the late Tony Anastasio's brother-in-law, Leo Lacqua, and his son, Joseph Lacqua (who was thus Marion Scotto's cousin). Keeping up the family connection, when the Lacquas expanded into real estate in 1959 with a company called Newbrook Enterprises, Inc., they took Marion Scotto in as a third partner, and possibly her husband also, although he continued to deny it even after the Waterfront Commission produced a number of building permits signed by Anthony Scotto on behalf of Newbrook, sometimes as president.

Since Court Carpentry, an employer of ILA labor, leased its premises from Newbrook, this in itself suggested some conflict of interest, but there was more to come. In 1964, according to the Commission's investigators, Scotto influenced the Kings County Lafayette Trust Company, a bank where $700,000 of Local 1814's funds were on deposit, to make an unsecured loan of $225,000 to Newbrook. This money was used by the Lacquas to buy the Englewood Country Club, in Englewood, New Jersey, which Scotto himself managed, in addition to his union duties, for two years (improving its image considerably, it was said, by persuading Thomas Eboli and other leading mobsters to resign their membership).

In the Waterfront Commissioners' view, this was sufficient reason for denying Court Carpentry a license to operate in the port, and they did not change their opinion when the Lacquas got around it by obtaining a State Supreme Court ruling that the Commission lacked the power to regulate firms such as theirs. Early in 1968, the Commission applied for powers to extend its jurisdiction over contractors performing services "incidental to the movement of water-borne freight," and in March, the Joint Legislative Committee on Crime convened a two-day hearing in New York City.

Scotto was one of the first witnesses to be called. Unusual precautions were taken to keep his testimony secret, even to the extent of taping brown paper over the windows, but Republican members of the committee confirmed afterwards that he had been questioned closely about his association with the Lacquas. Scotto was furious. The committee was being used as "a dupe," he said. The Waterfront Commission was "doing more dirty work against our people than management has ever done. . . . There is not a grain of truth in the wild allegations that form the alleged basis of this hearing."

His protestations were hardly confirmed next day when a vice-president of Kings County Lafayette Trust Company described Scotto's financial dealings with the Lacquas in some detail, but the budding scandal then slipped out of sight as the legislative process ground on and other matters came to the fore, including a disastrous eight-week national dock strike in the winter of 1968–1969.

In July, 1969, however, the lid blew off. Senator John L. McClellan, chairman of the Senate Subcommittee on Organized Crime, published in the Congressional Record a Justice Department chart showing Anthony Scotto as a Mafia captain in the Carlo Gambino family. It had been submitted to the House Appropriations Subcommittee by the FBI in 1966 to support a request for additional funds, but kept secret for three years to protect the Bureau's sources of information.

The story made the front pages from coast to coast. Scotto, of course, denied it.

"This isn't the first time a thing like this has been said against me, and I guess it won't be the last time as long as my name is Scotto and not Schwartz or O'Hara." (It was fortunate he did not say Ryan or Murphy.) "I am not in a position to question their alleged informant," he went on, "because I don't know who he is supposed to be. As far as I'm concerned, there's no truth to it. To me, it smacks of the vilification the Waterfront Commission started years ago. It's an anti-labor tactic."

True or not, his public career had suffered a check. From being photographed in the White House with Brooklyn members of Congress, including Hugh Carey, and sharing the dais with presidents at Columbus Day dinners; from founding an Independent Party in New York City to give John V. Lindsay another line on the mayoral ballot after Robert F. Wagner, Jr. and the machine Democrats lost the primary; from chairing fundraising drives, sponsoring free classical music concerts in city parks, and speaking up for civil rights, urban renewal, and other worthy causes, Scotto dropped quietly out of sight for a time.

But he still had favors to collect from a wide assortment of city, state, and national politicians. During the Lindsay administration in New York City, the result was a massive influx of public funds to modernize the piers worked by members of Local 1814, some of it diverted from projects already approved for other parts of the harbor. Representative (now Mayor) Edward Koch, for one, thought this Brooklyn bonanza smacked of "being no more than a political payoff."

That was in 1970, after it had become clear that while Scotto's career as a selfless crusader was over, or at least in abeyance, his powers behind the scenes were unimpaired. But it was still a bad year for him. The bills sought by the Waterfront Commission to widen its jurisdiction had finally passed the New York and New Jersey legislatures in the summer of 1969. Flexing his new muscle, Sirignano returned to the attack in January 1970, with a new series of public hearings, and a damaging new witness.

Salvatore Passalacqua had been fired from his job as foreman cooper on Pier 1 in 1965 for being "incorrigibly insubordinate and admittedly defiant of management"—or so the port's arbitrator found after Passalacqua appealed to the Waterfront Commission against his dismissal. Though he had not mentioned it at the time, he was now prepared to say that the real reason why he was fired was because he had refused an invitation, extended by Scotto among others, to join the Mafia family of Carlo Gambino.

Passalacqua's story was that he got the job in 1959 from Tough Tony Anastasio, to whom he kicked back $30 a month, sometimes passing the money on through Scotto. In July 1965, his pier boss told him that Joe

Colozzo, president of Local 1277 (and another Mafia captain, according to the Justice Department), wanted to see him on Sunday at the union's offices. When he arrived to keep the appointment, about 15 people were there already, including Colozzo, Anthony Scotto, and Carlo Gambino himself.

Asked by Commission counsel what Colozzo had wanted, Passalacqua replied: "He told me that the reason for this meeting was to introduce me to Carlo Gambino, because if there was anybody who deserved to become a member of the honorable family—Cosa Nostra—then he should know about it. So that we could, after following the tradition of the laws of the Cosa Nostra, and if I was willing to accept the invitation, they were ready to take me into the family as one of their peers. I told them I was not ready to give an answer on the spot."

"Did Anthony Scotto say anything to you at the time?" asked counsel.

"He asked me, 'Why don't you give an answer? What are you thinking so long about? Why don't you accept his invitation? After all, we also belong to the same family.' "

"Did Mr. Gambino say anything about Anthony Scotto when you . . ?"

"Yes, he told me that if I accepted his conditions, and I would have to submit to his orders, at the risk of my life."

"Whose orders?"

"To Anthony Scotto's orders."

Asked to comment on Passalacqua's testimony, Scotto said he felt sorry for him. "I think he needs psychiatric help. I have no knowledge of the meeting he alleges I attended."

On February 4, he appeared on subpoena before a public hearing of New York's Joint Legislative Committee on Crime to answer questions about his business affairs and to say, once and for all, whether he was or was not a member of the Mafia.

Instead, he refused to say anything, pleading the 5th and 14th Amendments 29 times before the committee's counsel abandoned the questioning as futile. In her turn, Marion Scotto did the same, bursting into tears at the witness table when asked about the real estate she had inherited from her father, Tony Anastasio; about the bank loans to Newbrook Enterprises, and her interest in Court Carpentry & Marine Contractors. Their attorney, Bertram Perkel, had to say for her that she was invoking the 5th and her marital privilege.

The reporters present were naturally curious. If he had nothing to hide, why had Scotto refused to answer the committee's questions?

"I have been so advised by my attorney," he told them. "I am sure the members will judge me on my record as a labor leader, and not on my part in the circus in there."

Realizing later that his confidence was probably misplaced, he attempted to explain his refusal more fully. On the advice of Bertram

Perkel, he had "reluctantly" taken the 5th, he said, because he had "testified to essentially the same questions previously." It was felt that "there was a good chance of my committing a technical error" if he had given new testimony.

This, of course, raised more questions than it answered. If he could deny belonging to the Mafia *outside* the hearing room, then why not *inside,* under oath? Scotto had never testified before (at least, not in public) as to whether or not he was a captain in the Gambino family, so why the apparent fear of committing "a technical error" like perjury if he could truthfully answer no? And anyway, just how "technical" *were* the discrepancies between the other answers he had given and those he might give now in the light of recent evidence?

Unsatisfactory or not, it was all the explanation Scotto was prepared to give, and he did the same thing again in April when the Waterfront Commission called the Scottos as witnessess at the hearing for which Koch had been pressing to determine if Court Carpentry & Marine Contractors should have a license to operate in the harbor. Indeed, they refused at first to appear at all. On March 30, Bertram Perkel appeared in their stead to move for the subpoenas to be quashed on the grounds of "prosecutorial misconduct."

When this failed, the Scottos duly appeared in person four days later, and duly claimed their 5th Amendment privileges to every question but one. They were prepared to admit only that they were married to each other. As most of the questions were directed toward showing that Scotto "indirectly received income" from the Lacquas, however, and as this had already been conceded by counsel, their reticence hardly mattered. Documentary evidence was introduced to show that Scotto had represented Newbrook Enterprises in negotiations for mortgage loans, in addition to using his influence to secure the $225,000 bank loan, and the hearing examiner had little choice but to find that "Anthony Scotto had at least an indirect interest in the business, and in the transactions of an employer whose employees his labor organization represented."

The examiner also found against the Lacquas, who had meanwhile transferred the assets of Court Carpentry to another of their businesses, CC Lumber Company, in a vain attempt to confuse the issue. They were not only in breach of Section 724 of the Labor Law, which prohibited employers from making business deals with union officials whose members were on their payrolls, but guilty also of "deceitful misrepresentation" in denying all knowledge of Scotto's activities on behalf of Newbrook Enterprises.

On these findings, set out in a 16-page report, the examiner recommended that the temporary stevedoring license issued to CC Lumber be withdrawn because the Lacquas "lacked good character and integrity," and that the firm's application for a permanent stevedore registration be denied.

Scotto found it "disheartening to think that individuals in business for a long time are being castigated because of their association with me," and three judges of the New York Court of Appeals were inclined to agree. In a dissenting opinion to the Court's rejection of the Lacquas' appeal against the Waterfront Commission's ruling, they saw no evidence that "Scotto had used his labor affiliations as leverage in the loan negotiations," and thought that "what is deemed objectionable amounts to no more than an ordinary incident of close family ties."

There was something in this argument. The Scottos had grown up in a closely knit Italian neighborhood where blood ties and friendship counted for more than moral squeamishness. Probably the only way to have avoided imputations of guilt by association would have been for them to repudiate their families, their social and business connections— almost their entire Italian–American inheritance, in fact—and to have moved away from Brooklyn.

Not many in their situation would have done so, or enjoyed much esteem if they had. It was unjust to assume, therefore, that because they remained, they necessarily took part in the criminal activities of their relatives and associates, or that they were necessarily incapable of acting in the wider interest of the community as a whole.

On the other hand, anybody in Scotto's shoes was necessarily required to be more careful than most to avoid obviously compromising situations, let alone conflicts of interest clear enough to be defined by law. This he had failed to do. More damaging still, he had also failed to reply on oath to questions about his associations and dealings that a state legislative committee and a state licensing agency were clearly entitled to ask of anyone in a position to act against the public interest. The inference to be drawn from this, and particularly his refusal to deny under oath that he was a Mafia capo, was plain enough for most people.

Content to leave the public stage to others until the dust settled, Scotto went down to the 1971 ILA convention in Miami Beach prepared to allow Gleason and his ticket another four-year term, provided delegates understood where the real power lay. And in case the employers, the government, and the nation were in any doubt as to how great that power was, when the ILA's contract expired on the last day of September, the longshoremen hit the bricks and closed down the East Coast and Gulf ports for 56 days before President Nixon finally resorted to the Taft–Hartley Act.

At Thanksgiving, Scotto distributed free turkeys to his members as a token of better things to come. A few weeks later, the employers settled with him and the wage-scale committee for a 41 percent increase in pay and benefits over three years, terms which *The New York Times* described as a "suicidal surrender to overwhelming union power."

In fact, it cost the employers nothing. The public paid, as usual, and to that extent, the deal represented a successful conspiracy between the negotiators rather than the surrender of one side or the other—just as it did in the case of the rackets. Though there was a clear distinction between the Field/Barone empire in the South and Scotto's northern kingdom, each had substantial interests in the other's territory.

Many of the major shipping lines operating out of southern ports were based in New York, for example, and so were most of the leading stevedores. In the same way as the ILA negotiated national wage settlements in New York, therefore, recognizing that the big names in the industry were active in all the principal ports, so also did the racket bosses in New York often arrive at national graft agreements covering their "clients" in the South as well. In such cases, adjustments had to be made by each group to reflect the other's "legitimate" sphere of interest.

But the "taxing" of stevedores was just the most obvious form of corruption. Reflecting the change in attitude toward the ILA's membership since 1953, the benefits won in successive contracts—improved welfare and pension schemes, guaranteed annual incomes, and so on—added up to a tempting new source of revenue to misapply. With the 1974 contract, the cash value of these employer-funded benefits exceeded $4 per man per hour, at a time when the ILA was claiming a total membership in excess of 135,000. Given that only 50,000 of these were working a 40-hour week at any one time, the value of the ILA's various benefit funds was therefore increasing at a rate of well over $1.5 million a day. (There was also a comfortable income from union dues, amounting to 8 percent of every longshoreman's pay, and 6 percent from the checkers.)

Then there was the workmen's compensation racket. By the mid-seventies, the annual cost to New York employers of compensating longshoremen injured on the job had risen to about $25 million. Some members of the New York Shipping Association were paying out $50 to $60 in injury benefits for every $100 in wages, and literally scores of cases had come to light of men found doing heavy work in other industries or engaged in strenuous sports while supposedly disabled.

The cost of these abuses was estimated by the Waterfront Commission at about $8 million a year, suggesting that one in every three claims was fraudulent, but to start with, the New York racket bosses saw very little of this money. After paying off the minor officials and crooked doctors who helped process phony injury claims, the principal beneficiaries were the individual members who filed them, which tended to undermine the whole object of the ILA from the mob's point of view. The problem was, how to take a solid slice off the top of the $8 million without the risks attendant on a thousand petty transactions with individual claimants. And if possible, how to do it in a way that would put the Waterfront Commission off the scent and avoid the bad publicity.

As usual, the answer was found in Brooklyn, in the subtlety of that new breed of union leader who could genuinely concern himself with the welfare of his members while milking his position for all it was worth.

Who paid for the abuse of workmen's compensation? The employers. Who, then, might be ready to pay for relief from that abuse? Again, the employers.

In the space of six months, there was a 42 percent drop in Brooklyn's accident claims.

The idea of making employers pay for the privilege of suffering less than they were being made to suffer already, and then publicly taking credit for reducing the level of abuse, opened up new vistas of opportunity for racket bosses everywhere, and particularly in the South, where some of these contract benefits were being introduced and funded for the first time.

In Miami, payroll and welfare rip-offs were the province of Cleveland Turner, for the larger membership of Local 1416 gave him more scope for these. If the port was busy and all 800 longshoremen and checkers worked a 40-hour week, Joe Teitelbaum and his fellow stevedores would pay about $100,000 a week into welfare and pension funds managed by the union's Florida administrators. But it was often hard to tell exactly how many *were* working. Certainly the payroll figures were not always a reliable guide, for Barone had schooled Turner well in the profitable art of "ghosting." Marine Terminals, the stevedoring subsidiary of Chester, Blackburn & Roder, for example, was believed to have Turner on its payroll under several pseudonyms and Social Security numbers.

Phantom employees could also help the stevedore cover the cost of his weekly payoffs. Already seething over having to pay for the right to work on Dodge Island at all, Joe now found that the "rent" increased even when he picked up extra business through his own contacts. Toward the end of 1972, an old business associate, Eduardo Garcia, came to see him one day with the news that the *Siboney* was coming back. This was a general cargo vessel, owned by Ocean Trailer Transport, a subsidiary of Reynolds Metals, that would make a weekly scheduled run to Puerto Rico and back, with Garcia acting as agent. The stevedoring contract, worth about $350,000 a year, was to be put out for competitive tender, but Garcia wanted to steer the work in Joe's direction as they had worked well together in the past.

Joe was naturally gratified, and it was left that he would get his rates together and put in a bid when the time came. But a week or two later, Boyle stopped by the office to say that Barone had decided he should have a new account. The *Siboney* was coming back, he said, and Joe should see Eduardo Garcia about it. When Joe replied that he had already spoken to Garcia, who wanted to give him the business anyway, Boyle was unimpressed.

Joe went to see Garcia. The account was his, Garcia said, but they would need $200 a week to take care of Barone, and Reynolds Metals would not go along with any payoffs. The best solution, he went on, was for Joe to put Garcia's brother-in-law, Frank Vidal, on his payroll as a phantom, to deduct tax, Social Security, union dues, and so on, and then give a check for the net amount of $200 to Garcia to cash every week for Barone. Fine, said Joe, but who was going to pay for it?

Garcia had thought of that, too. Reynolds Metals would pay for it. Joe would simply charge an extra half-hour for setting the ramp, and another half-hour for replacing it, and they would build Barone's $200 into the contract. Okay, said Joe, who really hated doing business this way. But what would that do to his competitive bid?

Garcia referred him back to Boyle, who saw no problem at all. Joe simply had to wait until all the other bids were in, and then Garcia would tell him exactly what he had to charge in order to win the contract.

And so it was arranged. When Garcia knew the price that Joe had to beat, he called him across the hall to his office with a secretary, who typed up both the bid and the contract for them to sign then and there.

As he left Garcia's office, Joe ran into Boyle and Barone. He had just signed the *Siboney* contract, he told them, quite unelated. Boyle congratulated him warmly. Barone said nothing. He rubbed his foot on the floor, then pulled up the leg of his pants to look at the sole of his shoe, as if he expected to find something sticking to it.

It was not long before Joe understood the full significance of this gesture. A few weeks later, soon after work had started on the new contract, Boyle stopped him in the hallway.

"The boys did a nice thing for you," he said.

"They did?"

"Well, they got you the *Siboney* account, didn't they? Now you ought to do something nice for them."

Joe opened his mouth to say that he would have won the account anyway, that he had already connived at a grubby little stratagem to provide Barone with $200 a week for it, and why the hell couldn't they just get off his back?

"What have you got in mind?" he asked.

"Couple of big ones?"

Joe rubbed his chest.

"Not all at once," said Boyle, misunderstanding. "Pay it off like the other. Two hundred a week."

Joe drove home in a rage, tackling the rush-hour traffic on the South Dixie Highway as though driving a tank. They now had him paying $600 a week, plus $15 an hour for the crane, for nothing he could not have done better without them. It not only went against everything he felt was right, they were also taking all the pleasure out of life.

He took a shower, and worked on his stamp collection. That usually helped, but not this time.

"You want to eat?" asked Ann, reading the signs.

"Nah, screw it."

"What went wrong today?"

"Nothing. I don't want to talk about it. That mother-fucker Barone just needs his fucking head kicked in, that's all."

Ann sat down with a sigh. "Joe, I've had enough of this," she said. "It's got to stop. I don't want to hear that kind of language. There's no need for it. And the kids don't have to be exposed to it. Not from you."

He tried to remember what he had said. "No, Ann. You're right." He was so disheartened his eyes began to smart. "I'm sorry."

"It's no good being sorry, Joe. You've got to do something. You're like a robot. You get up and go to work, that's all you do."

"I know. I'm sorry."

"Don't keep saying that. It's like you only come home when you've got nothing better to do. The kids don't know you. I don't know you. What kind of a man are you turning into, Joe?"

"I don't know, Ann," he said. "I really don't know."

Next day, he called Special Agent John Hexter, and suggested that he might want to look into what was going on between George Barone and Jack Sklaire, finance director of Chester, Blackburn & Roder. During the last two strikes, they had taken several trips together to Nassau, and CBR had been allowed to work its ships at Fort Pierce, a non-union port.

Big money was changing hands, he said.

8

Rebellion

BEN was no help. He believed in miracles. At least Manny Levy was a realist. If dealing with Boyle was a necessary condition for staying in business, then deal with Boyle. But Ben seemed to think they only had to do what was right, and if anybody tried to muscle in, God would strike them dead. Six million Jews had gone to the ovens believing that, said Joe.

Bullshit, said Ben. Six million Jews had gone to the ovens believing they could make deals with gangsters. What they had to do now was fight.

"What with?" Joe demanded. "Money? Bullets? You wanna commit suicide, go jump off the dock. Don't bother me."

"Losing is not the same as suicide," said Ben. "We beat 'em even if we lose. You're too fucking American, Joe. Sometimes it's noble to lose."

"Noble? What kind of horseshit is that? I'm a businessman. I can't *afford* to lose."

"Listen, going along with those guys is not winning. You know how some Jews survived? They worked with the SS."

"Oh, for Chrissake. What the hell do *you* know, you fucking Israeli? This is Miami, not Auschwitz."

"What do I know? I know something about you. I know you agree with me."

"Bullshit," he said uncomfortably. "And you better stop shooting your mouth off about these people. There's a grand jury coming up. That always makes 'em nervous."

It was humiliating. And his old friend Bob Richardson did nothing to help either. He was now with the Airport/Seaport Unit of the Organized Crime Bureau. With Special Agent John Hexter, he ran into Joe on the street one day, not entirely by chance, and bought him a cup of coffee.

"All right," Joe said. "I know what's on your mind, but don't start. I can't help you."

"You did already," said Hexter. "That was a good tip you gave us, about Barone and Sklaire."

Richardson nodded. "That's the kind of edge we need, Joe. Barone's ripping everybody off, but we can't get near him. He's got people frightened."

"Well, there's a reason for that."

"Right. He's a bad guy, and there's some bad guys working for him."

"That's part of it. But he's also making 'em rich."

"We know that, too," said Richardson. "When *he* goes down, they'll go down."

"If he goes down."

"No." Hexter shook his head firmly. "It's a federal case. He's targeted. He's up against the United States government, and he's gotta go."

"John's right. What we need is a place to start, Joe. Let us in on this thing, and we'll clean it up once and for good."

"Like they did in New York? I heard all this before. A dozen times."

"Joe, with somebody on the inside, somebody who can give us a real good handle on it, we can clean this up," Hexter said. "That I guarantee you."

Joe looked at them uncomfortably. "Man, I got a family to think about. Bob, remember that time Ann took a call from Field? She's never forgotten it."

"You'll be protected," said Hexter. "This is the federal government we're talking about. If we need the Marines in here, we got the Marines."

"Hey, don't think I don't *want* to help you." He scowled at his coffee. "It's just that I got a lot of people to consider."

"So have we," said Hexter.

"Yeah, but you don't know these guys like I do. They got the port like this."

He held out his hand and closed the fingers slowly into a fist, as Vanderwyde had done.

"That's why we came to you," said Richardson. "If *you* don't help us, who will? There's nobody else with balls enough to do it."

Joe squirmed. "If it was just me," he said, "it'd be different. Let me think about it some more."

He did. Often. It was nothing he could share with Ann, but he was trying to involve the family more these days in his working life—at least, in the parts of it that gave him pleasure. In the spring, they all went to Gijon, in Spain, where, on April 15, 1973, Ann Teitelbaum broke a bottle of Asturian cider on the hull of Yard No. 67, naming and launching her as the M/V *Morazan,* flagship of the newly fledged Conasa Line.

Three days later, driving home from a day at Garden State Park Race Track, William Murphy stopped for a red light on the corner of Fourth and Washington Streets in Hoboken. As he waited for it to change, two men in ski masks got out of the car behind him, ran forward, and fired eight to ten shots through the open window of his brand-new Cadillac. Murphy was still alive when the police arrived, but surgeons at St. Mary's Hospital later discovered that two of the bullets had caused irreparable brain damage.

Whether they knew it or not, Murphy's would-be assassins had done more than eliminate a fifty-eight-year-old vice president of the ILA. They had also knocked out of the box the old guard's favorite-son candidate to succeed Teddy Gleason as president—the only serious rival Anthony Scotto then had for the job. Certainly robbery was not the motive. Over $4,000 in cash was found in the trunk of Murphy's car, and several hundred more on his person.

Two weeks later, a likelier reason for the attack was suggested by the move of Prudential–Grace Line from Port Newark to the new Northeast Terminal in Brooklyn. Amid persistent rumors of bitter in-fighting between the New York and New Jersey Locals, the move meant a net gain of 600 jobs for Scotto's Local 1814, and a net loss of the same number for Willy Murphy, the ILA vice-president for New Jersey.

It was not the first time Scotto had lured a major employer across the harbor. In 1970, American Export Lines had moved from Hoboken to Brooklyn, a shattering blow to Murphy's pride as the loss on that occasion fell directly on his own Local 2. With Gleason's help, he had pulled every string he could find to prevent it, but without success. With his brother Michael, he had been heard to make all kinds of threats against Scotto if he ever again went poaching on their preserves.

On July 10, some three months after the attack on Willy Murphy, Michael Murphy was found dead in his West New York apartment with a .38-caliber revolver at his side and a gunshot wound in his left temple. Though he was right-handed, his death was put down to suicide.

Not unduly distressed by the news, Joe Teitelbaum had meanwhile taken his son back to Europe for the *Morazan*'s sea trials. Now fourteen, Mark enjoyed the experience as much as his father, and the two came home closer than they had been in years. A few weeks later, the whole family was again off on its travels, this time on the ship's maiden voyage to Puerto Cortes, her home port in Honduras, where the American Ambassador, Philip V. Sanchez, and the wife of President Oswaldo Lopez turned out as guests of honor for a dockside welcoming party. It was a proud and happy moment for Joe, the more so because of his distaste for what was happening in Miami, and on boarding the ship for the return journey, he embraced his Conasa partners, Virgilio Guzman, Oscar Martinez, and Guillermo Medina Santos, as though the four of them were brothers.

"You're a bit trusting with those guys," said Kessler, as they leaned on the rail, watching the coast of Honduras shrink into the sea.

"What do you mean?"

"I mean, they could steal you blind, and you'd never know. You got no way of checking on 'em."

Joe frowned. Then he shook his head. "Hey, I can't live like that. We're partners. I gotta trust them. They gotta trust me."

"Well, you know they can trust *you*. I just think you ought to have somebody down there keeping an eye on 'em."

"Then who's gonna keep an eye on *him?* No, let's see how it goes, for Chrissake. You calling 'em thieves already? They treated us like royalty, didn't they? Best of everything. First-class attention."

"That's what the goose says before they cut his liver out for foie gras."

Joe shrugged. "Why would they steal? You seen the manifest? We're on a floating goldmine."

Designed, as the earlier vessels had been, to Joe's own specifications, the *Morazan* was a partly refrigerated ship of 3,600 deadweight tons, with a good enough turn of speed to reach almost anywhere in the Caribbean from Miami in three days, and versatile enough to carry anything. Outward bound to Puerto Cortes, most of the traffic was general cargo in containers or trailers; on the in-bound leg, the loads were mainly bananas, lumber (mahogany logs, mostly), and frozen beef.

As she was his own ship, it was also gratifying not to have to pay anybody off for the account. For once, not even Boyle could claim that the boys had done "a nice thing" by allowing him to handle his own agency and stevedoring. With Manny Levy and Ben Mussary taking care of Eagle and PTO on a day-to-day basis, Joe escaped on the *Morazan* practically every other week, often taking Ann along with him.

After the first couple of trips, they had another reason for going. Joe was in Conasa's office in Tegucigalpa one day when Sister Maria Rosa came looking for help. With Father Willie, a Canadian priest, she ran an orphanage in the capital for about 200 children, surviving perilously on supplies donated by Catholic charities in the United States and very little money—too little, certainly, to waste on freight charges. Sublimely confident that God would provide, she managed to enlist Joe as His instrument in about 20 minutes. The children needed someone in Miami to receive and ship food, clothing, medicine, and other goods to Honduras, and Joe was it. Tickled by the idea of being the Jewish sponsor of a Catholic orphanage, he insisted on driving Sister Maria Rosa home so that he could meet the children himself.

They were of all ages from 18 months to 16 or 17 years, living 10 to a hut in conditions that seemed to Joe not much better than bare subsistence. Though well cared for, they looked thin to his eye, and their clothes, while clean and neat, had been handed down so often they were held together with patches and darns. He saw few toys, and most of those cherished but broken: a doll without arms, cars without wheels. The younger children in particular worried him. They were too watchful, too subdued. Unlike American kids of their age, they played almost guiltily.

By the end of the afternoon, he was ready to take them all home; or if not all, then one hut-full of new arrivals, still round-eyed and easily startled. When he asked Sister Maria Rosa how much it cost the mission to support each child, she told him about a foster-parent plan enabling families in the United States to sponsor an orphan in her care for $32 a year. In that case, he said, he would take the 10, and wrote her a check for $350.

Two weeks later, he was back again, this time with Ann and a huge load of groceries, clothing, and toys. Supplies from Catholic groups across the United States were already reaching him in Miami, and from then on, the *Morazan* rarely sailed without a consignment for the orphanage. Nor, even had he wished to, was Joe allowed to visit Tegucigalpa after that without spending some time with "his" children. On weekdays, when the older ones were at school, he would generally have to content himself with an hour or two of play and conversation in his fractured Spanish, but whenever he was there over a weekend, he would organize some kind of outing, perhaps to a baseball game, and buy them all popcorn and candy.

He and Ann were soon so attached to their foster children that they began to make plans for them to spend the following summer in Miami. They also thought seriously about adopting three of them, although Joe knew that both Washington and the Honduran government would make this difficult for them. On the other hand, he was on the best of terms with Guzman and his other highly placed partners in Conasa, who could probably pull a few strings for him.

He also needed to pull a few for himself in Miami. Manny Levy and Ben coped well enough when he was away, but there was a lot of money to find. He was still paying off the huge Jacksonville debt. There were payments on the crane, and on the *Morazan*. There were the ship's running costs, the payoffs to Boyle, and a payroll to meet of between $50,000 and $60,000 a week. There were also his relatives to support, who still took their cut though no longer engaged in the profitable end of the business. To keep Eagle and its brood aloft, Joe needed new accounts. And despite Ben's fuming and fussing, there was only one way to get them.

"Fred Field's in town," Boyle said one day, when he stopped by Joe's office to pick up the "rent." "You wanna see him? Say hullo?"

Joe would have preferred to kick his face in. "He knows I made my peace, right?"

"Well, naturally he does."

"All right. Then I wanna see him. Tell him he owes me a favor."

"You kidding? After all the trouble you gave us? He don't owe you nothing."

"No? How about the business you guys took away from me? How about Mamenic? I want it back."

"That's Eller's account."

"So? Move it."

"Listen, Mamenic's got their own man in there. Captain Murga. He's the guy you gotta talk to. He controls that business."

"Yeah? Well, who controls Murga?"

As if on cue, Field put his head around the door.

"Hey, Bill, what the fuck you doing?" he said. "We got a meeting with George."

He waddled slowly to the desk and rested his paunch on it.

"Hi, Joe. How's it coming?"

Joe hid his hands.

"Too little and too slow," he said.

"Yeah?" Field was not even remotely interested. "I heard you're doing all right now."

"Then you heard wrong. Now I'm in with you guys, I want my old accounts back. Like Mamenic."

"I told him he should talk to Murga," said Boyle.

Field yawned. "Could be Mamenic needs a new agent," he conceded.

"*And* stevedore?" Joe prompted.

"And stevedore. I know all those fucking squareheads. Their office is right in my building. Seventeen Battery Place. Then there's Gran Colombiana Line. That's a possibility, too. I hear they're looking around."

"Okay," Joe said. "Get me one of those."

Boyle frowned, but Field seemed faintly amused. "You can have Mamenic," he said, shooing Boyle toward the door. "That's easier."

"Bill says Murga controls that account."

"I'll take care of Murga. You just get your rates together."

"Okay. But don't go shitting me, Fred. Don't tell me you're gonna do it if you can't deliver."

Field rotated his bulk at the door, and quelled him with a stare. "Listen, prick. If I say you'll get it, you got it."

Behind Field's back, Boyle put his finger to his lips.

Joe sent his rates over to Captain Nicholas Murga in the morning, confident he had goaded Field enough to get results. A month later, he was not so sure, having heard nothing, and after six weeks without a word, he complained to George Barone in person. Either he was in with them, or he was on his own, he said. And if he was on his own, what was he paying them for?

Barone seemed to find the question in poor taste.

He called Joe out into the hall next day.

"It's not so simple," he said. "We gotta lotta pieces to put together here. First, you call Domingo Chomoro in Managua. He runs the line for Somoza. Make a date to go see him. Take your rates."

"Okay."

"Next, you stop fixing the *Morazan*'s containers in Honduras. You bring 'em here."

"What's that got to do with Mamenic?"

"You want the account or don't you?"

"I want it."

"Okay. Then Benny Cotrone gets the work."

"Okay."

"Also the *Morazan* will carry cargo for Mamenic. On Mamenic's bill of lading."

"You want the *Morazan* to go to Nicaragua? How come?"

"You got space, they don't. Their ships are full."

"You mean I can run Conasa freight in there? As well as theirs?"

Barone shrugged. "That's up to them. Maybe you can work out some kind of agency deal, so you don't compete. But don't horse around with these guys. Do this right, and you got yourself a half-million dollar account."

Joe went to Managua expecting to clinch the deal, but came back empty-handed and bewildered. Chomoro had not only refused to commit himself on the stevedoring bid, but wanted a 15 percent kickback on any Conasa cargo landed there, right off the top of the manifest.

"He's just a totally bad person," he told Boyle and Barone, and they laughed.

"Don't worry about it," Barone said. "He'll do like we tell him. Soon as we tie up equipment repairs for Miami, we'll put the whole deal together."

That was in March 1974. On April 5, Joe called John Hexter at the FBI with another interesting piece of information. He had discovered that George Barone controlled Don Julio Corporation, a welding firm on Dodge Island that accounted for a useful proportion of the port's on-the-spot container repairs.

Field and Barone had so perfected the repair racket that the executive council of the ILA had awarded them a national franchise for it. As general organizer, Field was now responsible for unionizing repairs and maintenance in every ILA port, North *and* South, with Barone as his official deputy.

The procedure, as developed in Miami, was classically simple. With a little help from the union, Florida Welding Services and Benny Cotrone's United Container & Ship Repair had been appointed official repair agents for the three main trailer and container leasing companies operating in the port. Under the terms of their leases, the shipping lines, their agents and stevedores were obliged to use either FWS or UCS for any necessary repairs, which the lessee, of course, had to pay for.

This, in itself, guaranteed a high volume of profitable business for the two firms, but Barone had drawn up a few extra rules to make it higher and more profitable still. FWS or UCS would decide what was a "necessary repair," not the lessee. No container or trailer could be loaded or unloaded unless a representative of one or the other company was present, the stevedore concerned naturally having to pay an "attendance fee" to cover this "inspection service." To make sure there was no cheating, any container showing signs of an unauthorized repair, however minor, could not be moved until the work was done again, also at the expense of the stevedore or lessee.

Applying these rules with adjustable diligence, Barone's inspectors could find something wrong with any container that passed through the port, unless, of course, the shipping line or stevedore offered Barone some compensating advantage for them *not* to do so. And as there was no special reason for favoring Joe Teitelbaum, even after he had made his peace through Cotrone's mediation, the Eagle/PTO repair bills were little short of astronomical.

None of his mechanics would touch a trailer or container, even to switch on the refrigeration plant. More impatient than usual, Joe did so himself one day, but an hour later, a mechanic came over from UCS to switch it off, and then, solemnly, to switch it on again. Joe and Ben Mussary had a good laugh about this and told all their friends, who laughed, too, but when the bill came in, the joke was on Joe. UCS's minimum charge was based on a guaranteed eight hours per call. Joe's moment of independence had cost PTO $150.

He threw the bill away.

Some weeks later, Cotrone came over to see him.

"Hey, Joe," he said. "You owe me twenty thousand dollars."

"The hell I do. For what?"

Cotrone spread a fan of copy invoices on his desk. "There you go. Stand-by on the ship. Attendance at the ship. Inspections. Service calls. Twenty thousand, give or take a couple of dollars."

Joe prodded through them with a disbelieving finger. "I never authorized these. I never saw 'em before."

"What can I tell you?" Cotrone shrugged. "They were sent to your office. Look at the dates. Now they gotta be paid."

"Bullshit." He started to get angry as he looked at them more closely. "These are all bullshit. If I *did* see 'em, I probably threw them in the waste basket."

Cotrone shook his head. "Well, you shouldn't have done that. They're past due, and I want my money."

"Fuck you, Benny. I'm not gonna pay these."

Still shaking his head, Cotrone left without further argument. Next morning, Barone called Joe out into the hallway.

"You owe Benny Cotrone twenty thousand dollars," he said.

"No, I don't. He just picked a number. It's bullshit."

"If you wanna query an invoice, do it when you get it. Now you got to pay the man."

"George, I paid him for the work he did for me. If anybody owes him for something else, it's not me. It's either the line or the agent. Let him go collect from them."

Barone fiddled with one of his hearing aids. "What kind of a dumb play is that?" he asked, obviously not certain he had heard correctly. "You're the stevedore. Cotrone works for you. You wanna *lose* that account?"

"No, I don't," said Joe, reaching in his pocket for an indigestion tablet. "You know damn well I don't. But I'm not gonna pay him."

"You wanna talk to Jay about it? Discuss it with him?"

"Not particularly."

"Okay. You don't wanna lose the account, and you don't wanna talk to Jay. I'll send Benny over to see you again. Maybe you can work something out."

They worked out that Joe would pay Cotrone $12,000.

Another time, when he cancelled leases on several hundred containers no longer required, there was an agreed total of $38,000 outstanding for legitimate repairs. When the final bill was presented, however, it came to $138,000, which he was again compelled to pay off, under protest, at the rate of $10,000 a month.

By such means, Barone boosted the volume of container repairs carried out by his members in the port to an estimated half million dollars a month, of which about $60,000 was kicked back to him and his colleagues. With similar arrangements in force at other ports, the total sum paid out in commissions like these amounted to several million dollars a year.

Meanwhile, in June, Joe had gone back to Managua to sign a contract with Chomoro. Mamenic's stevedoring in Miami was awarded to PTO. Eagle was appointed agent for Mamenic in Miami, and Amarnic became the agent for Conasa and the *Morazan* in Nicaragua. The container repairs for Mamenic and the *Morazan* were awarded to United Container Service, and the Miami trucking business went to Maritime Cartage. As for the unhelpful Captain Murga, Fred Field had him transferred to New Orleans.

It was a classic carve-up, even by the elevated standards of the ILA. Everybody scratched the next man's back, and an unsuspecting public paid for everything. When Joe asked Boyle how much the contract would cost him, over and above the weekly rent, he was told to get them three pairs of cruise tickets. It was all very friendly. Nobody was trying to screw anybody. It was just the way business was done on the waterfront. Just sharing the wealth.

Within two or three months, however, Joe found that *his* share barely covered his costs. Far from making the 20 percent profit he had anticipated from a half-million dollar account, he was snowed under with special charges and unforeseen expenses that reduced his Mamenic business to break-even point at best. Nor was his own Conasa Line panning out as expected. Though the *Morazan* was carrying useful loads back and forth between Miami, Honduras, and now Nicaragua, Guzman and his partners were still calling down huge sums from Eagle to cover their "expenses."

On one trip, the ship's manifest showed $45,000 in freight charges collectable in Honduras, far more than enough to cover every possible contingency. No sooner had it arrived in Puerto Cortes, however, than Guzman sent a telex to Miami asking for $20,000 more. It was the end of the honeymoon. After trying all day, Joe finally reached him on the telephone and plowed right through the usual flowery courtesies.

"What the fuck's going on?" he bawled. "It's like throwing money down a sewer."

"I do not like your tone," said Guzman coldly. "What are you suggesting? We have problems with the trucking, with special handling. Many emergencies."

"Guzman, you're full of shit. There's sixty thousand dollars revenue on that boat, so how the hell can you hack sixty-five for expenses? Tell me that, Guzman. Come on, talk to me. Explain it to me. Are you there, Guzman?"

The line clicked a few times and went dead. By the time the operator had reconnected Joe with Tegucigalpa, Guzman had "left for another appointment." Trembling with restraint, Joe called his accountant and instructed him to fly down to Honduras on a surprise visit to inspect the books.

More serious for his solvency was a sudden threat to the Nopal Line account in Miami, by far the most profitable segment of his stevedoring business. Joe had won it on his own initiative, flying to Oslo in April to make his pitch and bringing back both the stevedoring and the agency account. This was just a temporary arrangement, however. The Norwegians had explained to him that their policy was to divide these two functions between unrelated companies, so that once the line was operational, he could have one or the other but not both.

Joe had decided at once to keep the stevedoring, which promised to be more profitable, but giving up the agency also meant giving up overall control of the account, so that he approached the choice of agent with some care. After shopping around, he finally settled on Gus Hulander and Dewey Parker, two experienced shipping men whom he had known on and off for years. In September 1974, they founded Caribbean Agencies, Inc., to take over the Nopal Line agency from Eagle.

As almost their first official act, Hulander and Parker then informed Joe that Nopal's policy was to obtain competitive bids for all contracts, including the stevedoring. Abruptly revising his opinion of them, he demanded to know who would dare compete for *his* contract, and on being told that Neal Harrington was submitting a bid, choked on a rage so comprehensive that Ann turned him out of the house after two days with a warning not to come back until he was fit to live with.

He went in search of Bill Boyle.

"You asshole," he said tenderly.

Boyle blinked. "I love you, too," he said. "What's up?"

"You know what's up, you two-timing, double-crossing son of a bitch."

Boyle scratched his ear thoughtfully. "You go on like that and you're gonna hurt my feelings," he said. "You wanna tell me what's eating you?"

"No. I wanna see George. I wanna know what I'm paying you for. I wanna know why the more I give you guys, the more I get screwed."

"I don't know what you're talking about. And sit down, for Chrissake, before you give yourself a heart attack."

"I'm talking about your boy," said Joe, a shade less stridently, for Boyle seemed genuinely mystified. "The gimp."

"Harrington? Okay. I'll buy it. What's he done?"

"We gotta play games?" Joe registered scorn and disgust. "He's bidding on my Nopal account. You didn't know that? You didn't tell him to do that?"

"No, I didn't tell him to do that," Boyle yelled back. "Why would I tell him to do that? So you'd come hollering in here and give me a headache? Leave me alone, for Chrissake. You fucking guys are gonna drive me crazy."

"Then tell him to stay off my porch."

"Okay, okay. If he's after your cookies, I'll run him off, all right? That what you want? It's done."

"Okay. Son of a bitch took enough of my business already. You tell him to stay away from me."

"I'll take care of it, I told you."

Boyle took care of it. Next morning, Barone and Jay Vanderwyde stopped by to tell Joe that Harrington would withdraw his bid. The price of their intervention, however, was that United Container should handle Nopal's repairs, and Maritime Cartage the trucking.

Sorry, Joe said. Nopal required competitive bids on everything.

No problem, replied Barone. He would arrange for Florida Welding Service to bid high on the repairs. As for the trucking, Maritime Cartage was the only union firm in port, so they had no choice.

Not for the first time, Joe felt a pang for Harvey Sykes, who, after struggling for years to get ahead, had finally imagined he was going out on his own with Maritime Cartage, only to get eased out by Barone. But it was only a pang, for not even Sykes was being taken as badly as he was. Joe's accountant had come back from Honduras as though walking in his sleep, pinching himself, and when Joe heard what he had to say, it had the same effect on him. Without thinking to call ahead, he drove over to Mel Kessler's, walked blindly past his secretary into his office and sat down on the sofa.

"Looks like I've been screwed," he said.

Kessler eyed him critically. "You look like you've been run over," he said.

"You know what they did? Guzman and those mother-fuckers? They stole from me. They must have stole half a million by now."

"Bullshit. I mean, okay, they stole. I told you they would. All you do is fool around with those kids when you go down there. But half a mill? Nah. No way."

"Mel, I'm telling you. They been getting forty percent of the revenue. All the freight collect, okay? A lotta money. And all they have to do is run the office and pay the fucking mortgage on the boat. That's all. Every-thing else *I* pay for. Crew. Fuel. Insurance. The lot. And still I gotta send down ten thousand, twenty thousand . . . fifty thousand dollars. They're ripping me off, Mel."

He was really hurt.

Kessler sighed. "Then don't send any more. It's simple. Get an accounting. Send somebody down there to take a look at the books."

"I did that already. And now I'm gonna hire some fucking gorilla to bash their fucking heads in."

Kessler ignored this. If Joe had carried out all the threats he had ever made in the heat of the moment he would have filled the county's grave-yards single-handed.

"What did the guy say? They show him the books?"

"Books? What books? He couldn't believe it. There's no records, he says. They can't find the records. He don't know what the hell is going on. He says, 'I see expenses. I see checks. But where is this money going to? What is this corporation? What are we paying *this* for?' "

"And no answers."

"No answers. No books and no answers. You know what he found out? You won't believe this. *I* don't believe this. Remember those five tractors I sent down to handle the trucking? Sixty thousand bucks' worth of equipment, okay? You know what they did, those assholes? They transferred *my* fucking tractors to some cockamamie company they own down there, and they been charging me for trucking. With my own equipment. You like that?"

"Will you stop yelling?" said Kessler. "Now you look like you're having a stroke."

Joe checked his symptoms. "I'll kill 'em," he muttered, sitting down again. "Cocksuckers. I really trusted those guys. They're big people down there."

Kessler handed him a can of Coke from the bar. "Take it easy," he said. "It's only money."

"I'll sue 'em."

"Oh, yeah. That's a terrific idea. You want to sue the Honduran directors of a Honduran corporation in Honduras? Fine. Good luck, gringo. Let me know how you make out."

"Okay, okay." Joe tried to be calm. "So what do you think I ought to do?"

"Swallow it. Your first loss is the best loss. Take the ship and pull out of there. Start another route."

Joe looked at him doubtfully. He drank some of his Coke. Then he lit a cigarette, and immediately stubbed it out. Kessler went back to work on his papers.

"Maybe I ought to take a run down there first," Joe said eventually. "See if I can't straighten this out. I'm not saying you're wrong, but maybe I should give it one more chance."

"Okay."

As friend and attorney, Kessler always tried to give him his best advice. It was then up to Joe, as friend and client, to decide if he wanted to take it.

"Lemme use your phone."

It took the operator several minutes to connect him with the office in Tegucigalpa. Kessler meanwhile carried on as though Joe were not there.

"Hi. Gimme Guzman . . . No? Okay, I'll talk to Martinez . . . Martinez?" Joe's tone turned malevolent. "You mother-fucker. What the hell are you trying to do to me? I just got through talking to my accountant. And Mel Kessler . . . Don't give me any of that bullshit. I don't wanna hear it. I know what you've been doing. I'm coming down on the boat . . . Yeah, tomorrow. And you better be ready with some answers . . . I don't care. I'm coming down. And you and your asshole partner Guzman, you better be there."

He slammed down the telephone, and Kessler winced.

"How do you think I handled that?" Joe asked proudly. "Was it okay?"

"You were firm," said Kessler.

"Yeah. I'd say they got the message, wouldn't you?"

"Sure. And ten will get you twenty there's nobody home when you get there."

Joe paid him the $10 when he returned to Miami four days later. Guzman had been called away unexpectedly to Costa Rica; Martinez and Santos were taking care of client problems in Managua and Panama respectively, and Joe spent Saturday afternoon at the ballgame with Father Willie and the kids from the orphanage.

The following weekend, he flew down without warning and missed them again. Guzman was visiting with his brother-in-law, Colonel Policarpo Paz Garcia, chief of Honduran security forces, and Joe judged it best not to disturb them. If it had not been for his problems with Nopal, he would have waited until one of his partners showed up, but as things were, he sailed back to Miami on the *Morazan,* missing Fifi by three days.

Starting out in mid-Atlantic as the sixth tropical storm of the season, Fifi had been hanging around to the east of the Leeward Islands for nearly a week, a sullen, arcing engine of cloud, building cabbagey cathedrals high enough for jet winds to blast their tops as flat as mesas, streaming the debris out in plumes for a hundred miles. Far below, local winds nagged at her flanks like sheepdogs turning an unwieldy flock.

Around September 10, Fifi found her own axis and started to move, untidily at first, trailing squally fragments behind her, but spiraling tighter day by day into a towering, majestic vortex, seven miles high but made squat by the breadth of her base.

Now a full-fledged hurricane, she brushed through the screen of islands without much loss of energy, dawdled across the open reaches of the Caribbean, still picking up millions of tons of water, then swung abruptly north-west, spinning her winds at 130 miles an hour. Snagging her skirts on northern Nicaragua, she rolled around into the Gulf of Honduras, blackening the sky, and came ashore on September 17, roaring and shrieking like a thousand runaway locomotives, pushing a huge sea before her.

So vast was her system that two days passed before Fifi struck the northern lowlands of Honduras with her main force, but then, losing momentum, she began to break up on the higher ground of Belize and Guatemala, and finally collapsed in torrents of rain on the jungles and mountains of Yucatan.

Honduras, meanwhile, had declared a state of national emergency. Her banana plantations were flattened and stripped. Roads, railroads, bridges, and airstrips throughout the country had been washed away by flash floods that wrecked nearly 200 rural communities, burying some of them under seven feet of mud. Severely battered towns, like Puerto Cortes, were without electricity, running water or telephones. First reports put the total of deaths at over 7,000, and the number of homeless refugees at 350,000, all in need of urgent relief. At least 40,000 people were completely cut off by the flooding, many of them stranded on the roofs of their houses, a prey to snakes and starvation.

Ann dragged Joe almost physically from the shower when the news came through on the radio. Sick with worry about the children at Sister Maria Rosa's, he tried to get through to Tegucigalpa by telephone, but the circuits were either busy or out of action. He then called the Honduran consulate in Miami, and although its officials knew nothing about the orphanage, they were able to tell him that damage to the capital had been light. Relieved, he agreed at once to make the *Morazan* available for the carrying of relief supplies. The ship was at their disposal, he said. He was canceling all but priority freight until further notice.

Next morning, the cargo began to pile up on the dock. The situation in Honduras was so desperate that the United States government was using its Civil Defense communications network to help coordinate the movement of trucks, aircraft, and shipping throughout the Southern and Gulf Coast States. All day long, Joe loaded ambulances, airboats, portable generators, and containers stuffed with food, clothing, and medical supplies. His brains baking in the heat, he bustled on and off the ship and in and out of the transit shed and trailer park, hollering orders, improvising, exhorting, unstoppering bottlenecks.

Ann Teitelbaum, meanwhile, had launched a relief operation of her own. When Joe drove home late that night, sagging with fatigue, he found the garage full of groceries for the orphanage. With Marilyn, Mark, and Uncle Mutzie, she had spent the whole day canvassing friends, neighbors, and business associates for contributions. And they had not finished yet. By the following evening, when the *Morazan* sailed, she and Joe had spent about $5,000 on other essential supplies, and the whole shipment had been packed in one container consigned straight through to Sister Maria Rosa in Tegucigalpa.

About 50 miles out from Puerto Cortes, the captain called Joe to the bridge. The sea was littered with hurricane wreckage: uprooted palms, huge clumps of vegetation, splintered planks, and broken boxes, all bobbing and lifting on the swell as though an island had just sunk there. None of the crew had seen anything like it before, certainly not so far off-shore. They stared ahead in silence at a heaving carpet of flotsam stretching to the horizon, the Hondurans among them suddenly anxious to get home. But some of the palm trunks and balks of timber floating just awash at the surface were heavy enough to cripple the ship if they fouled the screws, and the captain took no chances. He picked his way into port some 10 hours later, with the twilight deepening behind them. The sheds and warehouses on the dock were battered and partly roofless. Etched against the last of the sunset, Puerto Cortes looked as though it had been bombed.

The illusion of war was heightened by the troops on the pier. On the way down, Joe had heard over the radio that there had been looting in the town, and that a curfew was in force. He also knew that President Oswaldo Lopez had ordered the army to take charge of the reception and distribution of relief supplies, and while he realized that the president had had little choice, the civil administration having been knocked out of action, he was ready to be surprised if half his cargo reached its proper destination. Joe had met too many Honduran generals to have much faith in their civic spirit, and his confidence was not increased when Virgilio Guzman drove up with a military escort to meet the ship.

It took Guzman a while to recover his poise after spotting Joe on the bridge, but the almost simultaneous arrival of two full gangs of long-shoremen and the sudden flurry of preparations for unloading distracted them both. When he came aboard to pay his respects, it was with a smile and an outstretched hand.

Joe ignored them both.

"We've got things to talk about," he said. "But not here. And not now."

"I agree." Guzman put his hand in his pocket. "This is not the time to air petty grievances."

"Stealing isn't petty, Guzman. Cheating a partner who trusted you is not petty. But that can wait," he went on, as the other turned to go. "I just wanna get this ship unloaded and on its way by first light. I'm counting on you for that."

Guzman nodded, hesitating. "A word of advice?" he said. "When you are in my country, you should be careful not to cause offense. Ask yourself, is it wise to say such things? These are serious charges. Perhaps you do not fully understand our ways."

"I do now," said Joe. "But forget that. I wanna call Tegucigalpa. I gotta find out if the kids are okay at the orphanage."

"I'm sorry. The capital is cut off except by radio. But the damage there is minor. You need have no fear."

"Then I'll call on the radio. You can fix that."

"No, no. Official business only. The relief work, you understand. Even for urgent messages, the delay is many hours."

"I could use the ship's radio."

"Yes, but who would hear you? I'm sorry."

Joe grunted. "Then I guess I'll have to go there. Can you get me a jeep or something?"

"I'm sorry." Guzman shook his head. "Is really impossible. All vehicles have been commandeered. It is an emergency, no? And it would take two days. The floods . . . Bridges down. Impossible."

Joe walked to the rail and thumped it. Below him on the apron, troops were breaking out some of the portable generators he had brought to augment the jury lighting on the dock.

"Then it looks like I'm gonna have to trust you again," he said bleakly. "But I want you to understand something. You cheat on me *this* time, and I will personally come down here and take you apart, piece by piece."

Guzman turned abruptly, but Joe caught him by the arm.

"You see that box?" he said, pointing. "It's consigned to Sister Maria Rosa at the orphanage. I wanna be sure it's gonna get there."

Guzman pulled free, brushing at his sleeve. "I will see to it," he said distantly. "I will make myself personally responsible."

"No," said Joe. *"I'm* making you personally responsible."

9

Casualties

THE death of Ben Mussary changed everything. They found him sprawled at the foot of a steel companionway with his head in a puddle of blood. An accident, they said. He had slipped on a piece of broken tile, fallen down the stairs, and bashed his brains out on a stanchion.

Joe did not believe it. Ben had spent his life scampering through ships, nimble as a mountain goat, never putting a foot wrong. His big mouth had killed him.

"I told him," Joe said to his father, the night before the funeral. "You heard me. I told him over and over. 'No pay, no play,' I said. 'You can't beat the system. *You* don't control our labor. *They* do. So make the best of it,' I said. 'Spare yourself the aggravation.' "

"He knew," Gus said. "He tried. He couldn't keep it down, that's all."

" 'You don't even have to know,' I told him. 'You just work the ships. Me and Manny, we'll take care of the rest.' But would he listen? No. Every time he saw those guys, he just had to pop off his mouth. Needle, needle all the time. 'What's eating him?' Boyle says to me. 'What's with this payoff bullshit? Don't he know there's an investigation going on? Son of a bitch is gonna get us all in jail, he keeps talking outa turn like that.' So I told him, I said, 'Ben, you wanna bitch, do it to *me.* You don't know who's listening. If these guys get busted for taking money, *we* get busted for giving it to 'em, understand?' 'Oh,' he says. 'Okay, I'll stay out of it.' So what does he do? Next time he sees Boyle, it's, 'Hey,

Twenty people must have heard him."

"I know," said Gus consolingly. "He didn't understand. He just didn't understand how it is in this country."

"They didn't have to kill him for it."

"Don't say that." In his anger, Gus pulled Joe around to confront him, face to face. "Don't even think it. You fell a few times yourself."

"Not with a grand jury sitting. Not after shooting my mouth off."

"Now you listen to me." Gus shivered with intensity. "And listen good. Not just for you. For Eileen and the kids and everybody, understand? Ben fell. He had a bad fall and it killed him. He slipped on a piece of tile and hit his head. Now you let him rest in peace."

Joe heard all his father was saying, and patted his cheek. "Don't worry," he said. "I'm not Ben. I know how to keep my mouth shut."

"All right. But sometimes you get yourself into things before you stop to think. Ben had an accident. Let it go at that. Don't think you got to do something about it. Think about your sister and the kids, what's best for them."

"Sure. I'll be careful."

Accident or not, Ben's death was the end of the line.

The morning after the funeral, Boyle stopped him in the hallway.

"Hey, I was looking for you yesterday."

"Yeah?"

"Yeah. It's that time again," he said cheerfully. "Got to keep the man happy."

Joe looked at his feet. "We buried Ben yesterday."

"Oh, yeah." Boyle rearranged his expression. "Yesterday was the funeral, right? How did it go? You get a crier?"

"What?"

"A crier. You know. Don't you people hire a crier for your funerals? Like a chief mourner?"

Joe pushed past him without answering. All right, he said. That's it. You watch yourself, Boyle. Now it's *your* turn. Now I'm gonna make a crier out of you.

He swore it over Ben's grave. That made it a decision, not just a fantasy of getting even. It was the first step, and probably the hardest one. As he was preparing himself for the next, the Strike Force came to *him.*

He was on the dock, in the middle of loading the *Morazan,* when he caught sight of Hexter, Richardson, and Jack Applegate, another OCB detective, just standing there, watching him.

"Hey, come on, fellers," he said, knowing every longshoreman in earshot was listening. "Some other time, okay? I'm busy."

He was not embarrassed. Investigators from the Organized Crime Bureau and the Strike Force were calling on every employer in the port as regularly as meter readers from Florida Power and Light. He really *was* busy.

"Won't take a minute, Joe," said Richardson easily. "The way you jump around, we gotta catch you when we can."

"Yeah, well, what's the matter now?" Joe led them off a little way. "If it's about those fucking guns again, I can't help you."

A consignment of Smith & Wesson .38s had disappeared from the transit shed a few weeks earlier.

"No, it's not that," Richardson said, in a normal voice, now they were out of earshot. "We got another problem, and we could use a little help."

Joe looked at them doubtfully.

"I know we talked about this before," Richardson went on. "And if I was in your shoes, I'd probably feel the same. But I don't think there's any risk in this. You wanna hear it?"

"Sure." He agreed as readily as if asked for a match. "Go ahead."

"We want to get somebody into Local 1922," Hexter said. "You know, under cover. So we figured the best way would be to put the guy to work someplace, and let nature take its course."

Joe nodded briskly. "You want me to give him a job, right?"

"Right," said Richardson, getting ready to argue his case.

"You got it," Joe said. "What's his name?"

"Uh, Vincent Ensulo," said Hexter, taken slightly aback. "Comes from New York. Nobody knows him down here."

"Good. Is he a cop or an agent or what?"

"No, he's a stool. But a good one. And he's put in some time on the waterfront."

"Fine. Send him over. I'll find something for him, and see what I can do about a union card. After that, he's on his own."

"Hey, listen. Appreciate it," said Richardson, but Joe was already walking away.

"For Chrissake," he yelled over his shoulder. "Half a million people dying in Honduras and you're bugging me about a couple of TV sets? What's wrong with you guys?"

Ensulo came looking for a job next morning, and Joe told Manny to put him in the warehouse. He was not much impressed. Ensulo was just the kind who *would* steal TV sets. He was fat, slovenly, and insolent, but at least no one would take him for a federal agent. Then Joe forgot about it. He sailed on the *Morazan* that evening for Honduras, and into a bigger disaster than Fifi as far as Conasa Line was concerned. He left the ship unloading in Puerto Cortes and flew back to Miami to see Mel Kessler.

"I gotta be crazy, getting mixed up with these people," he bellowed. "That fucking Guzman. If I find that asshole, I'll cut his heart out. Fifty-two thousand? They done nothing but rip me off. You need a company of Marines down there just to look after your fucking wallet."

"You want me to call the Pentagon?" Kessler asked patiently. "Or you want to tell me what happened?"

"Well, I'm *telling* you, for Chrissake. I get down there and start unloading the cargo, and along comes Quejo, the port director, and he hands me a bill for fifty-two thousand dollars. So I asked him, I said, 'Hey, what's this?' 'Those are landing charges,' he says. 'Landing charges? For what?' 'For the stuff you brought in after the hurricane,' he says. So I looked at him. 'Stick it up your ass,' I said. 'That was relief cargo. You wanna bill somebody for that, bill the government.' 'Oh, no,' he says. 'I have my orders. I gotta bill the ship. You pay, and then you get a refund from the government later.' He's playing the heavy, right? He's got a couple of hundred troops on the dock, and they're all so fucking bored, they're dying to shoot somebody.''

"Guzman's not there?"

"You kidding?" Joe rubbed his chest. "The captain's trying to raise him on the phone while I'm talking to Quejo. 'Give it to Guzman,' I tell him. 'He's the agent down here. He's got funds.' 'Oh, no,' says Quejo. 'He says to give it to you,' and he lays the bill on the table. I mean, it's a rip-off anyway, right? How can a ship that size rack up fifty-two grand in port charges on one trip? 'Look,' I said. 'I don't know how you're gonna work this out and I don't care. This ship's Honduran registry. She's carrying Honduran cargo for the Honduran government. She's owned by a Honduran corporation with Honduran directors, so why don't you take it up with them? I gotta get this ship unloaded and on her way.' 'Oh, no,' he says. 'This Honduran ship stays in Honduras till these charges are paid.' ''

Kessler pulled a face.

"Now you're getting the picture," said Joe. " 'The ship don't carry that kind of money,' I tell him. 'And I'm gonna dispute these charges anyway.' 'Fine,' he says. 'First pay the money, then dispute all you want. This ship don't move till the bill is paid.' So here I am. And what the fuck do I do now?''

Kessler leaned back in his chair.

"Send 'em the money," he said.

"*What?* No way."

"How much is the *Morazan* worth? Right now."

"Replacement cost?" Joe shrugged. "I don't know. Three and a half, four million. Something like that."

"Then send 'em the fifty-two thousand," said Kessler. "*Wire* it. And tell the captain to get the hell out of there. Something tells me you just made your last run to Honduras."

"Now wait a minute."

"You wanna lose the ship? I'm telling you. Send 'em the money."

"*Lose* it?" The pain in his chest was making it hard to breathe. "What are you talking about? I just want Guzman to pay, that's all. He stole enough to cover it, for Chrissake."

Kessler sighed. "Joe, figure it out for yourself. Guzman's in tight with the government, right? And the government sticks you for fifty grand. What happens if you don't pay?"

"You mean, they'll seize the ship?"

"You said it yourself. She's Honduran registry and Honduran owned. Not much we can do about it under U.S. law. What does a port authority do if an owner won't pay his bills? They sell off the ship, right? And you wanna bet who's gonna buy her? Real cheap?"

Joe pulled at his collar, waiting for the grip on his breathing to loosen. "You all right?"

"I'm okay. Just give me a second. I'm gonna fix that bastard. I swear to God, I'm gonna get him."

"You've gone a funny color," Kessler said, coming around the desk for a closer look. "You want me to call your doctor?"

"No, no. But I could use a cup of coffee."

"Sure. Anything. Only don't drop down dead in my office, that's all. I've got a client coming in."

By the time he returned with the coffee, Joe was in better control of himself. "If I pay this," he said, "I may wanna get away with one more trip. What do you think?"

"*I* wouldn't." Kessler scratched his ear. "What the hell for? You got equipment down there?"

"Yeah, but I think I can get some money out, too. I gotta load of urea fertilizer out of Port Allen. For the banana plantations. AID cargo. A hundred ninety-five thousand dollars in freight."

"Not bad. No way they can steal it?"

"No, sir. No way. That's not freight collect. That's cash money payable up front on presentation of the bill of lading. Right here in the United States. They won't even get to see it."

"Well, it's a nice piece of change. But I wouldn't want to risk the ship for it."

"Hey. That's U.S. government cargo moving under U.S. government contract. They wouldn't mess with that."

"If you say so."

"You know what I'm gonna do?" Joe cheered up suddenly. "First, I'm gonna bury Guzman's ass in fertilizer. Then I'm gonna charter the *Morazan* to Nopal Line. Won't make as much that way, but with Ben gone, I don't have the time to fool with her anyway. We'll make a nice profit on the deal, and no hassle."

Kessler smiled faintly.

Joe was gone for ten days, and returned with a draft contract from Nopal for Kessler to look over. But he had forgotten to tell Manny Levy to keep up with the rent in his absence.

"Where the fuck have you *been?*" Boyle demanded on Joe's first morning back, following him into the men's room. "You crazy? You know how much you owe? As of right now? You owe a thousand dollars."

"That *much?*" He whistled. "Mounts up, don't it?"

"You bet your *ass,* " said Boyle, who was much more agitated about it than he was. "And that's what's on the line here. Your *ass.* "

"Well, you see, I was down in Honduras a couple of times. Then I had to go to Oslo for a couple of weeks. Nopal's thinking of chartering the *Morazan* to go to Baranquilla and Curacao, and I think that makes sense. The kind of traffic we been . . ."

"Never mind all that shit." Boyle's beaky face was so stretched with annoyance he seemed ready to peck at Joe's head like an angry cockatoo. "What about the money? Oh, *fuck.* " He broke off, hearing voices and laughter in the hall. "I'll see you in your office," he said, and cleared his expression to greet Barone, who entered with a noisily sociable group of out-of-towners.

Union delegates, Joe guessed. Something about them reminded him of Ensulo. Returning to the office, he checked to see if their new warehouse-man was still on the payroll, and finding he was, made a note to ask Richardson how the investigation was going. It was time to get this show on the road.

"All right," said Boyle, barging in. "Where is it? I don't have much time."

"You kidding?" Joe sat back astonished. "I can let you have about twenty-eight dollars. That's all I got on me. Just gimme a couple of days."

"You don't *have* a couple of days." Boyle looked back over his shoulder, then closed the door behind him. "If I don't get the money today," he said confidentially, "the little guy's gonna come for it."

"Jay? Why? Come on, Bill. You know I'm good for it. But I gotta have a little time to get that much together. It's a lot of money."

However reluctantly, Boyle could always see the other fellow's point of view. "You don't understand these guys," he said, shaking his head. "I tried to cover for you, but they don't wanna know. They want their money. *Now.* And if somebody's gonna get their legs broke, it ain't gonna be me."

"Jesus, Bill. I can't just run out and cash a check for a thousand bucks." He was getting worried. "Look at the time. Fucking bank's gonna be closed before I get there. You gotta tell 'em."

"Tell 'em *what?* I mean, I gotta answer to these guys too, you know." Boyle thought for a moment, then rapped on the desk. "All right. Gimme a check. Make it out to cash. I shouldn't do this, but I'll try and wash it through Twin Express or the eye doctor. And you better hope they have the cash to cover it, that's all. Otherwise I don't know."

"Okay, Bill." Joe had his checkbook out already. "But George knows I'm good for it, too. I mean, what does he want? He's the one who won't deal with the family when I'm not here. And he knows I travel a lot."

"Listen," said Boyle, taking the check and examining it carefully. "All he knows is the rent gets paid every week." He folded it in two, and wedged it in a wallet two inches thick with bills. "They don't call him

'Nervous' for nothing. If you're gonna be away again, just gimme the payments up front."

"Okay, Bill. Thanks."

"Sure." He replaced the wallet before opening the door, and left with a parting nod.

Staring after him, Joe wondered what in the world he had thanked him for. It made him so angry, he picked up the telephone and called Bob Richardson, but he was out.

He left no message. He still had to think the next step through. There was certainly no point getting himself killed if Ensulo could give them what they wanted.

A few weeks later, Richardson came to see him anyway, with Jack Applegate. He could see they wanted another favor, but he let them get around to it in their own way.

"How's Ensulo making out?" Applegate asked eventually.

"I was gonna ask *you* that," said Joe.

"Well, he's come up with a couple of things," Richardson said. "But I don't think he can hack it."

"I don't think so either. I'm gonna have to let him go."

"Sure, Joe," said Applegate. "That's okay. No problem."

They looked at one another.

"Joe," said Richardson. "I'm gonna level with you. You know what we need? To crack this thing? We need one little piece of hard evidence."

"Like what?"

"Well, like, if we could tape a payoff, for instance."

"Yeah," said Applegate. "Something like that would get us started. It'd give us something to work with."

"Uh-huh." He swallowed, short of breath. "Uh, how would you use a tape like that?"

"Well, that depends. There's different ways."

"Like for instance?"

Richardson was also hesitant. "Well, if it was Boyle, say, and we had something like that, maybe we could get a court order for a wiretap. Tie in other people that way. Bring 'em back in front of the grand jury again. You know, confront 'em with it. There's a lot of different ways to go."

"Yeah," said Applegate. "Let's say we made a real good case against Boyle. He knows he's going down, okay? Well, then, maybe we can make a deal with him. If he helps us, when the time comes, maybe we'll let him cop a plea. Let him off light if he'll testify for us."

"That's it." Richardson nodded. "There's a hundred ways to go. But you got to start *some*place. You gotta have leverage."

Joe shook his head. "Boyle'd never go for that."

"He might," said Applegate. "You can't tell. It's better than twenty years in the slammer."

"No. They'd kill him. And not just him either. If they knew about the tape, they'd kill the guy that set him up, right?"

Richardson looked at Applegate. "That's not how it works, Joe. One payoff is nothing. A misdemeanor. We're not gonna get you killed for that."

"Hey, you're not getting me killed for *anything*. Let me tell you."

They laughed.

"No, we got a conspiracy going here, Joe," said Richardson. "A big one. To make the case, we're gonna need a whole bunch of witnesses who can put the total picture together for a jury, piece by piece. Not just one payoff here and another one there. I mean thirty or forty of 'em. Different people. Different places. Different times. All documented."

"Yeah, it's like a net," agreed Applegate. "There's maybe a dozen or twenty witnesses, all tied in."

"Right," said Richardson. "So what are the bad guys gonna do? They can't kill everybody. All the witnesses'll have protection anyway. And if you can't kill everybody, it don't make sense to kill just one. The case don't depend on just one."

Joe breathed deeply, steadying his pulse. "Right now it does," he said.

Applegate started to say something, but Richardson laid a hand on his arm.

"I won't lie to you, Joe," he said. "I'm not gonna tell you there isn't some risk involved. But look around you. Is there anybody else in this port with balls enough to do it? I don't think so."

"That's right," said Applegate. "You're the only one, Joe."

"How do I know I won't *stay* the only one?" he demanded. "I mean, where are you gonna get all these other witnesses from if they're in so tight with Barone? Suppose they *don't* cooperate. Where does that leave *me?*"

"They will," said Applegate, and Richardson nodded emphatically.

"Figure it out for yourself, Joe. It's a Taft–Hartley violation for a union guy to take money from employers, okay? But it's also a violation for employers to *give* money. And somehow I don't see guys like Chester and Sklaire taking a fall as co-conspirators with guys like Boyle and Barone. Once they know this whole deal is coming apart, they'll cooperate. We'll have to gag 'em to keep 'em quiet."

"Wait a minute," said Joe, unamused. "You're gonna get me killed here. You can't *tell* anybody I'm working with you. If that gets back to Barone, I'm dead."

"Hey, Joe." Applegate shook his head reproachfully. "Nobody gets to see a card in our hand till we're good and ready to play it, okay? All we do is worry 'em a little."

"Well, now you're worrying *me*. I can see myself caught in the middle here."

"Can't happen," said Richardson flatly. "Nobody knows about you till we're ready to go to trial, and then you're just one of a whole pack of witnesses. What Jack means is, once we got a tape, we can go to Harrington, we can go to Chester and shake their tree a little. See what falls out. Tell 'em we got some hard evidence of payoffs to take to the grand jury. Ask 'em about Boyle and Barone. How often do they see 'em? What do they talk about? Have they ever paid 'em any money? Remind 'em it's a federal violation. Ask 'em what they know about kickbacks, and buying contracts, and all that stuff. Let 'em think we're gonna subpoena their records. Make 'em see that if they don't cooperate, they're gonna become targets themselves, that we know who's involved in this. Make 'em understand that if they don't help us now, they're gonna get indicted with the bad guys for conspiracy, racketeering, corruption, illegal payments, tax evasion, and any other Federal and state violation we can think of. Okay? We'll kind of lean on 'em a little bit.''

Joe smiled wanly. "I feel like you just leaned on *me* a little bit.''

"That's just so you get the idea.''

Joe played with his fingers. "What do you want me to do?''

"Sign a consent,'' Richardson said. "We want to wire your office and tape the next payoff to Boyle.''

"Okay.''

That disconcerted them. It disconcerted Joe, too.

"But I won't testify,'' he added. "You gotta understand that. I gotta protect my family. I'll work with you, but I won't testify.''

Applegate smiled uncertainly. "Man, that's like ordering a steak dinner and then saying you won't eat it.''

"Never mind. A steak dinner can stick in your throat and choke you.''

"Yeah.'' Applegate grinned, and clapped him on the shoulder. "You're right. You're absolutely right.'' And then, because there seemed nothing else to say, he went on: "You know, you had us worried there. I didn't think we were gonna talk you into it.''

"You didn't,'' Joe said. "You better understand that, too. I was coming to you anyway. I'm doing this because I hate what those mother-fuckers have done to this port. I'm doing it for Ben. I'm doing it for my family. I'm doing it for myself. Not because you talked me into it.''

"Sure, Joe.'' Applegate was surprised by his vehemence. "Listen, I didn't . . .''

"I've had 'em on my back for eight years. And it's made me sick—I mean physically *sick*—paying off those bastards. Letting 'em tell me what to do. It's like a fist in my stomach when I think of it.''

"I know what you mean, Joe.''

"No, you *don't* know. You guys are just doing your job. You go home to something else. But for me, this is *personal.* Six years I fought 'em, and they damn near ruined me. Then I had to go along because shipping is the only business I know, and I love it. I'm not ashamed to say that. But it killed Ben, and it's killing me. And I've had enough. So don't think you talked me into anything. I *want* this."

Lying awake that night while Ann slept, he was not quite so sure. Suddenly his life depended on a bunch of cops keeping their mouths shut, and there was no one to share the insecurity. Ann's anxieties would be harder to bear than his own.

Next morning, the sight of Boyle in the hallway took his breath away, as though Boyle had only to look at him to read his secret.

"Hey, Bill," he said. "You gotta minute?"

"Sure."

During the night, Joe had also figured out that the best way to cover his tracks was to get in deeper.

"I hear PRIMSA's coming in," he said, closing the door of his office behind them.

"Puerto Rican Marine, right? Yeah, I heard that, too."

"Yeah. Their guy in New Orleans called me. Says he wants PTO to make a bid for the stevedoring."

"So?"

"So I want it. Can you get that for me? Will you ask George?"

Boyle looked guarded. "Well, I don't know," he said. "That's a big one. A real big operation."

"I can handle it. I've had bigger."

"Well, I'll ask around. Find out who else is gonna bid, okay?"

Joe waited until Boyle was in the doorway.

"If you find out what's eating the OCB," he said, "you can let me know that, too."

Boyle turned back. "You had a visit?"

"Bob Richardson was here with some other guy. Applegate."

"What did they want?"

Joe shrugged. "Did I lose any cargo lately? Have I heard about any payoffs? Usual thing."

Boyle eyed him for a moment, and again turned to go.

"Looks like they're gonna try again," Joe said. "Another grand jury or something. I didn't pay too much attention."

"Uh-huh." Boyle nodded. "Okay, Joe. Thanks."

Joe smiled as the door closed. He had enjoyed that. Thinking about things was sometimes worse than actually doing them. In a more confident mood, he settled down to work out the cash float for the day's operations. There were times when Eagle and PTO together needed as much as $40,000 a day to cover their payroll, fuel bills, and general port expenses. To raise it, he would first call his three banks to establish the position at each, and then generate the amount required by swinging checks between them, always with a wary eye on accounts receivable. When everything was going well, the two companies had been known to take in a half-million a week. On the spur of the moment, after finding out his cash position at Southeast First National, he made an appointment to see a vice-president of the bank that afternoon.

If he went through with a bid for PRIMSA, part of the deal would include building a special roll-on, roll-off ramp almost the size of a football field. The cost of this had already been estimated by the Line at about $350,000, but it was worth it. As far as Joe could figure out, the stevedoring account would gross around a million dollars a year and show a net profit of about $10,000 a week.

The bank thought so, too. When he returned to his office, late in the day, he had its agreement in principle to finance the construction of the ramp against a guarantee from the Puerto Rican government, who owned the Line.

Almost the first person he saw on entering the building was George Barone. He came bowling down the hallway toward him like a wind-up puppet, half-comic, half-sinister, shoulders hunched, feet splayed, arms swinging loose.

"In a hurry, George?"

"Going home," he said.

"Bill talk to you about PRIMSA?"

"Think you can handle that? It's big. Gonna need a special ramp and everything."

"I know. I already got the finance lined up. Just tell me what it's gonna take, George. I need this one."

Barone stepped back a pace, looking at him sideways. Then he rubbed his foot on the floor, solemnly lifted his pants leg, and, as Joe had seen him do before, inspected the sole of his shoe as if to see what had stuck to it.

"Heavy," he said. "Very heavy."

"All right, George. I understand. I can handle it."

Barone studied him, eyes hooded. "You been running late," he said.

"Running late? What do you mean, George?"

"You know."

"Oh, *that,*" Joe said. "No, that was just a misunderstanding. All cleared up now. I was away on a business trip."

Barone nodded, and after another sideways glance, walked past him.

He heard nothing then for several days. At the end of the week, Boyle came to see him.

"You still wanna bid on PRIMSA?"

"Bill, I need that one bad."

"Well, it's gonna cost you," he said. "You're up against Harrington, Eller, and Strachan Shipping."

"I'm not worried. Everybody knows I'm the best. I just wanna hear how much."

Boyle raised his right hand, and spread the fingers.

"Five," he said. "Up front."

"Five *thousand?*"

"Yessir." Boyle nodded firmly. "That's what it's gonna cost you if you wanna play with the big guys. And if you get the contract, then you pay more. The five grand is just to get in there with a bid."

Joe blinked. "But they already *asked* me to bid," he said. "PRIMSA did. Their guy in New Orleans."

"Joey," said Boyle patiently. "You wanna crack at this contract or doncha? I mean, it's up to you."

"Well, of course I do."

"Then it'll cost you five, okay?"

"Yeah, but suppose I pay you the money and I don't get the account. What the fuck happens then?"

"Then you get the next big one," Boyle said. "Guaranteed."

Joe whistled and shook his head a few times, frowning. Then he shrugged. "Okay."

"Good boy. You can give it to me Tuesday. When I come for the rent."

The Organized Crime Bureau wired Joe's office over the weekend.

On Tuesday, Joe had a $400 payment ready in his desk drawer—he was still undecided about the $5,000 entry fee—and the OCB was ready with an undercover truck parked nearby, but Boyle did not come. Next morning, Applegate and John Hexter came back in a different truck, but the suspense was fraying Joe's nerve. Being the bait in a trap was almost worse than being caught in it.

In the late afternoon, his secretary announced that Boyle was outside.

Joe licked his lips. "Tell him to come in," he said. "I'm not busy."

"He doesn't want to come in," she said. "He wants to see you in the hall."

Joe felt the sweat break out as he stared at her. Boyle *knew.* His breathing started to hurt. One way or another, this was going to kill him before he was through.

He went to the door with a questioning frown, and invited Boyle inside with a mock-courtly flourish. Boyle grimaced, showing his teeth, and with a glance up and down the hall, waved Joe out imperiously. It was a gesture that brooked no argument, and Joe went.

"I can't give it to you out *here,*" he said despairingly.

"Forget it," said Boyle. "Let's take a walk."

He set off toward the rear door of the building, and Joe followed. For all he knew, they were waiting to gun him down in the parking lot.

"What's this all about?" he demanded, as soon as they were outside. "Where are we going?"

"No place," Boyle said, slowing down. "I don't wanna talk inside, that's all. Fucking walls got ears sometimes." He was looking at Joe, but not accusingly. "Remember you told me you had a visit? Well, you were right. Fucking Strike Force is at it again, poking its fucking nose into everything."

"No shit." Joe was dismayed and relieved at the same time. "How'd you find out?"

"Oh, we got people downtown. And there's this fat fuck been hanging around. You seen him? Heavy, greasy-looking guy?"

Joe had a feeling he was being tested. "Ensulo, you mean? Yeah, I seen him. Manny threw him a couple of things to do for us in the warehouse. Felt sorry for the guy. Why? You telling me that's a *cop? Him?*"

"Well, I don't know if he's a cop or not. Could be working for 'em. Could be a snitch. Couple of guys seen him with binoculars. You know, hiding in the shed and spying on people."

"No kidding," said Joe indignantly. "Well, for Chrissake. If I see him again, I'll kick his ass right off the fucking dock."

"No, no. Don't do that. Don't do nothing. If he *is* a fucking snoop, that'll bring 'em down like flies. We been through this before. Just watch your step, and don't say nothing indoors you wouldn't want your own mother to hear."

"Well, okay." He was furious. "I got an envelope for you. You wanna come back for it?"

"What's that? The five grand?"

"No, the rent."

"Okay. Hold onto it. I'll let you know."

Joe drove home kicking himself for getting involved, for exposing himself to this lethal incompetence. If this was the OCB's idea of discretion, his life expectancy was about a week.

"What went *wrong?*" he hollered, when Applegate called him at home that night. "You kidding me? Vinnie Ensulo is what went wrong. They got him spotted . . . Yeah, he fucked up, the stupid, fat son of a bitch. You know what he's been doing? He's been playing hide and go seek on the pier with a pair of fucking binoculars. I mean, I'd die laughing, if he wasn't gonna get me killed some other way. Get him out of there. Asshole . . .

"No, I *don't* know when Boyle will come back for the money. He didn't say. Not with some fat snoop breathing down his neck. You can make book on that . . .

"Well, I'll think about it. You got 'em all upset now. And you better get all that crap out of my office. Next thing you know, they're gonna have some guy in there checking out the building for bugs."

He took the pains in his chest to a heart doctor, who prescribed some pills for hypertension and told him he ought to relax more. Obediently, he drove down with Ann to their townhouse in Key Largo on Friday night for a weekend's fishing, but without much luck, with Ann, the fish, *or* his nagging uncertainties.

On Monday, he returned to work with the clear priority of reinsuring himself with Barone. He called in at United National Bank and cashed an

Eagle check for $5,000, sealed the money—fifty $100 bills—in a white envelope, and went to look for Boyle. Finding him in the union office, he beckoned him outside and slapped the envelope into his hand.

"What's this?"

"Play money," Joe said. "Five thousand good reasons why I gotta get PRIMSA."

"Jesus Christ." With a startled look along the hall, Boyle stuffed the envelope into his pocket. "You're gonna get us all arrested."

Joe just smiled.

But that was all he had to smile about. Two days later, Manny Levy came into the office with a telex message in his hand and sat down in the corner like an old man.

"What's wrong with you?" Joe demanded, in no mood to listen to anybody else's problems.

"Guzman."

He tried to throw the message onto the desk, but it fluttered upwards and fell short. Neither made a move to retrieve it.

"What does he want now?"

After the last remittance of $52,000, Joe had told him he would send no more. The accountant had gone down for a last attempt to sort out the books, and again returned with no clear idea of Conasa's trading position. Now they were just waiting on the bill of lading for the fertilizer shipment before they took the cash, canceled the Honduras run, and left Guzman holding the bag.

Manny Levy shook his head.

"Lemme guess," said Joe, the bands tightening again around his chest. "Another fifty grand for port expenses?"

"Not this time." Levy could not stop shaking his head. "This time they just helped themselves."

"What are you talking about? Come on, Manny. What the fuck is this? Some kind of guessing game?"

"They took the money," Levy howled. "Read the fucking message. They telexed Washington, switched the shipment to freight collect and stole the fucking money. All of it. The whole fucking hundred and ninety-five grand."

Joe had been refusing to admit that possibility. "I thought you were watching that deal," he said mildly. His heart had stopped for a moment, but now it was getting ready to jump into his throat. "Didn't I tell you, keep an eye on it? Didn't I say that?"

"Who gives a fuck what you said?" Levy demanded miserably. "I can't hang around the telex all day. I got things to do. I mean, how the hell was I to know he'd pull a stunt like that?"

"Because it's Guzman, that's why. Now what are you gonna do about this?"

He was rather proud of his self-restraint. His vision had gone a little dark, and he could feel the sweat trickling through his hair, but anybody else would have been having a coronary or screaming his guts out.

"What do you mean, what am *I* gonna do about it?" Levy said "It's over. He's got the money. What do you *expect* me to do about it, for Chrissake?"

Joe rose from his chair, screaming his guts out. "You really wanna know? I expect you to get off your fat ass, and catch the first plane down there. And don't come back until you get the money or you kick his fucking head in."

Levy was not enthused by the thought of either course, but with Joe obviously torn between collapse and physical assault, he chose not to argue.

"Okay," he said. "Okay, okay. I'll go. But don't expect nothing. You know Guzman."

Joe dropped back in his chair, pressing his fist to his breastbone. "You tell Guzman from me. If he don't hand over that money, I'm gonna come down there myself and tear his throat out."

"Yeah," said Levy. "Great. That should do it."

"And do me a favor. When you get down there, check with Sister Maria Rosa. I been sending money, but I ain't heard nothing since the hurricane."

Joe took two of his blood pressure pills and went home early. Mel was right. No matter how badly Guzman had ripped them off, it was only money. Okay. A *lot* of money. But he was making a lot, and it really wouldn't hurt him. Not *badly*. It was the humiliation that hurt. So screw Guzman. He would stay calm.

He stayed calm even when Ensulo appeared in the office three days later. Manny Levy had flown back from Honduras the night before, refusing to talk to anybody, and Joe was waiting for him to come into work.

"It's not a good time, Vinnie," he said, waving him out. "I can't talk to you now."

"No, listen. It'll only take a minute. Just gimme a minute."

It was not the same Ensulo as had first come to see him. The New York hotshot, down to show the rednecks how things were done, had shriveled up a little.

"Got dumped, huh?"

"No, well, you see, they decided to call off the operation. This happens, right? I mean, like sometimes you see you're not gonna make it one way, then you try another. Happens all the time in police work. Win a few, lose a few."

"Ensulo," said Joe. "You're full of shit. You blew it. You screwed up the whole deal, and you could have got me killed. That I don't need. *You* I don't need. Good-bye."

"No, listen. These guys, they don't like seeing strangers around, that's all. A new face on the pier made 'em nervous."

"If you mean *your* face, Vinnie, I can understand that. Now get out of here. I got work to do."

"Come on. Gimme a break, will you? I know I can get in good with these guys. I need more time, that's all."

Levy appeared in the doorway, looking put out. "What's *he* doing here?" he demanded.

"Nothing," said Joe. "I told you, Vinnie. I can't talk to you now."

"Okay, okay. I'll catch you later."

Levy came into the room to let him pass.

"I don't trust that fat fuck," he said rudely, as Ensulo went through to the outer office.

"Oh, you gotta give a guy a break once in a while," said Joe, feeling he had enough enemies already. "But never mind that. What about Guzman? You see him?"

"Oh, yeah." Levy sat down, bristling with furious reproach. "Sure. I saw him."

"Well? Did he give you the money?"

"No, he didn't give me the money." His voice shook. "And don't give me any more of your bullshit, Joey, because I've had it up to here with Guzman *and* you. I must have been crazy, going down there."

"Well, where is it, then?"

"Joey, *fuck* the money. I could have wound up rotting away in some stinking jail for the rest of my life."

Joe snorted. "Guzman's a thief. How can *he* put *you* in jail?"

"Remember Garcia? His brother-in-law? He's head of the fucking Honduran army. 'This is *my* country,' Guzman says to me. 'The best thing you can do is leave. Right now. And forget this ever happened,' he says to me."

"Forget *what* ever happened?"

"So I left. In fact, you might say I fled the country."

"Manny."

"You seen those jails they got? Fucking death traps. So let him keep the money. I don't care."

"Manny," said Joe, clinging to the tatters of his calm. "How would you like a smack in the mouth?"

It took him several minutes to establish that Guzman had transferred the money out of reach before Levy got there. By then, they were both shouting.

"Well, where is it *now?*"

"Under his mattress for all I know," bawled Levy. "Why don't *you* go down and ask him?"

"Well, what did he *say,* for Chrissake? I mean, how did he explain it?"

"Expenses. They spent it on expenses. Cleaning up after the hurricane. Who knows?"

"What do you mean, who knows? You went down to find out." Joe caught hold of himself. He was right on the edge. "Manny, listen. Didn't you ask to see the supports? The invoices and everything?"

"Of *course,* I asked him," Levy wailed. "I mean, for God's sake, Joe, give me a little credit. That's when he started talking about Garcia, and how it was *their* country, and stuff like that. And by the way. The relief supplies? For the orphanage?"

Joe took a moment to readjust. "What about 'em?"

"They never got there. I checked."

Joe listened to the blood sing in his ears.

"I'll kill him," he whispered.

"Could have got lost," Levy said. "They're in such a fucking mess down there, it's gonna take years to sort out."

"No, no." Joe shook his head wonderingly. "How could it get lost? He said he'd take care of it personally."

"Oh, well. You know what *that* means."

"You think he *stole* it? Stole the kids' *food?*"

"Why not? You know what that stuff was worth down there? On the black market? Fucking army stole everything as fast as it went in. Ministers resigned. It was in the papers."

Joe mumbled something. He was in real pain from the pressure behind his eyes.

"Ripped off everybody," Levy was saying. "Even the Red Cross. So I don't see Guzman passing up a chance like that. I mean, I'm only guessing, but that's what it looks like to me."

Joe decided he was probably having a stroke.

"But what kinda person steals from an orphanage?" he said. "I mean, what kinda animal *does* that?" He stood up, knocking over his chair. "I don't know what to do."

"Do?" Levy laughed. "Best thing to do is forget it. We still got the ship."

"No." It was a howl of accumulated outrage. "Let 'em steal from those kids? No way. Best thing we ought to do is kill that son of a bitch. He deserves killing."

"Hey," said Ensulo, standing in the doorway. *"I'll* do it."

They stared.

"Sure," he said. "You want him killed, I'll do it for you."

Joe recovered first. "Fuck you, Vinnie," he said. "I told you to get out of here."

"No, listen. I mean it. The guy owes you money, right?"

"Fuck off," said Levy. "It's none of your business."

"Well, lemme try and collect. If that don't work, he gets hit, okay? I'll whack him out. Cost you ten big ones. Either way."

Joe and Levy looked at each other.

"Vinnie, I wouldn't give you a quarter," Joe said.

"Don't. When I do it, *then* you pay me. All I need is an airline ticket and a couple of hundred for expenses. Fair?"

Levy shook his head slightly. "Get him out of here," he said in an undertone.

"Yeah, Vinnie. Get the fuck out of here. I told you twice already. We got nothing for you."

"Okay." Ensulo shrugged his heavy, sloping shoulders. He had recovered some of his insolence. "Think about it. I'll come back tomorrow. See if you changed your mind."

Joe righted his chair and sat down. "What a world," he said, watching Ensulo step out into the hallway. "What a lousy stinking world."

"Yeah," said Levy. "Would he do it?"

"Kill Guzman? You bet your ass."

"No, no. Collect the money."

"How's he gonna do that? With the kind of protection Guzman's got down there. And suppose he did. Can you see him handing it over? For a lousy ten grand?"

"Well . . . At least Guzman wouldn't have it."

"That's true." Joe shrugged. If he turned Ensulo loose, Guzman *had* to lose. "I mean, can you *believe* that? Stealing food from little kids? Son of a bitch *deserves* to get his ass broke."

"No, no." Levy had changed his mind. "Suppose they catch him. Next thing you know, he'll be telling everybody we paid him to do it."

"Yeah, well . . ." Joe sighed.

"Forget it," Levy said firmly. "He's blowing smoke up your ass."

Thinking it over later, Joe decided Levy was right. Ensulo was just another bullshit artist. Made to feel small when the Strike Force fired him, the hotshot undercover agent was trying to give his ego a boost by playing the hotshot hitman. It was a pity. Every time Joe thought of Guzman and what he had done, he started to sweat.

But Ensulo came back next day as he had promised. Payment by results, he said. With a visa, a ticket, and expense money, he would either collect from Guzman, waste him, or both for $10,000, payable on completion.

Sure, said Joe. He was busy. He didn't believe it, but in case Ensulo was serious, Guzman had it coming.

A few days later, Ensulo called from New York to go over the details again, which made it seem even more like a fantasy, but Joe again played along, having nothing to lose.

After that, a gruelling succession of 16-hour work days put the whole thing out of his mind. Missing Ben bitterly, Joe was either clambering over cargo ships or supervising the turn-around of the three cruise liners now serviced by PTO when he was not fending off Mutzie and his cousins or sorting out the last-minute details of putting the *Morazan* into service with Nopal Line. And in the middle of all this, he heard that the PRIMSA contract had gone to Neal Harrington.

Tired as he was, he was too angry to let it pass. Five thousand dollars was not exactly confetti, but he had to keep cool. The pains in his chest never bothered him much when he was working on the dock, but he was sleeping badly again, and practically living on indigestion tablets.

Boyle was talking to a couple of his checkers in the union office, and winked at Joe in greeting.

". . . so the madam looks down at this basket case, this vet with no arms and no legs, and she says to him, 'Look, son, you can't come in here. This is a whorehouse. I mean, how are you gonna manage?' And the guy looks up at her, like this, and he says, 'Manage? Lady,' he says, 'how d'you think I rang the fucking doorbell?' "

Noticing that Joe was not laughing, Boyle punched one of the two playfully on the arm, and joined him in the hallway.

"Hey, you look like a man with a problem," he said cheerfully.

"I sure as hell don't look like a man with the PRIMSA contract."

"Yeah, I was coming to see you about that."

"To gimme back my five thousand?"

Boyle laughed politely. "I don't know, Joe. What can I tell you? They liked Harrington's bid better."

"Bullshit. He paid you more than I did."

Boyle's smile never wavered. "You can't always be a winner, Joe. It's like a horse race. But if you don't bet, you *never* win."

"Hey." He was getting hot in spite of himself. "You tell me five, and I give it to you. You tell Harrington something else, and you get that, too. What kind of a race is that, for Chrissake? I didn't lose. I got taken." It was a little strong. The whole point of paying the $5,000 had been to buy off suspicion, not arouse it by airing a new grievance. He forced a half-hearted smile. "So come on, cousin," he said. "Tell me it ain't so. Tell me I got a surprise coming."

"You go popping off in front of George like that," said Boyle, "and you'll get a surprise that'll put you in traction. I told you up front. The five was just for the chance to bid. Next big one comes along, you buy in straight off the bat."

"*Buy* in?" He reared up again. "What are you talking about? I bought in already. With the five thousand."

"Jesus." Boyle shook his head patiently. "Joe, how many times do I have to tell you? It cost five to make a bid for PRIMSA. This is something else."

Joe struggled to grasp what he was saying. "You mean, I gotta pay again? I still gotta pay for the contract when it comes?"

"Well, nothing is for nothing, Joe. I ought to charge you for keeping the others out."

It was said with such kindly concern for his failure to understand the basic rules of business that for a mad moment Joe felt he should apologize.

"Yeah," he said, breaking open a new pack of Pepto–Bismol tablets. "Yeah, I see."

"I mean, it's a pretty good deal when you think about it."

"Well, I don't know." He laughed painfully. "I think maybe it's better if you *don't* think about it."

As he walked back to his office, Joe kept telling himself that things could not get worse, but Ensulo was waiting for him. He had his passport, he said. As soon as he got his visa, his ticket, and a little folding money, he was ready to go. And did Joe have a gun he could use?

"Oh, Jesus." Between them, they were driving him crazy. "You can't take a *gun* down there, Vinnie," he said, as though about to cry. "The fucking country's a hundred years backward. They got icemen on the streets. Grab yourself an icepick and hit him in the fucking head with it or something. I mean, I don't know, do I? Just leave me alone."

For several minutes after Ensulo left, Joe sat collapsed at his desk, so tired he felt he must be dreaming. There was no point in living this way. Nothing was going right, and the demands being made on him were more than he cared to meet any longer. He was simply being whittled away, slice by slice. When Manny Levy came in, Joe told him he wasn't feeling well, and went home to bed.

In the next few weeks, he kept things as quiet as possible while he tried to decide what to do. There was no further word from the OCB, and after what had happened, he was in no mood to try anything else with them. When he was ready to start again, he would go straight to the FBI. Meanwhile, he kept Barone and the others off his back by paying the rent on time, and meekly sweetened the pot, at Boyle's request, with $6,000-worth of cruise tickets: six for Boyle himself, two for Vanderwyde, and two for the son and new daughter-in-law of Mayor Hans Tanzler, of Jacksonville. It was an expensive way to keep the peace, but still another crisis was blowing up.

Though a major stockholder in Eagle, Uncle Mutzie had left Joe and Manny Levy to run the business much as they liked after the Jacksonville debacle. With his son, Bobby Kratish, he had tried instead to cash in on the shore-based side of the container shipping boom by developing Eagle Trucking and a company called Tyler Leasing. Unhappily for them, however, the market had already peaked when they entered it, and both firms were soon struggling to survive as the shipping industry as a whole slid into recession.

Not being directly involved, Joe was not much concerned by their progress into bankruptcy. He even derived a certain wry satisfaction from lending Mutzie $50,000 to pay off the July 1975 installment on the notes outstanding against Tyler Leasing's trailers and containers, most of which were sitting idle in the firm's parking lot.

It was supposed to be a three-day bridging loan to tide them over. As

Joe had a $60,000 payroll to meet by the end of the week, he insisted on his uncle writing a post-dated check for the full amount, but when he presented it, the check bounced. And when he called Bobby Kratish for the money, he was told they didn't have it. They were broke.

Composing himself, Joe called Ann, and together they went to the bank and signed a personal note for $38,000, putting up a certificate of deposit as collateral. He then telephoned Mutzie, and on being told he was out, left a message to the effect that unless he and his son presented themselves at the office next morning with the money, he would have them arrested for passing dud checks.

They arrived at 8:30 A.M.

"You owe me fifty thousand dollars," he said, doing his deep-breathing exercises. He had been trying to slow his pulse rate down for ten minutes.

"Listen," said Mutzie. "I *own* this company. And I'm taking over."

It was July 23, the day Ensulo was supposed to leave for Honduras. With that on his mind, Joe was a little slow to take in what his uncle was saying.

"As of right now, *I'm* running things around here," Mutzie went on. "And there's gonna be some changes."

Joe frowned, but could not take him seriously. "I wouldn't let you run the men's room," he said.

Mutzie went and sat in his chair. "You got nothing to say about it."

But Joe had a great deal to say about it, particularly when he learned after a brawling half-hour of recrimination that the $50,000 was merely the tip of an iceberg of debt. One of the changes Mutzie had in mind was for Eagle to absorb Eagle Trucking and Tyler Leasing, along with unsecured losses amounting to close on half a million dollars.

This silenced Joe for a full five seconds. Made aware of the blood thumping at his temples, he felt for his pulse again.

"Mutzie, you're full of shit," he said distractedly. "Took four years to pay everybody off last time. There's no way I'm gonna get involved in this. Absolutely no way."

"Who asked you? You wanna leave? Leave."

"Now you're talking stupid. I don't have to listen to this. Why do I have to listen to this? Get the fuck out of here. I'll put the money through as a loan to you and Bobby."

"I'll tell you why you're gonna listen," said Mutzie fiercely. "Because if you don't, I'll fucking fire you."

"*Fire* me?" Joe honked with derision. His pulse was much too fast, and didn't seem all that regular.

"It's up to you. I don't wanna have to do it."

Joe swallowed once or twice. His mouth was very dry. "I own a piece of this business, too, you know. So does Gus. A *big* piece."

Mutzie smiled. "I already talked to Gus," he said. "Didn't I, Bobby?"

Another charge of adrenaline drilled through Joe's chest. He felt the heat of it rise in his face.

"*Gus* says you should take over?" he said, incredulously.

Bobby glanced at his father. "Well, he said Eagle should take the loss, Joe. He said it's all in the family, and he's right."

"We'll see about that," said Joe, choking. "You're just trying to drive me crazy."

He stood up shakily, frowning as the light dimmed, and went to the men's room. He had a pain in his back. Locking himself in a cubicle, he sat with his head between his knees. After a few moments, he *un*locked it, to be on the safe side, but nothing terrible happened, and as soon as his pulse steadied a little, he went back and called Gus from the outer office.

Fern answered. His father was sleeping, she said. He had had a bad night from all the worry. When Joe explained why he *had* to talk to him, she flew into a temper. Well, of course they had to take the loss, she said. In this cruel world, all they had was one another.

Joe went through to the inner office.

"Well?" said Mutzie complacently. "What did he say?"

"What did *who* say?" asked Joe, reclaiming his empty chair. "Let me ask you something. What are you gonna do if I call a stockholders' meeting?"

"Bury your ass," said Bobby. "We got the votes to do it."

"Before or after you explain why we got to take on a half-million dollar loss? We're a public company, right? The SEC could be interested in that."

"Yeah?" said Mutzie. "Well, maybe they'll wanna take a look at Conasa as well. What about the dough we dropped there?"

"Listen, that fucking ship's worth $4 million."

And off they went again for another furious gallop over the now familiar course, getting nowhere, settling nothing. There had never been much hope of a compromise, but now, neither side was even trying to persuade the other. They were just out to punish. Nose to nose across the desk, hardly listening to one another, each was absorbed in his own tirade until Mutzie said something about Honduras. This reminded Joe of Ensulo, wrenching him off balance so violently that he felt the pain of it like a blow in the back, sharp enough to silence him. As he lowered himself into his chair, he noticed the fingernails of his left hand were turning blue.

The others broke off unwillingly.

"What's wrong with *you?*" demanded Bobby.

"I don't feel so good," said Joe, breaking out in a heavy sweat. "I feel terrible. In fact, I'm having a heart attack."

"How do you know?" asked Mutzie suspiciously.

"Saw it on TV last week. How you can tell." He was surprised how calm he was. "Pains in the back. And look at my nails. Changing color. See that?"

"Oh, Jesus," said Bobby. "We better call an ambulance."

"No." Joe shook his head. He couldn't breathe. His chest seemed to have jammed. "It's a bad one. Drive me."

He still refused to panic. As they helped him out, he remembered to ask his secretary to telephone ahead to the bridge tender at the entrance to Dodge Island.

"Tell him, for God's sake, don't open that bridge," he whispered, "or I'm a dead man."

Half way to Cedars of Lebanon Hospital, he was sure he would die in any case. Working hard on his breathing, he was suddenly struck another, extinguishing blow on the breastbone. The pain was so lurid it scattered his wits in fright and amazement. Then came pressure, like an anvil crushing his rib cage. He felt it pushing him into the dark, and fought like a madman against it, terrified he might never find his way back. He knew when they reached the hospital, but not much more after that, except in painful fragments that made no sense.

He had suffered a severe myocardiac infarct that would almost certainly have killed him had they waited for an ambulance. As it was, he responded to treatment, and was discharged from the hospital after eighteen days.

What helped his recovery as much as anything was a visit from Vincent Ensulo on August 4. He had come to collect his $10,000, he said, but Joe could see he hadn't earned it.

"Where'd you kill him, Vinnie?" he asked, letting go inside. "In the parking lot?"

"Yeah. Right. With an icepick, like you said."

"Which parking lot was that, Vinnie? The one next to the office, or the one up the street?"

"Ah, the one right by the office there," he said. "He wouldn't give me the money, so I whacked him out. Pow! Hit him good. Right in the head. Just like you told me."

"Uh-huh."

There was no parking lot next to the office.

Soon afterwards, he went home, and for nearly three months did little but work on his stamp collection. He was no longer interested in the business. The crane and the ship meant nothing to him anymore. All he had left was a score to settle. He had been spared for a purpose, he felt. Field and Barone had destroyed the point of his life. Now the point of his life must be to destroy *them.*

By mid-September, he was getting restless, and welcomed company. In the evening of September 16 Bob Richardson and three other officers called at the house unexpectedly.

"Hey, Bob," Joe said, delighted to see them. "Come on in. I'm glad you stopped by."

"This isn't social, Joe," said Richardson, as he stepped inside. "We've got a warrant for your arrest."

10

One-man War

HE was accused of attempted murder, conspiracy to murder, and solicitation to murder Virgilio Guzman.

As they left the house, Richardson told Ann not to worry, that Joe would be home in an hour or so, and no one was indelicate enough to mention handcuffs. Joe walked between them to the car as if they were going bowling.

But he was bitterly aggrieved. Ensulo had played him for a sucker after he had tried to help the man. Worse than that, Richardson had not only condoned the double-cross but busted him on the strength of it. The pair of them had obviously planned the whole thing from the start. The day after his original offer to kill Guzman, Ensulo had come back to repeat the proposition wearing a body recorder.

"What the hell did you wanna go and do a thing like this for?" he asked, as they rode downtown. Mel Kessler had told him on the telephone to keep his mouth shut, but his sense of injury was too extreme.

"Don't look at me," said Richardson. "Ensulo works for the Bureau."

"Well, this is all bullshit, you know that, don't you?"

"He made tapes, Joe. No way you're gonna beat it. We gotcha by the balls."

"But he set me up, for Chrissake. You gonna put me in jail now? What for?"

"He made the tapes," said Richardson. "The Bureau hands us the case, and we gotta act on it. But that don't mean you're going to jail. No fucking way am I gonna put you in jail."

"Then where are we going?"

"Well, we gotta book you, Joe. Take your picture and everything. But that's it. Then I'll take you home."

"Yeah?" There had to be a catch. "Bob, what do you want?"

"You know what I want."

Joe rubbed his forehead in exasperation. "Well, I mean, it's just stupid.

I was going to the Strike Force anyway. Soon as I got back to work."

Kessler met them at Dade County Jail. After Richardson handed Joe over for processing, with instructions to hold him afterwards in an interview room until his bond was posted, he and Kessler went off with the other officers to discuss the case against him. It was the first Kessler had heard of the Ensulo affair. He had once told Joe that, if he wanted to play cop, he should first move Ann and the kids out of town.

"How does it look?" Joe asked, when Kessler eventually joined him in the interview room. "Can I leave now?"

"Sure. Bond's posted." He shrugged with the unconcern he usually affected when his advice had been ignored. "But you're not going to walk away so easy from the rest of it."

"You mean they don't wanna deal?"

"Well, of course they do. I never saw 'em so eager. I don't know what they want, but when they tell you, you better take a pretty hard look at it. Make sure you know what you're getting into."

"They wouldn't tell you?"

"No."

"Okay. What happens if I *don't* cooperate? That son of a bitch Ensulo is a police informer. I knew that when they asked me to hire him. So am I gonna ask a guy like that to kill for me? Do I *look* crazy? It's bullshit, right?"

"Maybe." Kessler eyed him thoughtfully. "Some of it. If Ensulo never left the country, there's no way they can prove attempted murder. Conspiracy? I don't know. Maybe. They say they got Manny on that as well."

"Manny?" Joe snorted. "Well, that *is* bullshit. Manny only talked to the guy just the one time. The *first* time. When he offered to do it for us."

"They say he was wired."

"Fine. But not the first time. If he *did* make a tape, it had to be next day when he came back to see me, the cocksucker. And Manny wasn't even there. It was just Ensulo and me."

"Okay. So maybe we can beat the felonies. That leaves solicitation. Richardson says it's open and shut. They got you for sure on that one."

"Yeah?" Joe turned himself off before he got angry. "For how long?"

"Solicitation? A year? It's a misdemeanor."

"Okay. So how much time would I have to do? *If* they got me. Six months? Eight? Hell, that's nothing. I could use the rest. Maybe I'll just beat this thing, and *then* cooperate."

"Well, that's crazy," said Kessler. "I mean, it's up to you, but I don't see the point. If you're going to work with them anyway, why put yourself through all that?"

"Well, maybe I don't *have* to make a deal. I mean, shit, the son of a bitch works for the FBI, and he offers to kill a guy for me. That's entrapment, right?"

"Could be. I'll have to hear the tape. But there's a couple of other people you ought to consider. If we go to trial with this, I don't think Ann's going to enjoy the publicity too much, do you? So why put her through that if you're going to give 'em what they want anyway? Doesn't make much sense."

"Neither does pleading guilty to something I didn't do," said Joe irritably.

"Okay. It's up to you. I'll do whatever you want. But if you're not guilty, you're not innocent either. What about the visa you got him? And the expense money?"

"I was calling his bluff, that's all. I knew he'd never do it."

Kessler smiled slightly. "Well, *I* believe you, Joe. But I can't promise a jury will. If you don't want to plead guilty, I could tell 'em you agree to a *nolo*. A *nolo contendere*. That just means you don't want to answer the charge, and it leaves the court free to sentence you."

"Will they buy that?"

"I don't know. I could ask. If it means you'll cooperate, why not? They're not looking to put you in jail. They're looking for leverage."

Joe grunted. He resented the whole idea of seeming to be compelled into something he meant to do anyway.

"They didn't tell you what they wanted?"

"No, and I didn't push it. I will if you want me to. Basically, they're saying they'll drop the felony counts and let you cop a plea on solicitation if you agree to work with 'em. They also promise to speak to the judge, which means you'll probably draw probation. On the other hand, we can go to court, and if what you say is right, maybe we can beat this altogether."

Joe shook his head. "Burns my ass," he said, "but I guess a deal is the quietest way to handle it. Only they gotta promise me probation. And no publicity."

"Then forget it," said Kessler. "They can't do that. The most they can do is promise to talk to the judge. And *not* to talk to the newspapers."

"Then *you* forget it," Joe shouted. "No guarantee, no deal."

"Fine. Don't get yourself excited. You want to tough it out, I'm with you all the way."

Joe checked his pulse, and thought for a moment. "Yeah," he said. "You're right. We all want the same thing, so let's get on with it. Let's deal."

Kessler drove him home. Ann was still up, not far from hysteria. Joe was so shocked to see her in such a state that before he realized what he was saying, he actually asked her if anything was wrong. And only when she started to cry did he begin to see what he had done to her. Never mind the heart attack. Trying to spare her worry, he had shut her out of so much of his life that there was nothing left but worry. What had begun as concern had ended as neglect.

Two days later, on Thursday, September 18, the *Miami Herald* and the *Miami News* both came out with bald, and consequently misleading accounts of the case under very similar headlines: EXECUTIVE ACCUSED OF SLAYING PLOT and EXEC ACCUSED IN MURDER PLOT. Coupled with several factual errors, for which the Public Safety Department seemed to be responsible, the story presented him in the worst possible light, as a vindictive murderer by proxy who, as the *Herald* pointed out, "could be sentenced to more than 30 years in prison if convicted." By 9 A.M., two reporters and a television crew were waiting outside in the street, and Ann had locked herself in the bedroom.

Then Richardson called, and Joe told him he had changed his mind.

"I just think I ought to fight this now and set the record straight," he said. "Mel's pretty sure we can beat this if we go to trial."

There was a pause.

"Have you talked to him about it?" Richardson asked.

"Not yet. Fucking phone's been jumping off the hook."

"Well, you go to trial and you're gonna get this kind of publicity every day for a week. I'm telling you as a friend. There's some pretty heavy stuff on those tapes. Ask Mel. He's heard 'em."

"All right. I'll talk to him."

"Okay. And there's something else. If Ensulo goes on the stand, he's not gonna lie . . . not under oath. He's gonna say you hired him knowing he was a police informer trying to get in the union. And I don't think Barone's gonna like that."

"Fuck," said Joe savagely. "These are bullshit charges, and you know it. So why don't you just drop 'em? I'll work with you. I was gonna do it anyway."

"I know, I know. But it's too late. We drop 'em, Barone's gonna know for sure you made a deal. We gotta go through with it now."

They settled the final details on October 16, 1975, at a meeting between Joe, Mel Kessler, Richardson, and Detective J. Lazzeri in Building 2148 at the western end of Miami International Airport, the headquarters of the Organized Crime Bureau's Airport/Seaport Detail. The State Attorney had agreed to accept a plea of *nolo contendere* to the misdemeanor and to drop the felony charges in return for Joe's cooperation in a waterfront investigation.

There was nothing more to think about.

At 6.30 A.M., Friday, October 17, he reported back to Building 2148, where Richardson, Lazzeri, and three other officers were waiting for him. He was in good spirits, neither unduly apprehensive nor foolishly overconfident. They recorded the serial numbers of the $200 he had brought with him for the payoff, and after he signed a consent form, strapped a Nagra miniaturized recorder to his right thigh with an Ace bandage, hiding the microphone behind his belt buckle. He was then shown how to switch the machine on and off through his pocket, and briefed on the way they wanted the conversation to go. Soon after 7, he left for Dodge Island, with a surveillance team following in an undercover panel truck.

Closing up as they crossed the causeway and bridge into the port, they parked more or less at the same time a few spaces apart. As instructed, Joe then switched on the recorder and made straight for the union office in the 1001 Building. He was not at all nervous. He just tingled, as though his blood were lightly carbonated.

Evidently cued by providence, Boyle was the first person he met.

"Good morning, Bill."

Boyle stepped back a pace. "Good *morning,*" he said. It was the first time he had seen Joe in three months. "How *are* you?"

"Feeling much better. All set now to go to work, although I gotta take it easy for a while. You know how it is."

"Right, right. But you sure as hell look in good shape."

"Yeah, I lost forty pounds. Off the belly." He patted it proudly. "You gotta minute? I need to see you."

"Sure, Joe. Sure." Boyle was getting over his surprise. "Come on. Let's take a walk." He put his arm around Joe's shoulders and steered him out into the hall. "What's all this shit about you getting arrested while you were sick? It was in the fucking papers and on TV and everything. Something about you trying to whack some guy out in Honduras."

"Yeah, yeah. It's all bullshit. I'm trying to sell my ship down there, and you know how it is with those cocksuckers. It's a set-up, but I'll beat it."

"Yeah? Shit. *We* didn't know. Why didn't somebody come and tell me?"

"I don't know. Looks like somebody's trying to hurt me real bad. I mean, they hit me with this just when I'm getting over a bad heart attack. Couldn't have done it at a worse time."

"Well, never a *good* time for getting arrested, right?" Boyle laughed, but half-heartedly. "And now Mutzie's taken over with that kid of his. We had our problems with them, Joe."

"Well, don't worry about it," he said, stepping outside as Boyle held the door for him. He glanced carelessly at the surveillance truck. "Let 'em take over their end. Nobody bothers *my* end. And that's what I want to see you about. Manny been taking care of you? How much do I owe?"

Boyle thought for a moment. "Sixteen."

"Sixteen? At two and two?" He thrust the envelope with the $200 into Boyle's hand, hoping Richardson's people were ready with their cameras. "Here's two hundred now."

Boyle stuffed it hastily in his pocket. "How much?"

"Two hundred. Two hundred for the boat. I looked over the book and saw we got behind. So that's two hundred. And I'll give you four hundred on Tuesday."

"All right."

"I appreciate it, Bill, because you covered me."

"Okay, Joe. I knew you'd wanna catch up when you got back from the hospital."

"Right. I'm going home now, but I wanted to come over and see you. How do you like the way I look?"

"Yeah, you look good."

"You know, I been out for three months? You know what kind of a heart attack I had?"

"Yeah, I know." Boyle was looking now to escape before he heard all about it. "Don't get yourself excited. Take it slow. And I'll see you next week."

"I understand." Joe winked. "I'll be gone Monday, now. Be here Tuesday."

He drove straight back to the airport building, dying to hear his first tape, but had to wait in Richardson's office while they copied it onto a standard cassette.

"Well?" he asked eagerly, when they came back with it. "We get 'em? Did I do okay?"

"You did great," Richardson said. "Just great. We got some noise on it here and there, and a few rough spots to figure out, but that's normal. I'd say you got yourself a base hit first time up."

But Joe was disappointed when he heard it.

"Shit," he said. "I didn't talk to him enough. We shoulda had a longer conversation. And I switched the thing on too soon. Most of that is just me walking around."

Richardson ran back the tape to the payoff, and played it again.

"You handled the money pretty good," he said.

"Nah." Joe shook his head disgustedly. "Too quick. I rushed the whole thing. Next time, I'll take him into the men's room and count the bills into his hand one by one. And I gotta get in closer. He's too faint sometimes."

Richardson laughed. "First time out? I don't know what you're bitching about, Joe. That's a good, solid tape."

"I don't think so. We wanna nail 'em for conspiracy, right? Okay. Do I talk about Barone? No. Do I talk about the fat man or the little guy? No. Do I make him talk about *any* of those people? No, I don't. Shit."

He drove down to Key Largo with Ann for a weekend's fishing. With the kids away, he had planned to mend a few fences, but he could hardly wait for Tuesday. Sitting out on the water in his 22-foot Seabird, he rehearsed endless gambits for leading Boyle on.

Promptly at 6.30 A.M. on Tuesday, October 21, he reported to Building 2148, and Richardson strapped on the recorder.

"Nervous?"

"Who, me? No." It was true. "I mean, I got a few butterflies, but that's good. Keeps you on your toes."

This time he waited until he was inside the building before switching on the recorder. And again he prickled with excitement, a faint, electric shiver of anticipation.

"Good morning, good morning," he said breezily, putting his head around the door of the union office.

"Good morning, Joe." Boyle looked grim. "Howya doing?"

"All right. Wanna take a walk?"

Boyle nodded, and joined him in the hall.

"Something wrong?" Joe asked.

"Your fucking family's driving me nuts," he said. "I don't wanna bug you with it, you been sick. But I think you ought to know."

"Well, now, tell me about it, okay? I've always been straight with you."

"It's the payments, Joe. That fucking Mutzie . . . 'What payments?' he says. 'I don't know from payments.' So *my* guys, they think you put him up to it. They think you *told* him not to pay. I mean, I know you been sick, and I'm trying to give you a break, Joe, but they're getting upset with *me.*"

"Listen. I'm good for it. A deal is a deal, right?"

Joe steered him into the men's room, and the swing door banged shut behind them.

"And another thing," he said, pretending to check the cubicles. "You know I'm not that stupid."

"All right," said Boyle, satisfied they had the place to themselves.

"I wanna clear everything up." Joe sidled closer, although there was a lot less background noise than there had been outside. "How do we stand right now?"

"With the two coming this Friday?"

"Yeah. That's *this* Friday." He brandished his roll of bills. "So what does that make the grand total?"

"Well, I . . . What have you got there?"

"Two hundred."

Boyle counted on his fingers. "That's four. That's sixteen."

Joe frowned. "I gave you two. It *was* sixteen. Friday I give you two. Now that'll make it twelve."

"No, no." He shook his head impatiently. "Sixteen *without* the part Friday."

"Ah. So . . ."

"It's two every week, right? So you still owe me sixteen."

Joe nodded. It was so easy. "I owe you sixteen. One other thing is bugging me, okay?"

"Yeah?"

"You told me that Turner is okay. So why is he breaking my balls?"

"For what?"

"I don't know. He hit me up for the extra man here. He wants two days' warehousing now for all the men on the containers. He's constantly breaking my balls."

"Well, they all got something to *do*," Boyle said. "But there's nothing to it. Can't you see what he's doing?"

"All right." Joe could see perfectly well. He was also behind in his payments to Turner. "But do me a favor. Will you please get him off my back? Please? As a favor?"

"Yeah."

Joe motioned to Boyle to hold out his hand, and started counting the bills into his palm.

"Twenty, forty, sixty, eighty, a hundred," he said, slowly and distinctly. "Twenty, forty, sixty, eighty . . . two hundred."

Boyle nodded. "Okay."

"Friday again?"

"All right. You mean, you're gonna double up? Should I tell 'em you're gonna do that or what?"

"Hey, fuck 'em all," Joe said. "You know I share the wealth. We all will enjoy ourselves."

He couldn't speak for Boyle, but he certainly was. Boyle turned to the urinals, unzipping his fly.

"Ah, George went to see Mutzie," Joe said, trying for more. "He told Mutzie I been a bad boy."

"When?" Boyle was astonished.

"When? Last Wednesday."

"If he's got something to say to you, he . . ." Boyle broke off as light dawned. "That was *me*. It wasn't George."

"Ah. All right."

"He didn't even go over there."

"Well, if there's something to say, say it to *me*. Please. 'Cause my relatives get all bent out of shape. I've been straight with you."

"You ain't got no problems, Joe. Okay?"

That was better, but still not good enough. He had two more tapes to make to complete his end of the bargain—one with Boyle and the other with Turner—but he seriously doubted if either would do more than scratch the surface of the case that *could* be made against them. It was too dangerous to force the conversation. One false note could ring their alarm and get him killed. Whatever was said between them had to flow naturally out of what each already knew about the other, and so much of what he wanted to record was common ground.

There was not enough to prove a conspiracy yet, and no saying that the last two tapes would produce any more, or even as much as the first two. Ideally, instead of trying to rehash old deals, he needed to negotiate a new one. To tape them actually asking for money as a condition for getting new business would lock them up nicely, and there was a chance he could do it.

Earlier in the month, he had heard that Zim Container Service, a new division of Zim–Israel Navigation, was planning to bring one of its big container ships to Dodge Island. After handling Zim's break-bulk service in Miami since the early sixties, Joe naturally assumed he would service its container traffic as well, but when he telephoned Captain Reuvan Ilan, Zim's operations manager in New York, he was surprised to hear that the agency and stevedoring contracts would be awarded through competitive bidding. Asked why there should be any question about who should do the work, Ilan said he would prefer to discuss the reasons face to face, leaving Joe in no doubt that two of them were Field and Barone. He was not particularly worried. His unsuccessful $5,000 bid for PRIMSA had guaranteed him the next big one, but it was another reminder of how conclusive their power had become in Miami. He sent off his bid, as Ilan had requested, and went to see Richardson to explain what was on his mind.

"We're not getting anyplace," he said. "I mean, how you gonna use those wires? You gonna arrest 'em or what?"

"We don't know yet. We'll see what we got when you finish, then they'll review it. But what do you care? After Tuesday, it's over."

"Come on, Bob. We didn't even get started. And if you wanna use those tapes in court, I gotta testify, so how can it be over?"

"That was the deal, Joe."

"Deal, schmeal. If I'm gonna testify, I gotta bury those guys so deep they're gonna fall over their beards when they get out."

"Don't worry," said Richardson soothingly. "You gave us something to work with. Now we'll get 'em good."

"Bob," he said. "You're shitting me. I'll tell you what we got. We got a couple of union guys on the take. And what's that? A misdemeanor. A fine and a year inside. Maybe. Fucking slap on the wrist, that's all. Then they come looking for me, right?"

"What's the matter? You think we're stupid? Whatever happens, we'll take good care of you."

"Bob, this is the fucking Mafia we're talking about. These guys are connected. If I stop now, it's like handing 'em a parking ticket."

Richardson grunted. "So what are you saying? You telling me you wanna go on with it?"

Joe had the impression he had not taken Richardson wholly by surprise.

"I mean I wanna make sure we clean this mess up once and for all," he said. "I didn't stick my neck out just so they could tread on it. But no more Ensulos, okay? Let's do it right."

"Sure." Richardson played thoughtfully with his pencil. "Does this go out of state, Joe? Because if it does, there's a guy you ought to meet."

"Then I ought to meet him."

"Okay. I'll set it up."

The Cleveland Turner payoff also went smoothly. Joe was now convinced he had a talent for undercover work. He managed to include a reference to the free cruise tickets Turner had asked for, and counted out $100 into his hand, making it clear that he expected this payment to take care of the problem he had complained of to Boyle. He also induced Turner to refer to Barone as his superior, as someone he had to "live with," and to agree to a further payoff in two weeks' time.

The fourth and last tape was the best of the lot. Joe went through his counting routine again with Boyle in the men's room, and even got him to agree this time to take a check instead of cash in settlement of the arrears, thereby setting him up for a prime piece of documentary evidence. To discourage any further delinquency, Boyle also invoked his reserve powers of intimidation with a first reference on tape to Vanderwyde.

"I got the little guy asking me questions about you," he said.

"Who you mean?" Joe asked nervously. "Jay?"

"Yeah," said Boyle, as though the enormity of the threat frightened even him. "It's true."

Special Agent Raymond Maria of the FBI was not at all what Joe had expected. Prepared for the usual Marine in a wash 'n' wear suit, he had to adjust to a tall, spare man in his thirties with the contained air of a bank executive considering a loan application. It was soon apparent that Joe was being paraded for *his* inspection, not the other way around. Making occasional notes, Maria took him through the whole story, from the voyage of the *Playmate* to his last meeting with Boyle.

Then he smiled, coming into warmer focus. "Well," he said. "I'll bet you're glad *that's* over."

"Over?" Joe's answering smile faded.

"You've done what you had to. Now it's up to us."

"No, it isn't. It's up to me. Without me, you're nowhere. You're on the outside looking in."

"The deal was four wires."

"Look, will you just forget the fucking deal?" he said irritably. "That don't mean anything to me. I was into this way before that, right, Bob?"

Richardson nodded.

"You see? It didn't start with the deal, and it don't end with it either. Now are you gonna help me or not?"

Maria tried another tack. "You discussed this with your attorney?"

"With Mel? No. He doesn't even know about the four wires."

"How about your family? Your wife, for instance?"

"Not a word. You think I'm crazy? *She'd* kill me."

"You could be putting her at risk, you know. *And* your kids."

"They are already. Anybody going up against these people has gotta know that and live with it. But that don't mean Ann's gotta live with it, too. There's nothing she can do, so why should I worry her? It'll be harder for her and harder for me."

"Not if you walk away from it."

"I can't." Joe understood now what Maria was trying to do. "They're not stupid. You guys start running with the ball, and sooner or later, Barone's gonna figure out who handed it to you. Any way you wanna use those tapes, I'm committed. I knew that before I started."

Richardson laughed. "Ballsy little son of a bitch, isn't he? Try to talk him out of something and he digs in like a dose of crabs."

"I just don't like unfinished business." They were doing a job on him again, but he didn't care. "My best shot now is to go the distance."

"Well, I needed to hear you say that, Joe." Maria was still very serious. "If you come in now, you're in till the finish, and I want to be sure you can handle it."

"That's not the problem," Joe said. "If *I* let *you* in, I wanna be sure you won't fuck up like you did with Ensulo."

He waited until Maria started to reply, then cut him off.

"You gotta understand something," he said. "Getting these guys means more to me than it does to you. I got more on the line for one thing. And I don't like being told what to do. Not by you. Not by them. Not by anybody."

"We'll be grateful for all the help you can give us, Joe," Maria said politely.

"Okay. I don't like a lot of bullshit either. And most of all I don't like paying a bunch of fucking crooks for the right to make a living on *my* waterfront."

"All right, Joe," he said. "It's your party. How far can you take us?"

"How far do you want to go?" Joe had yet to be convinced Maria was the right man for the job. He seemed a little conservative. "Like, for instance, I had the Zim people down here yesterday. They're bringing in a new container ship, and they want me to handle it for 'em. But that's not how it works. Barone wants Harrington to get the business, okay? Well, I got news for 'em. Harrington ain't gonna get it because Barone promised the next big one to me. Now when I ask him how much I gotta pay for it, you want I should tape what he says? Just for openers?"

Maria smiled.

"Yeah," said Joe. "That's what I thought. Couple of weeks after that, I'll have to go up to New York and sign the contract. And I never go up there without saying hullo to my old friend, John Caputo. I ever tell you about him?"

"Some," said Richardson.

"Well, he's my New York connection. And a lot of things that happen down here are settled up there. If we're gonna clean up Dodge Island, we gotta clean up New York as well. It's all one industry. So let's do it right, okay?"

Maria glanced at Richardson, who was smiling at the ceiling.

"Yes," he said. "I see."

"Yeah. I mean, Fat Freddy's got his own Local up there. So has Barone
—Tommy Buzzanca fronts it for him. And Bill Boyle is always running
up there. That's where guys like Tony Scotto make the big decisions,
okay? And Caputo is my main connection with 'em."

"You mean you pay him to steer business your way?"

"Well, not really. We done business together, yeah, but he's like a
troubleshooter. John's executive vice-president of Tilston–Roberts Corporation, which is a pretty big name in shipping. And he's a kinda liaison
man with labor. He keeps the wheels turning."

"So how does that help us?"

"How does that help us?" Joe leaned forward and tapped Maria on the
knee. "John is the key to this case."

Richardson laughed outright at the look on Maria's face.

"Something wrong?" Joe asked coldly.

"Hell, no," said Richardson. "Carry on. You tell him."

"Well, ten years ago, Caputo made me an offer," Joe continued. "He
said if I left my family and went in with his people, they'd make me the
biggest stevedore on the East Coast."

"So what did *you* say?"

"I told him, 'John, I can't do it. I can't just walk out on my father and
compete with him.' I said, 'I gotta turn you down.' 'Well, that's too bad,'
he said. 'But I respect your loyalty. And if circumstances ever change and
you wanna change your mind, you be sure and let me know.' "

Joe grinned at them expectantly.

"Who did he mean by 'his people'?" Maria asked. "Did he tell you?"

"He was talking about the Scotto group. After I turned him down,
Caputo told me Scotto went with McGrath, and Barone started pushing
all the business Harrington's way in Miami."

Richardson, who knew him better, saw what he was getting at. "You
telling us you're gonna call Caputo and tell him you want in with the
Scotto group? Bit late for that now."

"No, I don't think so. I think he'll go for it. I'll tell him, 'Hey, John. You
remember that talk we had? Well, I'm ready to swing.' If I have to, I'll
say I'm thinking of opening an operation up there in Brooklyn, and he'll
get me in tight with those guys."

Maria was silent for a moment. "You really think he can put you close
to Scotto?"

"I *know* he can," Joe said proudly. "And you know where *that* can lead,
right? Into Governor Carey's office in New York State. Into the United
States Congress. Maybe into the White House. So you tell *me.* How far
do you want me to take you?"

As Maria seemed abstracted, Richardson answered for him. "Well,
Joe," he said. "I'd say just about as far as you can go."

"Well, that's it, then." Joe nodded. "Hold on to your hats."

And that was the start of Operation Unirac (for union racketeering), the biggest criminal investigation ever launched by the United States government.

11

Second Front

ON the way to work next morning, Joe's elation fizzled out. He had just declared war on the mob. As he waited on the causeway for the upper works of a freighter to pass sedately between the raised bascules of the drawbridge, he suddenly saw the port as enemy territory. It was a curious shock; the familiar becoming unfamiliar. Dodge Island had fallen to Barone so quietly and so gradually that hardly anyone now questioned his sovereignty.

It was not a good thought to start the day. Joe had known all along that his life would depend on silence, but knowing it was not the same as feeling it. One word from Barone's "friends" downtown and he was an instant candidate for an "accident" like Ben's. He could "fall" through a hatch. A "malfunctioning" crane might flatten him with a container, or an "unsighted" trucker, backing up his rig, crush him against a loading bay. It was a lot to carry on his own, and already there were hints of something worse.

He had understood about the isolation he invited by going on, but the taste of it was unlike anything he had imagined. He was sealed off in himself, going about his business, responding to Ann and the kids as before, but frighteningly separate. He knew *them,* but nobody now knew *him.* Sometimes he would wake in the night and look at Ann sleeping as though from a parallel dimension, as though waking *to* a dream.

He felt no closer to the agents either, no compensating sense of fellowship. There were too many pretenses for him to keep up, and they were using him in any case. He saw it in the way they looked at him. They were not really interested in Joe Teitelbaum at all. They would act the same way whoever he was. Understanding this, he went to see Rabbi Herbert Baumgard of Temple Beth Am and told him the whole story.

Though not the most devoted member of his congregation, Joe had known him for 20 years. He was the one friend of the family in whom he could confide without endangering them both. In fact, it was the only relationship left to him in which nothing had to be invented or concealed.

More than that, it was vital that someone other than the agents should know what was going on, so that, in case of an "accident," his motives could be properly explained to Ann and the children. And they would take some explaining, for he was not only deceiving them, but exposing them to danger without their knowledge.

Rabbi Baumgard thought it courageous of him to shoulder so much for what he thought was right, and agreed he should follow his conscience, but Joe had an uncomfortable feeling afterwards that he had been seeking approval when what he really needed was absolution. On November 7, he taped another $100 payoff to Cleveland Turner, and a few days later, flew up to New York to sign the Dodge Island stevedoring contract with Zim Container Service.

With Barone 1,200 miles out of earshot, Captain Ilan was less constrained than he had been in Miami. Barone had favored Harrington, he said, because Harrington could also service the account in Savannah, Georgia—an explanation that astonished Joe. For all Field's bragging, he had never suspected that Barone's influence over Israel's national steamship line had grown to the point where they could nominate contractors for it in ports other than New York and Miami. But it gave him an idea.

If Zim planned to send its new container ships into Savannah, maybe Eagle should open a branch operation there.

Fine, said Ilan. He would prefer to deal with one firm, if Joe could get his act together. And if he cleared it with Barone.

Joe told him not to worry. It was essential to his plans to get Barone involved in every detail. And he smiled, because his first idea had just spawned an even better one. Ray Maria would go crazy if he could pull it off.

With the Miami contract in his briefcase, Joe called at 17 Battery Place next morning to see John Caputo at Tilston–Roberts. After his meeting with Maria and Richardson, Joe had called ahead from Miami to tell Caputo he was ready at last to cut a few deals, if his New York friends were interested.

"They're businessmen, Joe," Caputo said. "They're always interested. But I gotta tell you it's not like it was ten years ago. If you'd come in then, you could have had it all."

"I know." Joe looked around his office admiringly. "But I couldn't then. My dad needed me."

"That fucking family of yours." Caputo snorted. "They always held you back. And I gotta tell you, Joe. If you're still tied in with 'em and looking to do business with *my* people, then like forget it. After what they did to us in Jacksonville? No way."

Joe clucked, and shook his head. "I guess that *was* kinda raunchy."

"Shit. You were gonna sue the Brazilians and everything? Had us all going fucking crazy? Let me tell you, if you hadn't dropped that suit, they told me I was gonna have to go down there and dump you."

"Oh, Jesus. I never knew that."

"And don't ask me would I have done it, because I don't know." Caputo was only half joking.

"Then I won't ask. And don't worry. They're out. I've been offered a new port."

"Savannah?" Caputo nodded.

"How the hell did *you* know?" It was not 24 hours since Joe had first put the idea to Ilan.

"Because they offered it to us, dummy. And we couldn't take it on account of we got P & O Strat. I mean, that's all we need, right? Word gets out we touched an Israeli operation, the fucking Arabs would crucify us." He scratched his chin thoughtfully. "But that don't mean we can't work something out. You gonna take Savannah?"

"Thinking about it," said Joe warily.

"Well, you thought what it's gonna cost you?"

"I'm not worried. Figures look good. I got it covered."

"Yeah. So have we. Ever hear of James Stevedores?"

"Sure." It was a Tilston–Roberts subsidiary that served its parent company in the same way as PTO served Eagle. "They operate in Savannah?"

"Yes, they do. And they could use the work. Why don't you take the port and subcontract the stevedoring out to us?"

"Why don't I?" Joe laughed. "Because then you get half of what *I* got, and I don't get half of what *you* got. Unless you wanna give me a couple of your agencies?"

"Sure," said Caputo calmly. "Why not? Let's do it this way. You give James the stevedoring in Savannah, and we'll give you the agency there for Jakarta Lloyd, P & O, and Lloyd Brasileiro. How does that grab you?"

"In a very interesting place," said Joe. "I like it. Let's talk figures."

"Hold it. Fuck the figures." Caputo heard what he was saying, and held up his hands, smiling. "I mean, I *care* about the figures, but right now, I care a lot more about how you're gonna handle this. We're not talking Eagle, are we?"

"No, no." Joe thought fast. "We're talking corporation X. A brand-new company."

"Okay. And independent, right? With none of your fucking relatives in the picture. Because without them, you can go up the coast all the way to New York if you wanna."

"Right." It was getting complicated now. He would have to offer this to Mutzie, but he was pretty sure he could do it in a way that invited a refusal. Gus Hulander and Dewey Parker were naturals for a deal like this. It tied right in with the Nopal Line agency. "What about trucking? And container repairs? Ilan says Barone's people will handle it. That okay with you?"

Caputo hesitated. "Why don't you leave that one with me, Joe? I'll let you know. It's just that the Lacquas are moving in down there."

"The Lacquas?"

"Yeah. Friends of mine. They handle American Export and a bunch of others. Big people."

"Wait a minute. They're related to Tony Scotto, right? The Lacquas?"

"Yeah, well, it's all in the family. Joey Lacqua and Phil Lacqua are like Tony's cousins-in-law. Their old man, Leo, he's Marion Scotto's uncle. But it's not your problem. I'll let you know."

"Fine. Only what do I tell Barone?"

"Tell him what you like. It's no secret. We just gotta work out who does what, that's all."

"Okay." Joe wished he had been wired for this. "Now what about the figures? James has got to quote me rates so I can write Ilan a proposal. And they gotta be rates I can live with."

"Figures, schmigures," Caputo said. "I want my lunch."

Joe flew back to Miami that night, his head whirling with possibilities. Lining up a deal like this was doing him more good than all his anticoagulants and Transcendental Meditation put together. Next morning, Friday, he told Boyle that Zim had offered him Savannah, and within the hour, Barone came over with Vanderwyde. They took him out in the hall.

"Been doing yourself some good," said Barone.

"Yeah. I got the Miami contract."

"Yeah." That was no news.

"Maybe now you'll catch up with your fucking payments," Vanderwyde said, addressing the ceiling.

"I'm working that out with Bill," said Joe. "Give me a break, will you? I can't swing that much cash off the books all at once."

Neither of them replied. They just looked in opposite ways down the hall.

"Ilan's offered me Savannah," Joe went on. "I wanna know how you feel about that, George."

"Could be a nice thing for you. Nice piece of business."

"Yes, it could. But I wanna do the right thing."

"Then you better talk to Bill. We just made him the International vice-president up there."

"Okay, fine. If that's how you want me to handle it."

Barone glanced at him sideways, still facing away down the hall. "Go ahead," he said. "Take Savannah. We'll tell you what to do."

"Thanks, George. I'll get back to Ilan, then, and work out the details with Bill."

"Yeah, and call Benny Cotrone," Vanderwyde said. "He says you owe him."

"We're disputing some charges, Jay. He's killing us with all his fucking extras. And now Zim's coming in, I . . ."

"Look, just pay your fucking bills."

Not having looked at Joe once, Vanderwyde nodded at Barone and the two of them walked away without another word. But that was all right. Smiling to himself, Joe went back in his office to call Ilan and Benny Cotrone.

The next obstacle was Mutzie, and he took care of that next day, catching him exactly at his busiest, in the middle of servicing the *Mardi Gras.*

"Got a minute?" he said. "I wanna talk to you about Savannah."

"Savannah? Fuck Savannah. We got problems enough in Miami." He had the telephone in his hand, and three other people were waiting to speak to him. "Where's Bobby?" he bellowed through the open door. "Anybody seen him?"

"But Zim's ready to give us the business," said Joe. "And *you* don't have to bother with it. *I'll* handle this. I mean, it can't cost us much to set up there. Not more than a hundred thousand."

"You *crazy?* Look, somebody go and find him," he roared. "He's wanted on the phone. Urgent." Mutzie placed it to his ear. "I'm putting you on hold," he said sweetly. "Don't go away. And what the hell do *you* want?" he demanded of the first man at the door.

"I mean, it's not like Jacksonville or anything," Joe said.

Harassed as he was, the reference to Jacksonville claimed Mutzie's undivided attention.

"Once wasn't enough?" he said, amazed. "How many times do you want we should get our brains kicked in? Now get out of here, will you? No, not *you,* " he added, as the group in the doorway looked at each other. "Gimme that."

He held out his hand for the clipboard the man was holding.

"You telling me you don't *want* to go up there?" Joe persisted. "You don't *want* the Zim account in Savannah?"

"I mean you can stuff it up your ass," yelled Mutzie. "I wouldn't go there if Zim and United States Lines and American Export and Prudential–Grace all went down on their knees and paid me ten million dollars to go. Now will you get the fuck outta here. *Please.* "

By Sunday night, Eagle was out of the picture. To make doubly sure, Joe called Bobby Kratish and several other family stockholders to tell them about Savannah, and on hearing that Mutzie was against it, they were against it, too. He then drove over to Mel Kessler's house to talk about Problem No. 3.

"You wanna come in with me?" he asked, after explaining the situation.

"Sure. What do I have to do? You can have anything you want, except my money."

"Keep your goddamn money. All I need is somebody to give me an edge. I know those guys. Hulander and Parker are not gonna come in unless they got an equal stake. If I take forty percent, they're gonna want the same. So let 'em have it, I don't care. As long as you hold the odd twenty percent and vote it for me if you have to."

Kessler grunted. "What kind of dollars are we talking about? As working capital?"

"Not much. Fifty thousand? Less, probably. If we *do* need more, I'll front it."

"Why? Do this right, for a change. Make 'em pay. Ten thousand dollars for each twenty percent. Or at least get a commitment."

"Okay. Then write me a check."

"Take it out of my fee."

"What fee?"

"Well, I'm corporation counsel, aren't I? *That* fee."

"Oh."

"And listen. Bring Harvey in on this, too. Give the guy a break. He could be useful."

"Harvey Sykes?" It wasn't a bad idea. He knew shipping. He had worked with Hulander and Parker. "Any more out-of-work clients you want taken care of?"

"Just make sure you don't get to be one of them," said Kessler.

Monday was a busy day. Joe was on the pier at 8 A.M. to get the men started, and after breakfast at Howard Johnson's, drove around to Caribbean Agencies to put his proposition to Hulander and Parker. As he was offering them a 40 percent stake, for no money down, in a potentially very profitable company in which they would be the principal officers, plus four new steamship agencies, he anticipated little resistance, and encountered none. Harvey Sykes was then called in, and offered a job as consultant. As his first official act, he suggested that the new corporation be called Georgia Container Agencies, and when this was agreed upon, Joe took him to meet Benny Cotrone for lunch.

At his pared-down five feet four, Joe was amused to be seen with Sykes, who was about six feet eight inches tall, overweight, and effusively grateful for the opportunity. He escorted Joe into the Everglades Hotel like an ocean liner fussing around a tugboat.

Sykes had arrived in Miami from the West Coast in the mid-sixties to work for a cruise line operating out of the then newly opened Dodge Island seaport. Joe knew him casually, as he knew nearly everybody who worked in or around the port, but they had done no business together until early in 1974, when Sykes moved into trucking with Maritime Cartage, Inc.

Under pressure from Barone, the company was sold in the spring of 1975 to a group of investors that included Benny Cotrone's son Joseph, and two friends of Barone's from New Jersey: Frank Guido and Vincent James Fiore, Jr. Though supposedly retained for at least six months as chief executive to teach the new owners the business, Sykes was quickly eased out of office. From that time on, Maritime Cartage began to monopolize the trucking on Dodge Island, and Sykes to cultivate a nervous dread of Barone that bordered on the neurotic, although Joe found it quite reasonable.

Over lunch, Sykes was genuinely helpful in reaching a settlement with Benny Cotrone. Joe hardly cared, as it was now up to Mutzie to pay the bills, but he did care a lot about Problem No. 4: How to avoid getting caught between the irresistible Scotto and the immovable Barone when it came to handing out contracts for container repairs in Savannah.

He told Cotrone he was opening there, and Cotrone knew that already. He told him he had heard the Lacquas were moving in, and Cotrone had heard that, too. Joe then asked him straight out if he knew who would be doing Zim's repairs up there, and Cotrone shook his head. A meeting in Brooklyn between his people and the Lacquas had been scheduled for that very morning, he said, and "the word" would be passed down. He was plainly more interested at this stage in clinching the contract for Miami than speculating about one in Savannah, for he excused himself between courses to confer with Ilan on the telephone.

So far, Joe had no idea how much he would have to pay Barone for either the Miami or the Savannah contract. Nor had he asked, because Boyle had been out of town for two weeks, and Barone never bothered himself with such details. But as soon as Joe heard Boyle was back, he alerted Ray Maria, finagled an Eagle check to cash for $800, and set off on another recording session. This time, he took Bobby Kratish with him, partly because it was time some other member of the family faced up to the facts of waterfront life, and partly to shame Mutzie for the suspicion, obvious though unvoiced, that Joe was pocketing the money himself.

Boyle was not pleased to see them, although he took the check. Without saying so, he made it plain he would not commit himself to anything in front of a witness, least of all to a price for Savannah. This turned out to be annoying, because a day or two later, Ilan called to ask Joe to quote a break-bulk stevedoring rate. In addition to the container traffic, Zim had now signed a contract with Union Camp in Savannah to ship thousands of tons of corrugated board to Israel for packing citrus fruit, and he needed a price immediately.

Cornering Caputo in his office, Joe refused to hang up until he came back on the line with a firm price for the job from James Stevedores. It turned out to be $5.08 a ton. With some misgiving, Joe then called Ilan and quoted the Miami break-bulk rate of $6.04 a ton, allowing himself a margin of 96 cents. It sounded all right, but Barone's share had to come out of that, and Joe hated to settle on a final figure without knowing exactly what his costs would be.

On December 9, Barone appeared in the doorway and beckoned Joe out into the hall. The Zim contracts for Savannah were ready, he said.

"Okay. What do I do now?"

Barone blinked. "You go to New York," he said, as though to an idiot. "You sign them."

"Yeah, but what's it gonna cost me?"

"Don't worry about it."

"But George, I gotta know. I can't do business this way."

"I told him you'd go up tomorrow," Barone said, and he bustled off on his short, stiff legs, shoulders hunched, like a faintly disgruntled marionette.

Joe telephoned Ray Maria. They had not yet managed to tape a conversation with Barone, whose interventions were unpredictable, but Joe felt it was worth trying to confirm the details of this one by going over the ground again with Boyle. It showed more clearly than anything yet that the business of at least two Southern ports was directed by the president of the ILA checkers' Local in Miami.

Returning to Dodge Island with a Nagra recorder on his thigh, Joe looked in at the office for his messages and found Boyle there chatting with his secretary. He had called to collect checks for the dues and other union payments deducted from the payroll. As these accounts were up to date for once, Boyle's complaints about his relatives and the rent arrears were more muted than usual.

"If you don't want my family in it, you gotta let me maneuver the best I can," Joe said, as they set off for one of their little walks. "Yeah, I'll get you straight. That's no problem. But I'm ready to go into the Savannah operation. We're ready to sign the contract. All I need is the numbers."

"When you ready to go? Tomorrow?"

"I'm leaving for New York today to sign the contracts with John Caputo and Ilan. And you got to tell me what the . . . You know. In other words, I . . ."

"Listen, slow down. All right? Why don't you do it straight?"

Joe frowned. That wasn't what he wanted to hear. "What do you figure it?" he asked. "About ten grand?"

"I don't know."

"What?"

"I didn't even get with them. I haven't talked to anybody, you understand?"

"So nobody's really . . . You didn't talk to the fat man, then?"

"No, I didn't get to see him yet."

"All right. So nobody's really pushing for a price tag. All I have to do is just go ahead and get the contract?"

"That's what I would say."

"And then you and I will sit down and work out . . ."

"Later down the road, yeah."

They broke off then, smiling and nodding, as several passers-by greeted them in succession, and when they picked up their conversation again, Boyle was back on the subject of overdue payments.

"Just get me straight with this fucking thing *here,* will you?" he grumbled. "They keep asking me and asking me every time I go there. It don't look good for me. It looks like I'm doing something here."

"All right," said Joe, who found the idea of Barone and Vanderwyde suspecting their bagman of holding out on them very satisfying. It was a useful admission to have on tape, but he was determined to pin him down on Savannah. "I'll try. But I'm going to New York *today.* I'm going to sign the contract with John. You know I got United Container the repairs, and I got Maritime Cartage the . . ."

"That's if we can get them a contract up there," Boyle interrupted. "We don't know what's happening with Cotrone, if he's allowed in the fucking port yet."

"I'm talking about Miami so far."

"Oh."

"Up there, from what I understand, the Lacquas want Savannah. But I'm keeping . . . You know. You have to tell me who to make the contract with."

"Yeah, yeah."

"Ah, I talked to my guys, and I told them that the contract for Savannah could run maybe ten, if that's agreeable . . ."

"Listen, I told you. I'm not gonna commit myself until I get with them and talk about it."

"Right. . . . Just like we have a weekly deal here," Joe suggested craftily, "we'll have the same weekly deal in Savannah?"

"Yeah."

"Then the only thing we haven't squared away is the . . ."

"Up front."

Joe nodded. "When will you let me know this?"

"Maybe later this week."

"All right . . . Friday I'll get you even with the other thing."

Boyle was being very helpful. When he was not butting in with what they wanted him to say, he was supplying Joe with the cues he needed. Now was the time to ask about the president of the ILA Local in Savannah.

"Did you talk to Isaiah Jackson up there? So I get a contract at that end?"

"*Elijah* Jackson," said Boyle reprovingly. "You won't have any trouble, but I gotta go with you."

"You'll go with me?"

"Oh, sure."

"To sign the contract? So I have no problem with him?"

"Yeah, right." Boyle looked down at him, frowning. "And take it easy. Go slow, for your own fucking good."

Joe's heart bounded uncomfortably. "When you say go slow, what am I doing wrong?"

"For your own health. You're starting to look better now."

"Hey, I'm *feeling* better. But the fact remains, I'm putting together an operation, and you and I have always understood each other."

"No problems," said Boyle.

Ray Maria was delighted with the tape. With the others Joe had made, they could now connect Field, Barone, Boyle, and Vanderwyde in a pattern of extortion, and the breach he had opened in their defenses was widening with every recorded conversation. The Federal Strike Force agents in Miami had started to uncover, as Joe had promised, the interlocking segments of a very broad conspiracy indeed, and while they had the advantage of a man on the inside, there was everything to gain from having him explore as much of it as possible. Maria now arranged through the FBI's New York office to have Joe wired for his meeting with John Caputo.

Its ostensible purpose was to confirm the arrangement with James Stevedores in Savannah, and to discuss the possibility of extending it to service Zim container ships in Charleston and Jacksonville, but the Bureau was more interested in having Joe explore Caputo's relationship with Anthony Scotto.

For 12 years, the Justice Department had known more than it could prove against the boss of the New York waterfront, and for 12 months, the FBI had been monitoring his activities more closely even than usual. This was partly because Scotto had promoted his old friend Hugh Carey to the Governor's Mansion in 1974 (Carey had joined him in the union office on election night to watch the returns come in); partly because Carey and the Democratic majority in the New York Assembly had started to pay off their debts to him by introducing bills that, among other things, provided workmen's compensation funds to Local 1814's medical center, and weakened the police powers of the Waterfront Commission; and partly because the Commission had uncovered new evidence of wholesale corruption in the port, particularly in trucking and container repairs.

On the legislative front, alarm at Carey's bargain with Scotto had extended well beyond law-enforcement circles. The passage of bills through the Assembly designed to hamstring the Commission was seen by *The New York Times* as "a reflection of heavy campaign gifts to Governor Carey and other Democrats by waterfront interests. Undoubtedly, pressure will be heavy in the next session to move these death warrants for the Commission through the Senate. Success for that effort would invite a swift slide back towards the conditions that turned this bustling harbor into a pirates' nest a quarter century ago."

Against this background, and the general uproar in Washington over Teddy Gleason's recent blockade of American grain shipments to Russia, the FBI was naturally interested to see if Caputo could throw any light on Scotto's position in respect to any or all of these activities. And on

December 10, as soon as he disposed of his routine business, Joe jumped in at the deep end.

"How close are you with . . . with Tony, John?"

"Joey, I'm as close as, you know, anybody else. Follow me? He never commits himself one way or the other. But what are you . . ."

"What am I referring to?"

"Yeah."

"All right. Barone is in Miami."

"Right."

"All right. He kind of has his hand in Jacksonville. He says he's got his hand in Savannah, and he does, because Boyle has been moved up to Savannah now."

The reference to Savannah reminded Caputo of his promise to sort things out with the Lacquas.

"I cleared that with Phil and Joe the other day," he said. "About the container repairs? I said, 'Look, we really got to give this guy an answer.' "

"I'm also worried about the stevedoring, because . . ."

"We're there already," Caputo said emphatically.

"And . . . ah . . . ah, is Scotto protecting you there?"

"No, there's no problem there."

That wasn't clear enough. "My question is," said Joe, "are you the go-between man with Scotto?"

"I am."

"You are?"

"Yeah."

"Okay. Do you have to handle him?"

"It's all according to size, Joey. You know how these things work. When you're talking, you know, peanuts, he's not gonna . . ."

"I'm not talking peanuts." Joe was hurt. "I mean . . . Zim will give us Jacksonville and Charleston because of the military cargo going to Israel, and they trust us."

That led to a discussion of the other business they might expect to do together in those two ports, and how it might be necessary for Scotto to rule on who did what.

"Is he usually cut in?" Joe asked, seizing the chance to get back to the point.

"Who? You mean, Scotto?"

"Tony, yeah."

"Again, it's gotta be the size and the amount. If you're talking major cargoes, talking big ones, like *you're* talking . . ."

"Yeah?"

"He's got an in."

Joe nodded. That was more like it. "You'll handle that end?"

"I'll handle that end."

"Okay."

"Yeah."

"You see, I don't . . . I'm very careful now, John. I got a second chance to come around. I got my brains beat in in Jacksonville with my family."

"I know. I'm just glad that you have enough sense to talk the way you're talking, that you're not gonna go and say, 'Hey, I'm gonna do this and that,' and then fall flat on your ass."

"No way, baby. I blew seven hundred grand in Jacksonville when we went in without the blessing of the people. Now you know what I'm talking about?"

"Yeah."

But Joe proceeded to tell him anyway, describing Eagle's disaster there in detail so that Caputo could make it clear to Scotto that Joe had learned his lesson, that he would do nothing without his consent and protection.

"Supposing Zim says to me tomorrow, do you want Jacksonville or Charleston?" he said.

Caputo shook his head doubtfully. "Then you gotta . . . You're gonna have to stall. Because what I have to do is set up some kind of thing with Anthony right away, to see what we got here, and everything."

"Do you want me to go with you?" Joe asked hopefully.

"Not on the first one . . . I don't know how much Anthony will want to get involved."

But Caputo promised to see Scotto the following week, and after a few more assurances of his willingness to observe whatever rules were handed down, Joe closed his briefcase and left.

It was a good tape.

He signed the contracts next day at Zim's American headquarters in the World Trade Center, and flew home that evening. Now the pieces had been put together, it was time to unveil his great idea to Ray Maria.

"I'm gonna send Harvey Sykes to set up the office in Savannah," he said. The exhilaration had still not worn off. "Caputo's getting us space in the Whittaker Building. The same one they're in."

"Makes sense," said Maria.

"And I'm gonna need an operations man up there," he went on triumphantly. "I can't be in two places at once, can I?"

"I guess not. Who are you going to put in?"

"Well," said Joe. It was his big moment. "I thought maybe *you* could find somebody."

Maria stared. "You mean, an *agent?*"

"Why not?" He beamed. "I can teach him enough to get by. That's easy."

"Yeah, but will he get by Boyle and Barone?"

"I'll say he's my brother-in-law or something." It was the first time he had ever seen Maria at a loss. "Listen, the way I got this thing organized now, I could walk Mickey Mouse through."

Maria shook himself. "Okay," he said. "Let me talk to Washington. I'm not sure Mickey Mouse is available."

12

Digging In

THEY named their price two days later. Joe was on the dock, supervising the turn-around of the *Mardi Gras,* when Boyle called him over to his car.

"You want some numbers, right? For Savannah?"

"Yeah, Bill. We signed the contracts Thursday."

"Well, here's what it's gonna cost you. Fifteen thousand up front."

"Fifteen? Oh, wow."

"Plus one percent of the manifest. After that, it's twelve dollars a box for container ships, and fifty cents a ton for break-bulk."

"Oh, *shit."* Joe was dumbfounded. "I . . . Okay. I'll let you know."

"Let me know what?" Boyle stared up at him from behind the wheel, shading his eyes against the sun. "You asked me to find out for you, and that's it."

"Yeah, I know, Bill. But, Jesus. That's playing kinda rough."

Now he had delivered the message, Boyle was impatient to be off.

"Take it up with George," he said. "He wants to see you Monday morning. Ten o'clock."

"All right." Joe was trying to figure out if he could afford it. "And I wanna see *him."*

"Okay. But watch your step."

"Why? What did I do now?"

"You're way behind with the payments. I make it eighteen hundred you owe, and you said you'd get me straight."

"Eighteen hundred?"

"Yeah. With this week. So don't be surprised if he burns you a new asshole."

Ray Maria thought he should pay the $15,000, but not all at once.

"See how far you can stretch it, Joe. But I don't want you to push yourself too hard, now. It's a hell of a strain, working undercover. You let me know when you're ready to quit."

"Hey, listen," he said, rising as always to the bait. "Just tell me what you want, okay? I'll give him fifteen hundred a week for ten weeks."

"That'd be great, Joe. If you think you can handle it."

"I can handle it. And I'll tell you something else. You get me one of your guys for Savannah, and I'll fix it so *he* makes some of the payments. You like that?"

"I like it. Washington does, too."

"You heard from them?"

"They're sending two, three guys down tomorrow for you to look over. Not everybody gets to choose his own brother-in-law."

"Okay. I'll see 'em after I get through with Barone. And you *got* to wire me for this one. Because this time, I'm really gonna *bury* that son of a bitch."

But when Joe called on Barone next morning, with the Nagra recorder strapped, as always, to the inside of his thigh, it seemed more likely that Barone would bury him. Instead of leading him out into the hall, he sidled up to Joe with an odd, unreadable smile, and began to pat him lightly around the middle.

Joe suffered a momentary paralysis that probably saved him. It was the innocent response, attributable to surprise. The guilty one would have been to leap back at once out of reach.

"Pretty good, huh?" he said, standing his ground, though he felt sweat break out all over his body. "You, too, can have a shape like mine."

Then he pretended to understand what Barone was doing, and smacked his hand away.

"Hey, fuck you, George," he shouted, making fright sound like fury. "You gone crazy?"

"I just wanna . . ."

"Don't even talk to me. You out of your mind?" He turned to the door. "We got nothing to discuss."

That was the test. If Barone followed, it had been a routine precaution. If not, he knew Joe was wired.

Heart fluttering against his ribs, Joe took three or four agonizing strides down the hall before Barone called him back.

"I'm not running after you," he said. "You wanna talk about Savannah or doncha?"

Joe let his breath go slowly, and allowed Barone to catch up with him.

"You got something to say, say it. I got work to do."

"Don't get touchy. I gotta be careful."

"With *me*? George, I don't need this."

"Nothing personal. You wanna be careful, too."

"Yeah?" He reached out as though to pat down Barone, who stepped back, affronted. "What's the matter? Getting touchy?"

"All right, all right." Barone took him by the elbow, and they walked down the hall. "You straight now on Savannah?"

"Boyle laid the numbers on me Saturday. But hit me again. I wanna hear it from you, George. Fifteen thousand front money, right?"

Barone nodded, looking about him.

"How you gonna handle that?" he said.

"Installments. How else? You want I should write you a check? Fifteen hundred a week."

"Starting when?"

"First week in January. Plus one percent of the manifest?"

"Correct."

"And twelve dollars a box?"

"Right. Plus fifty cents a ton for break-bulk. And I mean prompt. You're way behind already."

Joe stopped, and Barone let go of his arm. "We're talking Savannah, right? The Miami payments are separate."

"No. You pay fifty cents a ton wherever."

"Hey! Bill didn't tell me that. What the fuck am I paying the two hundred a week for?"

"That's for other things. And who says you're paying it? I want that eighteen hundred cleared off before you start with Savannah. Otherwise you don't start."

"Now wait a minute. How much cash do you think I can swing every week? You guys are really breaking my balls here. And now fifty cents a ton for Miami as well? Shit. That wasn't the deal."

"The deal is fifty cents a ton," Barone said flatly.

"Come on, George. Gimme a break, willya?"

"You gotta break. You got Savannah. Now it's up to you."

"Well, let me think about it."

Barone shook his head. "No more bullshit. Just a yes or a no."

"You guys are really creaming me, you know that?" Joe was having a hard time hiding his excitement, but tried to look put upon. "And don't you do that again, George. Feeling me up like that. I don't deserve that from you."

Barone turned back toward his office. "You talk to Joe Cotrone yet? About the Miami repairs?"

"Yeah. But I didn't tell him he got it."

"Then call him up. Tell him."

"Sure, George."

Anything you say, George. Anything you say is being taped, and will be used in evidence against you.

He returned the recorder in a state of high elation, but Ray Maria had left for the airport to meet Washington's candidates for the role of brother-in-law. Unable to wait, Joe entrusted the machine to Special Agent Bill Heist and told him he would call back later to hear what they thought of the tape. He held out manfully for two hours.

"Hi, Joe," said Maria, when he was put through. "Listen, you know the Airport Lakes Holiday Inn? Can you make it over there around four? There's a couple of guys I want you to meet."

"Yeah, yeah. Sure. How about the tape? Really got the son of a bitch, didn't I?"

Maria hesitated, and Joe's spirits drooped abruptly. There had been quite a few unintelligible passages on some of the earlier recordings.

"Joe, you sure you switched the thing on? You remember doing that?"

"Oh my God. Well, of *course* I switched it on. It's not something I'm gonna *forget*, for Chrissake."

"Then the damn thing malfunctioned. I'm sorry, Joe."

It was too much to take in all at once. "We didn't get *anything?*"

"Nothing. Just a blank tape, dammit. Would have to be *that* one, naturally."

"Yeah."

"It was good, was it?"

"Yeah."

"That's too bad. It really is. But I'll give you a full debriefing on it."

"Yeah."

They were both silent for a moment. Then Joe said: "Just make sure it's working tomorrow."

"Don't worry. I'll check it myself."

He was suddenly furious. "Because I don't see getting myself killed for any blank fucking tape, all right?"

"Joe, I understand how you feel. It won't happen again."

"Okay. I can't go back to Barone, but I'll run it past Boyle again when I make the payoff."

"All right. But don't force it, Joe. Don't take any unnecessary risks."

"What do you think I've been doing all day?" After what had happened, he thought that was pretty funny. "You know that son of a bitch patted me down?"

"Did he?" Maria grunted. "We'd better cool it for a while. Forget Boyle."

"Hell, no. I gotta get *somebody* giving me the price on Savannah. I knocked myself out, putting this deal together. But no more foul-ups, okay? I'll see you at four."

He picked himself a Gentile brother-in-law for a change. Maria introduced him as Bob Carter, an agent from New York, and while Joe was pretty sure that was not his real name, he took to him on sight. He was in his thirties, studious-looking, and so bulkily constructed that the seams of his suit were in constant danger.

"You know any Jewish expressions?" Joe asked. "Say schmuck."

"Schmuck," said Carter obediently.

"Say, putzer yid."

"Putzer yid."

"Okay," Joe said. "He'll do."

Carter was to pose as Joe's ex-brother-in-law from Providence, Rhode

Island. According to the cover story they worked out together, he had been working as a taxi driver in Boston since his marriage to Ann Teitelbaum's sister broke up, and now, needing a steadier job with a future, had asked Joe if there was room for him in the family firm. After Joe undertook to teach him the essentials of the shipping business at a series of secret tutorials in the Holiday Inn, Carter flew back to Washington that night to flesh out his new identity with credit cards, fake family snapshots, a Boston chauffeur's license, and other personal papers. It was also agreed that Carter should meet Boyle for the first time in Savannah instead of Miami, so as to present him with a *fait accompli* rather than with a proposal that Boyle might conceivably veto, given his antipathy toward Joe's family.

But there was no reason why Boyle should not be *told* about Carter in advance. Next morning, Joe went to make his payoff with that intention in mind, a check for $800 in his pocket, and a double-tested Nagra recorder in his boot, in case there was any more patting down. With their last meeting in mind, he felt a distinct twinge of vengefulness when he spotted Boyle in the parking lot.

"I got eight hundred for you," he said distantly.

"Not here."

They fell into step.

"Next week, I'll give you another eight hundred."

"All right."

"And the week after, I'll give you another eight hundred, and then we're even. All right?"

Boyle grunted.

"Now I put my figures together last night, okay? So I'm confirming on the break-bulk operation. It's one percent of the manifest, and George and I agreed yesterday it would be fifty cents a ton in Savannah."

He expected to get slapped down for leaving out the Miami break-bulk, but Boyle just nodded.

"That's right. He told me that."

"He *did* tell you?"

"Yeah."

"Okay. In addition to what I gotta pay for Zim's container operation in Savannah, you get one percent."

"Of the break-bulk."

"Of the manifest."

"Okay."

"Twelve dollars a box. Fifteen thousand front money. Start paying it fifteen hundred a week for ten weeks. Clear?"

"Okay. When are you gonna start that? January?"

"January. The first week in January. Now here's what I'm gonna need from you. You're gonna be in Savannah, right?"

"Yeah. Pretty soon. I gotta get you top labor." With all the talk of money, Boyle was thawing out fast.

"You gonna take me to Ike Jackson to make sure?"

"I'll take you to Elijah Jackson, sure."

"You and I go alone?"

"Oh yeah."

"Okay. Now my brother-in-law . . ."

"You come up to my office," said Boyle expansively. "I'll show you my office."

"Right. My brother-in-law from Boston . . . my wife's sister's husband . . . I'm gonna put to work in Savannah. Get him off my ass."

"Okay."

"Will you put him in the union for me? The checkers' union?"

"I don't know if we can do that. They got seniority."

"They do, huh?"

"Yeah. Why don't you make him a super?"

"That's what I'll do." Joe was delighted with the idea. "I'll make him a super. I'll make him my terminal operator."

"That's it."

"Okay. And then anything . . ."

"He isn't a wise guy, is he?" Boyle had been seized with sudden doubt.

"No. He's a perfect gentleman."

"He's not gonna get out of line, is he? I mean, I *know* your family."

"The guy . . ."

"It's a very delicate situation," Boyle insisted. "It ain't like here, where we can cover up, you know."

Joe hugged himself. If there was anything wrong with *this* tape, he would personally strangle Maria.

"Let me tell you something," he said. "The guy's a gentleman. He's been kicked in the ass hard a couple of times, okay? He got laid off his job that he worked on for years and years and years."

"Really?"

"Yeah. The guy's been really kicked in the ass. So I'm doing a good thing for myself. I satisfy my wife after twenty years, and you're helping me keep peace with my family."

"Right, right," said Boyle, now bored. "We'll be working hand in hand, right? Let me take a piss."

Boyle wanted his money, and he was not pleased when Joe followed him into the men's room and gave him the check.

"Why can't you cash these?" he grumbled, launching them again on their familiar wrangle about Joe's embarrassment for ready money and Boyle's embarrassment with checks. As usual, each wound up seeing the other's point of view, and Joe went in search of his second target for the day, John Caputo.

He found him in his own office, talking to Jimmy Roberts, boss of James Stevedores. After an exchange of greetings, Joe took him for a walk over the same course he had just covered with Boyle.

"I don't like to talk inside," he explained.

"What do you mean?"

"Well, since, ah, the Waterfront Commission . . . Since they started talking about a Waterfront Commission down here, they been wiring the whole fucking place."

"Is that right?"

"Yeah." Joe laughed at his own audacity. "Anything is possible in this place."

The aim this time, as agreed with Ray Maria, was to question Caputo on the idea of starting up a joint stevedoring and agency operation in New York, a possibility touched on lightly at their last meeting. After working the conversation around to it, Joe again found Caputo cagey on the subject of Anthony Scotto.

"The whole thing, John, is the guarantee in New York," Joe said.

"With the labor?"

"Yes."

"All right, Joey. I'm not worried. Ah, I can't see any opposition at all, ah, opening up. But this is something else again you're gonna have to talk to Jimmy about."

"Yeah, but the thing is . . . If this deal goes through and we do make the stevedoring in New York, then you'll handle Anthony, correct?"

"Yeah, I'll take care of that situation."

"No problem?"

"Yeah."

"You'll find out how much the insurance policy costs?"

"Right, right, right."

"Full treatment?"

"Yeah. But I'll be very honest with you. First, you gotta convince Jimmy. He's the one that's gonna put the recommendation in front of the board, that either we go or we don't go."

"That's understood."

"Okay."

"But before any recommendation is made," Joe persisted, "you gotta have the blessing of The Man. You gotta have the insurance policy, and that's *your* end of it."

"Well, you gotta tell Jimmy that's your feeling. We had some conversation about it this morning."

"Okay. But you do agree with me that without the blessing of The Man, it ain't gonna work."

"Yeah, I told him that." Caputo's irritation was showing plainly now, but it was not against Joe. "I told him that. He can't see any reason why they would stop you. So I said, there's no way they would *stop* you. They'd let you in, but you'd end up with shit. You wouldn't get any help. You wouldn't get *anything.* I said, 'What he's looking for is a little bit of insurance.' I said, 'I have the policy for him.' I said, 'I have the in. I think I can get the conversation going. But in the beginning, I gotta figure out a way to do it without, you know, insulting The Man.' You follow?''

"Yeah."

It was the best Joe could do. He was still disappointed about losing Barone, and the Caputo conversation seemed to him to have moved them no closer to The Man in New York.

Maria and his Strike Force colleagues, on the other hand, were very pleased, particularly with the Boyle tape, which turned out perfectly and implicated Barone right up to the hilt. A case like this had to be put together piece by piece, they said. It was like a jigsaw puzzle with no picture on the box and a lot of the bits missing, but Joe was not to be placated. He just wanted to clean the whole mess up as fast as he could and get on with his life. The tranquilizers and anticoagulants his doctor was still feeding him were twice-daily reminders of what in retrospect were beginning to look like a lot of wasted years. With Chanukah almost on them, he felt his estrangement acutely, and a call from Caputo on December 22 did nothing to make it seem worthwhile.

He had been to see Scotto, he said, and told him that Joe was interested in expanding to New York, but the response had not been encouraging. Joe could have Charleston, Jacksonville, and other Southern ports, as well, if he wanted them, but not New York; at least, not yet. There were good reasons for this, but Scotto had not been prepared to discuss them.

Annoyed by the ruling, and doubly so because the call had gone unrecorded, Joe passed the information on to Maria next morning, but even as he was speaking to him, Caputo came through on another line.

He had spoken again with The Man, he said. Would Joe be interested in a *three-*way split of the South Atlantic and Gulf ports? Instead of just going in with Tilston–Roberts or James Stevedores, how about sharing the business with A & G as well? As A & G was a subsidiary of the McGrath organization, and as Anthony Scotto controlled McGrath's labor force, wouldn't that be just the kind of insurance that Joe had been looking for?

It was. Although this, too, had passed unrecorded, Joe called Maria back in considerably better spirits to tell him about the unexpected breakthrough. The next step, he said, would be a meeting in New York on January 13 to explore the idea. He might even get to see Scotto at last. And with that interesting thought, he said, the government's star undercover agent was signing off until the New Year.

Once or twice over the holidays, he succeeded in putting the whole thing out of his mind, but never for very long. He carried his other life with him like a secret deformity. He was not always conscious of it; nobody could see it, but it was always there. For once, Ann had no trouble persuading him to take her to Temple Beth Am. To her mild surprise, he even went there again by himself to see Rabbi Baumgard.

On January 5, he telephoned John Caputo to get things moving, and this time their conversation *was* recorded. Caputo was due to bring Joseph Lacqua down to Miami over the weekend of the Superbowl game, and the pretext for Joe's call, after reporting that he had the tickets, was to invite them to stay with him, if they wished, at the Key Largo townhouse. The real reason for it, however, was to get something on tape about Scotto's connection with A & G, and his interest in the proposed three-way split. In response to Joe's questions, Caputo duly supplied the confirmation they wanted, and went on to say that he was meeting A & G next day "to discuss the whole situation, both New York and the South Atlantic."

Three days later, Joe turned up on Dodge Island for the first time in two weeks, wired for another $800 payoff. It was later than promised, and again a check, but Boyle could hardly have been more accommodating. He pocketed the money with no more than a token grumble, and agreed to take Joe to Savannah with him in two weeks' time to introduce him to Elijah Jackson and the officials of Local 1414.

"All right. Another thing. Phil Lacqua called me again. He says he wants to do the container repairs in Savannah."

Boyle pulled a face. "We got two guys in there already. And now a third guy there?" He shook his head.

"I told him, if you want to go to Savannah, I can't make no commitments," Joe said virtuously. "You gotta go through Miami. That's what George told me to say."

"That's right."

"Okay. Who am I to use to do the repairs?"

"I'll give you a guy temporarily. Uh, either Great Southern or, uh, another guy that I'm gonna bring down."

"All right. 'Cause I don't want no . . ."

"No, no, no," said Boyle. "You're working for me. I'll show you. I'll take you by the hand."

Joe could scarcely credit what he heard, not even when the agents played the tape back for him afterwards. *He* was working for *Boyle?*

If the ILA's regional vice-president for Savannah could think, in all seriousness, that a major employer of dock labor was "working for me," Joe could only guess at the sort of feudal rights assumed by Fred Field in Mobile, say, or by Anthony Scotto in New York.

He asked Ray Maria how many more tapes of Boyle the Strike Force was likely to need. To go on recording payoff after payoff was beginning to feel like an exercise in overkill.

It was still early days, said Maria. Boyle was their key to Field and Barone, just as Caputo was opening the door to Scotto. Every word Joe could coax out of them, no matter how repetitive or irrelevant it might seem, could take on a crucial significance later. They learned something new from every tape. So would he mind carrying a recorder into his meeting with Caputo in New York on January 13?

No, said Joe, he wouldn't mind. In fact, that was the only reason he was going.

He was in a funny mood. The vindictive satisfaction he had taken in making the early tapes had mostly gone. The government was settling in for a long campaign, and where once the excitement and attention had been enough to carry him along, to keep going now called for other qualities. He had started to think about the future. But he still took pride in his work, and a cooler approach was no disadvantage. Obliged to start his body recorder as he went into the New York meeting, he wasted no more tape than he had to. As soon as Caputo repeated what Scotto and the Lacquas had told him about the possibility of joining forces, Joe moved in to pick him clean with professional precision.

"In other words," he said, "they're committed to A & G."

"Yeah. All the way through, I understand, to . . ."

"What do you mean, all the way through?"

"South Atlantic and here."

"Then how do I fit into the picture?"

"You can go in with A & G."

"And I can be their Miami boy?"

"That's right."

"In other words, let's call the spade a spade. The southern boys must be disputing stuff with the northern boys, and the northern boys wanna get tied up all the way down South."

"Yeah," said Caputo. "All the way through."

"Okay." Joe was not at all sure he wanted to be the spearhead of a Scotto thrust against Barone. "But they don't want me in the stevedoring business in New York."

"Let's put it this way. I've got a meeting tomorrow with Anthony and Joey, and I'm gonna ask Anthony a question. If Anthony will back us . . . right? . . . can you do it? One problem is that there's not enough for you to carry up here on the terminal."

"I got Nopal's auto carrier," Joe said doubtfully. "Which I've laid the groundwork for."

"Right."

"And I've got the Nopal break-bulk."

"Can I tell this to them? To Joey and Anthony?"

"Yeah. And I can get some of Zim's break-bulk, which I talked to Ilan about yesterday. Hey, John . . . understand. I don't *need* New York, okay?"

"Yeah, well, that's what I'm saying. If you want, I can push Anthony."

"Okay. But if you push Anthony, what does Anthony want? Does he want to be my partner?"

"I don't know. Ah . . ."

"Or does he want to put some of his guys in or what?"

"That might be," Caputo said. "He doesn't get involved himself. He'll put somebody in."

"See, I think that with Nopal Line's work in New York, I can get a big piece of the Zim break-bulk."

"Wait a second." He was trying to work something out in his head. "You got the break-bulk there, and you got the auto carrier. Where's the auto carrier going? Jersey?"

"Port Newark, right?"

"Shit."

"But I can move it to Brooklyn," Joe said, in a flash of inspiration.

"You *could?*"

"Yeah."

Caputo laid back in his chair, lacing his fingers behind his head.

"There's your ticket for Anthony," he said complacently.

"Okay?"

"All right."

"Then I can get some of the Zim break-bulk."

"Are you . . . . Do you think you're talking, between those two, about seventy thousand tons a year?"

"More."

"It is *more.*" Caputo was beginning to see something in this for himself. "Then with cars and that, you got enough to carry any terminal in New York."

"*If* I want it. But I want to make sure, John, that I don't get into an operation and get my asshole burned."

"Right, right."

"What I want to know is, do I have to take out an insurance policy with Anthony? How does he want to play this game?"

"Okay."

"I want the answers. I'm not going into New York alone. I'm not going in unless I have *him.*"

"Let me talk to him," Caputo said, lunging for the telephone. "I want to ask Joey if we can get together with Anthony maybe tomorrow before he leaves. Maybe I can have an answer for you then."

Joseph Lacqua was out, which led them to consider where Phil Lacqua now stood with respect to Zim's container repairs in Savannah.

"Phil told me he cleared it," Caputo said.

"Yeah? Well, as of last week, it was *not* clear. I have not made a commitment for repairs or trucking or anything in Savannah, and I have to make a move with Zim now."

Caputo clucked sympathetically. "Joey tells me that, ah, *he* would do it if Phil couldn't."

"Okay. But as of last Thursday or Friday, I talked to Bill Boyle, who was with Barone, and they told me there was no way that the Lacquas were moving into Savannah. That was *their* territory. Quote, unquote."

He sat back expectantly, and Caputo held up his hands in a gesture of surrender.

"Let me take what we have here, sit down with Joey . . . and I hope Anthony is in town tomorrow . . . and we'll sit down, and I'll go over everything with them. I'll lay it on the table with them. What you have in mind. What you *don't* have in mind. What you can do, and what you can't do."

"Okay. You'll talk to Anthony and Joey Lacqua, and then you'll tell me in Miami what's what."

"That's it."

Joe decided to push a little harder.

"The thing that has me concerned, John," he said, with a touch of calculated diffidence, "is I have the impression . . . to be quite frank with you, okay? . . . that there's an, ah, ah, inter-family fight between Barone and Scotto."

Caputo frowned. "Something's going on, yeah. Let me see what I can find out."

Joe tried to look glad to leave it at that. "Okay. Do your act. Because, hey, if all I have to do is stick to Savannah and Miami, I'm very satisfied, baby."

And that was about as far as Joe felt he could go for the moment. But there was more within reach. He sensed it in Caputo's change of attitude. Since outlining the business prospects for a New York operation, Joe had watched Caputo revise his former estimate of what lay between them. There was no hint now of the big-shot shipping executive doing favors for his small-time friend from out of town. If Joe read the signs correctly, Caputo had begun to see him as a contender, as someone to be cultivated. And if so, he could probably be persuaded to speak even more freely.

Joe decided to change the plan.

He had agreed with Special Agent Jim Abbott, of the New York FBI office, that he would decline Caputo's expected invitation to lunch, pleading a prior engagement to see a man about a crane, and report back to hand over the recorder. Now he decided to lunch with Caputo after all, although he still wanted to get rid of the recorder. Following instructions, he used Caputo's telephone to call the special number Abbott had given him, and rather enjoyed arranging, in Caputo's hearing, for the FBI to meet him outside the building at noon.

"I thought you were gonna have lunch with *me* today," Caputo protested as Joe hung up.

"John, I've got to get my hands on this crane."

"I understand," he said, smiling.

"But I tell you what. I don't really have to *eat* with the guy. Why don't I just run downstairs for maybe twenty minutes, see what he has to say, and then I'll come back and get you?"

"Great. You do that, and I'll take you to Ponte's."

"It's a deal."

At noon, Joe rode down to the lobby, and followed Abbott around the corner to his car, where Ray Maria was waiting. As case agent, he had flown up to coordinate this phase of the investigation with the Bureau's New York office. They then drove around for 15 minutes while Joe unstrapped the recorder and explained what had happened. Both agents agreed he should try to make the most of Caputo's expansive mood, and after arranging for the three of them to meet for a debriefing before he flew back to Miami that night, they dropped him off again outside 17 Battery Place.

He had a feeling he was getting in close to the center now. As much high-level shipping business was transacted over lunch at Ponte's Restaurant as in any New York union hall or steamship office, and his hunch turned out to be exactly right.

"I must have been crazy," he told Maria and Abbott three hours later. "I should have kept the wire."

Abbott looked sick. "Don't tell me. You met Scotto?"

"No. But I got the guided tour. John just walked me through the New York operation."

"Did he now?" Maria looked at Abbott, who turned on his cassette recorder. "Then you better tell us about it," he said. "While it's still fresh in your mind."

"All right. I'll run through it once, then ask me questions."

"Sure, Joe. Any way you want to do it."

"Fine. Are you ready?"

"Yeah, Joe." Abbott smiled faintly. "We're ready."

"Okay. We get to Ponte's. And it's like a class reunion. Everybody's there. Joey Lacqua. Sonny Montella. Carmine Vitole. Tony Morelli. Everybody. So we sit down and . . ."

"Did you know these people before, Joe, or did Caputo introduce you?"

"Never met 'em before in my life. He introduced me."

"Did you get to talk to them?" asked Abbott. "Or was it just social?"

"It was social. *And* I got to talk to 'em."

He was a little put out. They were supposed to ask questions later.

"Then we better take 'em one by one, Joe." Maria smiled encouragingly. "Let's start with Lacqua."

"Well, you know who *he* is. He's family with Scotto. He's his wife's cousin. And he's big. He's CC Lumber. He's Marine Repair Services. He's American Navigation, out of Baltimore. And he's tied in with Quin Marine, which is owned by McGrath. Him and Sonny Montella."

"That's big," agreed Abbott. "What did you talk about?"

"Football."

"Yeah, all right. But I mean . . ."

"We talked football, okay?" There was an edge on his tone. Who was doing the work here? Who was taking the risks. "He's coming down to Miami with John at the weekend, and the three of us are going to the Superbowl. That's how we were gonna meet, Joey Lacqua and me, but he was there in the restaurant. So we talked football."

"Did you say anything about Savannah, Joe?" Maria asked. "About the container repairs?"

"Yes, I did. I told him he'd got me in a jam, him and his people, and he had to get me out. I said, Barone had told me *his* group would handle repairs in Savannah, not Quin Marine. Not the Lacquas. So Joey tells me, 'Barone's got nothing to say. The contract belongs to us. Don't worry about it.' So I asked him to tell Barone that, because here I was, between a rock and a hard place. And he said the word would go down."

"Did you get a chance to ask him about starting up here in New York?"

"No. I didn't get one. I *made* one. I said I'd been kicking the idea around with John, and what did he think? So he says to me, 'It can be done. There's always room for a good man,' he says. If I want to go into the stevedoring business in Brooklyn, he said he'd arrange a meeting for me with Scotto. Only Scotto's out of town right now."

Maria whistled softly. "Hey, that's great, Joe. We'll have to plan that one *very* carefully."

"*You* will?" He was incensed. "Let me tell you something, Ray. *I'll* say when, where and how, all right? When I'm good and ready. I gotta get a deal together . . . a big one . . . before I take it to The Man. He's not just gonna shoot the breeze with me, okay?"

"Okay, Joe," said Maria patiently. "When I say *we*, I mean *you*, with your business and your safety to think of, and *me*, with the Bureau to think of." They had been through this before. "Now did he say anything else?"

"Yes. I'm just giving you the highlights."

"Okay."

"What about Sonny Montella?" Abbott asked.

"Heavy," said Joe. "He's muscle. Caputo told me, 'That's a violent man,' he said. 'Sonny's the type of guy you do business with, he's your friend, fine. But if you cross him, he's gonna come looking for you forever.' And I believe that."

"He wasn't friendly?"

"Yeah, he was friendly. They all were. Just didn't say much. He was there with Joey Lacqua, and sort of joined in with what *we* were talking about. Big guy. Very strong."

"Who's Carmine Vitole?" Maria's question was addressed to Abbott as much as to Joe.

"He's the tire man," Joe said, as Abbott shook his head. "John told me, every tire on every tractor and trailer that goes on a New York pier comes from him. He's a heavyweight."

"You talk to him, too?"

"Yeah, we talked a little bit about the tire business. Told him that's how my family got started in shipping. And then I met Tony Morelli."

"Okay." Maria knew him well enough now to recognize a revelation on the way. "Tell us about Morelli."

"All right. Morelli is Barone's associate in New York. One of 'em, anyway. He said he personally told Captain Ilan to give the Zim contract to me after Lacqua got the okay from Barone."

"Wait a minute. Lacqua *didn't* get the okay. Barone told you that himself."

"I know. Barone must have leaned on Ilan after Morelli talked to him."

"Right. But if Morelli wants Lacqua in there, then he's also tied in with the Scotto group, right?"

"Oh yeah. Gotta be. He's a New York boy. Well, a Jersey boy. But they're close, Barone and Morelli. You know what he said to me? He said, 'I hear you got Savannah.' So I said, 'Yeah, how do you know?' And he says, 'And you made your deal with Barone.' I mean, he's telling me, right? 'Sure,' I said. 'We got it all squared away.' And he looks at me. 'Fifteen thousand front money?' he says. 'Twelve dollars a box? Fifty cents a ton?' He's telling me the whole deal. So they're close all right."

"You think Barone told him?"

Joe shrugged. "Maybe. Maybe *he* told Barone. All I know is, they talked like they was partners."

"What do you know about him, Joe?" Abbott checked his recorder. "What's his background?"

"Morelli? He's a trucker. Handles Zim and a bunch of other steamship accounts. Knows Ilan. Knows Bob Partos, who runs maintenance and repair for Zim. And he's a consolidator. Got a big warehouse and packing operation up here. *Very* big. John told me Morelli prepares all the Ford cars for export that go through New York, so he's gotta be cutting up a few coins. I mean, that's big dollars."

"Yeah. Anybody else, Joe? Apart from Caputo and those four?"

"That's it."

"And those are the highlights?"

"Yeah. Plus the tape." He twitched again with irritation. "What's the matter? You don't think it's enough?"

"I think it's fantastic," Maria said gently. "This has really moved the whole thing along. We've got enough here to keep half the Bureau on the run for weeks. Right, Jim?"

"Right," said Abbott.

"But what about Barone?" Maria asked. "You gonna tell him you've been talking to these guys?"

"Are you kidding me?" Joe looked at them as if they were mad. "You trying to get me killed?"

"Well, I'm not saying you *should* tell him, Joe. But suppose Morelli does."

Joe came down abruptly. He was always edgy after these encounters, either precariously high on adrenaline or strung out with exhaustion. Sometimes both. It had been a long day.

"*If* he does, I'll handle it. I mean, Barone knows I'm working with Caputo. Can *I* help it if we meet these guys in a restaurant? What am I supposed to do? Run out the door?"

"I don't see any problem," said Abbott, who was naturally less concerned. "But let's run through it again, shall we?"

Joe caught his flight back to Miami with minutes to spare. He was more worried than he cared to admit about Barone. Though he could truthfully claim to have met Scotto's people by chance, it might still look like fraternizing with the enemy. And it did his heart no good at all when Boyle called him out into the hall next morning and he found Barone waiting for him.

"How'd it go?" Boyle asked.

"With Savannah? Fine. We're all set. First break-bulk ship goes in next month. The ninth or tenth."

"How about Zim Container?" said Barone, and Joe puffed out his cheeks. He was getting jumpy. Maybe he needed a vacation.

"Not before the end of March," he said.

"All right." Barone nodded. "Bill, you take him up next week to see Jackson."

"We're ahead of you, George," Boyle said. "We got that fixed for Monday or Tuesday."

It was news to Joe, but Boyle winked conspiratorially.

"And you better take that relative of yours," Barone said. "The one who's gonna handle the stevedoring and stuff?"

"Bob Carter?" said Joe. "Yeah, he'll be there. He's up there already."

Barone then bustled away, and Boyle watched him go, shaking his head slightly.

"You got something for me?" he asked. "You said Tuesday."

"You mean the first installment? I'll give it to you on Friday."

Boyle poked him gently in the chest. "Let's not have any trouble, all right? You're getting behind with the weeklies again. I'll be looking for you Friday."

With a body recorder strapped to his leg, Joe paid the first $1,500 on Friday morning, counting out the hundred-dollar bills into Boyle's hand, but when he tried to confirm the Savannah trip for Monday, he seemed hard to pin down—until Joe promised to pay for his airline ticket.

"All right," Boyle said. "But don't tell the other guy."

"Who? George? Why would I tell George? It's between you and me."

"All right."

While ripping the port off for millions, it seemed a little cheap of Boyle to hold him up for the price of a ticket, but Joe was getting used to that.

"Okay. We're leaving at eight-twenty on the Delta flight. Where will I meet you? At the airport?"

"Yeah. At the airport. And remember. I gave you the money for the ticket."

"Sure. I remember it well."

Barone came out to see them off. He was in an evil temper, burning to say something, but Gus Hulander was there. They chatted awkwardly for a few minutes, pretending not to notice Barone's furious silence, then Joe checked his watch.

"We better go," he said. " 'Bye George."

Barone would not look at him.

"You hear from the Lacquas?"

It was a snarl at the back of the throat, and Joe guessed he had heard from Morelli. He was glad to be leaving town, and suddenly grateful for Hulander's company.

"Me? No. Not since I got back. Why?"

"You stay away from them."

"Whatever you say, George. I just want somebody to do my repairs, that's all."

Barone jerked his head at Boyle. *"He'll tell you."*

Then he turned and stalked off stiff-kneed, short legs kicking out, and was lost in the crowd.

"What's eating George?" Joe asked innocently, as their plane taxied out for take-off.

Boyle made an exasperated noise, waving the question away. "Nothing. Just do like he says. Don't talk to those guys."

"Listen, they came after *me.* "

"I know that. So does he."

"Then what the fuck does he want? I mean, Caputo brings Joey Lacqua down for the Superbowl, right? They're friends. So what am I supposed to do? Say, 'No, I can't have a drink with you. Barone won't let me'?"

"He was *down* here? Lacqua? Oh, shit." Boyle breathed out noisily. "Look, I know you're working with Caputo, and all that, but don't get in with that crowd, Joe. For your own sake. It ain't worth it."

"Why?" Joe was all innocent concern. "What's going on?"

"Joe, I'm telling you this for your own good, okay?" He satisfied himself that Hulander wasn't listening. "Stay away from Brooklyn. Stay away from Scotto."

"I hear you, Bill," said Joe, still puzzled. "But where else do you look for business? New York is where it's at."

"Be patient, for Chrissake. Take it easy. You just been sick. You wanna expand, fine. But wait a while. What's wrong with New Orleans?"

"Nothing."

"Well, there you are. That's *our* area. That's our next port of operation."

"It's Fat Freddy's port."

"That's what I'm saying. You just keep away from those guys, like George said."

Boyle cheered up after that, and landed at Savannah full of bogus charm. He greeted Bob Carter, who had driven out to meet them, as if he had looked forward to nothing else for days. Prepared for the worst after Barone's performance at the airport, Joe had half-expected Boyle to unmask Carter as an FBI agent on sight, but instead, he took Carter's hand between both of his, squeezed it sincerely, looked deep into his eyes, and said:

"Bobby, my boy, if you're a friend of Joe's, you're already a friend of mine."

Carter responded with equal warmth, and the three of them kept up a stream of gossip, jokes, and family reminiscence all the way downtown. Joe was proud of him.

After a flurry of introductions in the new offices of Georgia Container Agencies, Boyle called the Reverend Elijah Jackson at the ILA Local, and on learning that he was out, left a peremptory message instructing him to report the moment he returned.

"Oh, boy," he said, slamming down the telephone. "I'm really gonna haveta whip these fucking niggers into shape here. Let's take a walk."

They went to Boyle's combined apartment and office at 204 Bay Street, where he sat them down, with a beer for Carter and a Coke for Joe, while he again called the Local. This time, he was told that the Reverend Jackson was on his way to meet them at Georgia Container Agencies, and would be there in 10 minutes.

"Now the son of a bitch can wait for *us*," he said, pulling up a chair. "You got yourself a place to stay yet, Bobby?"

"Well, no," Carter said. "Not yet. Haven't had too much time to look around."

"He's a real worker, this one," said Joe. "Never stops. And just about the most honorable guy you ever met."

"Well, that's good. You need that."

"Right. Every Jewish family needs a token Gentile. Right, Bobby?"

"I know someone who'll give you an argument on *that.*"

Boyle laughed. "She divorced you, right?"

"Yeah," said Carter ruefully. "Right."

Joe beamed. "So I called him up afterwards. I said, 'Bobby, what are you gonna do now? No job. No wife. What are you gonna do?' And he says, 'I'm pushing a hack in Boston.' I mean, can you believe that? A man with his capabilities driving a fucking taxi? So I told him, I said, 'Join us down here. We're opening in Savannah.' And here he is."

"Yeah, you'll like it here," said Boyle.

"And I wanna tell you something, Bill," Joe went on. "Bobby is the only one I trust out of my whole family. I want you to know that. When I'm not here, you do business with Bobby, okay? Nobody else. He'll look after you."

"Gotcha." Boyle grinned at Carter amiably. "Finish your beer," he said. "I'm gonna walk you over to Mr. Fixit's. He'll find you a place to stay. House. Apartment. Anything you want."

"Who's Mr. Fixit?"

"Tony Ryan. He'll take care of you. Like, I wanted a gun permit, okay? In Savannah, you fill in a form and you wait sixty days. Tony got me one in twenty-four hours."

"Hey, what about the Reverend?" asked Joe, who was worried about his labor.

"He can cool his black ass," said the Reverend's International vice-president.

They spent a jovial half-hour with Ryan in his lighting fixture store on River Street, and returned to the Whittaker Building just as Hulander was going to lunch with the office staff. Two men were waiting for them in the manager's office, he said.

Boyle led the way. As Joe followed him into the room, the Reverend Elijah Jackson rose to greet them. He was short, stocky, and beautifully dressed. His prematurely graying hair had been barbered to emphasize the breadth of brow, and his preacher's smile made dazzling by a gold star inlaid in an upper front tooth. Already standing beside him was James Reed, business agent of Local 1414.

With lunch in prospect, Boyle wasted no time. Seating himself behind the desk, he introduced Joe as a friend from Miami who was going to bring a lot of new business to the port, business that his brother-in-law, Carter, would manage for him. They were looking for top labor and good production, he said, and it would be Jackson's job to see that they got it.

Jackson then asked what tonnage they expected, and Boyle allowed Joe to explain that, besides the container traffic, which would build up to perhaps 90 a week within a few months, they also anticipated handling between 36,000 and 50,000 tons of Union Camp liner board a year, most of it in huge rolls.

This led them on to the scheduling of the ships, and the port facilities needed to handle this cargo, but Boyle soon put a stop to that. Looking pointedly at his watch, he asked Joe and Carter if they would mind waiting in another office for a few minutes while he spoke to Jackson and Reed in private. Neither objected, although they minded very much, and Joe killed time with a call to Miami for news of a ship he had loading.

After about 10 minutes, Boyle came looking for them.

"Okay," he said, standing in the doorway. "It's settled. Three hundred up front for Jackson. Plus fifty a week. Plus another fifty when you got a boat in."

"When there's a boat, he gets a hundred?"

"Yeah. Or if you got two boats, it's a hundred and fifty. You follow what I'm saying?"

"Sure." Joe looked at Carter. "How shall we do it? You want us to handle it here? Or out of Miami?"

"Here. Let's keep it separate, for Chrissake. You're fucked up enough in Miami already."

"All right. I'll shoot the money up to Bobby, and he'll take care of it."

"My pleasure," said Carter. "I'll just give it to him, regular as payday."

"No, no," said Boyle. "Give it to me. *I'll* take care of him. I got my reasons."

"Fine." said Joe. "That's it, then. You want us back in there? We don't have much time."

"Won't take a minute."

Boyle shepherded them back into the manager's office, and they all sat down again, smiling at one another awkwardly.

"Well." Joe rubbed his hands together. "I guess we understand each other, right?"

Jackson's gold star twinkled. "This is my superior," he said, looking across at Boyle. "What he wants is what he gets."

"Yeah," said Boyle, picking up the telephone.

"You will have our fullest cooperation."

"Yeah, good." He started to dial his call. "Listen, we're gonna be late for lunch with Union Camp, so I'll catch you guys later."

Jackson and Reed stood up meekly.

"Okay? I wanna talk repair shops, and I wanna talk pensions," he added, pointing the receiver at them.

Then he put it quickly to his ear as someone answered, leaving them to say their good-byes to Joe and Carter. As the door closed behind them, he finished speaking, and hung up.

"I fixed a meet this afternoon with Ray DeMott," he said. "Great Southern Trailer Corporation. They're gonna do your repairs. And the trucking."

"Oh," said Joe. "Good."

On the way over to the De Soto Hilton, Boyle explained that Teddy Gleason had given him Savannah to manage for the International, partly because Jackson was too inexperienced to deal with the port's employers on his own, and partly because he had turned for help to Landon Williams, the black International vice president in Jacksonville, who was trying to build an empire around his Local there. They were in the middle of a power play, but Joe was not to worry. Jackson had worked on the waterfront for 18 years, and knew what he was doing. He would make sure that Zim ships were handled by his top gangs.

The Union Camp executives were glad to hear it. So was Bert Ibos, boss of James Stevedores in Savannah, who joined them for lunch. In fact, they were all very impressed with Joe for being influential enough to bring with him an ILA International vice president who was ready to vouch personally for labor peace and efficiency. They also took to Carter at once, who sounded very knowledgeable about shipping after his study course with Joe at the Airport Lakes Holiday Inn.

Joe flew back to Miami, quite pleased with himself, and called Ray Maria from the airport.

"Relax," he said. "I got him in. And he did well."

Maria laughed. "I wasn't worried."

"And you know something? Looks like we got ourselves a nice profitable little operation all lined up there."

"Well, there you are. Who says crime doesn't pay?"

"I'll see you in the morning."

He woke at 6, ready for anything, and by 7:30, was looking for Boyle with a $400 check in his pocket and a Nagra recorder on the inside of his thigh, strapped high up as usual, close to the groin. It felt more comfortable this time. On the last few occasions, the Ace bandage holding it in position had been wound on so tightly that the machine had dug painfully into his leg, making it difficult to walk in his normal fashion. The less conscious he was of it, the better the tapes generally were.

Stepping out briskly across the parking lot, he took the rear entrance to the 1001 Building and headed down the hall to the union office, raising a hand in greeting to Vanderwyde's Cuban clerk, who was approaching from the other direction. Joe got there first, and waited for him, holding the door. As each politely motioned the other to go first, Joe felt the recorder slip. Too late, he tried to trap it between his knees. It fell down the leg of his pants and clattered on the floor.

They both looked at it. Then they looked at each other.

"Oh, my God," said Joe. He groaned. "My pacemaker. My heart."

Sighing and moaning, he bent down, unplugged the microphone lead, and stuffed the recorder in his pocket.

"Gotta get to the doctor," he mumbled, and set off at a clumsy trot, waving away the other's offer of help.

13

Maneuvers

"*IF* I live through this," Joe said, "what's gonna happen to me afterwards?"

"What do you mean?" asked Maria.

"Well, when you think we got enough. What happens then?"

"Then we arrest everybody and lock 'em up."

"Ray, I'm not kidding. As soon as these guys get indicted, they're gonna know what I did."

Maria studied his face. "You'll have protection. You're the star. We've *got* to take good care of you."

"How about *after* the trial?"

"Sure."

"For *life?*"

"Why do you think we've got a witness program?" asked Mike Levin. He was a small, neat Strike Force attorney who had sat in on most of Joe's debriefings recently. "Investigations like this can't happen unless people come forward and work with us. If we let anything happen to you, how much cooperation do you think we'd get in future?"

Joe shrugged. He was not worried about the theory. It was the practice he wanted to hear about.

"Listen," said Maria. "If you think, after all this, we're just going to say, 'Well, thanks a lot, Joe. You did a great job. Good-bye,' then I'm disappointed. I'm sorry you've got so little faith in the people you're working with."

"Okay." Now he felt guilty for mentioning it. "But these guys are connected, Ray. Will you give me a bodyguard or what?"

"That's up to the Marshal's Service," said Levin. "It's their program. It'll depend on how they read the situation when the time comes. But they'll work out a plan for you, don't worry about it. We won't let you down."

"Okay. It's not that I don't trust you."

"Sure," said Maria. "You want to try again tomorrow?"

Next morning, Joe tried again, this time with the recorder in his boot. He met Boyle on his way back from breakfast, and they went for their usual walk.

"Tony Morelli." Boyle was not his sunny, Savannah self. "You know him, right?"

"Yeah," said Joe. He had been trying not to think about Barone's performance at the airport.

"Well, yesterday he says to George you been running around New York with Scotto's people, telling 'em you can move Zim's break-bulk and all that, and he's really pissed off."

"Who? Morelli?"

"No, *George* is. Yeah, I know we talked about it," Boyle went on, forestalling his protests, "and I told him what you said about Caputo, and how you're working with him and everything, but he still wants to see you, and that's all there is to it."

Joe's mind silted up. "Anyhow, ah . . ."

"He's pissed off at you anyway," Boyle said. "You're way behind with the payments, like always. Now there's Savannah as well, and the next installment's due already."

"Here's a little bit of the, ah, delinquency."

"Okay." Boyle put the $400 check in his pocket without even looking at it.

It was yet another good tape, but with Barone suspecting him of a double-cross, Joe was not disposed to carry a recorder with him when they met that afternoon, in accordance with Boyle's instructions, at the ILA Welfare Fund office on Northwest 5th Street. He badly wanted a piece of positive self-incrimination from Barone, but Maria agreed it was just too dangerous. There was plenty of time, he said, which Joe found dispiriting.

He arrived punctually after lunch, and Boyle ushered him into a small private office with the air of a hangman allowing the condemned to precede him onto the scaffold. Inside, Barone was darting aimlessly about —two or three sudden steps, pause, turn, then two or three more in a different direction. One of these sudden dashes brought him nose to nose with Joe.

"You fuck," he said. There was a gurgle in his voice, and he cleared his throat. "Why don't you do like I tell you?"

He darted off.

Joe frowned. "Tell me what I did wrong, George."

"I'll tell you what you did wrong." He shuttled back by another route. "You been talking out of turn. Making me look bad."

"*Me?*"

He was all set to dispute this, but Boyle, standing behind Barone, shook his head vigorously.

"Jew prick." Barone was so angry he could neither keep still nor look at Joe for more than an instant. "Fucking me around. You don't ever learn, do you?"

"If you're talking about New York," Joe said, he hoped, with dignity, "I already told Bill what . . ."

"Never mind what you told him." He halted again, nose to nose. *"I'm* telling *you.* Cocksucker. You ain't meeting that fucking Scotto, understand? And that fucking Tony Morelli's got no right talking to you."

"George, I can't help it if . . ."

"And *you,"* he said. "You got no right talking to *any*body."

Joe gave up with a shrug.

"If them fucks call you again, you tell 'em, see *me.* "

"I already did that. I told 'em, 'That's George's territory. Talk to him about it,' I said."

"Because I gave you that fucking account, and I can take it away from you."

"I know you can, George."

"Fucking Scotto. You know what he's trying to do?" He rounded on Boyle, who hastily revised his blank expression. "He's trying to get Zim into Brooklyn, and he thinks this dumb Jew prick's gonna help him. Well, fuck *that.* I'm gonna have to set down some ground rules here."

"George, I wish you would," Joe said earnestly. "I've been asking and asking for that. I wish you'd just take me by the hand and tell me what to do."

Barone stared at him briefly, losing some of his momentum.

"You're part of the group, right?" said Boyle, moving in to distract the bull before he gored his victim fatally. "You're working for us?"

"You know it," said Joe gratefully. "I'm your man."

"Well, we decided we're gonna organize the office workers, right, George? Get 'em in the checkers' union. So if you're my man, Joe, we might as well start with PTO, okay?"

"Well, I don't know, Bill." He had expected help, not a stab in the back. "I don't have much to do with the office. You'll have to discuss it with my family."

"Fuck that," said Barone. "I don't talk to those mother-fuckers. You keep 'em out of it. I deal with *you.* "

"But Mutzie runs the office now. How the hell am I supposed to . . . Oh, fuck."

Boyle had put his finger to his lips.

Barone looked around suspiciously. "And what's all this shit about not paying fifty cents a ton break-bulk in Miami?"

"George, I told you. I handled that for years. I cover it in the rent. You want fifty cents a ton, okay. It's coming out of the two hundred a week."

Barone stopped in mid-dash, but a lot of the venom had leaked away. "You *what?"* He turned to Boyle, who shrugged. "You better think it over," he said darkly. "I gotta answer to my people. Don't make me look bad."

"I don't wanna make you look bad, George. I only wanna do what's fair. You think that's fair?"

Barone was looking at Boyle, as though trying to remember what else he had to say.

"The permits?" Boyle suggested.

"Yeah." Barone readdressed himself to Joe. "You still got your trucking permits?"

"Yeah. I got 'em. Why?"

"Okay. Jim Fiore's gonna call you."

"What for? He does our trucking already."

"Just do like George says." Boyle frowned at him to be quiet. "And while you're here, you might as well talk to Joe Zatto. Right, George?"

Barone shrugged, moving off at a tangent.

"How much insurance you carry, Joe?" Boyle asked. "For PTO and the ship and everything. How much would you say?"

"The premiums, you mean? I don't know. Hundred thousand a year, maybe. Something like that."

Barone came slowly to a halt, his back turned. Boyle winked.

"Then we got a guy here . . . Joe Zatto . . . who can maybe help you with that."

"Yeah," said Barone, his temper all gone.

Next morning, when Joe went to pay the second installment of $1,500, he found Boyle very pleased with himself.

"How'd you like the way I cooled that, huh? Settled him down."

"You did a good job," said Joe.

There were times when Boyle seemed as big a victim of Barone as anybody else. He was at least inconsistent. His weaknesses were human, whereas Barone's greed was not weakness at all but the core of his character. Where Boyle could be reached, Barone was unfeeling. To *relent,* for Barone, was weakness.

Joe counted the $1,500 into Boyle's hands in the men's room, and then, as he had promised Ray Maria a double-header on the one tape, he went on to Cleveland Turner's office to pay him $50 for the current week, and $100 off the arrears.

"That's a good deal, ain't it?" he said. "I think we're in pretty good shape, don't you?"

"All right," Turner said. "Everything's lovely."

Maria thought so, too, but Joe was not satisfied. He kept on taking these terrible risks, and the evidence kept piling up, but there seemed no real sense of urgency behind the investigation. He often wondered if the agents really understood his situation. It was just a job to them. They worked so many hours a week, plus overtime, and then went home to their private lives. But he was *never* off duty. At home or at work, there was never a moment when he was not deceiving somebody, and how long could he keep it up?

On January 31, he set Boyle up for a payoff from Carter in Savannah, and arrived there himself shortly afterwards with Harvey Sykes to supervise the loading of a trial shipment of liner board on a Zim freighter. Returning to Miami on February 3, he found that James Fiore had called to make a date with him for lunch that day at the Red Coach Grill.

His first impulse was to cancel, but as this was the call Barone had warned him to expect, he decided not to. It was another complication, but he was also curious to find out what Fiore wanted.

He wanted Joe to help him. The Miami trucking contract for Zim Container Service was not as safely gathered in by Maritime Cartage as Barone had led Joe to believe. Fiore backed into the subject by asking if Zim would pay its trucking bills directly.

"Yeah," Joe said. "After Eagle approves the invoices."

"Ah. Well, the man wants five dollars a box."

"The man? What man?"

"Barone." Fiore seemed surprised.

"You call him 'the man'?"

"Yeah. He likes people to call him that, you know, when they're talking about him, so they don't use his name all the time."

"I didn't know that."

"Oh, yeah. Like he says, the walls got eyes and ears. When you think you're safe is when you're not."

"He may have a point there," Joe conceded. It was one of the rare small compensations of a double life. "But how the hell are you gonna swing five a box? Zim knows your rates. You're ICC. You're working on a published tariff."

"Yeah. But I figure we can cover it by charging detention time. You know, for delays in picking up the cargo."

"And you want me to approve those charges on your invoices, right?"

"Yeah. That's it."

"Well, I don't know. I'll have to think about it. I mean, a lotta detention time can make the stevedore look bad, and that's *me*. How many different ways does he wanna slice this, for Chrissake?"

The question was too naive to deserve an answer. Fiore went on to say that Barone planned to ask the Interstate Commerce Commission to close down Miami's gypsy truckers. As he would have to show that Maritime Cartage would not then be left with a monopoly, it might be necessary for Eagle to activate a couple of trucks, as evidence of "competition."

To Joe's surprise, Fiore also revealed himself as a third contender for Zim's container repairs in Savannah. With his cousin, Bert Guido, he had been told by "the man" to move in there with a branch of Streaker Marine, a firm they had bought in Charleston. When Joe told him the Lacquas were also interested and that Boyle had already said the work was going to Great Southern Trailer, Fiore was equally bewildered. As they parted, he told Joe he would arrange a meeting with "the man" in the following week to resolve the question once and for all.

Then, Caputo called. He had just spoken to Sonny Montella, he said, and the Lacquas were going into Savannah over Barone's dead body, if that was the way he wanted it. Though not upset by the idea of Barone's dead body, Joe was genuinely worried about getting caught in the crossfire, and his alarm was not much diminished when Caputo called again two days later to say that the whole question had been referred to Anthony Anastasio for a final ruling.

Anastasio was the son of Frank Anastasio, one of the four original Anastasio brothers, who stayed on in Calabria after Albert and the others left for America. A trusted associate of Scotto's in Local 1814, and another of his wife's cousins, the new "Tough Tony" was said to take after his Uncle Albert more than his namesake. He was widely regarded as a last court of appeal, said Caputo, who had no doubt that Barone would back off.

Maria was unreservedly pleased with the news. Caputo's call had gone unrecorded, but the news of Anastasio's intervention was important enough to warrant confirmation, for it suggested that he was more important in racket circles than the FBI had previously suspected. On February 9 Joe signed a consent for the Strike Force to record his conversation, and called Caputo to ask him to arrange a meeting with A & G to discuss the idea of a three-way split. Having disposed of that, Joe returned to the guerrilla war in Savannah.

"You took me by surprise the other day when you told me you sat with, you know, Anthony Anastasio, and had dinner with him the other night."

"Right."

"You really knocked me on my ass. You're a heavyweight, John."

"Uh-huh."

"Anyhow, what is gonna happen? That's all I wanna know."

"Okay. I'll have to call you tomorrow 'cause Sonny and Joey are out. I'm gonna be with Sonny tomorrow, and if I have to, I'll have Sonny call you right from where we are. I know March 1 they're going in."

"Yeah? March 25 is when we commence the container operations in Savannah."

"Well, that's what I'm saying. If you just give me till tomorrow, I'll have him call. And if necessary, I can have him call the other guy, too. To tell him to lay off you."

"No, no." Joe choked on the idea of Montella trying to protect him from Barone.

"You see, John, I gotta stay on good terms with Barone here . . . Like Barone says to me, you know, 'I gave you the operation up there. I could take it away from you, too.' "

"Yeah."

"But when you talk about a guy like Anthony Anastasio, he's gonna tell *Barone* what to do. And I, you know, like you say, he's Joey's uncle. Fine.

I like this. This is good. It's good for *you*. But I don't want to be the poor schnook in the middle. I don't want Barone busting my balls. I mean, I like Joey, I like Sonny, but business has to be done in a businesslike manner."

"Hey, that's exactly what I say. If they're jeopardizing anything you're doing, I want to know, too, so I'll take care of that for you."

"No, but you see, I don't want it to jeopardize my relationship with you. That's why I want the big boy to give the ruling once and for all, so we know where we're at."

"Okay."

What was getting Joe down was his sense of having lost control of the situation. There were too many unknowable factors at work. After his call to Caputo, the agents hid a recorder in his boot and he went to pay Boyle the fourth installment of $1,500. He counted out the 15 marked $100 bills slowly and distinctly, and cheered himself up a little by drawing Boyle out on the subject of Bob Carter.

"What do you think of the kid?" he asked. "He's a good boy, isn't he?"

"Oh, yeah," said Boyle. "He's shaping up good, Joey. He's a nice, conscientious sort of guy."

"Right on."

"You know, a guy like that . . . You did a smart thing, hiring the guy."

"You're right."

Later that afternoon, Boyle telephoned to arrange a meeting in his office next morning between Joe and Fiore to settle the trucking problem. When Maria heard about it, he thought a tape might be useful, and Joe agreed to call in on his way there to get wired up. But he was restless that night, and when he finally dropped off, Ann allowed him to oversleep. He woke, already late, in a bad temper, and drove straight to the office.

Waiting for him was a message from Boyle, asking him to step over to Local 1922 as soon as he came in. Throwing it in the waste basket, he telephoned Maria to explain what had happened, looked through his mail, and finished his coffee before strolling over to see what Fiore wanted.

He was there with Boyle and the Vanderwydes, father and son. None of them spoke. As he closed the door, they just sat and gazed at him, their faces blank.

"What's the matter? Did I interrupt something?"

"No, no," said Boyle heartily. "Come in, Joe. Pull up a chair, and take your boots off."

Joe thrilled with alarm to his fingertips.

"What?"

"Take your boots off. Make yourself comfortable."

He managed an uncomprehending stare before the heat rose in his face. His throat closed up, and he swallowed convulsively.

"You *fuck*," he said, in an uncertain whisper. "You lousy fuck."

They waited silently.

He looked at them each in turn, mastering himself. Then he grabbed a chair, sat down, and wrestled off his boots, throwing them violently aside. A day earlier and he would have been a dead man. An *hour* earlier.

"I won't forget this, Bill," he said, teeth clenched.

Still no one spoke, but Boyle avoided his eye.

"Satisfied?"

He jumped up and emptied his pockets on the desk, scattering a handful of small change among Vanderwyde's papers. Then he unbuttoned his shirt and pulled it out of his pants.

"Okay now?" he demanded. "Or you wanna look up my ass?"

Jay Vanderwyde glanced at his son, and jerked his head toward the door. Butch stood up obediently, and on his way out, brushed against Joe, apparently losing his balance as he went by and needing to hold himself up. It could have been an accident, but Joe chose not to think so.

"Bastards," he said grimly, as Butch left. "I don't appreciate this. I got more to lose than you do."

He went to retrieve his boots.

"Don't get excited, Joe." Boyle tried to detain him, but Joe shook him off. "Just being careful, that's all."

"Go fuck yourself."

"Harvey sent word there's some prick walking around the pier with a wire on."

Joe straightened up slowly.

"*Harvey* said that? And you thought he meant *me*? What are you, crazy?"

"Joe, we're checking *everybody* out. We'd be crazy if we didn't. So now cool it, okay?"

Joe worked his heel down into the second boot, and started refilling his pockets.

"What the fuck does Harvey know anyway?"

"He knows somebody in the PSD," said Vanderwyde, less easily satisfied than Boyle. "*He* told him."

Joe's defenses took another sickening slide. "So?"

"So you got a case coming up. This thing in Honduras. Maybe they offered you a deal."

Joe looked into his glassy blue eyes. Whatever he said would be wrong.

"Jay don't mean it," Boyle said uneasily. "He's just telling you why we gotta be careful. Right, Jay?"

Vanderwyde did not answer, but he shifted his gaze to Boyle, and Joe unfroze.

"Yeah, well, I don't need this," he said, tucking in his shirt. "I'm really pissed. I've had it with you guys."

"Hey, Joe," Fiore said. "Where you going? We got things to talk about."

"Fuck you, too. I'm not in the mood."

"All right, Joe," said Boyle, his tone hardening. "Don't make a federal case out of it. We got a date next Tuesday, right?"

"I don't know. I'll see," said Joe, and he left.

That evening, he convened an emergency meeting with Mike Levin, Ray Maria, and his other Strike Force agents. There had to be some changes.

"I don't wanna rock the boat, fellers," he said, "but this is getting *dangerous.* That's the *third* close call I've had. I don't know if I'm gonna wear that thing on Tuesday."

"I don't know that we're gonna *let* you," Maria said. "I think we'll forget about body recorders for a while."

"You mean, you don't want me to make the payment?"

"No, I think we should keep things going, if we can. But no recorder. Think you're up to it?"

Joe bridled. "No problem. But I'm gonna tread water, okay? Till I see where I'm going. I let you guys in, and it's time *you* ran with the ball for a while. I'll fix it with Boyle for Carter to make the other payments in Savannah."

"All right." Maria looked thoughtful. "What about the weeklies for Boyle and Turner?"

"Fine. I'll take care of those. But no more wires. And who's this fuck Harvey Sykes knows in the PSD?"

"I don't know. We'll take a look at that. Could be some kind of feedback from the first tapes you did, or maybe even from the time Ensulo was here. I'm pretty sure there's no leak. Nobody over there knows what you're doing, except Richardson, and I'm not worried about *him.*"

"No, no."

As the next day was Friday, he took Ann down to Key Largo for a long weekend.

It was not a success. He was keeping too much from her, and she sensed it. They could not get comfortable together with each wondering what the other was thinking but afraid to ask. Several times, he caught her looking at him speculatively, and had to go off on his own to resist the impulse to tell her everything. In some ways, deceiving Ann was harder than deceiving Boyle or Barone. They were a threat to his life, but his distance from her was a threat to what made it worth living.

He had also begun to wonder what would happen when she *did* find out. In the beginning he had warmed himself with Hollywood-style fantasies of reconciliation, picturing Ann overcome with remorse for having misjudged him and added to his burdens. Now, in his more depressed moments, the misjudgment seemed more likely to have been his than hers.

On Wednesday morning, February 18, Joe collected $1,500 in marked bills from Ray Maria, and gave them to Boyle in the men's room of the

1001 Building. It was the fifth installment of the front money for Savannah. He would get the rest, Joe said, from "the kid." Raising no objection, Boyle asked how much was owing, under the 50 cents a ton formula, for Zim's first break-bulk ship in Savannah. Joe said it worked out at $882, but he need not expect to see the money until Zim paid *him.*

"Now tell me about Jacksonville," he said. "Looks like Nopal's going in there with African coffee, and we know Zim Container's looking at it. So what's it gonna take? Do I talk to Landon William up there, or what?"

Boyle sucked his teeth. "He's a bad nigger," he said. "He wants it all."

"What does *that* mean?"

"It means you better wait on it till I talk to George and the Fat Man. We been having trouble with that guy."

"Yeah? What kind of trouble?"

"Well, it's not like Miami, see? We don't have the same control. Not yet."

"Well, lemme tell you," Joe said. "Things are gonna run out of control down here, too, if you start organizing our office people. I told Mutzie, and he went crazy."

"Yeah. Well, we're going slow with that."

"Okay. Because that's a sure way to get everybody in an uproar."

There were other ways, too, as Joe discovered next day. After sorting out a crane breakdown that left a loaded container dangling perilously over the rail of the ship they were working, he found Barone and Boyle loitering purposefully in the hallway outside his office. It was plain to see they had not brought good news.

"Jesus," he said, still buoyed up by the charge he always got from working with ships and machines. "You look like your parrot just died."

Boyle held out two pieces of paper, and Joe took them doubtfully. They were the last two checks he had given them, for $400 and $300.

"What's the matter? You didn't cash 'em yet? You don't wanna take my money?"

There were no answering smiles.

"Look at 'em," said Boyle. "Look at 'em close."

Joe turned them over, frowning, and went rigid with rage. Now *this.* Each was marked "Unauthorized signature," and had obviously been returned by the bank.

"What the fuck is that?" Barone muttered.

"Yeah," said Boyle. "What the fuck is going on?"

Remembering his heart, Joe took a long, shuddering breath.

"Wait here," he said thickly.

He plunged through the door, slamming it behind him, and hurled himself into the inner office, as vengeful as a dybbuk.

"Did you do that?"

He slapped the checks down on the desk under Mutzie's nose, and stabbed them with his finger. His uncle glanced at them carelessly.

"Yeah," he said. "Yeah, I did that."

"You took my name off?"

"That's right. From now on, me and Bobby are signing all the checks. Nobody else."

"You know who's waiting out there?" Joe had never felt quite so hemmed in. "You know what you *did?*"

"Yeah, I know what I did." There was an edge on Mutzie's tone. "I saved the company a lotta money. And I don't give a fuck *who's* waiting outside. You wanna write any more checks for cash, do it on Georgia Container. Let Gus and Dewey worry about it."

"No, *you* worry about it. I gave those checks to Bill Boyle. He's waiting out there, right now, with George Barone, okay? You wanna go out and explain what you did? Or should I bring 'em in? It's up to you."

Mutzie grimaced. "Well, how the hell am I supposed to know what the . . ."

"You're supposed to *ask,*" Joe said. "Unless you're real anxious to put yourself out of business."

"Listen, if they threaten me, if they say anything out of turn, I'll call the cops so fast their heads'll spin."

"Fine. Maybe the cops'll work the ships for us, too."

"Listen, Barone wouldn't . . ."

"Be your age. He'll close you down in a week. And you know something? I don't care."

When he rejoined them in the hall, Barone was pacing again, having obviously passed the time abusing Boyle, who was staring, red-faced, into the middle distance.

"The bank made a mistake," Joe said. "I'll have the cash for you tomorrow."

Barone stopped in front of him, facing down the hall but aiming sideways glances at him from under his heavy brows.

"*You* made a mistake," he said. "You make too *many* mistakes."

"Like what?"

"First of all, no checks."

"Hey, finding that much cash every week ain't easy."

Barone wasn't interested.

"Second," he said, "you don't figure so good. How much you say we got coming on the Savannah boat?"

"Looks like eight hundred and eighty-two dollars."

"Not to me it don't. You take another look at that. I got the New York figures."

"Okay. Did Morelli also tell you when I'm gonna get paid by Zim?" he added, greatly daring.

"Looks like a lot more'n that to me," Barone went on, not seeming to hear. "On Monday, I'll tell *you* what's owing."

"You figuring long tons or metric?"

Again, Barone took no notice.

"Third, you don't listen to Caputo. I told you this. You listen to me. You wanna know about Savannah, ask *me.*"

"Then *tell* me, for Chrissake. I hear one thing up there, another thing down here. I'm caught in the middle of this fucking thing."

"Joey Lacqua? Sonny Montella? There's no way they're gonna get in there. You understand? They just didn't get the word yet."

"Bill." Joe appealed to Boyle, who looked pointedly away.

"Fourth," Barone said, "you fucked up with Fiore, but I'll take care of that myself."

"Yes, George."

"Right." That seemed to be all he had on his mind for the moment, but then he turned back. "Think about Georgetown," he said. "For Zim. They'll talk to you about it in New York."

"Okay. How about Jacksonville?"

"I'll let you know. You got your next ship in Savannah on the twenty-sixth."

"Thank you, George."

Barone was as well-informed as ever. Captain Ilan called the following day to tell Joe that the next break-bulk ship would arrive in Savannah on February 26. He also wanted him to think about Georgetown, and to meet Zim's Bob Partos in Savannah to settle the question of trucking and container repairs. Joe then collected $700 in cash from his Cousin Bobby, gave it to Boyle to cover the returned checks, and left for the weekend.

On Monday, February 23, Caputo called to say that the final ruling had at last come down. Container repairs in the Atlantic and Gulf Coast ports were to be carved up as follows: north of Norfolk, Virginia, the business belonged to Joey Lacqua and Sonny Montella; south of Norfolk, the territory was Barone's, or more strictly, Fred Field's.

Under their general directive from Teddy Gleason and the ILA's executive council to organize labor in the container shipping service industries, Field and Barone were technically empowered to regulate business in every ILA port, but, as Caputo explained, the Scotto group was too strong for them in the North. After years of dissension, a compromise had finally been reached that dealt more generously with the Southern group than Caputo had expected, but there were political reasons for that, he said, which they could talk about when they met in Savannah at the end of the week.

Joe could hardly wait. He loved nothing better than a good gossip about the inner workings of the shipping industry. Nor did Ray Maria at this stage of the investigation. He arranged for Joe and a hidden microphone to be installed in Room 304 of Savannah's De Soto Hilton Hotel. But there was also a more immediately practical reason for the meeting. After paying James Stevedores for loading the first ship, Georgia Con-

tainer Agencies had barely covered its costs. Ominously, James had made
no profit either, according to its boss, Jimmy Roberts. The gangs provided by the Reverend Jackson's Local 1414 had been too big, and the
tonnage moved per hour too small. The prospects for both companies
looked uninviting, therefore, unless Zim was ready to pay more, which
seemed unlikely, or unless Boyle could get them smaller gangs and
higher productivity, which was what Joe was paying him for.

It was Sunday night before Joe and Caputo at last settled down to talk
in Room 304. Both had a lot on their minds. Apart from everything else,
Joe now had to save his Savannah venture from going sour, while Caputo
was facing up to the implications of an executive reshuffle at Tilston–
Roberts.

"That fucking Barone drove me crazy," Joe said. "He took me up down
and sideways. Ah, quite frankly, I was surprised by what you said about
the ruling."

"So was I," said Caputo. "I was not only surprised, I was shocked.
'Cause I blew at Joey and Sonny. Ah, I laid it out. I said, you know, 'I told
the guy you were going in. Now all of a sudden you change. Why?' They
wouldn't answer. They said, 'Look, this isn't the time for us to go into
it.' I said, 'No, I wanna know why you're not going into Savannah. What
kind of bullshit are you giving us?' "

"John, the thing that really got me is, where does this leave us on a joint
operation with A & G? I gotta make a move in Jacksonville, with no
problems. I'm on the string with them. So what do you think? Does A &
G want to do something with us in Jacksonville?"

"No, they don't want to do anything at all. They're playing pussyfoot
around with everything now."

"In other words, they were actually told to keep out of this area?"

Caputo hesitated. "There is a possibility they're not coming down at
all. Yeah . . . You know what a fucking beating they must have taken
because of this?"

"Yeah."

"Ah, you know, it's more than just the local shit. You know what I
mean? The kids and the family? There's gotta be more to it, between
the assessment, the union, the fucking taxes, and the fucking voting. It's
just, ah, eventually Anthony's gotta take over from Gleason. He's gotta
take over. So what he's doing, he's cementing his relations all over the
fucking place, so when he *does* make his move, he's got North, South,
and Gulf."

"That's why he stays off Barone?"

Caputo nodded.

"You know," said Joe. "I've never seen you look so fucked up."

"I really am, I know," agreed Caputo mournfully. "I'm all fucked up
. . . Everything has been just collapsing all over the fucking place. The

office collapsed on me. I was the kingpin. Everything revolved around me, right?"

"Yeah."

"Not that I give a shit. I'm the president of marketing and sales and everything, but before I was wheeling and dealing, follow me? Now I can't maneuver . . . Ed Tilston's trying to make life easy for me, but he doesn't realize, by doing what he did, they took the whole play out of our hand. Even in New York, with the terminal shit. This new terminal we're trying to put together? I could have done that in five minutes."

"Scotto would have the whole terminal set up?"

"He could've done it. Ah, he just told me, he says, 'Don't even waste your time with it.' He said, 'When you're ready, you come and see us, and we'll set it up. No problems.' You know?"

"He goes right to the Port Authority, is that it?"

"Yeah, yeah. The other day, Sonny and Joey said, 'You wanna cause hardship for these guys? We'll give 'em all kinds of labor problems.' I said, 'Well, are you gonna cut off my nose to spite my face?' I said, 'That's ridiculous, don't you think?' "

"Yeah."

"Huh? I said, 'Why don't somebody talk to him? You know, have a talk.' Well, they did. Sonny and Joey went up and talked to him."

"They *did?*"

"Oh, yeah . . . So then Anthony . . . Anastasio, all right? The other day I was with him. I said, 'Anthony, you're gonna have to talk to Tilston.' And this guy is a fucking cuckoo clock, you know? He says, 'I don't give a fuck.' He says, 'You want me to go in the office and talk to him? I'll go right in the office.' I said, 'No.' I said, 'I don't want you to put the fear of God into him, you know, because you *do* that.' Tilston gets up tight, he don't know what the fuck end is up. He'll go crazy."

They both laughed at the vision of Anthony Anastasio leaning on a prominent New York shipping magnate.

"All right?" Caputo spluttered. "So he says, 'Don't worry about it. We'll straighten that cocksucker out if we have to.' I said, 'No, you can't *do* that. I mean, you *can't.* I said, 'You do that, they'll know right away it's coming from me.' I said, 'Anybody touches him, I'm in fucking trouble . . .' "

In the course of their conversation, Joe and Caputo also touched on longshore production rates in Savannah, divorce, the prospects in Jacksonville, Carey's connections with federally subsidized shipping lines, the labor position in Georgetown, the situation in New Orleans and Houston, Anthony Scotto's influence in West Coast ports, the 24-year-old blonde in Caputo's office, and Joe's family.

After two hours of this, Caputo yielded to Jimmy Roberts and his local manager, Bert Ibos, who wanted to talk to Joe about the lean pickings thus far in Savannah. During the third hour, and well into the fourth, they agreed on a new formula for sharing the profits, once the gang costs had been brought down, and to defer consideration of Jacksonville for 60 days while James sorted out its internal problems.

Joe flew back to Miami with Bob Partos, of Zim, who had been sent to Savannah by Captain Ilan supposedly to obtain competitive quotations for container maintenance and repairs. As soon as they took off, Joe bought him two double Martinis, and pumped him about Avner Manor, Zim's president in the U.S., who had hired a private investigator to look over the line's business connections.

"What's eating Manor?" he asked innocently.

"Ah, he thinks he's being ripped off."

They both laughed.

"It was the tire deal that did it," Partos went on. "Out in Chicago."

"The tire deal?"

"You didn't hear about that one? We bought a load of trailer tires in New York, okay? Paid, I don't know, ten thousand dollars. Something like that. Anyway . . . Turned out they came off our own fucking trailers in Chicago."

"They sold you your own tires?"

"Yeah. You like that?"

They again laughed companionably.

"Who did it?" asked Joe.

Partos shrugged. "Who knows? I guess that's why they hired an investigator. To find out."

"Well, is this gonna screw us up on repairs? I mean, I thought that was all settled, now the ruling came down."

"Sure, it's settled. It's just gotta look right in the files, that's all. I gotta get competitive bids, and all that shit. Means more fucking paperwork for *me,* that's all."

"You think *you* got problems? I got cargo to move. And I *still* don't know for sure who's gonna get the trucking and repairs."

Partos was surprised. "I thought you knew," he said. "You're gonna use Great Southern in Savannah. That's DeMott and Hodges. And in Miami, it's Maritime Cartage and United Container. That's who I'm gonna see. I mean, that's why I'm on this fucking plane, okay?"

"Well, well," said Joe. "Finally. I mean, Barone told me weeks ago, but I knew the Lacquas were interested, and I never thought he could keep 'em out."

"He's got Tony Morelli to thank for that."

"Morelli's that powerful, huh?"

"Well, they all had to give up *something,*" Partos said. "Tony's the one that swung it. Barone's not a piss in the wind next to Tony."

"Morelli's a real heavyweight, right?"

"They don't come much heavier." Partos finished his second Martini.

"Prepares all the Ford cars shipped out of New York."

"Yeah, I heard that," said Joe, signaling to the hostess. "That's *heavy.*"

"Yeah. And treats me like his adopted son, Tony does. He's gonna meet me at the airport."

"You mean, now? In Miami? Oh, wow."

On March 3, Joe reported to his heart specialist for a routine check-up. His electrocardiogram was not satisfactory, and he was advised to take two weeks' rest.

"If you don't," Ann said, "I'm leaving you."

14

Strategic Intelligence

WHENEVER he stopped to think about it, his family was still the only thing that mattered, but he rarely stopped. This time, however, he made an effort, and instead of two weeks off, took three.

Eagle and PTO could manage without him. More to the point, he could manage without *them.* He no longer felt it necessary to handle everything himself. As for Georgia Container Agencies, Hulander, Parker, and Sykes were quite capable of running the business; it had been set up that way. And for the moment, he was not even crucial to the investigation. The focus having shifted to Savannah, it was Bob Carter's turn to make the pay-offs and pile up the evidence. It was just the break Joe had been looking for. Not to be indispensable was a great relief. It was also a little disturbing.

On March 26, he appeared before Dade County Circuit Court Judge Leonard Rivkind to answer to the charge of soliciting the murder of Virgilio Guzman.

The circumstances were unusual. The State Attorney's office had accepted the idea of a *nolo contendere* plea, and agreed to recommend probation in return for Joe's cooperation in an investigation by the Dade County Organized Crime Bureau. This investigation had subsequently been taken over by the federal government, however, and for security reasons, the Strike Force, represented by its chief, Attlee Wampler III, *and* the Organized Crime Bureau, represented by Detective Bob Richardson, were anxious that neither the judge nor the State Attorney's office should find out who or what was being investigated.

This inevitably generated a certain warmth of feeling when they attempted to thrash the matter out at a preliminary hearing in Judge Riv-kind's chambers, particularly as Washington was now attempting to inter-vene in a matter of state law, and the confusion was in no way relieved when Mel Kessler, as Joe's attorney, made it clear he was equally in the dark as to the nature, extent, and importance of his client's commitment. With no immediate prospect of untangling the mess, Judge Rivkind shelved it, deferring judgment and sentence until July.

Boyle, meanwhile, had called Joe out for their first hallway conference in over a month. The Reverend Jackson's men had turned in their worst performance yet in Savannah.

Boyle would take it up with Jackson personally, he said, if Joe lined up payments nine and ten, which were both now past-due.

Joe replied that he would be delighted to give him the money if Boyle told Zim to pay its past-due stevedoring bills.

Boyle said he would ask Barone to attend to that if Joe paid off the Miami arrears, which now amounted to $1,800.

"Hey, Bill," Joe protested. "No matter how much I give you, there's always eighteen hundred owing. How about picking on some other god-damn stevedore in this port?"

"Aargh," said Boyle, disgusted. "All you fuckers are alike."

Ray Maria was now more interested in the way the investigation was broadening out through the Caputo connection. When Joe told him he was going to New Orleans on March 31 to confer with James Stevedores, and that Caputo planned to sit in on their discussions, Maria again ar-ranged to have Joe's hotel room wired with hidden microphones by the local FBI office.

Joe's main concern, however, was how to stay afloat in Savannah. He and James had about broken even on the first two liner board ships, but the third, the *Varda,* had proved a financial disaster. It had docked on St. Patrick's Day, a holiday in Savannah with the same sort of debilitating effect on local labor as Mardi Gras in New Orleans. But he saw Maria's point, and suggested he share the room at the International Hotel with Harvey Sykes, who was also attending the meeting. Sykes had dealt with Barone and Boyle in various capacities over the years, and Joe was pretty sure he could draw the whole story out of him in the course of their overnight stay.

He started sooner than expected. As they checked into the hotel, Sykes casually let something slip that drove all thought of business from Joe's head. As soon as they were alone upstairs, he took Sykes through it again for the benefit of the agents recording their conversation in the next room.

"What you're saying to me," said Joe, "correct me if I'm wrong, is that the Organized Crime Bureau has an investigation going on with the District Attorney's office?" He blinked at Sykes earnestly. "There's somebody who's a friend of Barone's, who told him there's an investigation going on here?"

"I don't know who told him," Sykes said. "I have no idea. All I know is, he has been alerted to the fact that organized crime . . . that there's an investigation. I think it's federal rather than state. Maybe it's not OCB. It's not, unless OCB is federally funded. I don't know about these things. Anyway, whatever it is . . ."

"He knows there's something going on."

Joe hoped they were coming through loud and clear. He would like to hear Maria talk his way out of *this*.

"Let me ask you something. You said your friend . . ." Joe broke off, seeing no reason to beat about the bush. "Did *you* do anything for George?"

"Sure. Many times."

"You paid him off?"

"Sure. For seven years now."

"Seven *years?*"

"For seven fucking years."

"You handled George personally?"

"Personally. And that's why they were nice enough to alert me about the investigation. I . . . I'm sorry. I thought everybody was aware of it."

"That may be . . ." Joe could feel his pulse was very agitated. "They never said anything to me."

"All right. Well, then. There's evidently no *reason* to say anything to you."

"Well, were they really worried about me?" This was for Maria's benefit. "They actually thought I would do something to hurt them?"

Sykes didn't think so. They worried about everybody, he said, especially somebody with strong religious beliefs, who put his family first, and disliked doing business their way.

"I don't dig it a little bit myself," Sykes went on. "But I do realize it *is* a way of life. And you either join it or you get off the train. There's only two ways to go."

"And you rode the train for seven years," said Joe mechanically.

"That's right."

"And then you left because of Fiore?"

"Oh, yeah. Sure. I called for a showdown. I told that fucking bum to get out of the office. I said, 'I'm making three-fifty a fucking week. That's all I'm taking out of this thing, to keep it alive and healthy. And you're coming here' . . . it's a fucking yo-yo who doesn't know how to spell truck . . . 'and you want five a week? Out of this fucking office, kid.' "

Joe nodded sympathetically. "Let me ask you a very direct question," he said. "I want an honest answer from you, okay? Was George getting so much a trailer, so much a haul, or so much a week?"

"You talking before or after?"

"Both ways."

"Before, so much a week."

"After?"

"Flat twenty-three."

"For a haul?"

"He'd make five thousand flat."

Talking about Barone had made Sykes uncomfortable. He got up and started looking behind the furniture, and running his fingers along the underside of ledges. Joe watched him grimly for a few moments, hoping the New Orleans agents knew their business. It was a very fine calculation he had to make now. If he played games with Barone a moment too long, he would go the same way as Ben, agents or no agents.

"What the fuck are you doing, Harvey?"

"I know," he said apologetically. "I'm just . . . I'm getting, ah, goosey."

Joe pretended not to understand. "You wanna go for a walk?"

"I'd like to go for a walk, yeah."

"Well, let me call my people here. Get this meeting set up."

Sykes was now tapping the walls.

"I've been advised to be goosey in closed quarters," he said. "I guess it's gotten to me. I'm an easy mark, I guess. I get goosey."

"Harvey, did you get goosey with *me?*" said Joe, as though catching on, and ready to be offended.

"Not with you. I get goosey with . . . Well, there's someone. He assigns a room for me. I get nervous, starting to panic . . ."

"Let me tell you something, Harvey. No one's ever been able to put their finger on me."

"I know that." Sykes sat down again. "You're not a chump."

"The reason I'm concerned," Joe said, "is, *I* gotta handle him. In Miami and up the coast . . . And I'm asking you, as my associate, basically to help me."

"Okay." Reassured, Sykes pointed to the telephone. "Let's call 'em, and we'll talk some more. I'll tell you some things that I firmly believe are disadvantages."

"Such as?"

"Jew versus Italian, number one."

"In what respect?"

"Loyalties. To the network. We're not part of it, and we never will be . . . I don't want to go into it any further."

"I read you," Joe said. "If you're an Italian, I kill for you . . ."

"For a dollar and a quarter."

"But if you're a Jew, for an extra ten cents."

"Exactly. That's exactly it."

"Let me ask you a question." Joe was still circling around their failure to warn him. "The one guy they have to work with is me, okay? Do I have their respect?"

"That you got. That you got."

"Do I have their trust?"

He hesitated to bring up the matter of his court appearance, but Sykes knew what he meant.

"Yes. This cemented it. You had it before, but they never knew for sure. I think now you got it for sure."

Joe hoped he was right, and telephoned Jimmy Roberts to fix their meeting for 3:30, giving himself another hour with Sykes.

"I've never had a chance to talk with you in Miami," he said. "Gus is there. Dewey's there. Everybody's there."

"Always, always."

"And I'm talking to you as a friend, you know?"

"Otherwise, I wouldn't say anything about any of this," Sykes said solemnly.

"I'm talking to you as a yid to a yid."

"That's what we're doing." Sykes was delighted with the idea. "That's exactly right."

"See, I wanted to talk to you because I remember you as making comments to me, 'That bunch of greedy bastards. You have no idea how greedy they are.' "

"I shouldn't have said it, but it stuck in my throat. And I was afraid it was gonna happen to you, too."

"Well, that's why I'm asking you, as a friend, what they did to you. *How* they did it to you. So I know how to protect myself."

Thus encouraged, Sykes launched into a bitter account of his ouster by Barone from Maritime Cartage, of how he had agreed to teach Fiore the business, only to find Fiore taking more out of the company than he was, and how Barone had tried to keep Sykes in line.

"I said, 'What the fuck are you doing to me? The one thing you're not going to do to me is put my nose in the shit.' I just . . . I shouldn't have done it, but I'd had it. 'You're not gonna do that to me.' He wasn't gonna kill my wife, I'm sure of that. He ain't gonna do that . . . I said, 'Don't tell me to help 'em, and then make me look like a fucking moron.' "

"So what happened?"

"He says, 'Well, do me a favor. Walk back up with me, and I'll come up with a smile. I'll let 'em think that I won.' I said, 'Fine.' They think he won, fine, but he knows that that's . . .' "

Sykes shook himself like a wet dog.

"Lying to me from the start," he went on. "And I said, 'I deserve something for seven fucking years of loyalty to you, and you put my nose in the dirt?' That's all. That's what could happen tomorrow morning with you."

"Let me ask you something. What did you do for him?"

Sykes was too angry to care. "Somewhere between sixty and seventy."

"Thousand?"

"In the last seven years."

"You mean, you made sixty to seventy thousand dollars for him?"

"Yes, sir. Yes. To him direct . . ."

Joe punched the bed in frustration.

"That thief."

"That cocksucker. That's what hurts. 'Cause he knows he's got you right by the balls."

"That's already got me up this wall. I'm coming across the ceiling."

They went on for another half-hour with this highly satisfying denunciation of Barone, his associates, and all their works, warming to each other more and more as they uncovered new areas of shared grievance.

"Harvey, you don't know how much I appreciate this conversation," Joe said at last, glancing at his watch.

"Well, I'm glad."

"Need you to do me a favor."

"Certainly."

"I need you to go downstairs, and I'll join you in the coffee shop in fifteen minutes. Twenty minutes max."

"Good."

"I paid a hundred and fifty dollars to learn how to meditate," he explained. "Ann meditates. Mark meditates. Marilyn meditates, and I meditate. Twice a day."

"And that can be a very wonderful thing," said Sykes uncertainly. "I'll be in the coffee shop."

Joe gave him a minute or two to get clear, then put in a call to Ray Maria in Miami, who was not much concerned. He thought Sykes had probably been talking about the supposed "leak" they had already discussed. As for the federal angle, officers of the Department of Labor had been questioning Barone on another matter, involving Fred Field, and the two things had probably run in together.

Nor did Maria attach much importance to Barone's failure to warn Joe as he had warned Sykes. Had Sykes himself shown the slightest mistrust of him personally? Despite feeling "goosey" and tapping the walls? No. Would he have talked as he had if Barone had planted the faintest suspicion of Joe in his mind? Never.

Joe allowed himself to be persuaded. He then checked with the agents next door to see what they thought of the conversation so far. The stuff was dynamite, they said. Later on, Joe might want to push Sykes a little more on the Italian versus Jew angle, for that really seemed to set him off. And it would also be interesting to find out how much he knew about Fred Field.

Fine, said Joe. No time like the present. He called down to the coffee shop, had Sykes paged, and asked him to come upstairs again for a few minutes before they left.

Eager to please, he stood by while Joe checked his briefcase.

"Remember what you said about Italians and Jews? Well, I tell you, Harvey, you gave me the answer."

"Good."

"Driving me bananas, okay? Actually driving me bananas. But when you said . . ."

"It sounds simple, and it *is* that simple. That's the answer for sure."

"But you know, John Caputo and I have been friends for twenty years."

"Right. And I'm sure *good* friends, and *close* friends, and warm friends, and sincere friends. That's right. But that doesn't . . ."

"But John's still an Italian, right?"

"That's exactly right."

"But you know how heavy he is?"

"Yeah, he's number one, and everybody knows it. Everybody that *has* to know it, knows it for sure."

"Number one for labor connections."

"Exactly, exactly. If he can't do it, it cannot be done."

"Okay," Joe said. "Let me throw something at you before we go to the meeting, all right? One of the things that we're here for . . . and I haven't mentioned this to you before . . . Jimmy Roberts wants me to get into the stevedore business with him in Baton Rouge. In the respect that I can get Zim's work. They have as much liner board going out of Baton Rouge as they do out of Savannah. This becomes Freddy Field's territory. Does that also become Barone's?"

"Uh-huh. Absolutely."

"Freddy got, you know, Harrington in New Orleans."

"We can do that in a minute. In thirty seconds."

"Come again?" Joe was interested in the "we."

"They can do that in one minute."

Joe shook his head in amazement. "What I didn't realize is how powerful Freddy Field is."

"Oh, sure. The son of a bitch. It's unreal for this day and age, it really is. The power is absolute. First, there's God, and then there's these guys, and that's how the power structure works. I think I gotta play ball. There's no other way. You gotta play ball."

"Okay." Joe snapped his briefcase shut, and sat down on the bed beside it.

"So what are you telling me, Harvey? To make sure I maintain my relationship, but never count on it because I'm not Italian?"

"That's exactly what I'm saying."

"The only security I have is Johnny in New York."

"Uh-huh. That's the only security. And even that . . . When the chips are down, he's gonna go with his people. I don't know the man personally. Maybe he's . . ."

"You gonna meet him tonight," said Joe, making ready to go.

"I mean, I don't know him *well* personally. I've met John before."

"Yeah."

"What I'm saying is that he may be an exception. He may tend to consider the friendship with the Jew boy more important than this other . . ." He shook his head. "But he can't. Even if he wanted to."

"His uncle won't let him," Joe said, indicating that Sykes should precede him to the door.

"Exactly. He couldn't do it. His whole forty-five years of life and upbringing are contrary to . . ."

"You know who John's uncle is?"

Sykes looked coy, his hand on the doorknob. "His first name is Tony."

Their meeting with James Stevedores went well, with Jimmy Roberts and Bert Ibos accepting most of the responsibility for the poor performance in Savannah. Then Caputo joined them, and dinner went even better, with all sorts of plans and joint ventures envisaged for when they got properly organized. Joe was well satisfied when he returned to the hotel just before midnight, and Sykes also thought it a good evening's work.

"It was an excellent meeting," he said, as they entered their room. "No question about that."

"How'd you like John tonight?"

"The man's crazy." Sykes looked down on Joe like a startled giraffe. "The man is a nut. I don't like to hear Mr. A's name mentioned."

"Did you hear what he said?"

"Gets me nervous. Yeah, I heard what he said. I tried not to. I wanted to get up and walk away. I . . . that gets me nervous. I get out of my league when I hear that, and I . . . I get very nervous . . ."

"Did you hear, he said, if we had to, if we had big problems, he'd call Anastasio?"

"Yeah. And you know what that means, though? His people don't come down and talk nice about what has to be done."

"They just come and *tell* you what has to be done, right?"

"You got two choices then. You can do it, or you don't live tomorrow. And that still exists in their aspect of the business."

They then spent some time congratulating themselves on how they had handled Bert Ibos, not damning him in the eyes of his employers for James's shortcomings in Savannah, but leaving no one in doubt that the responsibility was his, to be shouldered personally.

This took them on to other successful and not-so-successful negotiations in which both had been involved, arriving eventually at the case of Neilson Shipping, for whose stevedoring Joe had once made a bid, only to be told the price did not matter; the account was going to Neal Harrington. Joe was sure this had been on Barone's orders.

"George did say he was fond of Harrington?"

"I'm pretty sure," said Sykes. "Because it's a fact. He was then supporting Harrington strongly, and *will* for the entire relationship *we* have, because, in fact, he is a partner in Harrington. It doesn't show on the stock certificate anywhere, but he is a partner in Harrington and many other organizations."

"It isn't Barone. It's Freddy Field and Barone. And some other guys."

"The network, you know?"

"Hey, indirectly, he's a partner in *my* organization."

"Of course. The same thing."

"No," said Joe perversely. "He's heavier with Harrington than he is with me."

"Yeah, yeah."

"They *own* a piece of Harrington."

"Yeah, well. Remember, it's a solid eight-, nine-year relationship, for every day of that period, where *you* still have a level of independence where Neal does not. He became a part of the group early . . . But I give Neal credit, I really do. Up until lately, he busted his nuts. He worked from early in the morning till late at night. He done a lot of things that I consider truly unethical on a business level, but hard work he has done. Like you yourself."

Joe did not find the comparison pleasing.

"But, Harvey, look," he said, "everywhere he went, he had the blessing of Barone and Fat Freddy."

"Of course. For sure. But that doesn't take away from the hours and the effort the man put in."

"That's fifty percent of it. But the first fifty percent is getting the door open."

Sykes saw how the wind was blowing, and changed course.

"You betcha," he said. "If the door ain't open, you can put in twenty-four a day, and you won't get to first base. That's for sure. No, he's not clean competition now, that's for sure."

"Let me tell you something," Joe said. "Neither am I."

"You can't be," said Sykes, the perfect courtier. "You'd never get a piece of business."

"If I don't wheel and deal with George and his group, where would I be right now?"

"That's the name of the game . . . He's a very hungry, greedy man. He wants a piece of everything."

"He's got the whole fucking waterfront."

"And you don't know what else. *Related* to the waterfront . . ."

Sykes was enjoying himself as much as Joe. Both had spent their lives in shipping. Both were Jews in an industry run by Italians and Irishmen. Both liked nothing better than to talk shop. For a full hour, they discussed Barone's interests in the South, including the inside story of Fiore's take-over of Maritime Cartage, "the only trucking company," as Joe put it, "that's operating in Miami with the blessing of the Pope."

They talked darkly of what had happened since. About a mutual friend, a stubborn, gypsy trucker, who had been found hanged, and about seven tractors, owned by independents, that mysteriously caught fire on a parking lot one night. From there, they compiled a catalogue of recent dirty deals, alternating one by one, until Joe, yawning now that he had taken his medication, was moved to say:

"You know something about this business world? From the Waterfront Commission on down, they're all fucking crooks."

"Yeah," said Sykes. "You're right. There ain't one of them who ain't."

"Every one of them."

"That's for sure. That's what I meant about this business, Joey. I'll never be a whore. I'll never go that route. But there are times when you have to deal with people who are like that if you want to stay in this business, let alone survive. You got to do it. And that gives me a bad taste in my mouth every time."

"How do you think *I* feel when Bill Boyle walks into my office every week?" asked Joe.

"Believe me, I know. Ah, thank God, the man makes it as pleasant and painless as I guess he can, and I love him for that, because, ah . . ."

Sykes could see he was going wrong again.

"I gotta tell you something," said Joe flatly. "There's no such thing as 'painless,' and there's no such thing as 'pleasant.' "

"As possible," he suggested, but Joe would have none of it.

"It's, ah, something that has to be done, part of your fixed overhead, and you know what? There isn't one company on the waterfront that doesn't pay."

They ran through the names, comparing notes.

"Marine Terminals. Jerry Chester."

"That one," said Sykes.

"He pays."

"Eller for sure," Sykes proposed.

"Who, Erb? With Carey? Shit."

"Yeah, that's a certainty. Al Chester is extremely strong with George."

"Al Chester is, huh?"

On they went through the list.

"You take PRIMSA," Joe said. "They operate out of New Orleans. They operate out of New York. They operate out of Miami. Harrington's got it all. And that's all the Ferre family."

"What that cost me alone!" Sykes moaned. "It goes down to strictly Barone. Barone personally went up to New York and handled every facet, every piece of that. Personally. Every inch of it was George."

"I know," said Joe. "I know George handled it, because everybody had to come up with front money to bid on the contract. You know that. And I was told, if I didn't get that one, the next big one that came along was mine."

"Yeah, right. That's right."

"And then I got busted, and everybody found out, Hey! Joey is a decent guy, okay? And George broke his balls to get me the Zim deal."

"I know."

"But the greedy cocksucker was . . . I got the deal provided everybody I used was *his* guys. Well, here, do you believe that the man actually introduced me to Joe Zatto, the insurance man?"

"Sure."

"To handle all my marine insurance?"

"Oh, sure, sure. I'm telling you. His tentacles reach almost every-where."

Joe stretched out, lacing his fingers to cup the back of his head.

"Harvey," he said. "Ten years ago, when they first came to town, they offered me everything. And my family said, 'Fuck 'em.' Within one year, did we lose all of our business?"

"Exactly, exactly. You just can't say no to 'em. They make you a deal that you can't refuse. If you refuse, then you gyp yourself."

"And if need be, they kill you . . . I'm convinced that Fat Freddy got rid of Willy Murphy in New York."

He caught sight of Sykes smiling to himself, and frowned.

"What are you laughing at?"

"Yeah. I, ah . . ." Sykes threw up his hands. "Again, very conceivable."

"Okay. No proof, but conceivable?"

"Yeah, sure."

"Now you tell me Roberto hung himself in Miami. And Roberto was the one guy who was coordinating the gypsy NVOs."

"For sure."

Joe looked at him critically.

"What do you sweat so much for?"

"I'm nervous."

"Why you nervous?"

"That's the way I am."

"Every day like this?"

"No."

"You take tranquilizers?"

"No, I don't take pills. Nervous ain't a good word. I, ah, when I got a lot on my mind, I . . . I get fidgety, that's all."

Joe decided he had been punished enough for smiling.

"Well, you know," he said, "I sit up in the evenings, and I go through in my own mind what's happening. And how it's happening, and what to do about it."

"I'm not saying it was wrong," said Sykes, misunderstanding his offense. "Family first. I'll buy that till I die. Just again, it has its drawbacks, too . . . But your dad was a stevedore."

"My dad was a good stevedore."

The reference to Gus took him back to the old days, when his father would be called in by ILA officials to act as arbitrator, and on one occasion, even to help sort out the union's cash reserves, now held in First National Bank.

"You can imagine how much money they got in *there*," said Sykes.

Joe waved his hands, as though it were beyond computation.

"You know when the bank was breaking my ass with the notes?" he said. "These guys called, and whatever was done . . . I don't want to *know* how they did it, okay?"

"You don't have to know."

"To this day, I don't know how they did it. All of a sudden, the bank backs off, and agrees to take so much a week."

"It just took one phone call."

"One phone call."

"That's all. 'Hey, listen, we want you to do us a favor, for one of our friends.' 'What's the favor, sir?' And that's the whole conversation."

It was then Sykes's turn to reminisce about his early days in Miami, when he negotiated with Barone on behalf of the cruise line he worked for. In figuring rates and prices, he said, it had been necessary to allow, not only for union officers on the take, but for the employers' cut, too.

"You wouldn't believe what other little deals the cruise lines have for creaming off money, never to be shown anywhere," he said. "Every concession on the vessel has a cash return to either the principal or the general agent. Every meal sold got a kickback. Every quarter that went into a slot machine got a kickback. Every bottle of booze sold in the gift shop, or every bottle of perfume got a kickback. Everything in the concessions had a kickback on it. That one little vessel had enough kickback on it to put many thousands of dollars aside every trip. Right smack off the top."

"Tax-free money."

"Oh, yeah."

That reminded Joe of his own experience with passenger boats, and again of how Eagle's business had melted away after he turned down Fred Field in 1966.

"Harvey, within six months, they paralyzed me."

"Didn't you really expect that to happen when you told them no?"

"I didn't think they were that powerful. Maybe I was a neophyte. Maybe I was busy building ships, but it never really dawned upon me. They operate Miami. They operate New Orleans. Fat Freddy controls Miami. Fat Freddy controls New Orleans. And where's the headquarters? Right in New York. Bill Boyle's the bagman. He goes to Barone. And Barone goes to Freddy Field, and from Freddy Field, it goes right up to the top."

"And a piece is left for each, right along the line."

"And you know what, Harvey? Let them keep their piece. We'll go about our business very nicely, and give them their little piece. So long as they leave us alone, everybody's happy."

But Sykes was not entirely happy.

"I just again want to make one point," he said. "Then I'm gonna take a shower. Any negotiations with them, please make sure it's well protected. As far as the exchange of any currency, make sure the film isn't running, and the projector isn't going, and eye witnesses aren't watching. Be very careful."

"Hey, Harve."

"Huh?"

"This whole conversation is between you and me."

"That's the way it will always stay, wise man."

Joe clapped him on the arm, and went around him into the bathroom. When he came out a few minutes later, he found Sykes tapping again at the walls.

"What are you looking for?" he demanded, suddenly wide awake.

"I told you. I'm goosey."

"Hey, man," he said crossly. "The fucking room was locked."

"Yeah, I know, I know."

"You read into . . . Shit that don't exist. You read too many detective magazines."

"No," said Sykes. "I was given a small training program by George a long time ago, and he said, 'You are never to have conversations about this with any living soul. Because the walls have ears, and the halls have eyes."

"Harvey . . ."

"So nobody . . ."

"You talking to *me.*"

"That's what I say. The ears and the eyes—"

"You talking to *me.*"

Sykes puffed out his cheeks.

"If I didn't know I could talk to you a hundred and ten percent, and vice versa . . . Joey, I'm not concerned about that. I'm telling you, my concern is just, you know, we checked in here, and the room was predetermined. And if there's some listening devices or something like that . . ."

Joe waved him away in mock disgust, and got into bed.

"Mr. Sykes," he said. "Good night. I'm going to sleep."

That was the sign-off phrase he had agreed on in advance with the agents next door. He hoped they were still awake. Thinking over his marathon conversation, he was pretty sure he had sucked Sykes as dry as anyone could have done in a single session, and he was asleep before the other had finished his shower. But he woke first, around 7:15, and was dressed to go for a walk before Sykes even stirred.

Joe was hoping to find the agents and compare notes, in case there was anything he had overlooked, but there was no sign of them downstairs, and when he found he had forgotten to put his watch on, he went back to the room. As Sykes was now up and shaving, Joe decided to keep him company.

"Harvey, you think I gotta wear a tie?" he asked, looking at himself doubtfully in the mirror. "Or can I wear my sport coat without a tie?"

"Sure."

"I don't need a tie today, do I?"

"No. Absolutely not." Sykes was concentrating grimly. "One day, I'm gonna cut off this fucking mustache," he said. "It takes ten extra minutes to shave every day with a goddamn mustache."

Joe laughed. "Look at you next to me. In the mirror. How tall are you, Harvey?"

"Almost six eight, Joey."

"Six eight?"

"Yeah. I got a kick last night, with us three big fuckers and you, walking in there."

"Jimmy Roberts is what? Six five?"

"No, Jimmy is six seven."

"Six seven. And how big is Bert?"

"Bert's six six and a half."

"Okay. And here *I* am, five four and a half. I look like a midget next to you guys."

Sykes chuckled carefully, shaving the angle of his jaw.

"I get a kick out of it, I really do."

"How'd you like that guy last night? He says, 'I'm a country doctor.' He says, 'What are you? A basketball coach?' "

"Right."

They both laughed.

"Man, I slept good last night," Joe said.

"I was thinking about everything," said Harvey, splashing water in his face, "so I didn't fall asleep right away."

"What were you thinking about?"

"Everything that happened. Everything we said."

"Well, I thought it was a good meeting."

"You betcha."

Joe followed him into the bedroom.

"The big thing they have going for them is John," he said.

"Exactly, exactly."

"How'd you like that fucking Johnny? He says, you remember? 'You want me to call Anastasio?' He says, 'I'll call Anastasio and call Scotto, and have them go to Savannah and straighten that nigger out in two minutes.' "

Sykes looked stricken.

"I love Johnny's quiet approach to things, though. He doesn't look like he ever gets excited."

"Very seldom does he get excited," Joe agreed.

"That's beautiful . . . To me, he's a wild man in a quiet way. He doesn't come on loud and strong and boisterous, but there's nothing the man won't do."

"I tell you something. There's nothing he wouldn't do for me."

"Yeah, that's obvious. That is obvious."

While Sykes finished dressing, Joe called Eastern Airlines to book a flight back to Miami that night for the three of them, and then called Caputo to confirm the arrangements. As soon as he had finished, Sykes got on the telephone to see if he could make a reservation for them at Brennan's.

"It's the best breakfast in the world, Joey."

"Is that right?" He was not much interested. "John says we ought to just go sit and talk all morning and plan what we want to do. He's got plans, my ass. He's already got something in mind. What's your interpretation, Harve, of what they have in mind?"

"The pieces that you've got, plus the pieces that they've got, are the best pieces in the world. They got both the Gulf and South Atlantic."

Joey nodded eagerly.

"The whole Gulf area," he said. "And John could make the peace with the guy tonight to walk the Israelis through. You realize how many Israeli shipping companies are with Zim? There's Maritime Fruit. There's Overseas National. There's El Yama, the tanker fleet . . . What are you waiting for?"

"I can't believe it," said Sykes. "They said hold on a minute for reservations."

"I haven't had a cup of coffee this morning."

"Listen, I want you to get to this place."

'I'm gonna have a nicotine fit."

"I know. Ah, yes," he said, raising his voice. "I'd like to make a reservation this morning for two . . . Eleven thirty's the earliest? No, I can't wait that long. Okay, thank you." He slammed down the telephone. "Now do you believe this? Thursday morning. A nothing time. No tourists here, and you can't make a breakfast reservation? They got things like unbelievably prepared eggs with ham, like Benedicts, and all with flame . . ."

"Hey, what's wrong with a plain poached egg?"

"Listen with flaming grapefruit à la flambé with . . ."

"I don't go à la . . ."

"With champagne, wine, and all that jazz mixed in with fruit, with flaming bananas at the end, over ice cream, and all that . . . ahhhhh. It's a ten dollar breakfast, Joey, but I want you to try it."

Joe appraised him in the mirror, shaking his head.

"You know, Harvey," he said, "if you went on a diet and took off about fifty pounds, your back wouldn't hurt you."

"Yeah, I know. That's the same thing Bert told me yesterday, and he's right. And you're right."

Sykes was fighting hard to fasten a pair of elasticated supports around his ample paunch.

"I gotta do that," he gasped. "Ah, you cocksucker . . . fucker . . . Ah, fuck it. I don't need the goddamn things."

"You really don't."

"These goddamn things are too small anyway, and put too much pressure on it. I got the hungers. I can't wait anymore."

"Put your jacket on."

"Can't wait no more," he crooned.

"Let's leave. You done got your checkbook? Your ticket? Pipe tobacco?"

"Yeah, yeah. Ready to go. I need some more of these things."

Joe caught sight of the capsules he was putting in his pocket, and took them from him.

"*Damn*, Harvey," he said. "Them are elephant pills."

"Yeah, I know. That's for my back. That's called, ah . . ."

"I never saw a pill that big."

"That's the newest thing they found for, ah, arthritis and rheumatism, and all of that." He opened the door for Joe to precede him. "It's been very heavily promoted lately by Upjohn, who's making millions of dollars just on the . . ."

The door closed behind them.

In the next room, the agents listened out for a few minutes more, then shut down the recorder.

They looked at each other, and yawned extravagantly.

15

Baiting the Trap

AT the end of April, Joe and Mel Kessler took their wives to London on vacation. For Joe, it was like shucking off a suit of dirty clothes, and he bought a used Rolls Royce to celebrate. But before their three weeks were up, he was fretting to get back. There was too much unfinished business on his mind.

In spite of what Sykes and Maria had said, he knew Barone was suspicious of him. So was Vanderwyde. In fact, Vanderwyde was the main reason why he had yielded to Ann and agreed to take a break. When he had tried to give him $250 toward the rent arrears, Vanderwyde demanded a further $500, in terms that sent him straight back to the office to scrape it together. On returning with the money, he found Vanderwyde had been joined by Barone, and neither had said a word until Vanderwyde patted him down. That evening, Ann had proposed the London trip with the Kesslers, and Joe had agreed at once.

Thinking about it at a distance of several thousand miles, he concluded that paranoia was the main hazard of undercover work. He had himself told Boyle that the OCB had come to see him, and Boyle had later confirmed that the Strike Force was all over the dock. Why, then, would they need to warn him of the investigation, as they had warned Sykes, when he obviously knew about it already?

The body search was not so easily explained away. He was pretty sure that Vanderwyde did not make a habit of patting down Harvey Sykes before he talked to him. The postponement of his sentencing in the Guzman affair could have worried them, perhaps reviving suspicions of a trade-off, but the cause of their mistrust hardly mattered. Joe hurried back from vacation with the feeling that time was now definitely against him.

His first hallway conference was not auspicious. Barone observed that Joe was running well behind with his other commitments, but seemed to accept that this was Zim's fault for not paying its bills on time.

Tony Morelli had called him about it.

"That's why I haven't been pushing you," Barone said. "When you get paid, *I* get paid. But my partner, Jay, he don't give a shit," he added, in case Joe should think they were all as civilized about these things as he was. "Jay wants his up front."

Well, said Joe, Jay had asked for $3,600-worth of cruise tickets, and he would have to be content with that for the time being. One reason why Zim was so slow in paying was because they still had serious labor problems in Savannah.

At this, Barone rounded on Boyle so fiercely that the other stepped back a pace.

"You fuck," he said. "I told you to live up there if you had to when these ships work."

Caught off-balance, Boyle gargled his way into some sort of explanation, but Barone cut him short with a wave of the fist.

"I keep my word," he told Joe. "You'll get number one labor up there."

He also said that Houston and Charleston were the next ports on Zim's shopping list, but he was wrong for once.

When Joe flew up to New York two days later, he was told that a big Zim ship would be going into Mobile, Alabama, to load wood pulp, and that Georgia Container Agencies could have the stevedoring if he wanted it.

Joe wanted it.

The deal not only sounded profitable, but provided good cover for extending the investigation into still another port. But he approached the offer cautiously, using it, as he used almost every opening now, to probe the other side's position. Talking to Captain Ilan later in the day, he said he was definitely interested in Mobile, but before quoting rates, he would have to see how the land lay, and whom he would have to deal with. It was Fred Field's port.

Ilan knew exactly what he meant. Zim would negotiate a price, he said. What happened after that was Joe's business.

Meanwhile, Bob Carter was discussing the Savannah situation with Uzi Shaham, who had just been made vice president in charge of maintenance and repairs. After expressing serious reservations about Great Southern Trailer ("We don't wanna do business with people who use cement overshoes."), Shaham suddenly offered Carter the job of assistant manager, M & R, for all of North America. Zim's container and trailer repair costs were soaring toward the $2 million a year mark, and they wanted to bring in somebody they could trust to look at their problem areas, at ports where costs seemed disproportionately high in relation to traffic. Carter said he would talk it over with Joe.

There was never a doubt that he would take the job. To have an undercover federal agent working against Scotto in New York with $2 million-worth of repair contracts was like being given a free pass to the racketeers' club in every North American port. Acceptable to Zim as Joe's protégé, and with Boyle and Barone to vouch for him, Carter could now connect up the various waterfront cases proceeding independently in a dozen different Federal districts into one coordinated national investigation.

To try out the effect of his change of status, Carter accompanied Joe next morning to Tilston–Roberts. Arriving a few minutes after they did, Caputo picked them up in the reception area and led them through to his office.

"Did you get hold of Joey Lacqua yesterday?" Joe asked, as they were ushered inside.

"No, he wasn't . . . He's out of town."

"When will he be back?"

"He should be back . . ." Caputo trailed off, frowning at his battery of telephones.

"Every time I come in here," he said peevishly, "somebody's been playing around. I wonder if they're tapping my wires, for Chrissake."

"Fuck," said Joe, clutching his briefcase recorder.

But Caputo was already calling for the day's telex messages, and to get the conversation going, Joe told him about Mobile. Both agreed that all he had to do on signing the contract was to put a man in James's office there, with a sign on the door and a separate telephone number. Then Carter brought up the subject of his new job, describing it in a way that underlined not only his inexperience, but his willingness to take advice.

Caputo warmed to him at once. All Carter had to do, he said, was tell him which were the ports where repair costs were getting out of hand.

"Then I can meet with my people," he went on, "and say, 'Okay, look. This is what we'll do. We don't want to fuck around. We want to be able to do the job and make some money on the deal.'"

"Okay," said Carter gratefully.

"Now, if there's anything else that has to be done, all you got to do is just say, 'This has to be done,' or 'That has to be done,' and we'll get it done, all right?"

To illustrate the point, Caputo told them how the problem of the Tilston–Roberts terminal in New York had been resolved. Ignoring Caputo's advice, and a warning from Anthony Anastasio, the firm had moved part of its operation to Jersey. For a week afterwards, every truck waiting on line at the Brooklyn terminal had been ticketed by the New York Police Department. When the total of fines reached $4,000, Caputo said, Anastasio had telephoned to ask when the firm would be moving back to Brooklyn. As soon as it could get a pier, he was told. At which point, Caputo had directed the firm's attention to the pier which Anthony Scotto and he had had in mind for them all along.

"So if this is the chance," he told Carter, "you're on. Take it. And believe me when I say this: If you have any problem here, give me a call. If I can't straighten it out, I'll get someone who *can* straighten it out for you. All right?"

It was perfect.

"Thanks a lot," said Carter sincerely.

Another advantage of positioning Carter in New York was that it created an opening for a second, and possibly a third, undercover agent on Joe's payroll. It was not necessary to replace Carter in Savannah, now that he had paid Boyle the last of the front money, but Georgia Container Agencies was obviously going to need somebody in Mobile. And with the further possibility of expansion into Houston, Charleston, and, possibly, Jacksonville as well, the time was fast approaching when Joe might reasonably take on an assistant to hold the fort for him in Miami while he flitted back and forth between New York and the new branch offices, particularly as Manny Levy was now having trouble with *his* heart.

Joe flew home to report the Mobile offer to Boyle, and to ask how much it would cost him. Boyle didn't know offhand, but undertook to find out. Mobile was no problem, he said. It was run by Isom Clemon, president of Local 1410, a vice president of the International union, and "one of our boys." When Joe said he was anxious to inspect the port's facilities, Boyle offered at once to have Clemon show him around. Indeed, the news about Mobile and Carter's new job inspired a mood of such helpfulness that even Joe's past-due payments seemed temporarily unimportant.

Harvey Sykes, as usual, had the insider's explanation. Barone and Boyle were so pissed off at dealing with the Kratishes, even in the normal course of union business, that they were going to ask Joe to take the accounts and set up on his own. He would be hearing more about the idea in a few days.

Boyle's unnatural restraint over the rent arrears lasted until June 7. He then sought Joe out to tell him that the Zim contract for Mobile would cost $5,000 up front, payable in five weekly installments, plus $12 a box, 50 cents a ton, and one percent of the manifest, as in Savannah. And speaking of Savannah, he added, Joe had better come up with $1,000 in the next few days if he wanted the next Zim ship that put in there to be worked at all, let alone efficiently.

Having applied the stick, Boyle returned next morning with a carrot. The Fat Man, he said, wanted to know when Joe was quitting the family business. As soon as he made the break, Field was ready to put $100,000 into a new, Miami-based stevedoring company, with Joe as his front man.

Surprised, despite Sykes's earlier hint, Joe said he was pleased by their confidence in him, which was no lie after his recent qualms, and promised to think the proposition over carefully.

That was evidently not the right answer, for Boyle came back next day with the stick. Field had arranged for Joe to meet Isom Clemon in Mobile on the eleventh, he said, but Joe would have to go alone as Barone was insisting that Boyle personally supervise the loading of the next Zim ship in Savannah. Even *with* his personal attention, however, he could not guarantee that the ship would be worked to Joe's satisfaction without the $1,000 already mentioned. What Boyle proposed, therefore, was that Joe should bring Clemon, *and* the $1,000, to Savannah after inspecting the port of Mobile, so that the three of them could then conclude their business. And as both he and Clemon were going to so much trouble on his behalf, no doubt Joe would consider it appropriate to supply him with a round-trip ticket to Savannah, and to pick up the tab for Clemon's expenses as well.

Joe had no objection. The whole point of the investigation was to identify as many of the conspirators as possible and have them solicit illegal payments. He just wished the government would use its *own* money more often.

Isom Clemon drove out in his Cadillac to meet Joe at Mobile airport. Boyle had described Clemon as "the silent power" among black labor leaders in the South, conjuring up for Joe the vision of a more taciturn Landon Williams, a burly, brisk, commanding figure who might prove difficult to draw out. Instead, he was greeted by a lean, almost willowy man, about six feet tall, with a pencil mustache, a vaguely Oriental cast of feature, and a manner so "laid back" as to verge on the languid. Beautifully turned out in white shoes, white pants, and a MicMac shirt, Clemon struck Joe as being better suited to run a crap game than a longshoremen's union; an opinion he was given no cause to revise on closer acquaintance.

Far from being hard to draw out, he was an unquenchable source of reckless confidence.

"You know the score, Isom?" Joe asked, as they drove into town. "You know what's going on here?"

"I sure do," he said. "Bill Boyle done called me. He says you one of the family. He told me to take good care of you. And when the man says that, you ain't got no problems."

"Well, that's good to know, Isom. And let me tell you something. When people look after me, I look after them, okay?"

"*Okay,*" he said. " 'Cause I do like those little white envelopes coming in regular."

"Every two weeks, Isom. And when I'm out of town, one of my relatives will be working up here, and *he'll* take care of you."

Clemon settled back in the driving seat.

"You is a blessing," he said fondly. "You is definitely a blessing."

They toured the port, talking shipping, and Joe explained about the cargo he expected to handle.

"You gonna have my fullest cooperation," Clemon said. "The fullest. Fat Freddy, he's the main man in this port, and he told me. He said, like you gonna be the man in charge of the freight, like Sammy Gordon is the man in charge of the bananas." He pointed out a huge warehouse belonging to Southern Stevedores. "Him and Freddy. They unload all the bananas in Mobile. They all gotta go through them. They got the exclusive from the Port Authority. Nobody else unloads bananas here. Governor Wallace, he done give them the exclusive."

"George Wallace?"

"Oh yeah, yeah. Fat Freddy and Sammy and George is like this." He contrived to cross three fingers, and went on to describe a network of Southern political and business connections that Joe did his best to commit to memory. Many of the names were new to him, which made matters difficult, but he was not seriously worried. Ray Maria had arranged for the local FBI agents in Savannah to wire his room at the De Soto Hilton, and Joe was quite sure he could persuade his garrulous new friend to go over the ground again when Clemon arrived there next day. Joe flew out of Mobile that evening quite sure he had broken through to the political heart of the conspiracy.

Early next morning in Savannah, Special Agent Jack Wagner gave him a roll of 10 marked $100 bills; government money this time. They agreed that after passing these to Boyle in the men's room of the hotel, Joe would yawn and stretch as he came out to indicate that the payoff had taken place. He would also try to get Boyle upstairs to discuss Isom Clemon and his political connections for the benefit of the agents in the next room.

The second part of the plan proved impracticable, however, for when

Boyle arrived at 11:30 for an early lunch before the ship docked, he was accompanied by his wife, his daughter, and grandson, and by Ray DeMott and Jimmy Hodges, owners of Great Southern Trailer Corporation. Separating him from the crowd, Joe handed over the $1,000, and with a yawn for the watching agents, followed Boyle into the hotel dining room, resigned to a social lunch.

After a few pleasantries, however, Boyle's wife and daughter dutifully tuned out, and the conversation turned to Joe's deal with Great Southern Trailer. DeMott and Hodges were upset because Bob Carter, before leaving, had given some of Zim's trucking in Savannah to a rival firm, and Joe realized, as Boyle took him to task for this, that the meeting was for *their* benefit, not his. They, too, were paying off, and complaining, as he had often complained, because the business they thought they had paid for had gone somewhere else. Boyle had brought them along to justify the money they had given him, so they could listen while Joe was rebuked.

He then paid for lunch with one of the marked $100 bills, sent DeMott and Hodges about their business, and led Joe to the reception desk to find out if Isom Clemon had checked in.

"About Mobile," Joe said, as the clerk consulted his records. "We agreed five thousand, right?"

"No, it's not five. I talked to Freddy."

"No? How much then?"

"It's gonna cost you ten, my friend," said Boyle, turning away as the clerk shook his head. "Ten big ones."

"Oh, wow."

The taxpayers were definitely picking up the tab this time, but he pretended to be stricken.

"Well, listen," he said. "Can you take the five at a thousand a week, like we agreed, and then gimme a break before I start in with the second five? Like six months?"

"I don't know," said Boyle. "I'll have to ask Fred."

"Yeah, well, do that. Because otherwise, I'm gonna have to take a pass."

Boyle did not believe that any more than Joe meant it, but they had both spotted Clemon trucking across the lobby toward them. Turning up the wattage of his charm, Boyle shook him by the hand, but it was not one of his more convincing performances. Joe had noticed this before. Though officially equal in status, when a white ILA vice president met a black ILA vice president there was never a doubt as to who pecked first.

They spoke only briefly, as Boyle had to take his family home before getting down to the ship, but he stayed long enough to rule that Joe would pay Clemon $50 a week, plus another $50 whenever a ship was in. And he stayed a while longer when Clemon remarked that there was nobody in Mobile to handle container repairs. Maybe they should set up a corporation of their own to do it, Boyle suggested. Joe could provide the money; Clemon would guarantee a monopoly, and he would put his share in his daughter's name.

When Joe agreed to explore the idea over dinner, Boyle left, without including Clemon in the invitation. The omission was not accidental, and Joe bridged a slightly awkward pause by suggesting to Clemon that they move upstairs to his room. There was too much traffic in the lobby for them to talk in comfort, he said. You could never tell who was watching.

Clemon admired his caution, and as soon as they were settled, tried to repair his self-esteem by bragging again of his connections. He was particularly anxious that Joe, as a shipping man, should get together with his friend Dr. Frank Maddox, a bishop of the black Methodist church in Savannah, and Dr. Jim Smith, their New York business associate. Between them, he said, they had access to all kinds of commodities and facilities for trade with Third World countries.

To illustrate the sort of deal he had in mind, Clemon told a rather fuzzy story of how they had shipped a load of black cosmetics from Mobile to a West African country, and how the freight charges, amounting to some $960,000, had been paid to them in Switzerland, not in cash but in diamonds. Their attorney, who also happened to be the wife of a bank governor in the Bahamas, had then sold the diamonds for them in Amsterdam, transfered the money to Nassau, converted it into U.S. dollars, and finally delivered the proceeds, in cash, to Atlanta, where the partners were waiting to pay off their political allies and carve up the pot.

"Now in the State of Alabama," Clemon went on, hooking his thumbs in his armpits, "all the law enforcement office . . . in the whole State of Alabama . . . all the money . . . I'm on the board. I pay the gentlemen who wanna go to be State Assemblymen."

He laughed proudly, and Joe whistled.

"It's understood when you tell me about law enforcement," he said, "and they all do what you tell 'em to do, okay? Isom Clemon, State Supervisor . . . I hear you! But when you tell me that the government man will do what you say . . . That's the one at the head?"

"Hey, the Attorney General in the State of Alabama. I made him, did you know? Made him. He was a kid going to school, and when he finished law school and went with me to the convention in 1968 in, ah, ah, Atlantic City . . . I tell you, Bill Baxley's unknown, and he's one of the slickest guys in the State of Alabama. I got up on the regular floor in the State of Alabama, and I say, 'Here's twenty thousand dollars.' He said, 'I want that twenty thousand.' And here's the next Attorney General in the State of Alabama, and here's the next Governor. He's the power."

"He's gonna . . ."

"Yeah, yeah. The Governor. George will be out next month."

"Wallace?"

"Yeah. He be going to Washington next month. Sparkman going resign."

Joe shook his head in awe. Clemon's delivery was hard to follow, but he was getting the gist of it.

"Sparkman's gonna resign, and George gonna be the next Senator?"

"The next Senator."

"That's already laid out, huh?"

"Oh, we did that two weeks ago," said Clemon carelessly.

"I hear you. Now you tell me that Carter's part of the group, too, huh?"

"Sure! Sure! Now, his right-hand man . . ."

"Jimmy Carter's right-hand man?"

"Carter's right-hand man, he's one of *ours.*"

"He's one of our people, too?"

"You understand?"

"I hear you."

"You follow me now?"

"I got it all laid out."

"All right."

Clemon paused for effect.

"Now," he said. "Cloyd, he the one coordinate the whole shop for Carter in Georgia. His name's Cloyd Hall."

"Cloyd Hall?"

"Right. He coordinated it for him . . . I met him in California."

"You met Jimmy Carter in California?"

"California. Down on Parkway all afternoon . . ."

Joe paced up and down, shaking his head, speechless with admiration.

"Isom, you got all this?" He threw up his hands. "So let's be realistic. You, the heavy black man in the South, you got all the heavy black connections in the whole country."

Clemon smiled. "Me and you's brothers, right?"

"You understand what I'm saying? So . . ."

"Yeah, but in Alabama . . ."

"You is the heavyweight."

He nodded. "I'm the vice-president of all the labor in the State of Alabama."

"But Freddy . . ."

"Freddy is the big man. Freddy helped me more than anybody under the sun. Freddy come to Mobile and stayed six months. I say, 'I can get 'em all organized.' 'You what?' 'Yeah.' " Clemon laughed delightedly. "I walk in the Governor's office. He say, 'What you doing?' I say, 'I'm going organize every son of a bitch down on this dock.' He say, 'Go ahead.' I said, 'I need this, I need so and so . . .' You know what he said?"

"What?"

"Help yourself."

"God *damn,* Isom."

Warmed by Joe's admiration, Clemon went on to describe how he had delivered the labor vote to George Wallace at the last gubernatorial election, and how the Governor, in return, had surrendered the port of Mobile to Freddy Field, whom Clemon clearly regarded as the most powerful figure in the International union.

"They tell me that next time you're thinking of running Ralph Abernathy as president of the ILA," said Joe innocently. "Is that true?"

"Uh-huh."

"But that's gonna go to Scotto."

"I don't know," said Clemon. "It's Fred's deal. Whatever Freddy says . . . Me and Scotto was at the convention, and he was telling me, he says, 'Isom . . .' he says, 'now I'll be looking for your support.' And I say, 'Wait a minute.' I say, 'Now I'm already Freddy Field's. If he's right, I'm going ride with him. If he's wrong, I'm going stay with him till they get him out.' I said, 'I think you better talk to Freddy.' I said, 'Now if you and Fred could get down, you can do what you wanna do,' I said. 'But now, if Fred is on the other side of the fence, then *I'm* right over there. Now we don't wanna go and get our wires crossed.' "

Joe nodded.

"You know, I don't understand with Scotto," he said. "What does he want but New York? You could take Alabama. You could take Florida. You could take Mississippi, and all of 'em."

"All of 'em," agreed Clemon.

"And shit. Next to New York?"

"Uh-huh, uh-huh."

"Who gets . . . Who makes more money than Scotto?"

"Nobody."

"You know it, and I know it."

"That's right. Nobody. But what I'm saying now, and you know, old Scotto appreciated me telling him like that."

Clemon smiled reminiscently.

"Uh-huh. Do you think Scotto got a chance to be president?"

"Only if he makes right with Freddy. Freddy going be the balancing power needed."

Joe was beginning to find this reverence for Field rather irritating, but there was no doubt that Clemon, for all his incoherence, was a power in the South. Getting back to national politics, he told Joe how the Democratic machine that elected George Wallace had also won Alabama for Carter.

"I *pushed* ole Carter into winning," he said. "I put him in myself."

"So you gonna be right up there with the President."

"Sure. Right there. Right there."

With Joe's encouragement, the orgy of self-congratulation lasted until Boyle telephoned to say that he would meet Joe in the lobby at 6:30. This reminded Clemon that he was also expecting a call, and he took his leave, promising to return with Bishop Maddox around 8:30.

In contrast with lunch, dinner with the Boyles at the Downtowner Hotel was mainly social. They talked shop, of course, having nothing else in common, but the nearest they came to serious business was when Joe mentioned again that he wanted to open in Jacksonville.

Boyle winced with distaste.

"You're gonna deal with a bad nigger," he said.

"You mean Landon Williams? He's not in the group?"

"He's a bad nigger, that's all."

"What did he do?" Joe leaned forward avidly. "Last I heard, he was gonna be president of the South Atlantic District, then Buddy Raspberry got it. What happened?"

"He's a pushy black bastard, and who needs that?" Boyle looked around, then leaned forward as well, confidentially. "Know what he did? When Buddy beat him out? He goes to Fred, okay? He says, 'If I don't get to be president,' he says, 'I'm turning you in.' "

"No *shit.*"

"Would you believe that? Fucking nerve of that cocksucker? 'I'm gonna turn you in to the IRS and the Department of Labor,' he says. 'You and Cleve Turner both.' Black fuck."

"So what's Fred gonna do?"

"Well, what do *you* think?"

But Joe wanted to hear it. "You think Landon's gonna make trouble at the convention? In Chicago?"

"Listen." Boyle glanced around again. "That black mother-fucker better straighten out or he ain't gonna *be* at the convention."

"You mean, you're gonna kill him?" Joe suggested eagerly.

Boyle's expression shaded into disapproval.

"We'll do what we have to do," he said, waving his empty glass at the waiter.

A few minutes after 8:30, Joe pushed his way into the lobby of the De Soto Hilton, where Clemon was already waiting for him with Dr. Frank Maddox, a calm, prosperous figure with the confident presence of a man used to reassuring voters, stockholders, and congregations. Waving away Joe's apologies, he suggested they should go to Clemon's room to talk, but Joe was ready for that. Would they mind using his room instead? He was expecting a call from his wife, he said. His son had asthma.

Maddox readily agreed, and on the way up to Room 305, explained how fortunate Joe was to have caught him. He was leaving next day for Atlanta to attend a conference of his African Methodist Episcopal Church, of which he was vice chairman. Some 30,000 people were expected, many of them from the new nations of black Africa, with which they were closely linked. His church was the second largest body of Methodists in the world, he said, and predominantly black, although there were a few white brothers. More to the point, he added, "We are the largest organized body of minorities in the country."

Suitably impressed, Joe ushered his guests inside and called room service for a round of drinks. He then told Maddox what he had already told Clemon: that he had the ships if they had the cargoes. Oh, they had the cargoes all right, replied Maddox. They also had a company called Triworld International Ltd., based in the Bahamas and Nigeria. And under an agreement with the U.S. Maritime Administration, ratified by the Congress, 20 percent of the Federal government's ocean freight was available to those minority businesses capable of handling it.

The measure had been introduced by the Nixon Administration, which Maddox, as one of the South's leading black Republicans, had supported.

"If the Administration had stayed in," he said, "I was up for . . . I was being considered for Assistant Secretary of the Navy."

"*What* did you say?" Joe feigned astonishment. "Are you an attorney?"

"I, ah, read law. I sat on the bench for two and a half years. Juvenile court judge."

They all laughed.

"A juvenile court *judge?*"

"Uh-huh. Right here in Georgia. I was the first one. In Clark County."

"Is that right?" said Joe, marveling. "So you were right there with the Justice Department. And . . ."

"I stayed in the department, what? About seven years."

"And you would have been Assistant Secretary of the . . ."

"I was recommended," said Maddox. "Yes, sir, I was calling the shots."

Clemon leaned forward to make sure that Joe knew whom he was dealing with.

"Lemme explain this to you," he said, " 'cause it's politics."

"Yeah."

"Right. Politics."

"I'm hearing you."

"I'm on one side of the fence," said Clemon, "and he's on the other side. Well, we trade."

"Right," said Joe.

"Right?"

"Right."

"And we take one hand, and wipe the other hand. This is the only way we can make it."

"Frank, you can't make it no other way," agreed Joe, moved by this insight.

"I don't know any other way," said Maddox, but Clemon had not finished yet.

"Now, when Frank was in the Justice Department, I was opposed to him as a brother," he said.

Maddox nodded.

"Every major disturbance in the country, I was one of the chief mediators," he said modestly. "My area was conciliations, mediations, and arbitrations."

"I understand," said Joe, but Clemon cut him off.

"Right. Now Frank, with his membership and stuff . . ."

"Uh-huh."

"See, they wanted Frank back. Frank had the connections for making money."

"Right."

"They want to get into the, ah, ah, marketing business side of it, and Frank was the only one that could produce, okay?"

Before Joe could ask who "they" were, the room service waiter delivered their drinks. By the time he left, Clemon had forgotten what he was talking about.

"Now, the State Convention of Republicans is going to be here next week," said Maddox.

"Uh-huh," said Joe, handing him his Beefeater and orange juice.

"And I am going to open it up."

They all laughed appreciatively, none louder than Maddox.

"You see," he said, "our philosophy is this: We don't put all our chips in one coin bag. My wife is a Democrat."

"Oh, you're a smart one," Joe said, and they laughed even harder. "Now, Isom was telling me, he said, 'What about this boat of yours? Can you trade with Africa?' And I said, 'I trade anywhere in the world.' "

Maddox composed himself.

"You have any, pardon me, any feelings about what *part* of Africa you trade with?"

"Uh-uh." Joe shook his head. "Where do you *want* to trade?"

"We trade with money," Maddox said, sharing another laugh with Clemon.

"I said, *where* do you want to trade in Africa?"

"Well," said Maddox, serious again. "We going do some, you know, confidentially, we going do some South Africa trading. See, because I know that if I make enough money, ah, everything will be all right. And, ah, so, ah, I'm not saying that, ah, that I don't have some great feelings for the idea, but I'm looking for a marketable product that can economically move us forward. And it doesn't make any difference where it comes from . . ."

"Well," said Joe, who wondered if their Nigerian associates felt the same way. "I tell you what. I'm gonna put the boat at your disposal. And you tell me where you want the boat to go, and it'll be there . . ."

Maddox allowed they all understood where they were coming from, but he was still not ready to discuss specifics. When it came to handling major commodities, he said, the competition was rough on minority interests. He didn't want to get burned. During the sugar shortage, for instance, he had been sitting on a million tons of the stuff overseas, but couldn't move it. Their problem was transportation.

Well, that was why he was there, Joe said, with a touch of exasperation. All he did was operate ships.

Clemon had been watching Joe closely.

"Lemme tell you something," he said. "We fool around, and we been in this business the last twelve years, and when we start in it, we start in it with one idea and one goal for everybody who's gonna work. Comprehend?"

"Uh-huh," said Joe, totally bewildered.

"Him," said Clemon. "Cloyd Hall. And Marge DeWitt. And, ah, our head man there in New York, ah, Washington, ah . . ."

"Calhoun?" Maddox suggested.

Clemon shook his head. "I'm talking, ah, you know, in the Justice . . . I mean, out of the department."

"You mean, ah, yeah, yeah, okay . . . The director. Holman."

"Holman," Clemon said, relieved. "Ben Holman."

"Holman?" Joe frowned. "I heard of him."

Maddox laughed, a touch scornfully. "He's an assistant attorney general."

Joe pretended to swallow. "He's an assistant attorney general?"

"Right. Been there for the last eight years. I been thinking about moving him, but he's a friend. We going keep him there."

"You got that power, Frank? Can you really keep him there?"

"Right. I just say to the person that he ain't to be touched."

"That's right," said Clemon.

"I understand." Joe shook his head. "He's gonna be heavier if Carter goes in."

"Well, we got *that,*" Clemon said.

"One hundred percent," Maddox agreed.

"Lemme explain this to you now," said Clemon. "What I was thinking about, after you was telling about all these ships you own, and about that twenty percent what we know we can get . . . Thoughts commenced rolling through my mind . . ."

"Yeah," said Maddox. "Mine, too." He stared at Joe sincerely. "I been thinking about going along with you. I got the documents, the signed documents . . . I want Joey to sign them. I got 'em on file right here, and it's not really necessary to do, ah, ah, to even go there. Because when you demand your percentage, what you can produce, why go to the Maritime Administration and all the shit they got? Here's the ships, and my resources here. And here's my line of credit."

"Uh-huh," said Clemon.

"And here's my Dun and Bradstreet rating."

"Uh-huh, uh-huh."

"Hey, it's all over."

"What can I say?" asked Joe, lost in admiration. "The only thing you were lacking in was transportation, and here I am. What you gonna bring in?"

"I'll bring in coal," said Maddox, at last getting down to cases. "We got the contract with the largest electricity company in the South."

"Where you gonna bring this coal in from?"

"Africa."

"South Africa? You operate in the South African market?"

"Already, in a small way."

"Where do you want the boat? Then I can make a quick calculation. In like three minutes, I can tell you how long it'll take to get there, and the cost and everything."

They then spent rather longer than three minutes on the economics of ocean transport, for Bishop Maddox seemed fascinated by the profits to be made from running cargo in both directions.

"All right," he said. "Say you got a load, and I provide you with a load to come back. How do we talk? I mean, what . . . I'm really talking . . . I mean, now when I keep these ships on the move, I would probably want you to do something for me."

"Okay," said Joe, back on familiar ground. "Lemme tell you. You get a load going one-way down from the U.S., and you get a load of general break-bulk cargo, you're talking half a million dollars. So let's assume it cost two hundred thousand, all right?"

"Uh-huh."

"Here's three hundred thousand. You can do what you want. *Where* you want it, and *how* you want it."

Maddox tried to keep a straight face, but he looked at Clemon, and they both giggled.

Then Clemon got off on politics again, about how close he was to Governor Wallace, and how he had been one of 12 notables in the state invited to a private meeting with Henry Kissinger. Not sure how useful this was, Joe excused himself suddenly, saying he had to catch the hotel drugstore before it closed, and used the house phone in the lobby to call Special Agent Lou Stevens of the Savannah FBI in the next room.

"How's it coming through?" he asked.

"Loud and clear, Joe. Loud and clear."

"Lou, do you believe this?"

"Jesus Christ. Listen, Joey, do me a favor. Maddox is a Major in the Savannah Police Department, okay? The chief chaplain. And there's six black cops that just got indicted for shake-downs in the business district. See what you can get on that."

"You mean, you want more of this political bullshit?"

"Anything you wanna do, man. Just keep on rolling."

When Joe returned to the room, it was obvious they had come to some sort of decision in his absence, for Clemon tackled him straight away on the necessity for Triworld to act as agents for the ships he would supply. And when Joe assured them he had taken that for granted all along, Maddox finally showed his hand.

"We got a commitment of seventy million dollars a year," he said. "For moving commodities. That's in the first year, and it increases the second year. It increases each year. A twenty-year commitment."

"Of what?"

"Delivering coal, oil."

"From South Africa?"

"Right. You see, I got the . . . I got a thing on Nigerian oil, which is one of the richest countries in oil in the world . . ."

"Okay."

Joe looked at them wistfully. Somewhere in the middle of all this, there had to be the makings of a legitimate deal that might still be left standing when the FBI brushed away the flies.

"Now, how do we get paid?" he asked. "For the stuff that covers the labor?"

"Oh, well," said Maddox, as if that were the kind of petty detail he generally left to underlings.

"Government to government," Clemon said grandly.

Maddox nodded. "That's it."

"Bank to bank," said Clemon.

"Bank to bank," agreed Maddox.

"Does it have to be in money?" Joe asked.

Clemon shook his head. "It don't have to be."

"You want it in gold or diamonds? Something like that?" Maddox smiled understandingly, and Joe looked demure.

"Just like you say, okay?"

Maddox nodded.

"Now, you know, money deviates so much," he said, showing signs of developing the thought, but Clemon was still earthbound with the mechanics of earning it first.

"Now what we need," he said, "what we need to do . . ."

But Joe was with Maddox, and ignored him.

"He explained to me," he said, "that the last transaction was in diamonds, and they don't depreciate."

"No," agreed Clemon, giving in. "And then, then your silver's going . . . Silver is better than gold."

"Right," said Joe.

"Silver is better than gold, right?" Clemon was grateful for the confirmation.

"Right. Diamonds is better than all of it."

"And diamonds is the top," conceded Clemon.

"Top of the line."

"We gonna be in the market where we can do that," Maddox observed.

"I'm going have a diamond ring to set up on my finger," said Clemon happily.

"I want one up my ass about that damn big," said Joe, entering into the spirit of the thing. "So everybody can see me walking down the street." He took a few steps, bandy-legged, across the room. "Here I come."

"I'm gonna get me one," said Clemon, choking with laughter. "I'm gonna have me one made . . ."

Maddox tried to strike a more serious note.

"Well, of course, everybody's interested in having a diamond," he said. "But I'm gonna make sure that whatever it is, I can convert it to what I need at the time I need it."

"And what's better to convert than diamonds?" Joe demanded triumphantly.

"Nothing," said Clemon. "Nothing. Now, lemme get down to this point, then we'll talk or ramble all we want. You will look over this document, over this twenty percent?"

"That's what I wanna ask you." Joe was all business again. "When can I see the documents? I wanna have my lawyers look at it."

"Okay."

Maddox called Atlanta to speak to his contact, Jim Benson, whom he described as secretary of the Chamber of Commerce in Washington, D.C. While they waited for him to get through, Joe brought up the subject of Landon Williams, thinking to get the substance of his earlier conversation with Boyle on an FBI tape with a commentary from Clemon, but Clemon would only agree that Williams was "double-minded" and "crazy."

Maddox then rejoined the conversation, saying he would have to call again in a few minutes. All the people they needed to touch base with were in Atlanta, he said. He had spent the previous evening, for instance, with John Calhoun, President Ford's special assistant for minority affairs. Not to be outdone when it came to "politics," Clemon then launched into another of his largely incomprehensible anecdotes, this time about his dealings with President Nixon's special assistant, Bob Diamond, and was brought back to business only by Joe's insistence on seeing the shipping agreement which Maddox claimed had been concluded between the Office of Minority Enterprises and the Maritime Administration.

Maddox then tried and failed for a second time to raise his man in Atlanta. At this, Clemon proposed, and the other two agreed, that all the interested parties should bring their lawyers and advisers to Miami for a planning session at the earliest opportunity.

After that, there was little else to talk about. Joe asked Maddox in passing if he could help him get a stevedore's license in Savannah, as his relationship with James seemed to be deteriorating, and Maddox offered to go with him to see the city manager.

"And if he don't get it," he said musingly, "you know what happens?"

"What?"

"We better go to the Police Department. I'll talk to the new Chief of Police here. That's why they got me down there."

That reminded Joe of his promise to Agent Stevens.

"What about all them policemen that I read about yesterday in the newspaper?" he asked.

"Ah, they going be all right." Maddox dismissed it with a wave.

"How? Not what *I* read in the newspaper."

"Naw. See, that's another thing. You see, it's a different game. It's racially motivated, this department here. Now, there might be some, ah, some of these guys, ah, ah . . . It came from the old administration. The FBI conducted investigation, and when they conducted investigation, they didn't have enough evidence to even carry it before the federal grand jury."

"Well, that's typical of the FBI," said Joe, loud enough almost for his voice to carry to the next room without a microphone. "They come in and cause all kinds of shit."

As Maddox was not to be drawn further on the subject, Joe set about winding up the discussion. He was tired. Clemon was yawning, too, but he still had a final dose of political wisdom to impart. The Republicans had already lost the Presidential race, he said, because "all the people know what's going on. You understand what I mean?"

"Labor's going with Carter," Joe said sagely.

"*I* know it," Clemon said. "*You* know it. And when Carter go in, Cloyd Hall is Carter's number one man. He going be sitting right there. Right?"

"It could happen."

Joe stood up and stretched, and the others got to their feet. As a Republican from Georgia, however, Bishop Maddox was not prepared to yield the last word to a Democrat from Alabama.

"In the State of Georgia," he remarked, "we got a powerful friend in Herman Talmadge."

"You got Talmadge?" Joe said. "The U.S. Senator?"

"Right. We got him. I just got a man an ICC license here."

"Yeah?" said Clemon, impressed.

"And he been trying for years to get a license. So I just gave it to him."

He laughed modestly, and Joe pumped him by the hand.

"Reverend," he said. "It's been a pleasure."

He saw them safely to the elevator, then tapped on the door next to his for a word with Agent Stevens.

"Well? What do you think?"

"Oh, man. This shit is heavy."

"Okay. Well, stand by your machine. I got Jimmy Roberts coming in tomorrow."

That was a serious disappointment, however. Roberts's purpose was not, as Joe had supposed, to discuss the expansion of their partnership into Mobile and other Gulf ports, but to dissolve it.

"Joey, believe me," he said. "I love you. I think the world of you. But I gotta speak frank. We just ain't making any fucking money, Joey, and things are tight. To be honest with you, well, we're trying to, you know, tighten up on our, you know, bad investments."

Joe chewed his lip.

"If you can't make other arrangements in time," Roberts went on, "we'll go another. I'm not gonna leave you, you know, hanging. But that's what I'd like, to be honest with you."

Joe eyed him coldly. He was not used to being thought of as a bad investment. It was also necessary to keep Georgia Container Agencies afloat for the sake of the investigation.

As soon as Roberts left, he put in a call to John Caputo.

16
Feints and Skirmishes

At forty-four, Joe was learning all kinds of disturbing things about himself. One was that security bored him. While he truly loved his family, he loved them most when he was most in danger of losing them, and it was the same in business. He felt most alive in change and crisis. Though he complained, often sincerely, about the demands it made on his life, what finally bound him to the shipping industry was the ceaseless coming and going—a restlessness that perfectly matched his own.

But there were limits.

His decision to fight Field and Barone had been the right one because it was the inescapable one, given his temperament. But given his temperament, he had primed himself for a charge, not a siege. Eight months of emotional isolation and continuous exposure to the risk of discovery had pared the issue down to survival. Never mind the bullshit. Field, Scotto, Barone—all of them had to go before his stamina ran out.

He spent a whole day with Ray Maria, preparing the ground for the two new undercover agents sent down by the Bureau in Washington. The first of them, introduced as Special Agent Dick Aber (although Joe suspected, as he had with Carter, that his real name was something else), was already in training for the Mobile office, where he would pass as a second cousin of Joe's, but Miami presented a problem. The second agent, introduced as Bill Owens, would be working with Mutzie and Bobby Kratish, who knew all Joe's relatives, by blood and marriage, as well as he did. Owens needed a cover story for *them,* as well as for Boyle and Turner, and he needed it urgently for Miami was where Joe was feeling the pressure.

Lying awake that night, he suddenly remembered the oil survey ship that Eagle had fitted out some 10 years earlier.

"Hey, Mutzie," he said next morning. "I think I found somebody to help us out."

"Yeah?"

"Yeah. Remember that kid, that deckhand you liked, on the survey boat?"

Mutzie shook his head, reasonably enough, for there had been no such person.

"I don't even remember the boat," he said.

"You're losing your grip, you know that? The one we fixed up for Texas Instruments."

"That one. My God, that was *years* ago."

"Right. And this kid was on it. Bill Owens?"

Mutzie looked doubtful.

"Sure you do. Bright kid? Real hard worker? You told Ben he ought to hire him, but we didn't have room."

"Yeah, I do remember something like that. Yeah."

"Well, he remembers *you* all right. Sent his regards. I met him in New York last time. And he's looking for work."

"Yeah, but he's in New York."

"Don't worry," said Joe, disgusted. "He'll pay his own way down."

By afternoon, it was Mutzie's own idea to hire him, but Joe still had three weeks of Boyle and Barone to contend with before Owens could start, and they were pressing him hard for money. Almost every day, he had some new threat or warning to report to Ray Maria, although even Vanderwyde was beginning to understand that there was little Joe could do until he was paid by Zim.

From the start, James Stevedores had been slow to bill Georgia Container Agencies but quick to demand payment. Already pushing Zim for settlement of accounts past due, Joe immediately passed on each new set of charges, but these, too, were invariably held up while Zim questioned them, item by item. And as the flow of cargo was much faster than the flow of cash, the result was disillusionment for James, frustration for Joe, and baffled displeasure for George Barone.

Toward the end of June, GCA at last received $25,000 on account from Zim, out of which Boyle immediately claimed $2,000 toward the rent arrears, but Joe was determined to stall until Bill Owens reported for work on July 1.

On Owens's first morning, Cleveland Turner stopped by the office. He wanted $200 in cash and a pair of free cruise tickets for himself and his girlfriend. Joe took him inside, introduced him to Owens, gave him two

$100 bills in an envelope, and announced that his troubles were over.

"This here's gonna be my man in Miami," he said. "Don't deal with the relatives no more. If I'm not here, deal with him. And I don't want any more of these eighteen-, twenty-man gangs, okay? Fifteen is enough."

Turner put away his envelope, and shook Owens by the hand.

Boyle called for a little more finesse.

One afternoon, Joe went over to his office with Owens, who was carrying the money. Finding him out, they left a message to the effect that Joe had his overdue reports ready. An hour or so later, when Boyle came looking for his $2,400, Joe was tied up on the telephone, trying to arrange bond for a ship in Panama. He had given the envelope to "the kid," he said, who was working in the warehouse. But Owens had already left for the day, by prearrangement, and when Boyle returned to the office after a fruitless search, he found Joe had gone, too.

He called him at home that evening.

"Hey, listen," he said irritably. "The kid wasn't there. And I don't want him walking around with my twenty-four reports. I wanna get 'em in."

"Okay," said Joe. "No sweat. I'll send him around in the morning."

"No good," said Boyle. "I'm leaving early for Savannah."

"So he'll see you with it when you get back."

"Forget it. I know you. I wanna tell Fred you're up to date. You better have the kid meet me at the airport."

"Hey, come on, Bill. It's getting late," Joe protested. "I can't call the guy at this hour."

"Fuck that," said Boyle. "You better take this more serious. Call now. I wanna see the kid there at the gate with the money."

And that was that. Having demanded a payoff from Owens once, Boyle could hardly object to taking others from him in future. It was now Dick Aber's turn.

To prepare him for his role as vice president of Georgia Container Agencies in Mobile, Joe had arranged for him to spend a few weeks in New Orleans, training with James Stevedores, who had yet to act on Roberts's half-hearted notice of withdrawal. The next step was to introduce Aber to Zim, which Joe planned to do on July 20, when he was due in New York to sign the stevedoring contract and to discuss the line's plans for Jacksonville, New Orleans, and Houston.

On the Friday before his departure, the sixteenth, Caputo called to say that the Zim agency account in Mobile would not be awarded to Joe after all; just the stevedoring—the agency was going to A & G, the subsidiary of the McGrath Corporation, with whom they had previously considered trying to make a three-way deal. It was another mouth to feed, he said, but what the hell. It might also take them into ports they could otherwise never have touched.

Joe was rather pleased on the whole. It looked like the chance they had been waiting for to examine Scotto's links with McGrath from the inside, and it was also a rare opportunity for rubbing Boyle's nose in the dirt.

"When you leaving for Chicago?" Boyle asked him that afternoon.

"To the convention, you mean? I'm not going."

Boyle pretended to stagger. "Not *going?* What are you talking about? You gotta go."

"The hell I do. You buy your own fucking drinks. I gotta go to New York, get some money out of Zim. I got obligations to meet."

"Yeah, you do." Seeing he was serious, Boyle was seriously displeased. "You're behind with your payments again."

"Well, fuck you, William," Joe said warmly. "Fifteen thousand for Savannah, and I still got labor problems. Now ten more for Mobile, and I'm not even getting the fucking agency. All I do is pay out and pay out, and nothing comes back."

"Not getting the agency?" It was news to Boyle.

"No," he said, with a curl of pleasure.

"Who's getting it, then?"

"A & G, okay? McGrath. Fucking Scotto's getting it."

He would have liked a picture for a souvenir. Boyle actually swayed from the impact. His high color turned to mud, then flooded back again so vividly he looked as if he might have a stroke.

"I wanna know what I'm paying for," Joe grumbled, hugging himself. "Somebody's gotta take care of this for me."

Boyle wiped his mouth tenderly, as if Joe had slapped him. "I . . . I'll talk to George."

"Yeah. *Do* that."

Joe flew to New York on Monday evening, and checked into the Americana Hotel, where he confered with Carter and Aber on the tactics they would follow for the next two or three days. In the morning, he took Aber with him to Zim's headquarters in the International Trade Center, and stayed all day, working through a long agenda with Ilan that included the Savannah situation, and James's stevedoring charges; Mobile, and the award of the agency to A & G; the other ports Zim was soon to enter; the problems of splitting repairs and trucking between two or more firms in each port, and the money Zim owed him, which now amounted to close on $100,000.

The following day, he took Aber to meet Caputo, who welcomed him into New York's racket circles as warmly as he had Bob Carter. Bob Partos was now working for Sonny Montella at CC Lumber, he said, the company that Scotto controlled through the Lacquas. Montella was with Quin Marine Services which, Caputo claimed, Scotto controlled. Phil Lacqua, Joey's brother, ran Marine Repair Services, of Staten Island, with his partner, Vincent Marino, who was also related to Scotto by marriage. These were all people who carried a lot of weight, Caputo said.

None of this was news to Joe, but it was good for Aber to hear these things independently, and Caputo liked to talk. He went on to describe a $10 million project he was working on for Exxon Corporation, involving the bulk shipment of petrochemicals from Saudi Arabia.

"John, how do you handle something like that?" Joe asked, meaning how many ships would be involved, and how would he schedule them?

"Five percent," said Caputo, misunderstanding him entirely. "Cash. Up front."

Next morning, Joe flew back to Miami for his day of judgment.

In fact, it took only 15 minutes. Assured that Joe's continuing contribution was essential to a national crime investigation, Judge Leonard Rivkind was satisfied that "the ends of justice and the welfare of society" did not require that he "should suffer the penalty authorized by law." He accepted Joe's *nolo contendere* plea to the charge of solicitation to murder, and fined him $1,000, with a year's non-reporting probation.

The rest of the week was blessedly quiet, with the ILA contingent away in Chicago, but by the following Monday, it was business as usual. Boyle came over, in convalescent mood, to demand $1,000 by Thursday. If Joe was going to be away, he said, "the kid" could give it to him. He had also discussed Zim's agency arrangement for Mobile with Barone and Vanderwyde, and asked Joe to stop by the office next day for a ruling on that.

He got it in four words: No deals with A&G.

"Uh, okay, George."

Neither Barone, Vanderwyde, nor Boyle had offered him a chair. He stood before them as though before a court martial.

"I told Caputo the, ah, politics would have to be straightened out first. Before we could do anything," he added, at a near-shout.

Barone seemed to be having trouble with one of his hearing aids. He shook it, frowning.

"Right. That's good you said that. I don't want you making no deals up there."

Joe perched on the edge of the desk.

"Caputo puts me in with these guys," he said. "We talk. I see you. You tell me what to do."

"Yeah."

"Okay. Now what about Mobile? The front money. If A & G's gonna get the agency, I don't think it's right if . . ."

Barone gestured impatiently, like brushing a fly from his nose.

"You don't listen" he said. "Fuck A & G. You pay the money, you get the stevedoring and you get the agency, like I told you."

Joe looked to Vanderwyde for confirmation, then back again.

"You mean, you fixed it? A & G's out of the picture?"

"They weren't never in it," said Vanderwyde.

"Well, *I* told him that," Boyle said. "Didn't I tell you, see Jay?"

Joe shrugged.

"Anyway, we're gonna need twenty-five hundred for the first payment. At least," Boyle added hastily, catching Vanderwyde's eye.

"Okay. Well, I'm going up tomorrow to get Dick Aber started. Do we deal with Isom or what? I heard he got beat out as president."

Barone looked disgusted.

"Yeah," he said. "See Isom. George Dixon took over the Local, but you know how these niggers fuck around. Don't get involved. Isom's still boss up there. Deal with Isom."

As befitted his status, Clemon took them to lunch next day at the Malaga restaurant in Mobile. On the way there, Aber handed Joe an envelope containing four marked $100 bills, and Joe dropped it in Clemon's lap.

"There you go, Isom," he said. "Four hundred. Fifty a week for a month, makes two. Plus a hundred for the *Eshkol,* and another hundred for next week, makes four."

"That's my kinda 'rithmetic," said the silent power of the South.

"Okay. And, Dick, every two weeks, Isom gets his envelope, understand?"

"Right," said Aber. "Understood."

"And don't be late. Because if you are, and Isom calls, then you got trouble with *me.* "

"Don't worry. I'll take care of it."

"That's right," said Isom. "We all gonna take good care of each other, and have a real nice time."

The staff of the Malaga greeted them like royalty, the maitre d' and captain both asking after "Freddy." As soon as they were seated, Joe took this as his cue to pump Clemon for Aber's benefit about Field's local connections, notably with Governor George Wallace; the Port Director, Bob Hope, and U.S. District Judge Hand. This led them into the wider context of Southern politics, and among the other names Clemon dropped were those of Senators Sam Nunn and Herman Talmadge of Georgia and Governor Jimmy Carter's aides, Cloyd Hall and Phil Courtney.

"That reminds me," Joe said. "I wanted to ask you about this Triworld deal. What's happening with that?"

"Hey, we active," said Clemon cheerfully.

"Yeah?"

"Yeah, we been real busy on that. Look like we got a couple of deals cooking. We 'bout ready to start."

"Well, I been waiting to hear from you guys about the meeting," Joe said. "We were all gonna meet in Miami on this twenty percent deal, right? With the Maritime Administration?"

"Yeah, yeah. Right, right. We'll get to it. Frank, he got busy with his conference and all, and then Chicago, you know? But we got this fertilizer now. 'Bout fifty thousand tons urea fertilizer in San Diego. Cloyd Hall, he working on it. He just gotta make a few calls, then we ready to move."

"Does Freddy get a piece of this?"

"Oh, *yeah.*" Clemon was astounded he should ask such a question. "We gotta take care of the man."

After lunch, Clemon drove them over to see the Port Director, Bob Hope, and on the way back, they passed several hundred brand-new Army trucks lined up, nose to tail, on the dock.

"Hey, Isom," said Joe. "You get that military contract Fred was talking about?"

"Yeah, we got a piece of that. Right."

"Well, how the hell did he swing it? They were gonna ship 'em all out of Baltimore is what *I* heard."

"Well, you know Freddy," said Clemon. "He in pretty good with, ah, you know, them defense people."

Aber cleared his throat.

"Ah, what military contract was that," he asked.

"I'll tell you later," Joe said.

Clemon dropped them off at the hotel on his way home, and after making a few calls, Aber drove Joe to the airport.

"Looks like we got a streak going here," he said.

"Yeah, I'd say so. I'd say we got a couple of things to run with."

"You were going to tell me about that military contract, Joe. With the trucks?"

"Oh, yeah. You know, somebody's gotta take another look at that, Dick. Couple of months back, I saw Fat Freddy with Bill Boyle, and he says, 'Listen, Chrysler–Dodge are shipping three thousand trucks to Europe for the U.S. Army.' Replacements, okay? 'You wanna piece of that?' he says. 'They're going out of Baltimore, but I figure we can get a bunch of 'em for Mobile, or maybe Savannah.' "

"What's in it for him?"

"Well, that's what I asked him. 'Ten percent,' he says. That's around three hundred a truck, okay?"

"Oh, boy. Times three thousand? That's a nice piece of change."

"Well, let's say he only got two or three hundred of 'em, he's still not hurting, right? So anyhow, I told Ray Maria what Freddy said, and he says, 'Okay, I'll get right on it.' Comes back a couple of days later, says, 'Hey, Joe, you must have got it wrong. We checked with the Defense Department, and nobody there even heard about any contract for shipping trucks. Either he's blowing smoke, or you got it wrong.' Well . . . Okay. '*I* didn't get it wrong,' I said. 'I'm just telling you what *he* told *me.*' So I got hold of Boyle and said I'll take a pass and forgot about it."

"Until you saw the goddamn trucks on the dock there," said Aber. "Okay. I'll check on that."

"Yeah. Did I get it wrong? Or did the fucking ILA know what the Pentagon was gonna do before the Pentagon knew itself? I mean, that's heavy, right?"

"Yeah. That's heavy."

There was a lot to talk to Maria about over the next several weeks. Gus Hulander consulted Joe on a problem concerning four trailer-loads of Lorillard cigarettes for export that, under ILA contract rules, would either have to be unpacked and repacked on the dock by ILA labor before shipment, or, if that requirement were waived, entail substantial payments into the union's container royalty fund. Not caring much for either alternative, a Lorillard executive wanted to know if there was a third course. Joe said he would put the question to Boyle, as an officer of the checkers' union and vice president of the International.

Nothing simpler, said Boyle. For $200 a trailer, he would put them through himself.

Joe passed the word back to Hulander, who in turn cleared the arrangement with his client, and the trailers were duly nodded through. By arrangement with Hulander, the payoff was also nodded through to PTO as "extra handling charges."

Joe also had to keep Maria up to date about Boyle's plans for going into business for himself. Following their lunchtime talk in Savannah, he now wanted Joe to form a container repair company in Mobile, in which Boyle would hold a 40 percent interest through his daughter, Patty Kiernan. Joe and Dick Aber would each be allowed a 20 percent stake, while the remaining 20 percent would be shared between DeMott and Hodges, of Great Southern Trailer.

"Don't fuck around anymore with Scotto," Boyle said paternally. "We got it made up there. We got Integrated Container Service. We got Interpool, Container Transport International . . . We got everybody. Exclusive. A fucking monopoly, and Isom'll keep it that way. Scotto can't do nothing for you. It's our town."

"I'll think about it," Joe said.

"What's to think about? All you gotta do is buy a mobile repair unit, and Isom'll take you into every steamship company in the fucking port, for Chrissake."

"You wanna come up with forty percent of what it's gonna cost me? Or is that another story?"

"Shit," said Boyle. *"I'm* making *you* rich, and *I* gotta pay *you?"*

"Never mind rich. Just get me my money from Zim, and then we'll talk some more."

Zim's slowness in paying its bills was more than just an excuse for fending him off. Joe was feverishly juggling accounts to cope with a genuine cash crisis now, as Boyle well knew.

A few days later, Cleveland Turner asked Joe to come to his office, which was unusual, for he generally called at PTO to pick up his payments. As he sounded hungry, Ray Maria suggested they try him with another check, and when Joe sauntered into Local 1416's office to deliver it, he found Turner in earnest conversation with a City of Miami police officer, who excused himself the moment he saw Joe and left. Turner hesitated, caught at an awkward moment, then beckoned Joe into his private office, peeling off his jacket as he did so to reveal a holstered handgun in the back pocket of his pants.

"I got something for you," said Joe, dropping his check for $200 on the desk. Turner fingered it doubtfully. "I'll be gone again for a while, but that should take care of things in the meantime. Any problems, you just see Bill Owens, okay?"

Turner pushed the check back across the desk.

"You ain't got no cash?"

"Hey, nothing wrong with *that,* Cleve. You took checks before. Lots of times."

"Uh-uh. You gotta make it cash money, Joey. Can't take no more checks."

"Why?" Joe picked it up, hoping he looked offended. "You don't trust me all of a sudden? Shit."

"Ain't that." He leaned forward, and lowered his voice. "You wanna be careful, Joe. They got another investigation going."

"*Another* one?" Joe laughed, and pulled out his billfold.

"No, no. For real."

"The cop tell you? The guy that just left?"

"No, I heard federal this time. They say they gonna have another grand jury sitting."

"Well, that's news to me," Joe said. "Look, I only got a hundred and sixty. I'll haveta owe you forty."

"Well, that's all right, Joey. I know you're good for it."

"Yeah. I may be a little late doing it, Cleve, but I'm gonna take care of *all* you guys, believe me."

Maria agreed that Turner's information was pretty good, but Levin said it was not time to swear in a grand jury yet. The minute they started serving subpoenas, he said, the bad guys would stop what they were doing or run for cover. There was a lot more to find out before they all went underground, particularly in New York. Also in Mobile, said Maria. What was happening on the fertilizer deal, for instance?

On August 10, Joe made a recorded call from the Airport Lakes Holiday Inn to find out.

"Hey, Joey," said Isom. "How you doing, man?"

"Well, I'll tell you the truth. I'm busting my ass trying to get this fertilizer . . . you know, this urea . . . straightened out."

"Right."

"But I run into some problems, and I . . ."

"Where's your problem at?"

"All right. Now here's what I run into, all right? I called New York, and New York can position the boat for seventeen thousand tons."

"Uh-huh."

"I told 'em you had ten thousand tons spotted, and seven thousand tons more coming."

"Right."

"And New York wants to know, who is the shipper? New York wants to know who's gonna do the loading?"

"Uh-huh."

"New York wants to know who is gonna do the unloading, and who gonna pay the demurrage?"

"Okay."

"In case the boat is late."

"All right."

"All right?" asked Joe expectantly.

"Okay," said Clemon, as though the whole thing was now settled.

Joe blinked, holding the telephone at arm's length, then shook himself and started again.

"I've been trying to get hold of Cloyd Hall," he said.

"Uh-huh."

"I can't get him *or* Phil Courtney, either one, so I figured I'd call you."

"Okay. I'll get one of 'em right away and have 'em call you. What number you at?"

As Joe could hardly give him the Holiday Inn's number, he changed signals, and said *he* would try Hall again within the hour, assuming Clemon would speak to him first to explain the situation.

"Let's get down to some nitty-gritty," he said. "Okay?"

"Uh-huh."

"I wanna know how this thing's gonna be handled." Desperation was setting in. "Okay? I got it in my head what you have told me."

"Right."

"The three dollars a ton for you and Cloyd and me."

"That's all," Clemon agreed.

"Okay. And I got the five percent put away for Freddy and them."

"Right."

"Okay. That's covered."

"Covered," said Clemon.

"And the freight will be paid in Switzerland, just like we said?"

"Right."

"Okay. I gotta know which bank I'm going to."

"Okay."

That was all. Joe rapped himself on the head with the telephone, and tossed it on the bed. Maria smiled, and handed it back to him.

"How do I handle it?" Joe asked angelically.

"All right. Well, when you ask Cloyd . . . See, just tell him what bank it's gonna be, and the man out there will tell you."

Joe took off his glasses. Then he moistened his lips.

"Okay," he said, replacing his glasses. "Now who's gonna take care of Freddy? Me with the five percent? Or do I give *you* the five percent, and you and Cloyd take care of Freddy?"

"No, you just . . . You just hold that."

"Yeah. So I'll give that to Freddy directly."

"Right. Okay?"

"Okay. That's what I wanted to know."

"All right, boss," said Clemon, glad to have been of service.

Cloyd Hall was hardly more helpful. When Joe called, Hall explained how the urea 46 came to be in San Diego, but the loading and delivery arrangements, he thought, would be up to Joe and the buyer, when they found one. A couple of people were interested.

"I want to get into this," Hall said, "because I think we got a unique combination going, with Isom's long connections over the years of knowing what comes in and out of these ports, and then, uh, with my connections, in terms of, uh, bringing the business to Georgia, and my governmental contacts. If I can build up a situation where I can spot things that can be bought and sold, I'll be in a position to . . ."

"You've got some good governmental contacts?" Joe inquired, trying to salvage something.

"Well, see, I was Carter's special assistant for four years as Governor of Georgia," said Hall modestly.

"I didn't know that."

"Yeah. And although, when I say that, I want, uh, preface the remark that I would never, you know, do anything to, that would embarrass the Governor, or, or, or in any way make it non-ethical or non . . . or not legal. But the point is, the connections are there. In other words, uh, Congressman Andrew Young, one of the most powerful Congressmen in the Congress. Uh, and he's handled all of the Governor's minority support . . . Kind of a unique individual. He's big in Africa. He's big in . . . He's on the banking committee that's talking about Cuba."

"Yeah," said Joe, bored.

"These are connections that I have that, uh . . . Herman Talmadge, who heads up the agricultural in the Senate. Close friend. So really, not doing anything unethical, but just good business. I've got these kind of contacts. I've been thinking about how we can, we parlay these. People are making money, you know, by putting things together, and I have these contacts . . . We would like very much to put some things together. I think Isom would like very much to throw business, you know, your way on some of these things."

"I would, too," said Joe. "Isom told me, you know, about this other load of cargo that had carried."

"Right."

"And I'd like to be paid the same way. You know, right through Switzerland, which is beautiful. And he said I can ask you, and you'd even tell me which banker I should go to."

"Well, I hate to act ignorant on it," Hall said hesitantly. "I'll be glad to call Isom and, you know . . . In other words, I have not gotten into freight at all. I simply found the commodity that he wanted."

"Okay. But I tell you, it's getting to the point, Cloyd, where I'm getting tired of it. You know, I've spent like a thousand dollars on telephone calls on this."

"I see. And I'm . . . I'm embarrassed about it because it looks, it appears that we're more inept than we really are."

"Yes," said Joe.

Unable to bring himself to talk to Clemon again, he told Maria to have Dick Aber pursue it, if Aber was willing to risk having his brain softened. And a few days later, Joe received another call from Jimmy Roberts, of James Stevedores, that brought him back to sterner matters.

He was sorry, Roberts said, more resolutely than last time. He knew Joe was having trouble getting money from Zim, but Georgia Container Agencies now owed James about $150,000. And unless Joe could pay a large part of that off right away, James could not work his next ship, which was due in Savannah in three days.

17

Resistance Stiffens

THE whole juggling act had begun to go wrong, but he was tired of it anyway.

"I opened the door, didn't I?" he said to Maria. "Let in three of your guys? Who did that before? Who else gave you stuff like this? What do you want of my life?"

He called Savannah, and arranged for Southeast Maritime to take over from James Stevedoring.

Boyle almost had a seizure. Southeast belonged to another group, he said. If Joe knew what was good for him, he would cancel his instructions immediately.

Well, who was going to load the ship?

Harrington, said Boyle, and Joe laughed.

To calm him down, he sent Bill Owens over to Boyle's house early on Saturday morning, August 21, with $800 for the four trailer-loads of Lorillard cigarettes that Boyle had nodded through. Once a week, bag-man Boyle met Fat Freddy, Barone, and the others in the barbershop of the Holiday Inn at 21st Street and Collins Avenue, Miami Beach, for their carve-up of the take.

Monday morning, Boyle returned to the attack. Barone was mad at Joe about Southeast Maritime, he said, and madder still about the money owing, which included $3,500 due for Mobile. Barone would be coming over later to ream his ass about it, and on no account should Joe talk back. Boyle offered that advice as "a friend."

He returned after lunch, very sober, and escorted Joe into the hall. Barone, who had been zig-zagging up and down, paused and fixed his gaze disquietingly on Joe's throat.

"You got me very upset," he said, in his hollow, resonant baritone. "You trying to make me upset?"

"No, I don't wanna upset you, George." Nose to nose, Barone was not much bigger than he was. "And *I* don't wanna get upset either."

"Then you know what you gotta do. You call Southeast Maritime and tell 'em, thanks, but you got a deal with Harrington to do the work."

"George." He ignored Boyle's signals. "I told Bill, and now I'm telling you. I won't work with Harrington. Anybody else, fine. I mean, so long as their rates are okay."

Barone looked at him, as at an object of doubtful utility. Fred Field often looked at people the same way.

"You work with who I tell you to," he said carefully. "Either that, or you lose every goddamn piece of business you got. And I mean Zim. I mean Nopal. I mean Zonis. You understand what I'm saying to you?"

"Yes, George. And I'll work with anybody you say except Harrington. There, I gotta take a pass."

Barone decided not to hear this.

"Be a good boy," he said. "Don't make trouble. I'll tell you who to work with, you'll work with 'em, and we won't have no trouble." Having said what he had come to say, he had no more time or interest to waste on it. "Now I gotta meet Fred."

Taken by surprise, Boyle stayed long enough to wag a finger and warn Joe again not to argue before scurrying after him.

They returned a few minutes later. Barone had forgotten to mention the overdue payments. Had "the Jews" sent any money yet?

No, said Joe. Barone could do them both a favor by talking to Captain Ilan about it.

Barone was not pleased with this answer. Nor was Fred Field, according to Boyle. The best way to relieve the tension, he said next morning, would be for Joe to give him $5,500, representing $3,500 for Mobile, and $1,000 each for Savannah and Miami.

The best way to get that much money, Joe replied, would be for Boyle to persuade Zim to pay its bills.

The following day, Boyle returned to hint at stronger measures. Barone had gone to New York for Ed Cummiskey's funeral, he said.

"Cummiskey?" The name meant nothing to Joe.

"Yeah. Rich Kenny died. You know, the president of George's Local up there. 1804?"

"I didn't know that."

"Yeah. So Cummiskey and his partner got whacked out."

Joe could not see the connection. "Why?"

"Why? Because he had a big mouth."

Joe shook his head. "Bill, you trying to give me some kind of a message, or what?"

"I'm just saying you better work with Harrington," Boyle said, avoiding his eye. "George went up there special for the funeral."

"You mean, it's like the Roaring Twenties, right? You kill somebody, then send a big bunch of flowers?"

"What can I tell you?" He hunched his shoulders. "You come up with some money, Joe, and that'll relieve a lot of tension."

He was back again on Thursday, the fourth day in a row. He wanted Joe to agree at least to have lunch with Harrington when he called, but Joe refused. He would take the call, he said, but he had other plans, which was true. He had promised Maria he would try to record a conversation with Captain Ilan before he returned to New York, and another with Harvey Sykes.

Wearing a Nagra body recorder for the first time in almost six months, Joe took Ilan on a tour of the new warehouse and container storage area just allotted to PTO on the southeast corner of Dodge Island, and tried to line him up as an ally in his dispute with James.

"Barone says to me, 'Hey! Why haven't you paid James?' I said, 'I haven't paid James, two reasons. First, James has to live with the contract that he made with me. And secondly, I'm not banker for Zim. When Zim pays me, I will pay James.' "

"Yeah," said Ilan.

"So Barone says, 'Hey, you know, you're holding out on me now.' I said, 'Well, I can't help it. I don't have my funds.' So he started to lean on me. He said he was gonna see you at the convention. Did he see you?"

"He wasn't there. And you know something? I want to give you a very good tip, see?"

"Go ahead."

"Further you stay away from him, further you make less deals with these guys. My advice to you is to stay away. He is bad news now."

"Who is bad news now?"

"Barone. Don't say I said it."

"I'm talking to you."

"This is for your own health, okay? They know a hell of a lot," said Ilan, with heavy emphasis. "They know things *I* don't know . . . I were you, I would say, fuck it. You don't need this kind of help, okay? You can live honestly, and make money."

"I tell you something, okay? You can believe this if you want, but Barone turns the labor on and off here."

"Okay. We know that."

Joe shook his head. In one breath, Ilan was warning him to stay clear of Barone, and in the next, conceding Barone's power to put him out of business. He came back to his troubles with James, but Ilan grabbed his arm, and brought them both to a halt.

"There's a fucking story going on," he said, "and I can't imagine where it came from. Somebody was yapping. You know, those guys are so stupid. They're talking all over the place, and always in the worst places. Like Ponte's, and all these places."

"Yeah."

"You know that there's three tables bugged in Ponte's? And there are five bugs at the bar. And the public phone is bugged, you see."

"Yeah, yeah."

"And it's no joke, because these bugs and these tapes are, I think, is a federal order."

The more he talked about it, the more unhappy Ilan made himself. He also seemed a little irritated by Joe's problems with James, and paid only perfunctory attention to PTO's new container facilities.

"Listen." Ilan lowered his voice confidentially. "I can only tell 'em I've been down here and ask you whether there was any payoffs, and you assured me there were not. You can prove it in the books."

Joe clapped him on the back.

"I go one step further than that," he said. "Here is a case where James is trying to charge extra money that they are not entitled to, and I refuse to pay it. Is that enough?"

"That's good enough," said Ilan, satisfied. "Very good."

Ten minutes after returning him to the parking lot, Joe set out on his second tour of PTO's new yard, this time with Harvey Sykes, and by car because his feet hurt. As they drove out to the site, he explained how he had just taken Ilan through the files to show him that James was trying to overcharge by $60,000, and how Boyle was pressing him to replace James with Harrington.

"So I said, 'I'm not working with Harrington.' He says, 'At least talk to him.' What do you think Neal asked me a ton?"

"Five-fifty?" Sykes suggested.

"Would you believe eleven-twenty-five a ton? To do stevedoring? And he says, 'That's my price,' and I told him, 'It's out of proportion.' "

"*How* much?"

"Eleven-twenty-five . . . . He says, 'That's my price.' "

Sykes blew a derisive raspberry.

"Okay," he said. "You talked to him. Now fuck him."

"Okay, I talked to him. Now what do I do with George?"

As Sykes saw it, Ilan had to say whether or not he was committed to James through some deal in New York they knew nothing about. If not, then Barone had to come up with an alternative to Harrington.

"He owes you two things now," he said. "He owes you a good stevedore up there, with labor. And he owes you to keep you the fuck out of a battle with Scotto's bunch."

Joe shook his head. "You know what Bill Boyle says to me? And this is between us, huh?"

"Bill is a good boy," said Sykes. "I love Bill. He says a lot of things out of school that could really hurt him. When he feels for you, he goes to bat for you."

Joe stared him into silence. "Yesterday, Bill comes up to me, and he says, 'You know this guy Cummiskey in Jersey?' I said, 'Who's he?' He says, 'He got whacked out because he had a big mouth.' "

Sykes gaped, and Joe nodded grimly.

"So I said, 'What are you telling me, Bill?' He said, 'Work with Harrington.' How do you read that, Harvey?"

Sykes was genuinely shaken.

"That sure don't sound very promising," he said. "I never heard Bill talk like that one day in my life."

"But that didn't come from Bill."

"No, of course not. He wouldn't tell you that on his own. No way." He pulled himself together. "You can't work with Harrington at eleven and change," he said flatly. "It ain't there."

"I'd rather give up the whole business," said Joe. "I'd rather close the fucking doors and go out of business."

"Up there?"

As Sykes realized that a substantial piece of his livelihood was probably in jeopardy again, his color rose and his eyes widened in alarm.

"We're not gonna let that cocksucker squeeze us out up there," he said viciously. "We all put in too much fucking blood and sweat to really get the goddamn thing going to let these bastards squeeze us out. George owes us *something.*"

"*Us?*" said Joe distantly.

"Forget me." Sykes lost his composure entirely. "George owes *you* something . . ."

"Do you think Ilan lied to me when he says he didn't see George? You think he *did* see him?

Sykes shook his head. "I don't think Ilan's gonna lie to you. He's an Israeli. No, I think that's the Barone bullshit. I don't think he saw him at all. I've seen George do that a thousand times, to impress somebody with his position. 'I've told that cocksucker that I'd put him in fucking cement if he . . .' And he never saw the guy. I've seen him do that many times."

"But he's not beyond killing you either."

"No, no, no. That's for sure. I'll look you in the eye and tell you that's for sure." He laughed uncomfortably. "But George has to know that he got you into this. You've been playing his game for a long time, and you've taken care of him royally. You're on his team. And it's time for him to support you on this thing." An unpleasant thought struck him. "Unless he *can't.*"

Sykes considered that possibility for a moment.

"If he looks you in the eye, and says, 'Joey, Scotto is too fucking big. They're squeezing. I know I got this for you, and I know you've taken care of me, but I can't buck the fucking guys up there. I'm not big enough . . .' "

Joe had been left some way behind. "George knows I could have wheeled and dealed," he said, "and I could have walked right out of the courtroom. But I took a rap."

Sykes was surprised he even mentioned it.

"You could have had him busted for a long time," he agreed. "You'd have died as a result, but you could have had him busted, and he knows it. Ah, I think your answer is very simple. It ain't easy, but it's simple. You sit him down, and you tell him where you stand now, what the problem is. Hey, look, George ain't gonna put you with someone where you can't make a buck, 'cause then *he* can't make a buck."

Joe massaged his chest. He had caught up now with what Sykes had said earlier.

"What if the Scotto group goes to him and says, 'These are our bills, and we want them paid in full.'?"

Sykes tried to think of a reassuring answer, and failed.

"Then you pay them, my friend."

"Sixty *grand?*"

"If it has to be, my friend, it has to be. If they say, 'This is what we're gonna get,' and Scotto backs 'em, then you pay it, Joey."

"Pay it?"

Harvey nodded. "There's no such thing as you don't pay it."

"Then you fucking well die, that's what you're saying to me?"

"That's all. Exactly."

"Fuck it," said Joe savagely. "Who needed this?"

Half the time, Joe could hardly remember if he was playacting or not. So much of what he had said and done over the past year had been aimed just at getting people to talk, building the case. After his heart attack, he had meant to go out on his own, not caring particularly what became of the family business, but the investigation had kept him working for Eagle almost as hard as ever; his pride was now so involved, he could no longer tell how much it really meant to him, or how far he would go to defend it.

His feelings about the Savannah business were just as mixed. In a sense, he *had* gone out on his own with Georgia Container Agencies, but the investigation had again determined his choice of associates and his methods of doing business. Now that James Stevedores had pulled out, and the whole edifice was crumbling, Joe's first impulse was to get clear before it fell on him. His second impulse was to run around as usual, shoring it up.

A week later, Zim–Israel suspended all payments for stevedoring in both Savannah *and* Miami until a settlement had been reached, and hinted broadly at the possibility of hiring James directly to work its ships in Savannah, cutting out Georgia Container Agencies altogether.

This induced a terminal case of the jitters in Gus Hulander and Dewey Parker, who now faced having to pick up their 40 percent of a likely $100,000 loss. Looking around for someone more deserving, they settled on Mutzie Kratish, and sought to persuade him to take over their stock in GCA by reminding him of Eagle's dependence on the Nopal Line account, which they controlled.

Smarting already from the suspension of Zim's payments for the Miami stevedoring, and now threatened additionally with having to make good the losses of a company he had wanted no part of in the first place, Mutzie naturally communicated his disquiet to the rest of the Teitelbaum/Kratish clan, who were soon considering Joe's problems with all the passionate concern of a lynch mob.

Barone's family now ganged up on him as well. Although Dick Aber delivered one $3,500 payoff to Boyle in Wilmington, North Carolina, and Bill Owens paid Boyle $2,000 more in Miami a few days later, James Vanderwyde moved in on September 10 with a demand for six suites for Fred Field on the *Carnivale* for its Christmas cruise, and $4,000 for Mobile. He also wanted Joe to call Benny Cotrone to discuss the possibility of "doing something together under one roof." Looking into eyes as expressive as blue glass marbles, Joe asked no questions, although he could not imagine what they had in mind.

Barone explained a few days later, when he and Vanderwyde met Joe outside the office of Hulander's Caribbean Agencies.

"I hear Hulander and Parker are thinking about going into the stevedoring business," he suggested slyly. "You hear that?"

"Don't surprise me." Joe had already figured that as a possible move.

Barone did not answer directly. "We gotta make some changes, all right?"

"It's those fucking relatives of yours," said Vanderwyde.

"Jay's right. You can't do business with people like that. They ain't reliable."

"And they got big mouths," said Vanderwyde.

"Right."

Benny Cotrone now emerged from Caribbean Agencies, and seemed surprised to see them. Barone jerked his head, signifying he should join them.

"All right," said Joe. "What do you want me to do?"

Barone looked at him reflectively.

"The way I see it," he said, "you got three ways to go. You can quit, and work for Benny here. That's number one. *Or,*" he went on imperiously, as Joe started to object. "Or you can merge PTO with Benny's operation. *Or* you can sell PTO to Maritime Cartage. Those are the three."

Joe's heart began to labor. Sweating a little, he leaned casually against the wall.

"PTO is owned by Eagle," he said, without a tremor. "Eagle is a public corporation owned by my family . . . *controlled* by my family, excuse me. So it may not be possible."

"Then it looks like number one, don't it?"

"Me working for Benny, you mean?" He did a breathing exercise. "How about Benny working for *me?*"

Barone shrugged. "Work it out any way you want."

He nodded to Vanderwyde, and they started to walk off.

"Hey, wait a minute," said Joe.

Cotrone touched his arm, shaking his head. "Forget it," he said. "Don't bother with him. Son of a bitch."

"Who?" Joe had always thought of Benny as Barone's errand boy. "You mean, George?"

"Yeah. Greedy cocksucker. I hate the fucking union."

Cotrone had aged a lot in the past few years. He was also half-blind, with cataracts in both eyes.

"What's it all about, Benny?" Joe felt almost sorry for him. "You gonna buy Neilsen Shipping?"

"You heard that? Did they tell you?"

"No. They told me I gotta leave my family and go to work for *you,* okay?"

"Bullshit."

"So what do you need, Benny? A hatch boss? Stickman?"

"It's all bullshit." He gestured vaguely. "Let me tell you something. I'm the oldest in the family. The oldest. And Barone, he can't do nothing.

I got the okay from Carlo himself. Anything I want is okay. So he can't make me do shit."

"Who's Carlo?"

Cotrone almost smiled. "Who's Carlo?" He thought Joe was joking. "Yeah. Told me that himself. 'Anybody gives you a hard time,' he says, 'you come to me. You earned that consideration.' "

"Carlo *Gambino* said that? The big boss himself?"

"Sure. And they know it, those cocksuckers. They're careful with me." He tapped the side of his nose, and winked. "So waddya wanna do, Joe? You wanna come see my son, Joseph? You wanna talk a little bit?"

"Maybe. You buy Neilsen Shipping, you get Neilsen's stevedore license, right?"

"Yeah."

"Okay. Well, I'll tell you. I gotta take a little trip. When I get back, we'll talk some more. Maybe I'll buy *you* out."

"Listen. It's talkable. It's all talkable."

That afternoon, he told the Strike Force he was leaving.

"Where are you going?" Mike Levin asked.

"Oslo. Then I'm gonna stop off in London for a few days, and after that, we're all gonna have a serious talk about my future, okay? I wanna know what's gonna happen when we go to the grand jury."

"Well, I wouldn't worry about that," said Levin. "We still got a fair way to go."

Joe looked at him with dislike.

"Don't tell *me* not to worry," he said. "I been doing this for a year. I *know* when to worry. They're moving in. And if you guys think you're gonna stand around and make notes while they bust my balls, forget it. I got other plans for 'em."

He took Ann and the Kesslers, and stayed away for two weeks. There was no hurry this time. The worst had already happened. Everything was falling apart, but nothing could be settled without him.

He returned from London to find that Zim was still withholding payment; that it had hired James Stevedores to handle its ships in Savannah; that Hulander and Parker expected Eagle not only to indemnify them against loss, but also to buy in their investment of $11,502; that the family would hold him personally responsible for every penny the venture cost them; that Boyle was demanding $4,000 for Mobile and $1,000 each for Savannah and Miami, and that Fred Field wanted two more tickets for the *Carnivale*'s Christmas cruise. In the circumstances, there seemed little point in holding back. With Ray Maria and Special Agent Joe Frechette listening in, he called Landon Williams, president of Local 1408, Jacksonville, and vice president of the International.

They arranged to meet on October 5 at the Americana Hotel, Miami Beach, where the ILA was conferring with employers for the second time in two months over the container-ship clauses of the master contract, which otherwise still had a year to run. Joe was ready to wear a body recorder, but Maria thought it too dangerous. Williams was no Isom Clemon. He was tough, shrewd, and cautious. Better to wire the car. Joe should take him out to dinner, and they could talk on the way.

The FBI's electronics experts worked on Joe's red Buick for two days, converting it into a mobile recording studio, but as he drove over the Causeway to keep his appointment with Williams, the car's radiator hose split, and he arrived at the Americana steaming, literally and colloquially. With no time to make repairs or alternative arrangements, Joe tipped the doorman $2 to top up the radiator, and hoped for the best.

He had plenty of time to let the car cool off. The lobby was crowded with people he could hardly ignore, including Fred Field, Sam Gordon, the banana boss of Mobile, Isom Clemon, and Bill Boyle.

After chatting with them, he bumped into Ed Heine, Jr., president of United States Lines. He was crossing the lobby with a tall, lean man who wore the slight, public smile of visiting royalty.

"I think I know you," Joe said to him, after greeting Heine. "I think we have mutual friends."

"That's very possible," he said.

"You're Anthony Scotto, right?"

The other nodded, and shook his hand politely.

"I'm Joe Teitelbaum. I gotta talk to you."

"Not now, Joe," said Heine. "We're going into a meeting. Some other time, okay?"

Becalmed in the hubbub, Joe watched them go. He had nothing against Scotto personally, but he had just shaken hands with the man he had to destroy.

It was another 20 minutes before he disengaged Landon Williams and steered him through the crush to the entrance.

"Can't talk in that zoo," he said, handing the doorman his ticket for the Buick. "Ain't safe. Let's wait till we get in the car."

"You think it's safe in a car?" Williams in a business suit looked like a millionaire pro line-backer turned investment counselor. "Shit, they got all kinds of bugs they put in cars."

Joe choked a little.

"Think I don't know that?" he wheezed. "I got five cars, okay? I never use the same one twice running."

"That's kinda safe," Williams conceded. "But you still wanna be careful. They got things they can just drop in there . . . like when you're parked, you know? . . . and then they take it out after, and like you never knew it was there."

"Man, you're full of shit. You watch too much TV. You wanna check it out, be my guest."

Williams did, in fact, look into the back of the car before seating himself in front, but Joe knew there was nothing to see. He was more worried about the risk of the motor seizing up. It sounded all right, and there was no steam, but their dinner table at the Newport Hotel was a mile and a half away.

"They told me you own a Rolls Royce," Williams said.

"Yeah." Joe waited for a gap in the traffic. "Had it shipped over from Europe."

"But a lousy Buick's good enough for me, right?"

"No, for *me*. I'm a truck man. All that fancy shit makes me nervous." He gunned the car out of the driveway, then slowed at once to a jogger's pace. "But if you wanna Rolls Royce, maybe I can help you."

Williams looked out the window disdainfully.

"If I wanna Rolls Royce," he said, "I'll go right out and buy me one. Okay?"

"Sure, Landon. I know that."

"Yeah. Like I just bought myself a new home up there. Cost three-hundred-thousand dollars. And I send my kids to private school."

"You're doing good, Landon."

"Yeah. See this suit?" He held out his lapel. "Silk."

"Yeah," said Joe. "Very nice."

"Okay." He settled back. "Now what have you got?"

"Coffee. African coffee. Seven, maybe ten thousand tons a month." Joe fancied he could hear a hissing noise in front. "And now Zim–Israel's talking about sending a boat in there, so I don't want no problems. I want good labor, and I want labor peace. Guaranteed."

"No sweat. I can do that for you."

"Fine. Now do I work through Boyle or what?"

"Fuck Boyle," said Williams irritably. "You deal with me. That's *my* port."

"Well, that's what I heard." The hissing was getting louder.

"Yeah. Talk to Isom Clemon, you're talking to Fred Field, right? Talk to Uncle Tom Cleve Turner, that's Field again. But in Jacksonville, you talk to *me.*"

"I hear you, Landon. Loud and clear."

At least, he hoped so. It depended on how close the microphones were to the leaky hose.

"Okay. What are you gonna need?"

"Well, I tell you. I'm gonna need an office. I'm gonna need a girl in it. And I'm gonna need a stevedore's license, okay? What's it gonna take?"

Now Williams could hear the hissing, too. He leaned forward, cocking his ear.

"What's that?" he said. "That whistling?"

"Fucking hose split as I was driving over. Don't worry about it."

Williams shrugged. "Ten cents a ton. Minimum guarantee, two-fifty a week."

Joe scratched his nose. "Thousand a month basic? Nice piece of change. Pay for the kids' tuition, right?"

"The hell it will. That's fifteen grand, plus extras."

"Well, let's get you started, then."

Joe fished in his inside pocket for the white envelope Bill Owens had given him, and pushed it across the seat.

"Here," he said. "To show a little good faith."

Williams opened it, counted the money and pushed it back.

"Check this over," he said.

"Huh?"

There was a red light up ahead, and as they rolled to a stop, Joe flicked through the envelope.

"Four hundred, right?"

"I was looking for this." Williams held up his hand, spreading the fingers. "For two weeks?"

"You're right." Joe pretended to be vexed with himself. "Tell you what. When I bring my man Dick Aber up to meet you, I'll give you eleven hundred. One to make up the difference, plus another full month. Okay?"

The hissing was quite loud now, and wisps of steam blew back alongside the car as they moved off.

"Okay," said Williams. "But I only do business with you. That's a rule I got. Like with Strachan Shipping, I know Jerry Fox. With Southern Shipping, I know Carl Opper. With Georgia Container, I know you. Nobody else. You follow what I'm saying?"

"Yeah. Gotcha."

"Bring in anybody you want, but don't try to deal with me in front of them, understand? Last time somebody tried to set me up, I had to call Chicago."

"Yeah? You mean, you had the guy killed?"

Williams sniffed. Steam was puffing out around the hood as though from a tailor's press, but they had reached the restaurant.

"*I'm* here," he said. "The other guy ain't."

With some more water in the Buick, Joe got Williams back to the Americana after dinner, but half way home, the car broke down in another cloud of steam and refused to restart. A few minutes later, a cab stopped to pick him up, and he called Special Agent Frechette from the first public telephone they reached to arrange for the FBI to recover the car and recording gear.

Next morning, when he called to find out what was on the tape, Frechette told him they now had incontrovertible proof that his radiator hose had split.

Then Georgia Container Agencies collapsed.

Under continuing pressure from Hulander and Parker, Uncle Mutzie caved in and dictated a letter, which Joe co-signed, holding them "safe and harmless" in any legal action that might be brought against GCA, and agreeing to buy back their stock at par.

He did not do so quietly. At the top of their considerable lungs, a male-voice chorus of Kratishes invited Joe not merely to step out of the business, but out of their lives, and also out of this world, if he had any sense of decency.

Declining the invitation, with a few counter-suggestions, Joe made his own position equally clear. He was ready to sue James Stevedores, John Caputo, James Roberts, Tilston–Roberts, Gus Hulander, Dewey Parker, Uncle Mutzie, the entire family, singly or collectively, and anybody else who got in the way, for breach of contract, commercial conspiracy, fraud, and whatever else he could think of unless a prompt and satisfactory settlement was reached over the Zim stevedoring bills—a threat that alarmed everybody except the Strike Force.

On October 7, Harvey Sykes came over from Caribbean Agencies to advise Joe that Jimmy Roberts was flying in from New Orleans next day to meet with them all in Hulander's office for a last attempt to resolve the affair amicably. Asked how he read the situation, Sykes thought Joe should meet James halfway or "risk losing it all." From Joe's beleaguered position, this seemed rather like advising him to pay off the mortgage as the house was burning down.

Overnight, the FBI wired Joe's briefcase, and in the morning, he found himself on trial. The meeting had been called by Hulander and Parker, not so much to negotiate, but so that Joe and Roberts could confront each other, with Sykes acting as moderator, witness, and friend of the court. Zim was not represented, for it took no position—other than refusing to release any money against the bills outstanding from GCA until James's attorneys confirmed in writing that agreement had been reached.

The stakes were high, but both sides remained calm and reasonably friendly, for each was familiar with the other's position and even felt some sympathy for it. Joe's argument was that he had entered into a contract in good faith, and expected both parties to live up to it; that he had contracted to bill Zim at a fixed rate per ton, and therefore required James, as his subcontractor, to bill *him* at the fixed rate agreed to verbally by John Caputo, without the tens of thousands of dollars in extras that had been tacked on.

Roberts's position, on the other hand, was essentially that James had found the original terms impossible to live with, and that Joe had agreed to vary them in an effort to make the job pay. The sums billed in excess of the original terms were, therefore, either covered by his verbal agreement or represented the cost of extra labor or machines ordered by GCA or Zim at various times.

To this, Joe replied that he could not reasonably be expected to finance James's mistakes or its failure to achieve a reasonable rate of production, and that many of the disputed extras had in any case been charged incorrectly or unwarrantably. Furthermore, whenever he had found it necessary to adjust a bill from James, he had sent a copy of his letter explaining the reasons for doing so to Caputo, who had told him he would take care of it.

For two hours, the discussion went around and around, returning again and again to the central role of John Caputo. Roberts was no more anxious than Joe to drag him into the argument if it could be avoided for Caputo would then be placed in a most invidious position, but there was clearly no other way in the end of determining who was in the right.

Never doubting the outcome, Joe waited confidently while Roberts placed a call to Caputo in New York, but it was soon apparent that his confidence had been misplaced. When Caputo evidently suggested that Roberts should put Joe on the line, Joe first wanted to know what position he had taken.

"He says he doesn't know anything about the rates," said Roberts awkwardly. "Nasty situation."

Joe clenched his jaw.

"I'd rather speak to John face to face," he said grimly.

After that, there was not much left to talk about. Joe had put so much into his role with Caputo that he could not have felt the stab in the back more sharply if their friendship had been genuine. He called him as soon as he returned to his office.

"You son of a bitch," he said. "You left me in the middle."

"Hey, Joe. I'm sorry, man. They took it out of my hands."

"You gave me your word, you cocksucker. You left me holding the fucking bag."

"Listen, Jimmy went over my head. There was nothing I could do."

"Fuck that. *I'll* tell you what you should do. You should tell 'em you made a deal with me in their name, and they're bound to it like you are, you son of a bitch."

"Come on, Joe. Get off my back. So the deal went sour. What do you wanna do? Make me look bad? They're still gonna want their money, and then I can't help you. Is that what you want? Or do you wanna settle it, and we'll work something out? I mean, let's be grown up about this. There's lots of ways I can help you get it back, you know?"

"No. Don't help me. Your kind of help I don't need. You just helped me lose about a hundred and twenty grand, you fuck. And don't give me that bullshit about people going over your head. All you gotta do is get somebody in there to talk to 'em. You know who I mean."

"Joe, you don't know what you're saying."

"I'm saying, stand by your shit, John. If you can't do it yourself, get somebody to help you."

"Forget it. I couldn't do that even for me. That way, somebody's gonna wind up in cement."

"All right. Then I'm gonna sue, John. I'm gonna sue you. I'm gonna sue Jimmy. I'm gonna sue James Stevedores. And I'm gonna sue Tilston–Roberts. I'm gonna sue you for every fucking penny. Plus punitive damages. Okay?"

There was a silence.

"You do that, Joe," Caputo said sadly, "and you're gonna start something you can't finish."

"It *is* finished. I lost it all anyway, so what the fuck's the difference? You didn't keep your word."

At the time, Joe neither knew nor cared what Ray Maria or Mike Levin would think of this, but, as it turned out, they were quite pleased. It would be interesting now to see what sort of pressure, if any, Caputo could bring to bear on Joe through Barone. It might show just how much power the New York group really had in the South. With Bob Carter still undercover at Zim developing the case against Scotto, Joe was no longer really needed up there.

Nor was he carrying the sole burden in Miami any longer. Dick Aber and Bill Owens had taken over much of the day-to-day progress, while squads of other agents, most of them unknown to Joe, were fanning out through the other Atlantic and Gulf ports to explore the leads that he and his agent "relatives" had turned up. From the first day of his private war, every new suspect identified had provided a new circle of associates to be investigated, and so on, to the point where the FBI was now engaged in the largest single investigation ever mounted by the U.S. Justice Department.

In Savannah and Mobile, Aber was doing as much damage as anybody. He had developed a good case against DeMott and Hodges, of Great Southern Trailer, for conspiracy and violations of the Taft–Hartley Act, inducing Ray DeMott to admit during a taped telephone call that he was paying Boyle off at the rate of 30 cents an hour for every man he employed. Aber had also ensnared yet another ILA union president with his final payment to Boyle for the Mobile contract. Unable to collect the $4,000 himself, Boyle had arranged for Robert Bateman, president of the Charleston Local 1422-A, to pick the money up from Aber and bring it on to him in Norfolk, Virginia.

Joe's meeting in Savannah with Clemon and Bishop Frank Maddox had produced several interesting leads, but Aber soon found that Clemon, whose inability to grasp even the simplest idea correctly was a source of endless bewilderment to himself as well as his associates, had muddled them up. His business partnership with Governor Jimmy Carter's aides, Cloyd Hall and Phil Courtney, for example, was quite separate from his involvement with Maddox and Dr. Jim Smith of Triworld International

Ltd. The former arose from Hall's desire to cash in on his political connections, as he had explained on the telephone to Joe, and was not, therefore, subject to "commissions" to either Field or Boyle, whereas the arrangement with Triworld was subject entirely to their blessing, and, therefore, to a substantial piece of the action.

Not that anybody was in much danger of getting rich as a result of Clemon's contribution to either enterprise. An elaborate oil deal, for instance, from which Hall, Courtney, and Clemon expected to share a brokerage commission of 4 cents a barrel on deliveries of up to 650,000 barrels a day of light Arabian crude eventually foundered, after several delirious weeks of discussion about how they would spend the money, for a number of reasons: partly because Hall, whose belief in his power to make a fortune with a few telephone calls was matched only by his faith in Clemon, delegated all the practical arrangements to him; partly because Clemon, misunderstanding everybody and only dimly perceiving what was required of him in any case, took the wish for the deed and duly assured the others that all was in readiness when, in fact, nothing was; partly because the "buyer" they found in Houston turned out to be as phony as they were, and partly because the "supplier" they were relying upon had never had any oil in the first place.

Landon Williams was an altogether more formidable proposition, however, as Joe and Aber discovered again when they flew into Jacksonville on October 20 for a second attempt to record a payoff. Taking no chances this time with split hoses, the FBI provided them with one of its own bugged cars, a briefcase recorder for Joe to carry into the meeting, and $1,100 in marked $100 bills, which Aber handed to Joe in an envelope as they drove in from the airport.

Williams kept them waiting for several minutes, and when he did appear, excused himself while he returned a telephone call from Anthony Scotto. Apparently, Williams had asked Scotto—not Field or Barone—to stop PRIMSA, the Puerto Rican government shipping line, giving its repair work in Jacksonville to any firm but United Trailer Services, the local arm of Benny Cotrone's business, run by his daughters, Laura and Francesca.

"We always take care of our own," Williams explained as he hung up, and went on to indicate, by now superfluously, that United Trailer would also handle Joe's repairs in the port. They then went over the business forecast they had already discussed in Miami Beach, and after Williams arranged for representatives of a local trucking firm to come over and meet them, Joe raised his eyebrows and said:

"Can we talk? Let's go for a ride."

Williams regarded him sourly.

"Yeah," he said. "Leave your man here."

Aber shrugged, as if it were all the same to him, and Joe reached for the briefcase.

"You don't need that either," said Williams.

Joe could hardly insist. As they left the building, he made straight for the Bureau's bugged car, but Williams caught him by the arm.

"I'll drive," he said, pointing to a white Cadillac. "I got a phone in there, if the office needs me."

Joe hoped the agents were taking pictures, for they would have to make do with that.

As they drove away, Williams took one hand off the wheel and rubbed his thumb and forefinger together under Joe's nose.

"Yeah," said Joe. "I got it."

Scowling, Williams leaned forward to turn up the air-conditioning and switch on the radio.

"You fuck," he said. "Next time, you're gonna wind up in traction sucking soup through a straw, you Jew son of a bitch. I told you. I only do business with you."

"Hey, man. Don't be so fucking touchy. The guy's gotta be here. He's gonna run things for me."

"I don't give a fuck *who* he is, *where* he is, or what he does," said Williams. "If he's gotta problem in this port, he can call me anytime. But I only do business with you. And I ain't gonna tell you again."

"You're right," said Joe. "Here's eleven hundred, like we agreed."

Without bothering to count it, Williams took the money, one-handed, from the envelope, and leaning across, tucked it under the rubberized floor mat on Joe's side.

Aber was furious.

"We fucking blew it again," he said, on leaving for Mobile later that afternoon, but, as Joe told Mike Levin next morning:

"Williams still caught his tit in the wringer. Dick gives me the money as we're going in, but I don't have it on me afterwards. He made a search. And I was never out of sight for a minute. Okay? That's number one. Number two, you got pictures. What's wrong with that?"

"It's better than nothing," agreed Levin, though plainly disappointed. "Maybe if Williams gets used to seeing him around, Dick can hang in there for the next payoff."

"Maybe Dick can," said Joe. "Me, I like drinking soup with a spoon."

He, too, was disappointed. It was his only real failure in a year, which made him the more anxious to oblige when Levin remembered something else, just as Joe was leaving.

"It's not urgent or anything," he said, "just something to bear in mind. We're coming up dry on some of these people, and I'm wondering if we've got all the basics right. You know, like their full names, date and place of birth. Stuff like that."

"Yeah? Who, for instance?"

"Well, Fiore, for one. Sykes. Hulander. Parker. Those'll do to be getting on with. And we could use some handwriting samples as well, if you get the chance.''

"How about fingerprints?''

"Yeah, fine." Levin laughed politely. "But you know, don't push it. Just bear it in mind in case the opportunity comes up. There's no hurry.''

Joe was back inside an hour.

"Hi," said Levin. "Forget something?''

"Me? No.''

He shook five small pieces of paper onto the desk from an envelope.

"I got Boyle in there as well," he explained.

On each piece of paper was written the full names of one of the four men Levin had mentioned, plus Boyle's, along with their respective dates and places of birth.

Levin stared at them, as though confronted by witchcraft.

"Is that their handwriting, too?" he asked.

"Well, of course it is. That's what you wanted, isn't it? And don't touch," he added sharply, as Levin reached out to make sure they were real. "They got their fingerprints on 'em.''

Levin sat back, bewildered.

"Joe, how in the world . . .''

"Well, I got lucky," he said. "They were having a meeting in Boyle's office, so I gave 'em each a piece of paper and told 'em what to write.''

"Yes, but didn't they think that was . . . strange?''

"No. I told 'em Ann and me were throwing an astrology party. And I said they couldn't come unless they gave me what she needed for their horoscopes.''

18

The Big Buildup

THEIR fortunes were written, not in the stars, however, but in federal wiretap transcripts. Joe never did throw an astrology party. There was nobody left on Dodge Island whom he cared to ask, and as the days went by, fewer and fewer who would have come if he had. His stubborn refusal to withdraw the threat of a lawsuit against James Stevedores was setting everybody's teeth on edge.

Barone came to see him about it twice. On his first visit, he said he would ask Scotto if he could help with the problem. Surprised by the offer to mediate instead of the usual bald instruction to settle, Joe asked if this meant that the territorial dispute between the two groups had at last been resolved. Yes, it did, said Barone. Scotto would keep out of the South, except by agreement. In return, the six International vice presidents controlling the South Atlantic and Gulf Coast ports had pledged Scotto their votes when the time came to elect a successor to Teddy Gleason.

On his second visit, Barone was not quite so accommodating. He was on his way up to New York to see Scotto, he said, and Harvey Sykes agreed with him that the chance of a settlement would be much improved if Joe stopped threatening to go to law. Meanwhile, whatever the outcome, his problems with Zim were no longer acceptable as an excuse for not paying the rent. Joe thanked him for his trouble, wished him luck with Scotto, and suggested he invite Sykes to jump off the dock.

By the end of another week, it was obvious to Joe that Barone was avoiding him. When he went to see Boyle about it on Monday, November 1, he learned that Barone was back but tied up in meetings.

There was still no word by Wednesday, when Boyle called for the rent.

"Where's your fucking boss?" Joe demanded.

"Well, he wants to talk to you, Joe, but he hasn't had a minute. He's in and out of meetings all the time."

"In two whole days he can't find a minute for a phone call?"

"You know how he is. He never talks on the pipe. But he'll get around to it. Maybe tomorrow, if I tell him you're up to date."

"What do you mean?"

"What do you mean, what do I mean, you schmuck?" Boyle tried a comradely laugh. "The October rent is what I mean. You wanna get his attention, give him a green signal."

"I ain't giving anybody another fucking quarter," said Joe indifferently. "Not until this thing with James is straightened out."

Boyle walked away shaking his head.

Harvey Sykes was the next to try. He had wanted to come sooner, he said, but he had been tied up with Barone.

"The man wants to see you, Joe, but he just hasn't had a chance. He told me to tell you that."

"He say what happened with Scotto?"

"No, he probably wants to tell you that himself."

"Well, if he's got time to see *you* but not me," said Joe contemptuously, "I guess I can draw my own conclusions."

Sykes looked uncomfortable. "Well, all he said was, you better call off the lawsuit because you're making some bad enemies. And he's right, Joe. You can't beat him *and* Scotto, not both together. That's for sure."

"Well, I got news for you, Harvey. Fuck him. Fuck Scotto. And fuck you, too. I'm *not* gonna pay. And I *am* gonna sue."

Sykes walked away, shaking his head.

The fact that Barone was still avoiding him could mean only one thing: that he had failed, or perhaps not even tried, to get Scotto to intervene. And without that, there was no reason in the world why Zim should change its position.

Boyle practically admitted as much the next time he came over for the rent.

"All right," said Joe. "Where is he? Back ten days, and I still ain't heard a fucking word."

"He's busy. And one's got nothing to do with the other. This is separate."

"Separate?" He honked with derision. "Bullshit. I told him, I said, 'You get your money when I get mine.' If he won't back me against those people, then I gotta sue 'em for it. Simple as that."

"Look, Joe . . ." Boyle groped for some way to get through to him. "In his *mind,* it's separate," he said. "You know how he gets when he's nervous. I can't always handle him. Or the little guy. You don't know what I have to go through."

"Well, now you're just breaking my heart."

"Lemme tell you something. Sometimes I have to give 'em my *own* money, just to cover for you guys. You don't understand what I have to do to keep things quiet. But I got my limits, Joe. I try, but you make it hard for me."

"What do you want, Bill? Sympathy? Okay, you got sympathy. But don't ask for money till he gets it for me. He said he was gonna talk to Scotto."

Boyle clasped his head, as though trying to reason with a fractious child.

"You still don't understand, do you? Nervous ain't getting in any fights with Scotto over *you.* Let's be grown up, for Chrissake. You know what he's got at stake here?"

"Do *I* know?" Joe pretended to buckle at the knees. "This is unreal. Do *I* know what *he's* got at stake? Jesus Christ. *I'm* the one that's getting fucked. I been paying out for years. Mr. Nice Guy. Gone along with you all the way, and for what? First problem comes along, first time I turn around and say, 'Hey, man, I'm hurting. Help me out here,' what happens? Nothing. He won't even talk to me. It's just, 'Too bad, Joe. Gotta be grown-up about this, Joe. And P.S., don't forget to pay the rent, Joe.' Well, fuck that. And fuck you, too. I've had it."

"You finished?"

"Yeah. Finished. It's all gone. And I don't give a shit anymore."

"Joe, you got the wrong attitude. He's not gonna fight with Scotto over this, but there's other ways to skin a cat."

"Like going into business with you in Mobile? Thanks a lot. I'm tired of being the fucking cat."

"Have it your way." Boyle was offended. "He's not gonna fight with

Scotto, but you handle him right, and he's gotta owe you something.
That's all I'm trying to tell you."

"Like what?"

"Well . . . You wanna get into the repair business? Take any port you
want. And no front money. Houston, Mobile . . . Name it, and I'll fix it
for you. All you gotta do is drop this fucking suit against James, which
is getting everybody upset."

"Bullshit. You think I'm gonna do it *again?* Lay out another hundred
and fifty grand to get started someplace else, and then have you guys fuck
me over some more? You gotta be crazy. First, get me my money. *Then*
we'll talk."

Boyle chewed his lip.

"Joe, we always been friends," he said. "I done my best for you, and
we always got along. Okay. Now I'm telling you . . . in a friendly way.
Don't make waves. All right? You make waves, and they're gonna roll
right over and drown you. And there's gonna be nothing I can do about
it. You understand what I'm saying?"

"Shit, I'm drowning already," Joe said, who understood very well.
"You seen the gangs I been getting? They're killing me. How come
Chester and those fucks at Marine Terminals always get short gangs and
me never?"

"You seen Turner lately?"

"Listen, I paid that guy all these years, he can't wait a little bit till I get
my money? Same story. Gets tires for his girlfriend's fucking car. Cruise
tickets. And what do *I* get? Full gangs."

"Yeah," said Boyle. "Cruise tickets. That reminds me. You got those
tickets for Fred yet? Whatever you do, don't screw up on that one."

Joe had had enough. It made no business sense to carry on like this, and
as for the investigation, he seemed to be covering the same old ground,
over and over.

"I'm gonna get myself killed," he told Ray Maria. "If I stay in, I gotta
sue. If I sue, they gotta kill me, because otherwise it's all gonna come out
in court. And they'll *do* it. You know they will."

"But Joe, they're going to want their money if you stay in or not, aren't
they?"

"Jesus Christ." He threw up his hands. "You guys are as bad as Barone.
What are you telling me? Don't rock the boat or we'll throw you to the
fucking sharks? Shit. Anybody takes the loss, it ought to be the government."

"I doubt Washington sees it that way," Maria said calmly. "But if you
think you've got a case, then go ahead and sue. That's your right as a
citizen. You've also got a right to the fullest protection the law provides."

"Yeah. Great. Stake me out as bait and see who comes along for a piece
of my ass. Thanks a lot."

"Then what do you want to do?"

"You wanna know what's gonna happen?" he said. He shrugged helplessly. "I'll tell you. *I* won't pay James. Mutzie will. And then he's gonna come after *me* for the money."

"Fine. Then *he* can sue *you,* and everybody's happy."

"I've had enough, Ray. It's been a whole fucking year. I don't think there's much more I can do for you."

"No, I don't think there is." Maria smiled at his astonishment. "We were talking about that this morning. Don't be surprised if we pull Bill Owens and Dick Aber out in the next two or three weeks."

Joe laughed uncertainly. "You mean, you're getting ready to move? You got enough?"

"Not quite yet." Maria put a hand on his arm, as though worried he might rush into the street to spread the good news. "We still want to know what Sykes is up to. And what Cotrone's got in mind for Neilsen Shipping. And how Fiore fits in. Things like that. Another month, maybe. Two at most."

"Then you start hitting 'em with subpoenas?"

"Could be. Depends on New York. They've still got a lot to do up there."

"Uh-huh, uh-huh."

"But it's your party, Joe. If you wanna stick around to see how it all comes out, we'll be glad to have you."

Joe eyed him almost fondly.

"You fuck," he said. "I brought you this far. I guess I might as well take you all the way."

All fired up for the final act, he was then frustrated, for nothing much happened in the next several weeks. The running, sniping, griping war with his relatives edged them closer and closer to the settlement he had predicted, and just as predictably, Boyle came back again and again for money, trying first to goad him with the news that Sykes was after the Nopal account, and then to shame him with the news that he had paid Isom Clemon $400 out of his own pocket. On top of that, Boyle said, Joe owed him $1,000 for the cigarettes, $1,000 for Savannah, $2,000 for Miami, now November had passed, and the final $2,000 for Mobile.

He had forgotten the tickets, Joe said. The Christmas cruise tickets for Fred Field were going to cost about $6,200. Mike Zonis, of Carnivale Cruise Line, had refused to give him a break on the price. And if Boyle thought Joe had a spare $12,000 to give him, he must still believe in Santa Claus.

Boyle said he would call Zonis and straighten him out. Meanwhile, Joe should get the tickets, and they would work out a formula to pay for them.

Knowing how short a lease they now had, Joe was willing to pay them as much of the taxpayers' money as the government chose to give away.

The pressure, in any case, had eased. Bill Owens left at the end of November—let go, Joe told everybody, because business was bad—and Dick Aber was leaving, ostensibly for the same reason; indeed, his last official act for Georgia Container Agencies was to mail $2,400 (the final payment for Mobile, plus the $400 Boyle had paid Clemon) to Boyle's home in Fort Lauderdale.

They all knew Joe was strapped for cash, and rumors of a settlement pending between Mutzie and James Stevedores had also relieved their anxieties about a lawsuit. It was almost like old times when he went to Boyle's office on December 2 to pay him $800 of the $1,000 owing for the cigarettes, and to arrange for six more trailer-loads from Lorillard to be passed through. Next day, he was rewarded with the offer of an opportunity to bid for the stevedoring account of Trailer Ship Line.

That was interesting. The Cotrones had acquired a 40 percent stake in the line a couple of months earlier with their purchase of K. Neilsen Shipping, whose own stevedoring division had continued to handle the account. If it was now up for grabs, that presumably meant Cotrone had dropped the idea of a merger with PTO, and that Sykes, representing Hulander and Parker, had failed to interest Cotrone in his attempt to grab the Nopal Line business.

"The Cotrones have that account," Joe said innocently.

"Benny will do like the man tells him," said Boyle.

"I also heard Harvey Sykes was after it for Hulander. Those guys'd do anything to get hold of a stevedore's license and rip me off."

"Listen, forget them. You want this or dontcha? If not, it's going to the gimp."

"Harrington? Shit. You go on feeding him like this, the guy's gonna wind up talking to the Anti-Trust Division. Gimme a few days. I'll go see Joe Cotrone. If he's closing down his stevedoring, maybe we can do a deal."

"Yeah," said Boyle cordially. "Good idea."

To avoid further rumors, family complications, and doubts about his seriousness of purpose, Joe took Bobby Kratish with him when he went to see Joseph Cotrone on December 10. Though not in so many words, Cotrone virtually admitted that his family had bought Neilsen Shipping for its stevedore license with a view to starting a joint venture with Hulander and Parker of Caribbean Agencies. The Cotrones had lost a lot of their enthusiasm, however, when they found that Hulander wished only to lease their equipment and license, and the stevedoring business was now for sale again at the very reasonable figure of $350,000. With the blessing of their "mutual friends," Cotrone added.

Joe happened to know that the whole Neilsen company had changed hands for $250,000, which put Cotrone's price for the stevedoring division at least $100,000 out of line, but that was all right. If their "mutual friends" were involved, a word from them was all it would take to put the

deal on a more realistic footing. Indeed, when Joe returned to his office
and found a message asking him to come over to Local 1922 as soon as
he got in, he assumed that that was what Boyle wanted to talk about.

Confident of his welcome, Joe sauntered into another court martial,
with Fat Freddy presiding. Whatever it was they had been discussing had
not made Field a happy man. Immobilized as usual by his own bulk, he
sat in silence, waiting for someone to trigger his malevolence. It hung on
the air like humidity, an oppressiveness infecting even Barone, whose
eyes kept straying in Field's direction, as though alert to disown what
Boyle was saying at the first sign of trouble. Only the two Vanderwydes
seemed unaffected; Jay because he could no more adapt himself to his
master's moods than a lead-weighted sap could cut bread, and Butch
because of his father.

Boyle turned to greet Joe with visible relief, his face red and shining.
"Hey, you got Fred's tickets for him?"

"You wanna talk about that *now?*" Joe glanced at Field, wishing Boyle
a compound fracture. "I just got back from seeing Joe Cotrone."

"What's to talk about?" Boyle sensed a chance to redirect Field's displeasure. "You gonna tell me there's a problem now?"

"Yeah," said Joe stoutly. "There's a problem. It's like six thousand
dollars-worth of tickets, and that's too heavy for me. Zonis wants full
rate."

Everybody looked at Field, who slowly lifted his head to look at Joe.

"What the fuck is this?" said Boyle. "You told me you'd take care of
it. Fucking weeks ago. They're for Fred, I said, so don't screw up. Didn't
I say that?"

"Yeah, you said that. And I'll tell you something else you said. You said
you'd call Mike Zonis and straighten him out because he wouldn't give
me a discount."

Everybody now looked at Boyle.

"Yeah, well, I did that," he said. "But the mother-fucker wouldn't talk
to me. He said he'd only talk to you."

"Yeah? We'll see about that." Joe picked up the telephone and dialed
the number for Carnivale Cruise Lines. "He'll talk to you, don't worry
about it. Mike Zonis, please. Joey Teitelbaum."

Enjoying Boyle's discomfort, he waited to be put through, then
launched into rapid Yiddish as soon as Zonis came on the line.

"Malchamuvos vil reden tzu dir," he said. "The kiss of death wants to talk
to you. He wants the tickets, but he doesn't want to pay for them."

Without waiting for an answer, he held out the telephone to Boyle, who
took it with the air of a man much put upon.

"I've gone as far as I can go," said Joe apologetically, half-listening with
the others as Boyle explained to Zonis how important Field was. "Business is off. Cash flow, forget it. I got this problem with James. I got Mutzie
on my back . . ."

He turned up his hands, appealing for suggestions, solutions, anything.

"Listen," Boyle said. "We give favors, we get favors. Ten percent is nothing. It's no good."

"I got no room to maneuver," Joe went on. "And now the *Morazan.* I gotta put her in dry dock. You know what *that's* gonna cost me? For repairs? And loss of charter? Shit. And now you want me to do something with Cotrone as well? I mean, you guys got me over a barrel here."

"Yeah?" said Boyle, redder still and sputtering. "Well, when contract time comes around, don't expect any breaks from *us.*"

He thrust the telephone back at Joe, as though disclaiming any further responsibility in the matter.

Field, still immobile, appraised Joe ruminatively, pushing out his lips.

"Fuck you and your Jew friend," he said, in a bored tone. "You will repent."

Joe shook himself free of his stare.

"Hey, Mike, listen," he said, half-turning away. "We got a serious problem here."

"No, *you* got a problem," said Zonis, very excited. "I don't know what he wants from me. It's the one chance I have to make money, the Christmas cruise. I'm not gonna give him six-thousand-dollars-worth of tickets."

"Hey, cool it, okay? It's not gonna kill us. I'll split it with you. How about that?"

"No," he howled. "It's full rate. I'll give you ten percent. You're the stevedore. *You* pay it."

"You kidding? I don't *make* six thousand."

"Hang up on the mother-fucker," said Field imperiously. "I'm not going. If he *gives* 'em to me now, I won't go. So fuck you and your Jew friend together."

Joe was confused. As far as he knew, Field had always been going to get them free. Boyle avoided his eye.

"Yeah, yeah, Mike . . . I'll talk to you later," he said, and hung up.

They looked at one another, waiting for Field. When it dawned on them he had nothing more to say, they all started talking at once, and all stopped at once.

"You settled with James yet?" Barone demanded furiously.

"*I* haven't," Joe said. "Mutzie has. I'm going up to New York next week to sign the papers."

"Good," said Boyle. "It's about time, for Chrissake. You got a lot of catching up to do."

"When I get *my* money, you get yours. Now does anybody wanna hear what happened with Cotrone, or don't you?"

"Just a minute." Barone was glaring at Boyle for having interrupted him. "You gonna see Ilan up there?"

"That's why I'm going, George."

"Then you be careful what you say to him. Don't tell him nothing. He's been making a lot of trouble."

"Yeah? What kind of trouble?"

"Just do like I tell you. I'm up there myself next week. Anything happens, you call Tommy Buzzanca. He'll know where I'm at."

The telephone had rung while they were talking, and Field himself had picked it up, waving off Butch Vanderwyde. Now he half-rose from his chair and dropped back again, reddening in the face and chopping at the air with his free hand.

"That mother-fucker," he whispered, his voice curdling. "Cocksucker. That Irish son of a bitch."

He smashed down the receiver and rubbed his forehead shakily, shading his eyes.

Jay Vanderwyde touched his shoulder. "You all right, Fred?"

Field uncovered his face. Its color was alarming, like raw liver.

"That was New York," he said.

It was hardly more than a croak, but Vanderwyde seemed to understand. Catching Joe's eye, he jerked his head toward the door.

"Get that mother-fucker Durant on the phone," Field panted, and Boyle leaped to obey.

Vanderwyde propelled Joe into the hall, nodding and winking.

"I'll come and see you in a minute," he said. "Wait in your office."

"Sure, Jay," said Joe, as the door closed in his face.

It was his best moment in more than a year. He was fiercely pleased—to see Field in trouble, to deny him his cruise, and to know the one secret worth all of theirs. No matter how bad the news from New York, it could never be as bad as the news they had coming.

Vanderwyde came over about 20 minutes later, but refused to be drawn.

"Fred's okay," he said. "Just a little problem he's got, that's all. They'll take care of it."

"Anything I should know about? As I'm going up there?"

"No, it don't concern you. And you know, you shoulda given him the tickets. What's six thousand to you?"

He sounded reproachful.

"Hey, come on, Jay. I lost my *ass* already. I lost so much fucking money this year I don't know why I'm even *talking* to Cotrone."

"Because you're a smart boy."

"Yeah? Well, Cotrone doesn't think so. He thinks I'm stupid. I mean, I went over the books. And like they bought Neilsen out for a quarter of a mill, okay? You know what he wants now? Three-fifty. Now you tell me, Jay. What happened in a couple of months the price should go up forty percent? That's crazy, right?"

"Yeah, well . . ." Vanderwyde nodded sagely. "If he wants to keep the hundred for himself, that's one thing. But if it's a little division, that's something else. You better talk to George. *He* knows. He'll get you some answers on it before you go see Cotrone again on Friday."

"Yeah," said Joe, who had told nobody that a further meeting had been arranged for Friday. Cotrone was still working both sides of the fence. "But Jay, I don't know where to turn right now. I mean, I gotta find another hundred grand from someplace for the *Morazan.*"

"Well, maybe I can help you there," he said off-handedly. "What you got for collateral?"

"I got the crane. Equipment."

"She got good earnings?"

"The crane? Yes, she does. You mean, *you* can handle that, Jay? A hundred grand?"

"Sure, I can handle it. You kidding?" He reached out and ruffled Joe's hair. "You be a good boy and do like I tell you, and you'll never go wrong."

The gesture left Joe speechless for a moment.

"How much will it cost me?" he asked faintly.

"For a hundred grand? Two thousand a week."

"For how long?"

"Three years."

Joe held up his hands and pretended to cower.

"Hey, thanks a lot," he said, laughing. "I'll let you know."

Afterwards, Joe called Ray Maria, who was not surprised to hear about Field's outburst. A New York grand jury, he said, had just indicted him on three counts of accepting illegal payoffs, totaling $124,500, from United Brands.

"Hey, you mean, it's *started?*" said Joe, riven with relief, excitement, and dismay. He wasn't ready yet.

"No, no," said Maria. "That's another case."

"Ah, Ray. You should have seen his face." He felt a pure contentment. "Looked like a fucking eggplant in a business suit."

"Yeah, I figured it might spoil his Christmas."

"Yeah." Joe pulled himself together. "Okay. Now I gotta do it to Barone."

First they had to decide whose money they were going to use. Zim owed Georgia Container Agencies and Pierside Terminal Operators about $180,000, of which about $125,000 was earmarked to cover the disputed bills from James Stevedores. After agitating strenuously for the uncommitted balance of $55,000, Joe had won a promise that $25,000 would be released to him in New York on Tuesday, December 14, and, as he told Bob Carter at the Americana Hotel on Monday night, he was not parting with a cent of it. If the government wanted him to give Barone the $8,700 he was now supposed to owe him, then the government would have to find the money, and fast, because he was leaving for Jacksonville first thing Wednesday morning.

The government found the money. It was the first, best, and probably the only chance the Bureau had of trapping Barone himself in the act of extortion. All the omens were good. He was hungry for money. The sum was substantial. He was unscreened by his usual retinue of acolytes and bagmen. With Washington's approval, the New York office of the FBI mounted a maximum effort.

The money was placed between a two-volume set of *The Joy of Sex,* and wrapped in pink Christmas paper, with a pink ribbon. Joe's room was then wired with microphones, in the expectation that he would invite Barone up there to receive his present, and a recorder connected up to the telephone for Joe's call to the union office.

Barone was not available. His lieutenant, Thomas Buzzanca, president of Local 1804, promised to have him call Joe back as soon as he was free, and that left nothing to do but fret it out. The delay was potentially very awkward. It was already late in the afternoon, and a reasonable interval would be needed between Barone's call and his meeting with Joe so that the squad of agents standing by could be properly deployed.

He called shortly before 7 o'clock, just as Joe and Carter were about to give up.

"Hi, George," said Joe. "How are you?"

"Fine. Yourself?"

"Good. Can you talk for a minute?"

"No, I'm in a meeting. I'm . . . I got my membership meeting. I just ran out to get you before seven. You going to be in the morning around?"

"No," said Joe, pulling an agonized face at Carter, who was listening in on the recorder's monitor. "But let me tell you something, all right? Listen to me. I got my money from Zim."

"Yeah."

Barone sounded hesitant and distant. The easiest way to infuriate him was to try to talk business on the telephone.

"And I got a Christmas present for you," Joe said, deciding to risk it. The man had to be coaxed uptown somehow.

Barone mumbled something about it not being his concern, and for a moment, Joe was afraid he had lost him. But then he came back to propose a meeting in the lobby of the Americana later that night, and Joe breathed out again.

He took a ride uptown with Carter in a government car to have dinner in an Italian restaurant, and came back by cab, timing their arrival at the Americana for a little after 11:30. A few blocks from the hotel, they both gargled with whiskey, and as they climbed out onto the sidewalk after paying off the driver, they were talking and laughing rather louder than usual.

This attention to detail was not misplaced, for Barone had watched them arrive. They greeted him effusively, and Carter steered them into the Lion's Share lounge, for reasons that Joe heard about later. The bartender and waitress were both agents, and so was a prowling hooker in a broad-brimmed black hat. But Barone was not alone either. As Joe accompanied him into the lounge with Carter, he noticed two men watching them from the bar, and when one of them waved, recognized Thomas Eagleton, an old friend of Barone's whom Joe had met in Honduras.

The two did not join them immediately. Joe ordered drinks, and in a confidential vein, launched into a long complaint about Zim and the bitch of a day he had spent there, trying to get his money. Barone, at his most affable, agreed that Zim had been causing them all a lot of problems lately. Still, he said, he *had* managed to get Ilan to release some of the money owing to Joe, and it looked as though a final settlement was not far off.

"Yeah." Joe winked. "You wanna take a walk with me, George?"

"What for?"

Barone glanced at Carter, frowning.

"Oh, don't worry about Bobby. Bobby's all right, aren't you, Bobby? Me and George are gonna take a little walk, okay? You look after the drinks. We'll be right back. Come on, George. I got something to show you."

He got up, swayed slightly—careful not to overdo it—and turned toward the lobby without waiting to see if Barone would follow. After only two or three steps, he knew it was not going to work, and looked back.

"What's the matter?" he demanded, with a nice touch of querulousness. "You don't want your Christmas present?"

Joe's voice was a shade too assertive for Barone to risk an argument in public. He got up without a word, and followed Joe into the lobby.

Certain now that they had him, Joe headed for the elevators, but Barone took his arm suddenly and thrust him against the wall, ignoring his expostulations.

"You nearly did a stupid thing," he said, looking at Joe's throat.

"Me? What did I do?"

"Don't you talk to me on the pipe about nothing, understand? Just hullo, I wanna see you, good-bye. That's all."

"Well? So? What did I say? I didn't say nothing. I just said . . ."

"Don't talk." He poked Joe gently in the chest. "Listen. Learn something. They got the fucking phones bugged, okay? I gotta tell you that? So you don't say nothing to me about money. And you don't say nothing about any fucking Christmas present."

"Oh." Joe pulled a face. "Hey, man, I'm sorry. I was just excited about getting some money and everything. I didn't mean nothing."

"You wanna explain all that to some fucking cop? Just don't call me no more. Not ever. You wanna see me, tell Boyle."

"Sure, George." Joe hung his head.

"And there's something else," said Barone. "Don't drink. It makes you kinda loud."

"I don't drink, George. Never in my life. I just been celebrating a little bit." He saw Barone relax, and went on playing the fool, pointing upwards in an eager, questioning sort of way. "Okay? You wanna go get your present now?"

"Shit." Barone stepped back out of reach. "You don't listen. This is New York City. They could grab me with the money right on the fucking street."

"I don't understand." Joe shook his head. He refused to believe it. The son of a bitch was going to walk away clean. "I mean, what do you want me to do?"

"I want you to be a good boy and take it back to Miami. I'll get it from you there. We'll have lunch. At Fiore's place."

"What, Hendrick's? In Coral Gables?"

"Right. I wanna talk to you about Neilsen Shipping, and what we're gonna do with that."

Joe allowed himself to be piloted back to the bar.

"I don't know what's to talk about," he grumbled. "I told Jay. Cotrone's a thief. He's asking too much fucking money."

"Yeah. Well, Cotrone don't know it yet, but the price is three-twenty. He gets two-seventy. I get fifty."

"Hey, George. I don't *have* that kind of money, I keep telling you. Plus Neilsen ain't worth that much."

"Don't worry about the financing," Barone said. "We'll take care of it."

Joe met Carter's eye as they rejoined him. They had not been gone long enough for the plan to have worked. But Eagleton, meanwhile, had introduced himself to Carter, and Barone now reintroduced him to Joe as executive director of the Metropolitan Marine Maintenance Contractors' Association. The last time they had met, Eagleton had been involved with Barone in a scheme for manufacturing raincoats in Honduras to undercut the union shops of Seventh Avenue and Broadway. Now, in less obvious partnership, he was responsible for negotiating labor contracts with the ILA on behalf of New York's waterfront service industries.

His companion, whom Barone introduced as John Sullivan, had the build and conversational gifts of a nightclub bouncer. When they moved to a table to be more comfortable, he remained at the bar, drinking steadily and keeping an eye on the comings and goings until the place closed at 1 A.M.

As they left the bar, Joe drew Barone aside for one last try.

"George, do me a favor. Take the money? Nothing's gonna happen. It makes me nervous, running around with so much cash."

"It's all right," he said. "I'll see you in Miami."

"I'm not *going* to Miami, George. I'm gonna be in Jacksonville, remember?"

"That's okay. I trust you." He winked at Carter. "Howya doing?"

"Fine, George. Just fine."

"You're a good man, Bobby, so I'll tell you something. You too, Joe. Ilan's handing everybody up to save his own fucking ass, all right?"

"Yeah?" said Joe.

"Yeah. Including you," Barone said.

Joe looked at Carter. They did not have much to show for their evening.

"Well, George," he said sadly. "As long as I have you to take care of me, I don't worry."

Barone gave him a sideways look, then the benefit of the doubt, and left, flanked by Eagleton and Sullivan.

Two days later, Joe's doctor in Miami told him his blood pressure was up again. There was also bad news from Mutzie. The Cotrones had double-crossed them. While supposedly negotiating to sell Neilsen Shipping, they had put in a competitive bid for the Nopal Line account, based on figures Joe himself had provided in his bid for Neilsen's Trailer Ship Line.

This hurt Joe's pride. He had no intention either of buying Neilsen Shipping or of putting up with Mutzie after the investigation went public, but the Cotrones deserved a finger in the eye, and he went to see Boyle about it on December 17. But Boyle was not only unimpressed by the Cotrones' unethical behavior, he compounded Joe's grievance by demanding $2,000 for the rent.

That weekend, Joe drove down to Key Largo for the holidays with Ann, Marilyn, and Mark. As Barone had not seen fit to call or even leave a message about their proposed lunch at Hendrick's, Joe was no more interested than the Strike Force in rewarding his negligence with $8,700. He let Boyle worry about it for nearly two weeks before calling him at home on the evening of December 29. Ray Maria, as usual, listened in on the tape recorder monitor.

"Bill?"

"Yeah?"

"Joey here."

"Oh, for Chrissake. Where the hell have you been?"

"Key Largo. I told you last week my wife's family was coming to town."

"Yeah, but I didn't say . . . Listen, I didn't tip my mitt where you were. *I* know where you were. The other guy . . . you know, Twinkletoes . . . is asking me. I said, 'He's out of town. He has his family.' "

"Uh-huh."

"And he's bugging the shit out of me."

"Is that right?" Joe was glad to hear it.

"Oh, Jesus. I went around. I told Mutzie, and of course, Mutzie, playing it smart, he says, 'I don't know. You know, he's someplace.' I says, 'You see Joe, tell him I'd like to see him.' You know, or get in touch with you, or let me know where I can see you, or what you are doing."

Boyle seemed unable to make up his mind whether he *had* known where Joe was or not, and Joe was not about to help him out.

"Uh-huh," he said encouragingly.

"And it mostly comes from Nervous. Twinkletoes."

"You mean George?"

"Yeah."

"Well, does Barone want to see me?"

"Well, yeah. He says, 'Jesus Christ, Bill, get after him with that.' I said, 'Now wait a minute, George. First of all, I have to find him.' That's how I've been stalling him. I said, 'He's got family down, and he had to go see a few attorneys.' "

"Uh-huh, uh-huh."

"And then he called. He said, 'Jeez, I thought he was gonna . . .' I said, 'Hey, George. I told Joey that you would call him that same night to set up a luncheon appointment the following day' . . . which was Thursday."

"But Barone never called me."

"He never called you, you know? So now . . ."

"When I met George in New York . . . You know the story, okay?"

Joe went through it again anyway, about how Barone had been afraid to take the money, and their proposed lunch date.

"In the meantime," he said, "I come back to Miami, and I find out about this double-cross with Benny Cotrone."

"Well, he knows all about that one."

"Okay. Then I want to sit with George. I got the money, that's no problem. But I want to sit with him because I'm really upset with this Cotrone deal."

"Yeah, sure. I think the other guy's able to straighten that out, you understand? I think he's got something in conversation to talk to you about."

"Who, George?"

"Yeah. That part's okay. But you know what you're doing to me? You make me look bad with him."

"How?"

"Well, because of the situation that you did up above. Then I'm supposed to come to you and say, 'Listen, Joe, you and *I* are supposed to do these things.' "

"Well, Bill, I had it in New York. What did you want me to do with it, you know?"

He winked at Ray Maria. This one was going well. Barone might be too smart to do it to himself, but having Boyle do it to him was the next best thing.

"I understand that, but get my point, Joe. I don't like to blow my horn, but this is the way they think. You never . . . Not one time could you ever do anything there with him. You understand that?"

"Yeah."

"Right? So now when he says, 'What's he trying to do? You know, that would get me in a lot of trouble,' I said, 'Well, the fellow meant well. Sure of that.'"

"By trying to give him something in New York?"

"Yeah."

"It's like a one-way street, you know? Who gets all the heat? You get it from your guys . . ."

"Yeah."

". . . and I get it from *my* people. Okay?"

"Right. Yeah. We're the buffers."

"Exactly. And, ah, what else I want to say to you? That Cotrone. There's no way that he can have what he wants, you know?"

"He's getting the pressure put on him. Wherever it's coming from, I don't know."

"Well, George said he was gonna lean on him."

"Yeah. Well, I think that is what it is. And it came from upstairs. That's what I make out of it that makes any kind of sense to me at all. Because George has a funny delivery, you know? You gotta first know this guy to find out what he's really talking about. Because he gives you bits. Then I always know when he's reneging. The little guy'll tell you the same thing."

"Understand." Joe looked at Maria to see if there was anything else he should bring up. "Well, look, I got it. Tell him I got it."

"Yeah, yeah. Don't worry about it. I just like to touch bases with you so I know how to scramble a little bit."

"Yeah, right." Maria was scribbling something on a pad. "Well, do me a favor. Tell George that you spoke to me in Key Largo."

"Okay."

"That you and I will get together on Tuesday."

Maria showed him the pad. He had written: Field. Tickets.

"All right," said Boyle.

"Ah, one thing, okay? Is Freddy pissed at me about the tickets?"

"Nah, I straightened that out."

"Well, if he *is* pissed at anybody, he should be pissed at Zonis, because . . ."

"Yeah. Well, we have a way of doing . . . you know. I'll explain to you when I see you. I'll tell you what we have in mind."

"Well, I know what he said. He says, 'You and that fucking Jew friend of yours are gonna repent.'"

"Well, he didn't mean it actually. He's got to say that to you. Zonis will be coming to me very shortly. You know, it isn't too far away."

"In September he needs a new contract, right?"

"That's right. Anyway, he looks like a real shit-ass vice-president," Boyle added, suddenly vicious. "Fucking holes in his shirt. He smells.

He's fat. What has this guy got that they need this fucking schmuck?"

"I . . . I can't answer you." It was almost funny, but not quite.

"Impossible. He's an obnoxious-looking fucking man. For a business."

"What can I tell you? William, have a very happy New Year." He put his hand over the mouthpiece. "Only don't count on it," he added, and Maria smiled.

"And you, too," Boyle was saying. "And you have a good happy New Year, and a good healthy one, and everything is gonna be okay, Joseph. Don't worry about it. We'll always get a little aggravation in this fucking business, but you never let it get you down."

"I hear you," said Joe.

He was back at work on Tuesday, January 4, 1977, resolved to give Boyle a little more of the aggravation he had been so philosophical about. He refused to talk to him or to part with any money until he spoke to Barone. Boyle said he was making things very embarrassing for him, but returned on Wednesday with Barone in tow.

Joining them in the hallway, Joe again registered his complaint that while the Cotrones were outwardly negotiating in good faith to sell their business to him, they had gone behind his back and tried to steal a major account. As he went on and on about their duplicity, about the payoffs he had made, and the protection he felt entitled to, Barone fidgeted back and forth with mounting impatience, and finally cut him short.

"Look," he said, coming so close that Joe smelled the warmth of his breath. "If Joey Cotrone fucks with the Nopal contract, him, his father, his sisters, they're all fucking dead, okay? That's yours."

"Okay." Joe eased back a pace. "But they couldn't have done it without Hulander. And that means Harvey Sykes has got a hand in this someplace."

"Forget Harvey. I'll take care of Harvey. What else?"

"That's it, George. Get Cotrone straightened out for me, and that's it. I'm happy."

"All right. Now you straighten out, too. Make *me* happy, okay?"

He rubbed his fingers together suggestively and scurried off, with Boyle at his heels.

Boyle called soon afterwards to say that Joe now owed them $10,700, and that Nervous was waiting next door for his money. He had to have it that day. Joe said he would go and get it, but he knew it was already too late in the afternoon for Ray Maria to set up the payoff. He therefore left word at his office that he was going to the doctor, and went home instead.

Next morning, he presented himself at Local 1922 with $4,000, and a new, miniaturized recorder strapped to the inside of his thigh. Boyle greeted him with only partly feigned dislike, and followed Joe into the hall.

"You know, last night, he called me up to see what had happened with you? Why don't you just tell me you're not gonna come back?''

"I had to go to the doctor, and then I had, uh . . .''

"Yeah, but just tell me about it. I go back in there, he says, 'He's fucking me around again. Our talk didn't do any good.' ''

"That's bullshit. How about Cotrone? Did George go over there?''

"Oh, yeah. I went first to talk about another matter, and they come in right after us. They said, 'Stay here.' Wanted me to hear this, you know? Pretty cute, George.''

"He really leaned on him, huh?'' said Joe, closing the door of the men's room behind him.

"Oh, yeah," said Boyle, checking the cubicles. He flushed two of them, so the noise of running water would jam any bugs that might have been planted overnight.

"I got four Gs here." Joe waved the envelope. "All I got left. The rest of it I used for Marilyn's tuition. By the end of the month, my CD is free at the bank. I'll open it up, and bring you the rest of it then.''

"Oh. Okay. You got me, you know, the monthly?''

"I'll take care of that Monday.''

"All right. 'Cause I laid that out to George. That's the truth. Get him off my back.''

"There's two thousand," said Joe, as he finished counting it into Boyle's hand.

"Okay.''

"There's four thousand," he said, completing the count. "Right up front. And I'll take care of the rest later.''

"All right. That should do it. See, Joey, he's a pain in the balls. You've no idea. You know, he's not like Jay and me. He's one of those fucking, *demanding* guys. 'Well, maybe you got there too late,' he says. I said, 'I didn't get there too late.' I can get into an argument very easy, and then he won't talk to you for days. 'Maybe you didn't go when you said you were going.' I said, 'Ah, yes, I was there. He couldn't get out. He had two meetings. He couldn't go the first time. The second time I come back,' I said, 'somebody in the office told me he went to the doctor.' So there's a lull in the conversation. Then he says, 'He's fucking me around.' I said, 'Well, I don't think so.' And then I got to go before all of them when I get this. I'm the bad guy. That's the truth, Joey.''

"You cover everything, right?''

"Yeah." Boyle flushed another toilet moodily. "I don't get anybody in bad with 'em, and I come up with it 'cause I know they're good for it. And I like peace and harmony.''

"Hey, man. I'm breaking my balls, okay?''

On their way back to the office, Boyle said he had attended a meeting of the employers' association the previous day with Cleveland Turner, who had wanted to know why Joe was not a member.

Joe reminded Boyle that Barone had told Pierside Terminal Operators *not* to join in case he needed to use Joe as a wedge in negotiations.

"Well, that's right," said Boyle.

"Yeah," Joe said. "Turner called *me* yesterday."

"Yeah?"

"Yeah. And he says, 'Christmas done came and went.' "

They both laughed.

19

Surprise Attack

THEN it was all over.

And suddenly everybody wanted to talk about his future.

He was the government's principal witness, said Mike Levin; the essential linkman in the complex criminal conspiracy that lay at the heart of the case. His testimony would place the main conspirators in a pattern of graft and corruption involving the nation's major ports. Joe's safety was therefore a matter of critical importance. As soon as the story got out, the other side would be as anxious to see him dead as the government was to keep him alive.

In the opinion of Mike Levin, John Evans, the Special Attorney who had joined Levin from Washington to work on the case, Ray Maria, Attlee Wampler III, head of the Miami Strike Force, and all the other agents and attorneys involved in 17 different Federal Districts, Joe ought now to disappear, to go quietly underground, protected by the U.S. Marshal's Service, until called upon to testify before the grand jury and then at the trial itself.

"No," Joe said.

He was worried about how to break the news to Ann.

"We've been married twenty-two years, and I've no idea how she's gonna take it." Rabbi Baumgard had not been prepared to speculate either. "All I know is, Ray, when I tell her, *you* better be there or *she's* gonna kill me."

Maria and Levin did not appreciate the joke. Something like 900 subpoenas were about to be served on shipping and ILA officials, organized crime figures, and other potential witnesses in one massive, coordinated sweep from Portland, Maine, to Brownsville, Texas. A federal grand jury had been empaneled in Miami, and was scheduled to open its hearings on February 8. Once the investigation went public, they said, it would be impossible to keep his part in it a secret, and therefore next to impossible to keep him alive if he refused to cooperate. The only sensible course was to take advantage of the Federal Witness Program, which had been devised precisely to cope with this kind of situation.

"No," Joe said.

He thought Ann might appreciate more what he had done, and better understand his reasons for keeping her in the dark, if she heard about it from someone other than him, from someone whose word she would have to respect.

"Mike, do you think you and Ray could be there when I tell her? And Attlee Wampler?"

There was something Joe should know, Maria said. They were going to confront Bill Boyle with overwhelming evidence of his guilt to see if they could turn him into a government witness. They would offer him at least partial immunity and full federal protection in exchange for his testimony against Field, Barone, Vanderwyde, and others. To have any hope of success, they would have to play him some of the more damaging tapes, identify Carter, Aber, and Owens as Special Agents Robert Cassidy, Richard Artin, and William Oliver, and generally make plain the central role that Joe had played in his downfall. If the idea miscarried, it would inevitably set him up as a priority target for reprisals, which in turn made it absolutely essential that he be a good fellow, and do as they suggested.

"No," Joe said.

In the first place it was stupid. He knew Boyle better than they did. There was no way he was going to flip. He was not the type. They would simply tip their hand a lot sooner than they had to and give the whole bunch that much more time to regroup and cover its tracks.

"And in the second place," he said, "unless you can offer me a better deal than that, I won't even testify *myself.*"

They argued about it every day for a week. Then Maria arranged for Frank No, head of the U.S. Marshal's Witness Protection Program, to fly down from Washington to meet Joe at the Airport Lakes Holiday Inn and set him straight. What they were going to do, No said, was give him and Ann a new name, a new identity, and resettle them in another part of the country. The government would naturally pay all their expenses, take care of any other problems that came up, and keep an eye on their children. It was not an ideal solution to the problem, No conceded, but several hundred Federal witnesses had started a new life under the program, and could now face the future with a reasonable sense of security.

Joe laughed. He could think of nothing adequate to say.

"You're all fucking crazy," he said.

"Well, I'm afraid that's it, Joe. There's no other way we can *guarantee* your safety. How long do you think you'll need to get your affairs in order?"

"Now wait a minute." They actually seemed to be serious. "Lemme make sure I understand what you're saying. You want me to change my name and leave Miami, right? You want me to give up my kids. Give up my business. Give up my friends and my home. And if I do all that, you'll help me start over someplace else. Is that it?"

"No point beating about the bush, Joe. We'll get you and Ann together again with Marilyn and Mark as soon as we think it's safe, but that's about the size of it, yes."

He was utterly dumbfounded. He had never in his life conceived of a treachery so fundamental, so extravagant, and yet so mean.

"I don't understand," he said, determined to be reasonable. "I risk my neck. I take you by the hand through a racket you never been able to touch before. I help you clean up the waterfront, and this is the thanks I get? You gotta be kidding me."

"Joe, you don't . . ."

"Forget it. I don't even wanna talk about it anymore. If you ask people to come forward and work with you, you're gonna have to do better than *this*. In fact, if you ever wanna see *me* in court, you're gonna have to do better. I mean, I been royally screwed in my time, but you guys make Field look like a fucking amateur."

"Now come on, Joe. What did you *think* was going to happen? How else are we supposed to look after you?"

"That's *your* end of it," he said. "You'll have to work something out, won't you? I seem to remember somebody telling me this was the U.S. government I was dealing with. If we needed the Marines in here . . . and all that bullshit."

"Joe, we got a plan that works. It'll keep you alive. I know it must sound a little rough to you right now, but give it a chance. Come into the program until the trial, say. Then we'll look at it again. After all, what are we talking about? A year? Maybe you'll find it's not such a bad deal after all."

"You know, I just don't *believe* this. You guys . . ." He broke off in disgust and bewilderment. "Let's say *two* years, all right? I know this case. And then what? After I give my testimony? It's take it or leave it, right? No thanks. I don't buy that. I've given up enough already. I'm not giving up any more."

He stood up to go, and they looked at one another.

"You want to give up your life, Joe? There's a good chance of that if you don't come into the program."

"Go fuck yourself. I've been threatened by experts."

"Then take a vacation. The Strike Force is going to have its hands full. Take Ann on a trip. Make yourself scarce for thirty days. No harm in that, is there?"

Joe looked back from the door.

"All right? A little vacation on Uncle Sam? It'll give you a chance to think this over quietly . . . talk it out."

Studying their faces, he finally accepted that nobody cared. In spite of everything he had done and failed to do, he had believed all his life in truth and justice and the American way, and nobody cared. He felt faintly ridiculous.

"Sure," he said.

That evening, he started to square his conscience. He told Ann he was leaving the family business for good at the end of the month, and that was no lie. He had just had another big fight with Mutzie, he said, which was pretty nearly always true. And now he wanted her to go with him to Texas for a few days as he had been offered an important job with a steamship company in Houston, which was really the whitest of lies, for the FBI had asked him to confer with its agents there about the investigation going on in the port. Afterwards, he said, they could take a few weeks off to drive through the Southwest and California, if she would like to.

Ann responded like a prisoner released from solitary, unbelieving at first, but then with a mounting charge of excitement that made Joe wonder if, rather than easing the blow when it fell, he was instead softening her up for it.

On the morning of Tuesday, January 25, 1977, Operation Unirac went public. Several hundred agents moved in simultaneously on every ILA union office and scores of waterfront companies from Maine to Texas to serve close to a thousand subpoenas, some commanding the attendance of officials before federal grand juries in Miami and New York, the rest requiring the production of union and company records by the truckload.

In the evening, Attlee Wampler III and Mike Levin drove out to Joe's house to help him break the news. Marilyn was away in Gainesville, at the University of Florida, but Mark was home, and Joe sat him down next to his mother before taking a deep breath and introducing his visitors. He was so strangled with apprehension, he could hardly speak.

Ann went white when she heard who they were, but recovered quickly as he gabbled on, and took the story fairly well, he thought. There were moments, while Wampler and Levin were stressing the importance of what he had done, when she seemed almost proud of him, particularly when she realized that the Guzman affair had had nothing to do with it. If it had not been for her and the children, she said, Joe would probably have gone to them 10 years earlier.

How much of that was keeping up appearances, and how much an indication of acceptance and forgiveness, Joe could not be sure. He did not press the point after Wampler and Levin left, sensing it might be better if he gave her time to reflect on the past 16 months in the light of what she now knew.

Next morning, Bob Richardson was at the airport to see off Mr. and Mrs. Joe Katz (Federal Witness Coordination No. 1935), who were traveling first to Gainesville, for a serious talk with their daughter Marilyn, and then on to Houston and a four-week vacation.

As case agent, Ray Maria had been sorry not to accompany Wampler and Levin the previous evening, but he had had another engagement. With Special Agent William Oliver, better known on Dodge Island as Bill Owens, he had driven up to Fort Lauderdale to confront William Wallace Boyle with conclusive evidence of his guilt.

Having had his records subpoenaed that morning, Boyle was not as surprised as he might have been. He listened in bleak silence for two hours while the agents reviewed the case against him, and then, as Joe had predicted, showed them the door.

While this was going on, the FBI was having slightly better luck with Isom Clemon in Mobile. Still posing as Dick Aber, Special Agent Richard Artin had asked Clemon to meet him in his room at the Sheraton Inn to discuss a little business. While they were talking, two other agents arrived, by prearrangement, and treated both of them as suspects, advising them of their rights and of the nature of the investigation in progress. Asked if he had ever taken any money from Aber, Clemon hotly denied it, expecting Aber to back him up. Instead, Special Agent Artin produced his credentials, and Clemon lost his head.

Unlike Boyle, who was just then refusing to say anything, Clemon now admitted taking money as "a consultant." Everything else he denied, including conversations recorded on tape. No, he had never said he had any influence over President Jimmy Carter, the President's mother, Lillian Carter, or U.S. Senators Sparkman, Nunn, and Talmadge, nor had he ever called Governor George Wallace for money to pay off a federal judge. Yes, he was trying to put an oil deal together with the President's former aides, Cloyd Hall and Phil Courtney, but he had never mentioned a five percent commission for Fred Field, nor had he told Teitelbaum about South African diamonds being used for payoffs with the help of a banker's wife from the Bahamas.

Wednesday, January 26, was another busy day for the Miami Strike Force. On their way over to interview Harvey Sykes on Northwest 36th Street, Special Agents Joseph Frechette and Edward Turner stopped at Eagle Tire Company on Northwest North River Drive to tell Joe's "good" Uncle Issy about his nephew's undercover work for the government, so that he could pass the news on to the rest of the family. Uncle Issy was not impressed. He thought Joe was a schmuck to risk getting himself killed.

Harvey Sykes was not very impressed by the investigation either. He knew nothing of any payoffs or shakedowns, he said. He had been listening to that kind of talk on the waterfront for years.

Meanwhile, Special Agent Arthur Gill was calling on Neal Harrington, president of Harrington & Company and Atlantic Stevedoring, at his office on Northeast Second Avenue. Harrington flatly denied giving money or gifts to any ILA official, even though some *had* indicated from time to time that he ought to "share the wealth." Nor had he ever "bought" any favors or contracts, he said. The only tangible courtesy he had ever extended to union officials was the occasional use of a company pass to a Miami Dolphins football game.

Jeremy Chester, president of Chester, Blackburn & Roder, also had to be persuaded that the government meant business. When Bob Richardson and Special Agent John Hexter called that morning at his office on Northwest 70th Avenue to serve subpoenas, his first response was, "Oh, you're still at it?" But after hearing an outline of the government's case, he had to admit they had gotten it right this time.

"It doesn't appear that you overlooked anything," he said, acknowledging that payoffs were routine throughout the industry. Employers were forced into it, he claimed, by the ILA's "stranglehold" on the waterfront.

In contrast, Special Agents William Oliver and Robert McVey could scarcely get a word in edgeways with Eduardo Garcia, sometime general manager of Ocean Trailer Transport, the Reynolds Metals' subsidiary that operated the *Siboney,* and now general manager in Miami of Prudential Lines. As soon as he heard why they were there, Garcia began to unburden himself so volubly that the interview spilled over to a second, and then a third day.

He admitted almost eagerly to a history of illegal payoffs going back to the start of his association with Barone in 1971, and unraveled a tangle of shady business connections between half a dozen prominent waterfront firms. He also wanted to know if he could avoid testifying before the grand jury and instead make his first appearance as a witness at Barone's actual trial. Remembering what had happened after earlier leaks of grand jury testimony, he feared for his life if word got out that he was cooperating with the government. In any case, he was going to buy a gun to protect himself. Barone and the ILA ran the Port of Miami like "a police state," he said.

One of the firms Garcia mentioned was Florida Welding Services Corporation, of Northwest 66th Street. According to his estimate, it handled about a quarter of the container repair business in the port, working mainly for container leasing companies. When Special Agents Donald Rivers and Robert Payne called there on the morning of January 26, they found Ray Kopituk, president, Oscar Morales, vice president, and Dorothy Kopituk, secretary-treasurer, courteous and helpful, but totally unaware, they said, of payoffs, sweetheart contracts, or any other corrupt or improper business practice involving anyone anywhere at any time.

On January 27, the same two agents interviewed Laura Cotrone at the offices of United Container & Ship Repair, Northwest First Avenue. In the absence of her father, Sebastian "Benny" Cotrone, who was recovering from a cataract operation, and her brother Joseph, who was busy on Dodge Island, she was managing not only United Container, which handled about 65 percent of the port's container repairs, but also Florida Refrigerated Truck and Trailer Service Company.

She willingly described some of her family's recent business transactions, including the sale of the Bay Container Repair Company in New Jersey to Umberto Guido, a cousin of Jim Fiore's, and president of the Metropolitan Marine Maintenance Contractors' Association, of New York; the pending sale of the Bay Container Repair Company of New York to Vincent Marino, a cousin of Anthony Anastasio; the purchase of United Trailer Services in Jacksonville, and of K. Neilsen Shipping in Miami. She was also the sole owner of L.C. Lashing Company of Brooklyn. Her father, she said, had known Anthony Scotto and Anthony Anastasio for many years, but she had absolutely no knowledge of any payoffs or corrupt business practices, either in New York or Miami.

Benny Cotrone said much the same thing, only more picturesquely, when Special Agents Robert Friedrick and James Fanning visited him at home in Hollywood, Florida.

"I hate the guts of the unions," he said. The only payments he made to them were the dues deducted from his employees' paychecks. If Barone or Boyle asked him for money, he added, "I would bust their heads. Or get *my* head busted."

The New York Times picked up the story that morning under a front-page headline: "U.S. Summons 350 in Two-Coast Inquiry on Pier Kickbacks." FBI Director Clarence Kelley was prepared to say only that a major investigation was in progress, but *The Times* had a shrewd idea of what was going on. The government was after Anthony Scotto again, having just indicted Fred Field for taking money from employers.

"You're going to tar and feather me," Scotto was quoted as saying. "There's no way that Joe Blow can come up and say that he's given me a nickel."

A day later, and with obvious access to inside information, the *Miami Herald* of January 28 filled in some of the background to the story. "Probers Look for ILA Payoffs," ran the headline. The focus of the inquiry, its report said, was on "systematic payoffs by businessmen to certain union officials controlling ports along the East and Gulf Coasts." Beginning in Miami, the inquiry had spread to other ports, the paper went on, and was now "being called the biggest labor probe since the Justice Department's efforts against Jimmy Hoffa and the Teamsters."

Among the businessmen interviewed by the FBI that morning about "systematic payoffs" was Alvin P. Chester, president of American Marine Industries, who denied all knowledge of payoffs or other improprieties involving Chester, Blackburn & Roder or Marine Terminals and officers of the ILA. He liked Barone, he said, because "you know where you stand with him."

Special Agents Richard Artin and William Coggin, meanwhile, were questioning Robert Lee Bateman, president of Local 1422A, in Charleston, South Carolina. In no position to deny transporting a $4,000 payoff from Artin in Mobile to Field and Boyle in Norfolk, Bateman admitted receiving several cash payments from Boyle to ensure "labor peace" in Charleston for Umberto Guido and James Fiore, of Streaker Marine Services, and DeMott and Hodges, of Great Southern Trailer Corporation.

By the weekend, the flurry of activity touched off by the subpoenas began to subside as government attorneys, accountants, and agents set about the formidable job of examining hundreds of tons of union and company records in the light of the evidence already in their possession. The next phase of the investigation was scheduled for February 8, when the Miami grand jury would convene for its opening session with a dozen witnesses in attendance, including Boyle and Eduardo Garcia. But on February 4, Ray Maria picked up the first hint of a counterattack. Garcia came to see him in a state of near-panic to report that Barone had just taken him for a walk up Northwest Second Avenue.

He had made no threats or suggestions as to the testimony Garcia might give to the grand jury. He had simply talked in generalities about the investigation, and then informed him that "they had got Bill Boyle" because Joey Teitelbaum had been "wired." Having solicited Garcia's condemnation of this treachery, he had gone on to say that he, Barone, had nothing to worry about because he had done nothing wrong, and after soliciting Garcia's agreement to that, too, he had gone on his way, leaving Garcia thoroughly unnerved and his usefulness as a witness severely undermined. Added to his previous qualms about possible leaks, the encounter rendered him tongue-tied, hesitant, and reluctant even to confirm the information he had already provided.

The setback was minor, however, and immediately offset by an unexpected bonus. Less skilled in the techniques of intimidation than his master, Boyle now tried to break out of the trap by eliminating the two principal witnesses against him but succeeded only in *adding* two, in the persons of Ramon DeMott and James Hodges, who had both been summoned to appear before the grand jury on February 22.

About a week before his own appearance, scheduled for February 8, Boyle asked them to meet him at the Ramada Inn in Savannah. They were not anxious to be seen in his company, having broken the law themselves by paying him off, and still less eager to discuss the case in public.

"It makes no difference," Boyle told them, in the hotel's crowded lounge. "They got me already. The Jew set it up. We would like to . . . we have a contract on the Jew. It'd be nice if he wasn't around on the twenty-second, right? Him *and* Aber, both."

To their increasing alarm, Boyle went on to explain what he meant. As they were all in this together, he was offering them a contract on the lives of Joe Teitelbaum and the man they now knew to be Special Agent Richard Artin of the FBI. If anything went wrong, Boyle said, "they" would look after them. "They" had people everywhere.

DeMott was so nervous by now that he went to the men's room, and the meeting broke up. Next day, he and Hodges went to see their attorney, who, in turn, approached Michael Levin in Miami with a view to making a deal. On February 15, each agreed to plead guilty to a Taft–Hartley violation, carrying a maximum penalty of one year's imprisonment and a $10,000 fine, and to cooperate fully as government witnesses, in return for immunity from prosecution on other, more serious charges.

Knowing nothing of this, Boyle had meanwhile presented himself before the grand jury on February 8. In response to Levin's questioning, he told the jurors he had worked on the New York waterfront, in the restaurant business, and as manager of a Long Island golf club before moving to Miami in 1965. On July 1, 1966, he had gone to work for George Barone as business agent of Local 1922, and a year later, had been elected secretary-treasurer, a position he had held ever since, adding to it the office of International vice president at the end of 1975.

With every appearance of candor, he then described his duties, and went on to discuss his salary and expenses until it suddenly occurred to him, after categorically denying he had ever accepted money from employers, that he had been committing perjury for the past several minutes. He then left the jury room to confer with his attorney, Michael Maisin, and upon his return, declined to answer any further questions on the grounds of possible self-incrimination. In fact, Boyle's denial was the last direct answer to a material question that Levin was able to get from any of the principal conspirators in front of the grand jury. Profiting from Boyle's experience, Barone and the others invoked their Fifth Amendment privileges as soon as they appeared, refusing to admit even that they knew one another.

That was not unexpected. Considerably more annoying was what appeared to be a second success for Barone's psychological warfare. Having given nothing away at his first interview, Harvey Sykes had since refused to discuss the case with anybody but his attorney, as was his right. The story was going around, however, that he had told Barone he would refuse to testify before the grand jury even if offered immunity from prosecution, apparently preferring to risk jail for contempt than Barone's displeasure.

How much of this was protective coloration, and how much an expression of genuine solidarity with the racketeers was open to doubt. The betting on the government side was that a couple of months to reflect on the prospects of martyrdom, perhaps to no purpose, would restore Sykes's native flexibility, and with several hundred witnesses to examine, Levin was in no hurry. But it was worrying. Except for Joe and the agents who had worked with him, everybody else on the waterfront could be pressured as easily by Barone as by the government, and a clear pattern of intimidation was starting to take shape, backed by a proven readiness to kill.

This, of course, made Joe's testimony, already central to the case, still more vital, and the question of his safety correspondingly more pressing, but nobody knew for certain where he was. He had been reporting in only when he thought of it.

Without telling anyone, he and Ann returned home from "vacation" on February 23.

The trip had gone well, he thought. Ann seemed to understand why he had deceived her and to be ready to face their uncertain future. There were also signs of a new independence in her attitude. She was clearly determined to have at least an equal say from now on in matters that concerned her, but he felt closer to her than he had for years. What they both badly needed was a chance to settle down again, which naturally ruled out the idea of relocation or any such foolishness.

The first call he made on returning home was to Bob Richardson.

"Bob? Joey."

"Hey, man. Howya doing? How's the vacation coming?"

"Oh, great. Just great. Ann and me, we had a wonderful time, let me tell you."

"Well, that's good news, Joe. Because I don't mind saying I was kind of worried about you two. Where are you now?"

"We just got in. Not ten minutes ago."

"You're *back?*" The alarm in Richardson's voice was unmistakable. "You mean, you're *home?*"

"Sure. Why not? Something wrong?"

"Goddammit, Joe. Why didn't you tell me you were coming? You should have let me check the house first, for Chrissake."

"Why?" he asked lamely, knowing the answer. "I'm not worried."

"Well, you should be. I'm coming over."

"At this hour? Come on. Can't it wait till morning?"

"No, it can't. Call Ray Maria. He'll fill you in."

Maria was equally displeased when Joe called, and on hearing about Boyle's talk with DeMott and Hodges, Joe could understand why. He promised not to tell anybody else he was back, and Richardson helped him double-check the doors and windows. That was all right. He was ready to take reasonable precautions. But Miami was his home, and Miami was where he was going to stay. He told Levin and Maria so next morning, refusing point-blank even to discuss the Witness Protection Program as outlined by Frank No, or to leave town again while they took the matter up with Washington. He was not just being stubborn, he said. He hadn't beaten off the mob just to let the *government* drive him out.

A few hours later, Bob Richardson called to say he had been assigned to act as Joe's bodyguard for the time being. Like it or not, they were about to become inseparable. He would pick Joe up in the morning, stay with him all day, and take him home at night. Joe could explain this to Ann any way he wanted, Richardson said, but if he ever left the house without him, Joe would also need a bodyguard to protect him from his bodyguard.

"Well, that's okay," said Kessler. "As far as it goes. But do they think hitmen work union hours or what? I better talk to those guys."

"You really think it's that serious? What do you think I ought to do, Mel?"

"*Now* he asks me."

"What's the matter? You don't think I did the right thing?"

"It's Ann I'm thinking about. If I'd known what you were doing, I might have helped you build in a little protection up front, before you went ahead and committed yourself." He shook his head in self-reproof. "I should have guessed you were up to something."

"Are you proud of me for what I did?"

"I don't know if I'm proud or mad. I'll let you know when I figure it out. In the meantime, I better have a word with Levin."

"You don't think I did a good thing?"

"Joey, what do you want me to say? I'm your friend. Anything you do is all right with me, and I'll help you all I can. Sure, you did a good thing. I just don't think you really thought it through, that's all. I think you got suckered into this because you never learned how to back off from anything."

"I don't agree," said Joe. He was not offended. He had wondered about that himself. "I know what I'm doing. These guys are gonna go to jail. And when people find out what's been going on, I think there's gonna be some new legislation. The shipping business needs cleaning up."

"Fine. I hope you're right. Until then, you better get under the bed and not come out for a year or two."

Joe grunted. "You heard from the family?"

"Have I heard? Your mother calls me every day."

"How about Gus?"

"He's okay. I talked to him a couple of times."

"That all? Nobody else?"

"Mutzie. *He* called."

"Yeah?" He laughed. "Wants his money before somebody whacks me out, right?"

"Wrong. I'll tell you what he said. He said, 'I may hate the little bastard, but we'll stand behind him.' Okay? Don't put 'em down, Joe. You're the kind of family that fights a lot but nobody else gets to join in. He didn't even mention the money. I guess he figures you'll need it if you have to relocate, or something."

"Hey, wait a minute." Joe straightened up sharply. "Don't *you* start. I'm not going anyplace. I told Levin. I said, 'You wanna know why I did this? I did it because I got tired of Barone and those guys pushing me around,' I said. 'Now *you're* trying to push me around. And I'm getting tired of that, too. You want me to give evidence? Fine,' I said. 'Glad to do it. You think they'll try to kill me? Okay. I'm an American citizen. I'm going about my business in my own country and helping you catch these guys. So protect me. Otherwise, why do I pay my taxes?' "

"Joe, it's not as simple as that."

"Yes, it *is* as simple as that. The government *owes* me. I didn't have to do this. I *gave* them this case. I gave them a handle on the biggest crooked operation this country's ever seen. And now they're telling me to give up everything I ever worked for? Including my *children?* In a pig's eye."

"Joe . . ."

"I gotta call myself Joe Katz, and go wash dishes for a living in Sioux Falls, or something? Bullshit. My name's Joe Teitelbaum. I worked on the waterfront all my life. What else do I know? I told him, 'Forget that. I'm not hiding in any closet,' I said. Or under the bed either. 'Things will be what they will be,' I said. 'You and Barone will both know where to find me. I'm not running. I'm not hiding. You do what you gotta do,' I said, 'and I'll do the same.' That's what I told him, and now I'm telling you. So don't waste your breath."

Kessler sighed. "Well, I guess I *am* kind of proud of you at that," he said.

"Okay." It was really all he had wanted to know. "As far as I'm concerned, it's business as usual."

"Well, now you *are* talking crazy. *What* business? You don't *have* a business. Mutzie doesn't want you. And even if he did, the first time you set foot on Dodge Island, cops or no cops, they'll have to scrape you off the bottom of something heavy."

"Did I *say* Dodge Island? The only reason I stayed as long as I did was to nail those assholes. No, I'm talking about the river. Nobody's gonna bother me there. The union can't get in for three or four years yet, and the government'll have it all cleaned up by then."

"Oh, yeah. Sure."

"You know that piece of land we got next to Eagle Tire? The vacant lot? That's five and some acres. There's enough river frontage for two boats at once, and plenty enough room for a big apron, and a warehouse, and a parking lot as well. So that's what I'm gonna do. I'm gonna build myself a new terminal."

"Uh-huh. And what are you planning to use for money?"

"Oh, I figure we can find some when the time comes. I got a deal cooking in the back of my mind, so don't worry about it."

"Joe, you don't even know you can get the land. Who does it belong to? Eagle Tire?"

"I'll get it. I'll go sit with Uncle Issy. If he says yes, the others will go along. I'll guarantee 'em five thousand dollars a month, say, and they'll go along. It's found money, right? Lot's not doing anything. They got no plans for it."

"Oh, Jesus," said Kessler helplessly. "You *sure* you don't want to wash dishes in Sioux Falls?"

Joe was quite sure.

By the middle of April, he had put the deal together. Every member of the family holding stock in Eagle Tire had signed an agreement leasing him the land for a guaranteed $6,000 a month clear. He had also concluded an agreement with his old friends Ray Thompson and Barbara Evans, of Pioneer Shipping, assigning *them* the lease for 20 years in consideration of a partnership and a 20-year employment contract as terminal manager. Pioneer would finance the construction, but save itself the capital cost of the cargo handling equipment by leasing Joe's crane, the one smuggled back from St. Croix, and his seven forklifts, taken from PTO on Dodge Island in settlement of a $63,000 loan that the company had never repaid.

By June 1, when his contract with Pioneer went into effect, Joe could easily have forgotten about the investigation but for the constant presence of Richardson at his elbow. Ann, too, hardly mentioned it anymore. Outside of the family and those immediately concerned, no one knew anything about Joe's part in it, the story had dropped out of the newspapers, and she had picked up her life again much as before. But Richardson never missed a day.

Harvey Sykes was also being careful. Sooner than risk having to testify against Barone, even in secret, he had invoked his Fifth Amendment privilege in response to every question Levin put to him at his first grand jury appearance. Expecting that, Levin had then applied for a court order directing Sykes to testify under a grant of immunity from criminal proceedings based on his testimony. This was granted on June 16, but when Levin recalled him to the jury room, Sykes again refused stubbornly to answer his questions. This time, however, he was defying a court order, and on June 28, he was committed to the Federal Correctional Center at Perrine until he purged his contempt.

He held out for six weeks, appearing before the grand jury on August 10 after giving the court a written undertaking that he would now answer any and all questions put to him.

Asked if he had ever given money to Barone, he said: "I have never paid George Barone one penny in my whole life."

He did, however, admit to paying "a few thousand dollars" to William Boyle in 1970 or 1971 for various "favors" that fell conveniently outside the five-year period covered by the Federal Statute of Limitations.

Asked why he had told the court he was too frightened to testify if that was all he had to hide, Sykes said: "I felt that it might be endangering myself by testifying to anything that jeopardizes another person's position, particularly in the ILA union." When asked if he was frightened of Boyle or Barone, however, he said no.

Though naturally dissatisfied with his answers, Levin arranged for Sykes's release from custody, pending yet another grand jury appearance in September, but it was now Joe's turn to face the music again. On September 1, the precarious peace of the summer, based largely on his public anonymity, was abruptly destroyed by a front-page story in *The New York Times.*

It was not a complete surprise, for Nicholas Gage, then the paper's specialist in organized crime, had telephoned him for confirmation of a so-called "leak" about the investigation from the FBI's New York office. Taken off-guard, Joe had tried to cover up, referring Gage to Levin and hoping the problem would simply go away, but seeing the story in print was a big enough shock to remind him uncomfortably of his heart. That he should have been mentioned at all was bad enough. What made it unbearable was that he emerged without credit; not as a reluctant crusader risking his neck in the public interest, but as a crooked businessman cooperating with the FBI to save his own skin.

Clearly misled by his "sources," Gage credited Cassidy/Carter with most of Joe's achievements, and described the origins of the case in terms that Joe found demeaning as well as inaccurate.

"The agents asked Mr. Teitelbaum for information about his contacts in the waterfront union," the story ran, "but he refused to talk, sources said.

"The agents then obtained a court order to install an eavesdropping device in Mr. Teitelbaum's office, hoping to catch him conspiring to make payoffs to union officials. They did not accomplish that, according to the sources, but the agents did record a conversation he had in which Mr. Teitelbaum allegedly plotted to kill a competitor in Honduras.

"The FBI turned over the tapes of the conversation to the local district attorney, who had Mr. Teitelbaum picked up on charges of conspiracy to murder.

"After Mr. Teitelbaum realized the nature of the evidence against him, he reportedly asked to see the agents who had once sought his cooperation. When they arrived, he reportedly asked cordially, 'How can I help, gentlemen?' "

Badly scooped, reporters from Miami's newspapers and television stations badgered Joe all day for his comments, and after reading the *Miami News* that afternoon, he was seriously tempted to set them straight. Unable to add much in the few hours available, the paper could only rehash *The Time's* story for local consumption with most of its inaccuracies intact, softening the blow to this small extent:

"A source close to the investigation said Teitelbaum was assisting the FBI in investigating waterfront corruption in Miami, Mobile, Savannah and New York, where FBI agents infiltrated port businesses. The FBI trained Teitelbaum in using electronic devices so he and Cassidy could monitor conversations with union leaders, the source said."

It was something, but not nearly enough. By the time he cornered Levin and Maria after that day's session of the grand jury, he was furious enough to believe that the "leak" had been deliberate, although he was not quite clear in his mind about what purpose it might have served.

"You know what this is doing to me?" he bellowed. "Never mind about my reputation. Never mind I'm trying to get a new operation started. I know you don't give a fuck about that. But what about my family? What about Ann? How's she gonna face people? You gotta let me talk to these people."

"Joe, that's out of the question."

"Then *you* do it. It's your fault. You said there'd be no publicity. *Somebody's* got to set the record straight."

"You want to throw the whole thing away? You want the case thrown out of court because you can't wait to tell the media you're a hero? You want to see Field and Barone and Boyle and all these other people walk away from this? After all you did?"

"But they're making me look such a schmuck. I gotta sit still for that?"

"It's good practice, Joe. There's only two ways they can go. They can kill you or discredit you. One or the other. The defense is going to hit you with anything it can dig up, in *and* out of court, so you better get used to that."

"And I gotta take it? They can say anything they want, and I can't say nothing to defend myself? What kind of a deal is that?"

"Joe, there's only one place for the truth to come out. In court. You start talking to the newspapers before you tell it to a jury and you'll play right into their hands. The only way they can beat this is if somebody on *our* side does something stupid."

"Shit. Ann's gonna kill me."

"She may have to get on line, Joe. You thought any more about the Marshal's Program?"

"No."

Next morning the *Miami Herald* made him feel a little better. Its front-page story at least credited him with a central role in the case, and quoted another "source" as saying that he had started to work with the FBI *before* the Guzman affair. Still more mollifying was the first public suggestion that what he had done was commendable.

Three days later, Joe learned he had been sentenced to death.

20

Pyrrhic Victory

"WHO told you?" asked Kessler. "Ray Maria?"

"Right. I'm out at the terminal, and Uncle Sam comes over. 'Maria wants you on the phone,' he says. 'It's important.' So I go see what he wants, and he hits me with it."

"What exactly did he say?"

"Huh?"

Joe had several times caught himself just sitting blankly, not thinking at all.

"What did he say?"

"He said, uh, he said, 'Partner, I've got something to tell you. Someone is trying to kill you. We just got word from New York. There's a contract out on you. They know you're supposed to go to the grand jury soon, and they don't want you to testify.' That's what he said."

"So what do they want you to do?"

"What do you think? Go underground."

"You going to do it?"

"In the middle of building a terminal? You crazy? Let me ask you something. You think maybe they're trying to *frighten* me into the witness program?"

"I doubt it. They don't have to play games."

"Well, I don't know. I don't go for this bullshit they keep handing me about a leak in New York. What do you think, Mel? Are they just using me?"

"Who? The government? Well, of course. You're the best tool they've got."

"That's all I am to them? A tool?"

Kessler shook his head fondly. "Joe, you're their number one witness. They're worried about your safety. You think they're going to give your name to the newspapers? That's paranoid."

"Maybe. But maybe they need the publicity to put pressure on these guys. Maybe they figure to kill two birds by scaring me into the witness program at the same time. That's possible, isn't it?"

"Anything's possible, Joe."

"They got other witnesses now. Some of 'em in the program. I'm not so important anymore. Maybe they can afford to hang me out for bait and see who comes nibbling around."

"Before you even go to the grand jury? Nah. Besides, they need you to authenticate the tapes you made. That's their whole case. You're getting jumpy, that's all. Maybe you should do like they say."

Joe looked disappointed. "I got a terminal to build, Mel, and I'm not leaving. I told 'em that."

"And what did *they* say?"

"They said, 'Well, you're presenting us with a problem we don't know how to handle.' And I told 'em, I said, 'I'm sorry, but that's the way it is. The rest is up to you. You're big boys now.' And then I came here."

"Richardson with you?"

"He's out in the car."

Kessler scratched his ear.

"Maria's right," he said. *"Now's* the dangerous time. *Before* you go to the grand jury. If they can whack you out now, they'll put a real crimp in the case, which is why I think the government's on the level. Why don't you just do what they want, go underground until you testify? That's no big deal."

Joe shook his head.

"Once they get me into the program," he said, "I won't get out until after the trial. And that could be a couple of years. Once I'm in, they can feed me any kind of bullshit they want, and I'll have to go along because how will I know if it's true or not? And after that, I'm finished. I got nothing to bargain with. That's number one. Number two, it's convenient for *them,* not for me, and I figure *I'm* the one who ought to be considered here. I agreed to work with 'em. I didn't agree to give up everything I got in the world. I want to stay with my family, and I want to build my terminal. I think I'm entitled to that."

"Yes, you are," said Kessler. "But face the facts, Joe. So far, you've been lucky. Now you've got a couple of killers looking for you, and unless you duck out of sight for a while, there's not a whole lot the government can do about it."

"I made my bed, Mel. I'm gonna lie *on* it, not under it."

"You stay out at the terminal, Joe, and all you're going to lie on is a slab."

"Maybe." He shrugged. "And maybe I'll have another heart attack tomorrow and wind up there anyway. I'm not gonna hide, Mel. I can't live like that."

"Maybe you don't have a choice."

"Oh, yes. I can choose."

"What about Ann?"

"She'll be okay. Anything happens to me, I know you'll look after her."

"Oh, for Chrissake. You're beginning to sound like you *want* to die."

"Well, why don't *you* face the facts?" he said, stung. "You think they're gonna let me walk away from this? Program or no program, if they don't get me *before* I testify, they're gonna get me after. They got to. If they don't, it's gonna encourage other people to do the same thing I did, and they can't afford that. I don't know when or how they're gonna do it, but they're gonna do it."

Kessler chewed his lip. "Not if you're in the program."

"Mel, Mel." He held up his hands wearily. "That's just gonna kill me another way. A slower way. This is better. I'm not afraid of these people."

"All right." Kessler eyed him in silence for a moment. "I'll call Levin. See what he means to do. Are you going to tell Ann?"

"What? About the contract? No. Are you crazy? And don't you say a word either."

"Hey, it's *your* life, Joey. I'll tell you what I think, but I won't interfere."

"I know, man. And they could be wrong, couldn't they?"

Any small hope of that was snuffed out a few days later. Joe and Ann took Richardson and his wife to dinner on Saturday night at Plantation Yacht Harbor. Half way through the meal, Joe happened to look up toward the entrance of the restaurant, and everything stopped. His jaws. His heart. His breathing. Richardson followed the direction of his gaze, then looked at him inquiringly.

"Anybody we know?"

Joe refocused on Richardson, playing the question back to himself.

"Yeah," he said. "I know him. His name is Sullivan. He was with Barone in New York."

Richardson glanced thoughtfully around, and saw no immediate problem.

"Okay," he said. "Stay here. Don't get up. Don't do anything. I'll take care of it."

Still smiling, he pushed back from the table and got to his feet.

"Where you going, honey?" his wife said.

"Gotta make a phone call," he said. "Just remembered something I had to do."

When Joe looked again, Sullivan had gone.

A couple of State Troopers followed them home after dinner, and next morning, an unmarked car was parked a few feet away from their door with two men inside reading the Sunday paper. They stayed there all day, and escorted them back to Miami.

"Who are those men?" Ann asked.

"They're FBI agents."

"Are we in danger?"

"Not really. They don't want any more stories in the newspapers. They're to keep the reporters away."

He could see she did not believe him, but she said nothing more, and after that, there were two agents with him at all times.

Then there was some good news for a change.

On September 18, Fred R. Field, Jr., described by the prosecutor as "a clever, corrupt, powerful union official," went on trial in New York for taking $124,500 in payoffs from United Brands Corporation.

Three senior executives of United Brands testified against him under grants of immunity. The payments were delivered personally to Field at his New York apartment by Beverley K. Hachman, director of labor relations. The payments were authorized by Wilbur Laur, vice-president, who had since become senior vice president of USM Corporation, of Boston. The cash was provided, and concealed in the books, by Edward F. Gibbons, vice-president of finance, who had since become president of F.W. Woolworth Co.

Impressed, no doubt, by the credentials of these witnesses, if not by their readiness to break the law, the jury found Field guilty on September 28 of all 10 counts of conspiracy, racketeering, payoffs, and tax evasion. According to *The New York Times*, "he appeared shaken by the verdict."

Joe was elated by it. He also learned that day that Washington had decided he was to have "in-place" protection from the U.S. Marshal's Service.

"What does *that* mean?" he asked Levin suspiciously.

"It means you got lucky," he said. "It means that, starting tomorrow, you'll be guarded around the clock by U.S. Deputy Marshals. You'll have four with you at all times. They'll be held responsible for your safety, so we expect you to cooperate with them fully, and do exactly what they tell you."

"Four? Oh, man. You mean, every time I have a business meeting, I gotta take four armed men with me?" Secretly, he was rather tickled by the idea. "What the hell are people gonna think?"

Levin smiled faintly. "They're going to think they better not argue with you."

On October 14, Levin called to say that a Justice Department attorney by the name of Gerald Shur had flown in from Washington expressly to see Joe, to thank him for what he had done, and to meet his family. Fine, Joe said. Anything the government could do to make him look good in Ann's eyes would be very welcome, he added, and Levin, a married man himself, responded with an understanding laugh.

That evening, Shur arrived at the house with Frank No. Joe's defenses went up as soon as he saw them, but having prepared Ann and Marilyn for Shur's arrival, he could hardly turn them away.

"Your husband has done a great job," Shur said, when they were all seated in the living room. "I want you to know that, Mrs. Teitelbaum. You can be proud of him. Working under cover, in constant danger . . . That puts a terrible strain on a man, even when he's trained for it, and Joe never was. It takes a special kind of courage and determination, and I'm here to say how much we respect and admire you for it, Joe."

"Thank you."

He was watching Ann, though pretending not to, but she showed no sign.

"You may not realize it, Mrs. Teitelbaum," Shur went on, "but your husband has enabled the United States government to break up a criminal conspiracy that has stolen billions of dollars from ordinary American citizens like yourself over the years. If this was wartime, he would certainly get a medal for what he has done, and I mean that very sincerely."

He smiled at her, very sincerely.

"But not for what he's doing now," he added. "Now, I'm afraid, he's doing a *bad* thing."

Joe saw what was coming, but was helpless to prevent it.

"I know what you mean," he said, "but can't we talk about that some other time? Why don't I come by the office tomorrow and . . ."

"*I* don't know what he means," said Ann. "What is it, Joe. *Are* you doing something wrong?"

"No," he said balefully. "And somebody is gonna pay for this. They're still trying to make us leave, that's all. And I won't do it. I don't even want to discuss it. In fact, I'd like both of you to go now."

"For God's sake, Joe," Shur said, meeting him head on. "Your family has a right to know. There's a contract out to *kill* you."

Ann sat up straight, and Shur turned to her, softening his tone.

"Tell her about it, Joe," he said. "You must. It's only fair."

He could hardly bear to see the expression on her face. He sat down and got it over with, explaining what had happened and why the marshals were guarding them. When he finished, Marilyn looked at her mother, who seemed frozen and abstracted, as though none of it had anything to do with her.

"Well, what should we do?" Marilyn asked.

"You must leave," said Shur. "All of you. And at once."

"No, no," Joe said. "*You* leave. Right now."

"You know what could happen?" Shur ignored him. "You know what *I* could do . . . and I'm just an attorney? I could fly over this house in a helicopter and kill you all with a dynamite bomb. Or I could shoot a bazooka into the house and kill you all. You think the marshals could stop me? Forget it. Now *I* could do that, and I'm not a professional killer."

"Well, I don't know, man," said Joe bitterly. "You're doing okay."

"You've got no right to keep them here, Joe."

"But I'm getting married next month," said Marilyn, trying to laugh.

"Then I'll tell you what you should do," Shur said. "Get in a car with your fiancé and go away with him. Forget school. Make him take you away somewhere. I'll bring you back next month for the ceremony, but that'll be the end of it. You must all leave here."

"Listen," said Joe, so choked with outrage he could hardly speak. "This is *my* house, you son of a bitch. You're abusing my hospitality."

"Joe, you know these people better than anybody. You know what I'm saying is true."

"He's just trying to scare you, Ann," he said. Her silence frightened him. *"They* can't make me go, so they want *you* to do it." As he watched her face, his chest began to hurt.

She cleared her throat.

"But where will we go?" she asked politely, as though she had not heard a word he had said. It was a nightmare. He wanted to throw them out; she wanted to hear what they had to say. He sat back, rubbing his breastbone.

Frank No answered, as he had answered Joe at their first meeting. He would help them find a new area, and settle them there under a new name. It could not be on or near the waterfront, nor could Joe have anything more to do with the shipping industry. Their children were grown, fortunately, and already leading their own lives, so that the separation should not prove too painful. The government would, of course, pay their moving expenses, and allow Joe $768 a month, tax free, until he got started in some new occupation.

"But what will my husband *do?*" she asked, bewildered. "He's worked on the piers all his life. He's forty-five years old, and that's all he knows."

"Joe's a smart, resourceful man, Mrs. Teitelbaum," said Shur. "He's proved that. He'll make it. I've got no worries about that. He'll start something new, and he'll make it. You can't keep a good man down."

"We could make a farmer out of him," No suggested jovially. "How about that, Joe? Sit on the porch and watch the corn grow? After what he's done, Mrs. Teitelbaum, your husband can make a go of anything he puts his hand to, I'm sure of that."

Instead of laughing in their faces, she asked them what would become of the house and her car, almost as if she were taking this seriously. Joe did not interrupt, for she was entitled to have her say, but it was stupefying to listen to them, to hear No explain that the government could not help them dispose of their home, that she and Joe would have to do that themselves, in the usual way. She started to cry silently, looking from one face to another, trying to understand what they were saying, and unconscious of the tears running down her cheeks.

"All right," he said, stirring himself. "That's enough. You did what you came to do. I hope you're satisfied."

"We won't be satisfied, Joe, until we've got you and your wife safely under cover somewhere. That's all we're trying to do. That's our job."

"Yeah. But it's *my* life. And this is *my* house. And I'm asking you for the last time to leave."

"All right, Joe." Shur stood up to go. "I'm sorry, Mrs. Teitelbaum, but you had to know the facts. You are all in serious danger."

"Yeah, you *said* that. You made your point."

"The marshals will do their best, but we can't protect you properly while you remain here. It's my duty to tell you that. I hope you understand."

She nodded, closing her eyes, and Joe stepped between them, shooing him and No toward the door.

"Talk it over with your husband, Mrs. Teitelbaum," Shur said over his shoulder. "And let's hear from you in the morning, Joe."

"You'll hear from me," he said grimly. "You'll also hear from my attorney."

He returned to the living room, and Ann blew up in his face. Her long resentment at being kept in the dark, her fears for him and the children, her bitterness at having their lives disrupted, came together like fuse, detonator, and charge.

He had done this terrible thing to make himself look big, she said. It was an ego trip. To get his name in the newspapers, he was willing to see his wife and children killed. He had ruined her life, and for what? So he could boast about how important he was, and show off in front of people? He was always saying how much he loved her and the children, but he loved nobody but himself.

Marilyn tried to intercede from time to time, but after a while, she gave up and went to another room. All along, she had seemed to understand better than either Ann or Mark what he had done, and why. He promised himself a quiet talk with her later, when the storm blew over, but Ann was in no mood to spare him her full catalogue of grievances. When he attempted to defend himself, he provoked her. If he stayed silent, it inflamed her. Too guilty to reply in kind, he tried to cut her short by walking out, but she followed him from room to room, lashing him with every wounding remark she could lay tongue to, vengeful and unreachable. That night, they slept apart under the same roof for the first time in 23 years.

It was mid-morning before he managed to get Levin on the telephone.

"Now you tell me the truth," he said. "Did you know what they were gonna do, those sons of bitches?"

"Which sons of bitches?"

"Shur and No. You know what they did? They came over to my house last night, and they terrorized my wife to the point where they actually ruined my life."

"Joe. You're exaggerating. We just made a mistake not telling her the truth up front, that's all. She'll get over it."

"Oh, yeah, we made a mistake all right. So did they. I'm not gonna testify. Those guys destroyed my marriage, and I'm gonna sue 'em. Just who the hell do they think they are, coming into a man's home like that, and frightening his family half to death?"

"Joe, will you listen to me for a minute? First of all, they told her the simple truth. She *is* in danger. So are you."

"Yes, but there's ways of . . ."

"Just a minute. Let me finish. Second, nobody can just walk into a man's house and destroy his marriage with a couple of minutes' conversation. Not unless there's something wrong already."

"Bullshit. I don't buy that."

"Think about it. You're very different people. You told me that your-self. You've had counseling. She made you see a psychiatrist. I think your marriage was already in trouble, and this just brought it to a head."

"I don't accept that. They didn't have to scare the shit out of her so she blamed *me* for it."

"Well, I don't know, Joe. I wasn't there. Anyway, what are you going to do?"

"Do? Nothing. You can all go fuck yourselves."

When he got home that evening, he found Ann had been at the wine.

"You're going to get us killed, Joe," she said piteously, "I don't under-stand you. Why did you *do* it?"

"Jesus Christ." He sat down heavily, in despair at last. "I can't take any more. You're gonna have to work it out for yourself, Ann. I don't *care* what happens."

"You never *did* care, Joe. I see that now. If you cared, you never would have done this."

"Look, I'll put the house in *your* name, okay? And the cars. Everything's gonna be in your name. Only you gotta leave me alone. I don't feel good. I can't handle this anymore."

He turned and went out again. With two of his marshals in the car and two more following, he drove over to Ray Maria's house.

"I'm not gonna testify," he said. "You fucking people are no good. I try to help you, and you ruin my whole fucking life."

"I heard what happened, Joe." Maria nodded sympathetically. "I'm sorry. I am really. It was Washington's decision. But you can understand it, Joe. If anything happens to you, it would pretty well blow the case. You've got to try to see it from their point of view."

"No, I don't. They gotta see it from *mine.* Fuck the case. That's all you guys care about. *I* don't count. Ann don't count. All that counts is the fucking case. Well, it doesn't with me. You made me look the worst kind of schmuck in the papers, and now this. So fuck it. I'm not gonna testify."

"Joe, I know you won't believe me, but they're trying to do what's best for you. They really are. The only way we can take care of you and be sure you're safe is in the program. I know that's hard to take, but it's the truth."

"Look, Ray. The witness program is for criminals. It's not for people like me. It's for guys who are gonna go to jail otherwise. For them, it's a good deal. For me, it's a disaster. For me, it means giving up everything. And I'm not gonna do that, Ray. I don't care *what* happens. I'll take what's coming. If they kill me, they kill me. I'll live day by day, and I don't wanna hear any more about it."

"It's the best we can do, Joe."

"Well, it's not enough. And now you fucked up my marriage as well, so I'm not gonna testify. You can do what you like."

On November 16, he testified for four and a half hours in front of the grand jury.

After nine months, Levin and Evans had burrowed deep into the body of organized crime on the South Atlantic and Gulf coasts, working closely with U.S. Attorney Robert B. Fiske, Jr. in New York, who was coordinating the investigation from Norfolk northwards. Among the scores of witnesses called to appear, Santos Trafficante, Jr., boss of Tampa and power broker for the Southeast, had traveled to Miami to make another of his ceremonial invocations of constitutional privilege before the grand jurors, and so had Carlos Marcello, his opposite number in New Orleans. In fact, Marcello had appeared twice, to explain his connection with the now defunct Container Service Corporation of Miami, which had used the threat of labor troubles to obtain repair work at extortionate prices from local shipping firms.

Harvey Sykes had also been back for a second time to walk the knife edge between the dangerous truth and contempt of court. Suffering from intermittent attacks of selective amnesia, he could remember most things that fell outside the five-year Statute of Limitations, but hardly a word of his conversation with Joe in New Orleans some 18 months earlier, even when Levin read from the transcript of the tape recording. He had never made any payoffs to Barone, he said. If he had told Joe he had done so, it was because he knew Joe wanted to hear that, and he was just trying to ingratiate himself.

When James Vanderwyde appeared, he had forgotten even his own address. He agreed, readily enough, that Local 1922 had employed him as office manager since its formation in 1966, but was vague about his duties. He had "to see that everything's kept up to date." For that, the 325 members of Local 1922 had paid him a salary of $23,150 in 1976. He also admitted that the president of the International, Teddy Gleason, had appointed him "a coordinator," which meant that "whenever they ask me to go someplace, I go and do my duty, whatever they ask me to do."

Sebastian "Benny" Cotrone remembered where he lived all right, but not how to spell his first name. He showed a fair grasp of his business interests, however, although he could not vouch for the accuracy of his personal records because he was "a lousy bookkeeper."

George Barone, in contrast, was prepared to tell the grand jury no more than his name and address, both of which he knew and could spell. After every subsequent question, he asked to be excused to confer outside the jury room with his attorney, David Rosen (among whose other distinguished clients was Meyer Lansky). Barone would then return and decline to respond on grounds of possible self-incrimination. This applied even to admitting any connection with the ILA.

The questions were therefore more interesting than the answers. Referring him to a conversation he had had with Special Agent Cassidy, then Bob Carter, at Miami Airport, in which Carter had spoken of transferring some of Zim's work to Marine Repairs, the Staten Island firm run by Phil Lacqua and Vic Marino, Levin reminded Barone of his response: "You stated to Special Agent Cassidy, if that were to take place, 'Anthony and I would have to sit down again.' The question is, who is Anthony, and why and what would you have to discuss?"

Barone's answer was, "May I see my attorney?"

Despite the shyness of Field, Barone, and their accomplices, Levin and Evans were blocking out a huge canvas of business, social, and political corruption embracing the whole Southeastern rim of the United States. But a few days after Joe's own first appearance before the grand jury, Anthony Scotto reclaimed the spotlight for himself in New York with an almost contemptuous twitch of political muscle.

Having taken over Field's job as general organizer of the international union, he prevailed upon his old friend Governor Hugh Carey, whose political career he had sponsored and financed since Carey's days as a Brooklyn Congressman, to nominate another old friend, attorney Bertram Perkel, as New York's Commissioner for the two-man, bistate Waterfront Commission, the port regulatory agency whose most implacable foe, almost from the day of its inception, had been Anthony Scotto.

In the middle of a massive federal investigation of waterfront racket ties with the business and political establishment, it seemed almost deliberately provocative, as though Scotto were publicly defying the Justice Department to tamper with the sources of his power. The office of Commissioner had fallen vacant upon the retirement of Joseph Kaitz, but Carey's choice of a Scotto associate to succeed him seemed even to some Democratic politicians to be like putting a fox in charge of the henhouse. The only serious challenge ever offered to the ILA's grasp on the port had come from the Commission, and a former ILA attorney seemed, on the face of it, among the candidates least likely to maintain its investigative zeal. The office was also one of the most lucrative patronage jobs at the Governor's disposal, paying $37,000 a year for his nominee's part-time services.

None of this surprised Joe Teitelbaum, whose most immediate problem as the weeks went by was a growing sense of isolation. Working under cover, he had often felt acutely isolated by the need for secrecy. Now that everybody *knew* his secret, he was beginning to realize he actually *was* isolated.

Ann noticed it first. About a week after Shur's attempt to scare them into leaving, she and Joe had settled into an exhausted truce. She was a long way from forgiving him, but they had lived together for 23 years, and Marilyn was about to be married. Though frightened and resentful, Ann was no more anxious than Joe to abandon their home, family, and friends in Miami, but as the wedding preparations went ahead, it began to look as though their family and friends might be abandoning *them.*

Her own parents and relatives had been so scandalized by the publicity that she knew she had to give them time to get over it, but that hardly applied to Joe's family. When Manny Levy, his cousin and former business partner, actually refused an invitation to the ceremony, she knew there was more behind it than outraged respectability. And he was not the only one. As the day drew closer, others began sending their regrets, paring the guest list down to the hard core of those too close to Marilyn and her fiancé to have an excuse for not coming.

Then she noticed that people in their neighborhood would cross the street as she approached, or look the other way when they could or plead urgent engagements when they could not. Nobody would ride in her car when offered a lift, and at Hadassah meetings, the women she had always thought of as friends would break off their conversations when she went to join them, or eye her surreptitiously when they thought she was not looking. It was the same in Key Largo at the weekends. Though nobody actually said anything, the standing invitations they had once had to drop in at any time were being withdrawn, and people *they* asked over to the house were now mostly too busy to come.

At first, Ann read this creeping ostracism as disapproval for what Joe had done, or what had been written about him in the newspapers. But then she understood that people were frightened. If Joe was in danger, *she* was in danger, and except for the Kesslers and a few other old friends, they were not willing to share it with them. In some complicated way, knowing this made her feel braver.

Joe took longer to feel the effects because most of his waking time was spent at the terminal, where the staff of Pioneer Shipping protected him as closely as the marshals. Nor were Pioneer's customers much deterred. One account was lost, and a certain amount of new business was perhaps placed elsewhere because of him, but this was more than offset by the calls he received from shippers expressing their satisfaction in learning of at least one honest man on the waterfront.

It was after work that he began to feel it, and at the weekends. The Kesslers did their best to take up the slack, but for much of the time, Joe and Ann had to rely on each other for company. And on the marshals.

The romance of traveling everywhere with a close escort had quickly faded. Every two weeks, a new 16-man detail of deputy marshals drawn from all parts of the country would take over, working four-man shifts around the clock. Some of them resented the risks they ran, feeling he should be in the witness program. Others found the assignment a welcome change from courtroom duty or transporting prisoners. Some told endless Jewish jokes among themselves, but always just in earshot; others felt sorry for him, saying he should not trust the government for it would drop him as soon as his usefulness had ended. Some were officious and obstructive; others, tactful and accommodating.

Sometimes, Joe had to look after *them*. The marshals were never very happy when he went out fishing from Key Largo in his Seabird. They were inclined to think of her more as the Sitting Duck, bobbing about alone on the ocean, and would often ask the Coast Guard to have a cutter standing by. They would also search the boat thoroughly before letting him on board, sometimes with dogs trained to sniff out explosives. Once out on the water, however, the roles were often reversed. Few of them were deep-water fishermen, and some were very poor sailors. There was a certain melancholy satisfaction, Joe found, in feeding seasickness pills to an anti-Semite, and on one occasion, 20 miles out from shore, a positive pleasure in dumping a particularly unpleasant deputy over the side to cool off before he got sunstroke.

So far, his bodyguard had had little to do, despite the lurid prognostications of Shur and No. It was a quiet winter, with only occasional public reminders of the grand jury investigations still grinding along, month by month, behind closed doors.

Early in January 1978, a separate federal inquiry into the activities of Edward J. Heine, Jr., whom Joe had met in Miami with Anthony Scotto, led to charges against United States Lines of making illegal payoffs to ILA officials, politicians, and shippers amounting to about $1.5 million.

In Newark, New Jersey, where another federal grand jury had just indicted 10 persons for corruption in the waterfront trucking business, Sea–Land Service Inc., pioneers in container shipping, was also being prosecuted for making illegal payoffs between 1971 and 1975 amounting to no less than $19 million.

In Miami, however, all remained outwardly peaceful until March 2, when *The New York Times* once again stirred the local media into action with another front-page lead story, this time by Anthony Marro, of the paper's Washington Bureau.

Under the headline, "Federal Indictments Expected Soon in East and Gulf Coast Dock Inquiry," he wrote:

"After more than two years of investigation in Atlantic and Gulf Coast ports, Federal prosecutors in Miami are planning to seek about two dozen indictments charging a cross section of labor union and shipping industry officials with corruption . . ."

After naming Scotto, Barone, and Boyle among the primary targets, Marro went on to quote James B. Adams, the FBI's deputy associate director for criminal investigations, who said: "What makes this so devastating is that there's only one real victim—the consumer. Everyone else can get out of what he has to lose by passing the cost along," and these added costs amounted to billions of dollars.

As evidence of progress, Marro cited the imprisonment of Robert Dalton, former boss of an ILA Local in Boston, for embezzling $84,000;

the conviction of two Customs House brokers in Charleston for corruption, a case affecting half the cargo entering the port; the ILA welfare fund fraud in New Orleans, for which 56 people were awaiting sentence; Fat Freddy's problems with United Brands in New York, for which he had been sentenced to a year's imprisonment and a $50,000 fine; and the recent indictment of Isom Clemon in Mobile on 35 counts of theft from ILA pension funds. He also made the point that venal shippers were in trouble, too.

"If this project is successful," said Marro's anonymous Justice Department source, "it may change in dramatic ways the way business is done on the waterfront, because it will make shippers realize that it's not just a matter of paying the money and passing along the cost to consumers —that they face a real threat of prosecution if they do."

Toward the end of the story, Joe Teitelbaum was mentioned as "the subject of a separate investigation" who began cooperating with FBI agents in Miami "and allowed them to use his office as part of an undercover operation."

Although less wounding than the original *New York Times* story, this passing reference still did him scant justice. He had just astounded the grand jury for a second time with further details of his exploits, and by continuing to deny him credit for them, *The Times* had turned the screws unwittingly tighter. Now more than ever he needed to appear in a better light in order to bolster Ann's morale and shame their former "friends." Several times in the next few days he came close to making a statement to the Miami papers, but Levin narrowly dissuaded him. With a little more patience, he said, Joe could have the best platform in the world for telling his story—a witness stand in Federal court—and the most attentive audience in the world: a jury empaneled because of his efforts to hear the charges brought against his enemies.

One of the reasons why the news media were still getting him wrong was because Vincent Ensulo had surfaced again. NBC-TV had stumbled across him in New York while putting together a series of documentary programs on the waterfront after the story broke in September 1977. With no official source prepared to confirm or deny his claims, the producer had put Ensulo's head in a black bag and shown him to America as an anonymous member of the Carlo Gambino family and an active FBI informant.

Asked, on camera, what he knew about the investigation, Ensulo said he had started it, that he had been hired by Joe Teitelbaum to kill a banker in Honduras, and had used that to turn Joe into an informer. "This is my case," Ensulo said proudly.

It would have been wiser, perhaps, for him to have given credit where credit was due. Ensulo was then working as a taxi driver in New York under the name of Vincent Ennisie. On April 14, 1978, as he was leaving a coffee shop on 57th Street at 11th Avenue, he was shot four times in the back at close range, and died in Roosevelt Hospital.

Jimmy Breslin wrote his eulogy. Ensulo was "The Stool Pigeon Who Sang His Way to the Hit Parade," and after that, who could doubt that the killing proved Ensulo had told the truth? Joe Teitelbaum's role in the investigation was now irremediably tarnished as far as the media were concerned. Ensulo had not merely stolen his thunder, but lined him up as number two for the hit parade, although subtler methods were called for in his case to neutralize the bodyguard of marshals.

A few mornings later, on arriving for work at Pioneer's terminal, Joe found that someone had poured acid on his crane during the night, disabling the controls. Fortunately, the ship he had expected to unload was late, and by the time she tied up, he had completed the necessary repairs, otherwise he would have had to send for Jack Hoersch, whose mobile crane Joe generally rented whenever he needed more than one.

Later that morning, Hoersch drove over to see *him.*

"Hey, Joe," he said. "The marshals here?"

"Yeah." Questions along those lines always commanded his undivided attention. "Why?"

"Well, I'll tell you. Some guy called last night, and said he'd give me fifty thousand dollars if I dropped a box on your head."

"Well, well," said Joe, understanding now about the acid. "I appreciate it, Jack. That's a better rate than *I* pay you."

He left it to the FBI. He was determined to get on with his life as best he could. If he allowed himself to dwell on all the possible ways the other side might get to him, it could only become a burden; he would be as well off in the witness program. Besides, he knew there was worse to come. From what Levin was saying, and from the play the investigation was now getting in the press, it was clear that the grand jury was about ready to indict. Once Field and the rest saw the charges against them, they would know the only chance they had was to silence him before he could testify.

On April 17, *Newsweek* magazine reported at length about "Crime on the Docks." Two primary targets, it said, in "the biggest single probe in the Justice Department's history" were Anthony Scotto and "tough-talking George Barone," boss of the Miami docks, which seethed "with just about every form of waterfront corruption."

The *Miami News* ran its own curtain-raiser on April 24, quoting a local source as saying, "This is going to make *The Godfather* look like a family picnic." Getting the issue exactly right, reporter Bill Douthat wrote that "the Justice Department's job has been to document a system of racketeering that has existed on the nation's docks for decades . . . The Port of Miami is the center for a number of wide-ranging racketeering schemes . . . Modern-day pirates plunder the cargo and revenue of the port, and the losses are passed on to the consumer in higher shipping rates."

An even stronger hint of what was to come emerged in Federal court on May 9. Eugene Schaefer, former warehouse manager for Coordinated

Caribbean Transport (CCT), admitted perjuring himself before the grand jury in December when he denied paying Boyle $600 a month on behalf of his employers for "labor peace." He had little choice but to plead guilty, for the government was prepared to offer the testimony of Hector Calderon, the firm's principal, who had admitted ordering him to do so, and was now cooperating with Levin and Evans.

This indication of the weight and scope of the coming indictments was confirmed in Washington toward the end of May by the then Deputy Attorney General, Benjamin R. Civiletti. Asked about the Justice Department's attitude toward organized crime, he cited the waterfront investigation as evidence of its zeal, suggesting, as *The New York Times* put it, "that the results would show it to be one of the government's more impressive efforts in recent years." The Department was now, he said, "about three weeks from surfacing that investigation in a dramatic way in one area of the country."

In fact, it was about two weeks. On June 7, 1978, the federal grand jury in Miami returned a sealed indictment charging Field, Barone, Boyle, Vanderwyde and 18 other persons with conspiracy, racketeering, extortion, tax-law violations, and other crimes. Bench warrants were issued in U.S. District Court for their arrest, and these were served by federal agents, starting early in the morning of June 8, the day on which Aleksandr Solzhenitsyn would denounce the West in his Harvard commencement address as slack, evil, and consumed by greed.

The indictment, a formidable document of 128 pages, charged under Count 1 that George Barone, Robert Bateman, William Boyle, Alvin P. Chester, Jeremy Chester, Isom Clemon, Francesca Cotrone, Joseph Cotrone, Laura Cotrone, Sebastian "Benny" Cotrone, Fred R. Field, Jr., Vincent James Fiore, Jr., Max Forman (an accountant once employed by the Cotrones), Neal L. Harrington, Elizah "Elijah" Jackson, Dorothy O. Kopituk (Florida Welding Services), Raymond C. Kopituk (FWS), Oscar Morales (FWS), Cleveland Turner, Cornelius "Butch" Vanderwyde, James Vanderwyde, and Landon L. Williams—the defendants—"willfully and knowingly conspired, combined, confederated, and agreed together, with each other and with persons known and unknown to the Grand Jury . . . to corruptly control and influence the waterfront industry of various ports in the United States . . ."

Still on Count 1, the grand jury cited no fewer than 211 overt acts committed by the defendants between 1966 and February 1977, in furtherance of the conspiracy. Of these, 110 were conversations or payoffs in which Joe Teitelbaum participated on behalf of the government. A further 21 conversations and payoffs were separately documented by the three FBI agents he had brought into the investigation under cover, so that about two-thirds of the list, and in that sense, two-thirds of the government's case, was directly attributable to his efforts.

Count 2, involving the 17 principal defendants, also depended very heavily on Joe's testimony. Under this count, the grand jury accused them of conducting the affairs of their criminal enterprise through a pattern of racketeering activity, basing the charge on all the other counts in the indictment, which in turn rested for the most part on the list of overt acts accompanying Count 1.

Taken together, the two counts lay at the heart of the government's case. Under Title 18, United States Code, a conviction on both would render the defendants liable, not only to substantial terms of imprisonment, but also to the permanent loss of union office and/or the seizure of their business interests—a matter of no small consequence to Neal Harrington, the Chesters, the Cotrones, the Kopituks, and Oscar Morales. The risk of outright forfeiture would have a stronger deterrent effect on other waterfront businessmen, it was thought, than even the prospect of jail or some combination of jail and fines.

The indictment then continued on through 68 more counts, charging the defendants, separately or in combination, with extortion, witness-tampering, and violations of the Taft–Hartley law, the pension fund law, and the Internal Revenue Code.

As Deputy Attorney General Civiletti had predicted, the effect was dramatic. The story made the front pages of every major newspaper in the country, and ran all through June 9 on network radio and television from coast to coast.

The New York Times, which had led the media coverage from the start, was quick to remind its readers that the arrests ended only one phase of an investigation that still had Anthony Scotto in its sights. Its reporter, Anthony Marro, also noted that Fred R. Field, Jr. had surrendered in New York on June 7 to start serving his one-year sentence in the United Brands case "at almost the same time as the grand jury in Miami was indicting him on additional charges that could, if he is convicted, result in maximum sentences of 72 years in prison and $180,000 in fines."

In Miami, the press had a field day.

"Dockside Crackdown Begins," the *Miami Herald* announced overnight on June 7, before the indictment had even been unsealed. "We're dismantling a huge criminal monopoly where free enterprise did not exist," an investigator was quoted as saying. "Every management person we charged thought he was getting an advantage over a competitor."

The paper also began to apportion the credit more fairly. "As the indictment was being returned Wednesday," the story continued, "the man who reportedly started it all continued business as usual. That was despite efforts by the Justice Department to get him to accept protective custody in hiding.

"Joseph Teitelbaum, who headed his family's Eagle shipping company in Miami, became a government informant in 1975 . . . The government has reportedly spent tens of thousands of dollars in around-the-clock protection of Teitelbaum and his family. Teitelbaum wouldn't comment on his role, but allowed news photographers to take pictures of him at work at Pioneer Shipping on NW North River Drive.

A few hours later, on June 8, there were more pictures, this time in the afternoon paper, the *Miami News.* Barone, the Vanderwydes, and the Cotrone sisters were shown in handcuffs on their way to jail. Thirteen of the 17 arrested by that time had already appeared before U.S. Magistrate Herbert Shapiro, and been released on bonds ranging from $10,000 to $25,000.

The next morning, the *Herald* appeared with a four-column, front-page headline: "Dockers, Businessmen Charged in Plot to 'Control Waterfront'." Next to it was a two-column picture of George Barone, again in handcuffs. Underneath was a picture of the FBI's Director, William H. Webster, with a quotation from a statement released in Washington on June 8: "The investigation is the largest labor probe by the Justice Department in history. It revealed a systematic scheme of payoffs, kickbacks, buying and selling contracts, embezzlement, extortion and threats that went on for nearly 12 years."

It was good strong stuff. The story, by Ron LaBrecque, analyzed the indictment in relation to the main defendants, providing a thumbnail sketch of each, and again did something to restore Joe's wounded pride.

"The indictment clearly shows," LaBrecque wrote, "that the effort of one man who turned government informant, Joseph Teitelbaum of Miami, was instrumental in getting the investigation going . . . Throughout the indictment, Teitelbaum is named as an intermediary between union officials, businessmen and undercover FBI agents."

Elsewhere in the paper, the restoration of Joe's good name was taken a stage further by columnist Charles Whited.

"Violence, extortion and other abuses long have been part of the ILA," he wrote. "And time and again, union leaders have been the target of corruption probes, but to little real effect. But finally, some three years ago, Miami shipper Joe Teitelbaum, now 46, whose father, Gus, started the family's waterfront business in the 1940s, grew weary of constant involvement in payoffs, bribery and fear. Joe Teitelbaum, whom I regard as a courageous man, blew the whistle to the FBI. What followed, of course, was the most massive probe into union racketeering ever mounted by the U.S. Justice Department."

The magnitude of the case, and the belated public recognition of Joe's part in it, was helping a lot with Ann. It was quite obvious at last that he had not endangered her and the children for any trivial or self-seeking purpose. Nor was she in much danger now in any case. By one of those quiet, unofficial concordats sometimes concluded between law-enforcement agencies and organized crime, Joe's family had been declared off-limits, and the marshals had long ago given up following them around. But this limited immunity certainly did not extend to Joe, and the day-to-day strain of living under these conditions had kept Ann in a state of continuous apprehension. Prepared for another sensitive patch in their domestic relations when the indictment was returned, he had not bargained on another hassle with the Marshal's Service as well.

It began on June 7, when the grand jury returned its indictment. Ray Maria called Joe at the terminal and asked him over to his house that evening to meet with Attlee Wampler and Michael Levin.

Knowing that meant trouble, Joe arrived late, in an irritable mood.

"I've been working all day," he said. "I'm tired and I wanna go to bed, so let's not play games."

"Fine," said Levin, who was tired himself. "The marshals are pulling out."

"They're what?"

"Washington's lifting your protection, Joe," said Wampler. "They say you won't cooperate."

"Won't cooperate? What the fuck do they think I've been doing for three years?"

Levin shook his head. "The marshals say you don't listen to them. You go where you want. You do what you want. They say you're a walking target, and you're going to get their men killed. So they're pulling out."

"*Now?* With the indictment coming? What kind of timing is that, for Chrissake?"

Levin and Wampler looked at the floor.

Joe had not allowed himself to think much about the day when he would be left alone. He knew the Strike Force would do anything to keep him alive and cooperative until the trial, but it did not control the Marshal's Service. He also knew that Don Forsht, head of the Marshal's office in Miami, had recommended to Washington that his men be withdrawn if Joe refused to relocate.

"They were supposed to leave today," said Wampler, "but I talked them into staying until Monday."

"Fuck 'em," said Joe, choking up. "They can *go* today as far as I'm concerned."

"Don't be such a hero," said Levin crossly. "Why don't you take a vacation or something?"

"I can't spare the time. So forget it. I'm not running."

"Well, what *are* you going to do?" Wampler asked.

"I'm gonna go home, take a shower, and go to bed. And *you're* gonna have to decide how bad you want me to testify."

Joe was not as unconcerned as he sounded. He knew as well as they did that Washington was not really worried about the marshals. It was worried about the expense, and that was a bad omen. The Strike Force would look after him if it had to until the trial; Wampler and Levin were not about to throw away three years' work. But after? The chance of persuading the government to consider some sort of longer-range protection suddenly looked a lot slimmer.

Then the media did him a good turn at last. When the story broke, Brian Ross of NBC-TV News, called. He said he had heard from a friend of Joe's in the Public Safety Department that there was talk of the marshals pulling out.

Then he had heard right, Joe said. And as far as he was concerned, they could do as they liked.

The result was a prime-time segment on NBC's June 9 networked evening news program in which Ross examined Joe's situation. Noting the continued presence of the marshals, Ross observed that the government had apparently "backed off its threat to stop protecting Teitelbaum because it was getting too expensive . . . A squad of U.S. marshals has been protecting him around-the-clock for the last nine months, at an estimated cost of a half-million dollars. Teitelbaum said today he has been told the protection *will* continue, but he still doesn't know for how long."

Joe himself was then shown on Pioneer's dock, saying: "I really don't know what their intentions are, as I stand here talking to you now. I was only told that the marshals were going to continue to be with me through today, and that they were not going to pull out . . . Something was going to be done."

Ross went on to quote a Justice Department spokesman in Washington as saying that the whole thing had been "a mix-up, a case of bad timing," and that the government never intended to leave Teitelbaum out in the cold. "But Teitelbaum and his family say that they want it in writing," said Ross, "and that they won't take new names or move away."

Joe then reappeared, this time at home with Ann.

"If I were gonna relocate," he said, "I would have run before, not after, the fact."

"If anything happens to my husband," Ann added, and she paused, trying to be fair-minded, "I'll put a great deal of blame on the government."

Ross signed off with the thought that while the government was trying to think of a cheaper way to protect Joe, the FBI was investigating the offer of $50,000 to a local crane driver to drop a container on his head.

And that was that. The issues in the case were all but discounted. What came through unmistakably was that Washington had shown itself ready to risk the life of its own chief witness in order to save a few bucks; that it was playing dirty pool with a brave little guy who was not afraid to stand up for his rights against either the mob *or* the government.

With that impression planted in the minds of many millions of Americans across the country, Deputy Attorney General Civiletti confirmed next day that the government was indeed looking for a cheaper way to protect Teitelbaum, but that there was no question of withdrawing his bodyguard until a suitable alternative had been worked out.

It was a victory for Joe, and an expensive loss for the government in more than just the financial sense. A lot of damage had been done in a vital area of public confidence. As Ron LaBrecque wrote in the *Miami Herald*'s follow-up story on June 10, "some Justice Department officials fear that even talk of withdrawing protection will have a chilling effect on other potentially cooperative witnesses."

The reporters and photographers were out again on June 15, to watch him work the M/V *Mereghan V,* just in from the Bahamas. As he walked the ship and dock, supervising the unloading of her cargo, 17 of the 22 defendants were entering pleas of not guilty at their arraignment before U.S. Magistrate Peter Palermo in the Federal courthouse. (The other five —Fred Field, Isom Clemon, Neal Harrington, and the Cotrones, father and son—would also plead not guilty when arraigned in the following week.)

Joe declined to discuss the case with reporters, but confirmed that he meant to carry on as usual, "no matter what." He was not afraid. "My biggest problem today," he told the Herald, "is fixing the fuel transfer pump on the ship. I find my solace in my work, and my family's support."

His family's support, however, was conditional on his getting a commitment from the government about his future protection. As Ross had indicated on NBC-TV News, Ann wanted something in writing, and she asked Joe about it every night, as soon as he got home. But Joe was not sure how best to broach the subject and kept putting it off, until one day early in July, another emissary from the Marshal's Service in Washington gave him the perfect opening.

"I don't particularly like you," he said to Joe. "You pulled that stunt on TV, and now you're gonna get sixteen of my men killed."

"That's bullshit." Joe had heard all this so often he was not even annoyed. "There's never more than four with me, and two of those are usually sleeping in the car. So don't give me any of your bullshit about sixteen. It's two. And I don't like you either."

"You think you're worth two men's lives? Just because you wanna play hero?"

"I'm not playing anything," Joe said, bored. "I'm just trying to hang on to what I worked for all my life. I wasn't gonna let a bunch of crooks take it away from me, and I'm not gonna let the government do it either. Don't worry about your marshals. I'll look after 'em for you."

"All right."

He sorted through the papers in his briefcase, and tossed one of them onto the table.

"That's a release," he said. "A waiver. It just says that because you refuse to enter the program and relocate, if anything happens, we're not responsible. That you're doing this on your own."

He took a ballpoint pen from the inside pocket of his jacket, laid it on top, and pushed the document toward Joe.

"That's funny," said Joe, sitting back in his chair. It was another of life's golden moments. "I was just gonna ask *you* to sign a letter guaranteeing that the marshals will stay with me until the trial and the appeals are over."

They regarded each other for several seconds.

"Joe, that's crazy. We won't give you that. We can't."

"Okay." He shrugged. "Then I may not testify," he said carelessly, and the other looked appalled.

Levin was appalled as well. The very idea of anything happening at this late stage to undermine a case that had absorbed him to the almost total exclusion of everything else for two years had him reaching for Joe's throat.

"What the hell are you talking about?" he demanded. "You can't *not* testify. You'll be held in contempt of court and go to jail."

"Well, that won't do much good, will it? If I go to jail, I won't last a night."

"Joe, you don't understand. If a judge orders you to testify, you'll testify. If you don't, he'll imprison you for contempt. It's got nothing to do with the case. He won't know or care what you've got to say. He'll only be concerned about upholding the authority of the court. Now be sensible."

"Mike, you're just talking wild." Joe had always had a good feel for other people's bargaining positions. "It's very simple. Ann says she's gonna leave me if I don't get a piece of paper saying the marshals will stick around for a while after this is over. Not for ever. Just for a reasonable time, that's all. So just get me a piece of paper . . . a letter will do . . . and there's no more to be said."

"Joe, I don't have the authority to make a commitment like that. Be reasonable. We're not going to let you down, you know that."

"Do I? I know *you* won't, Mike. But I don't trust your employer anymore."

"We've got that sorted out now. Washington says the marshals stay."

"Yeah, but for how long? *You* can't tell me. Tomorrow, Washington could say the marshals leave, and they'll leave. So I've got to do what's right for *me*. If Ann wants a piece of paper, then I gotta get a piece of paper."

Levin bit down on his temper.

"I'll talk to Attlee," he said shortly. "We'll take it up again with Washington."

"Thanks, Mike. If you can get on it right away, I'd appreciate it."

"Look, a decision on this is going to take time, Joe. We'll probably have to go to the Attorney General himself before we get an answer. I'll do the best I can, but you'll have to be patient. And for your own sake, Joe, don't say anything to anybody about not testifying, okay? Don't even think it."

"Well, I'm a sick man, you know," Joe said delicately. "I've got a bad heart. And this is putting me under a lot of stress."

He could see Levin understood him perfectly.

In fact, physically, Joe felt better than he had in years. His blood pressure was almost normal; his indigestion had gone; he was sleeping well, and he could not understand it. Ann was still skirting a breakdown. A couple of professional killers were stalking him. A grateful government was all set to wash its hands of him as soon as he had served its purpose, and he felt fine. Worried, disillusioned, disappointed, angry—but fine.

Having everything out in the open at last had made the difference. No matter what anybody else thought or said, he had done right. He *knew* that. And corny though it sounded even to himself, knowing it made anything possible and everything bearable.

At the end of July, Robert MacNamara, Jr. called Joe from Washington on behalf of Senator Edward Kennedy. They wanted him to appear before the Senate Permanent Sub-Committee on Investigations to testify during a week of public hearings in August on organized crime in South Florida.

To feel appreciated at last at that level was heady stuff. He agreed to go to Washington for a preliminary interview, not only with MacNamara, but with an aide of Senator Henry Jackson's, who wanted to talk to him about his problems with the witness protection program and the Marshal's Service. Fine, said Joe, delighted with the idea of getting some action in the capital on the two questions that most concerned him. Wonderful.

"Impossible," said Ray Maria. "No way. That's out, I guarantee you. You're not going to Washington."

"Why not? I said I would."

"To testify in public? And maybe blow the case? Forget it. I'm going to hang up on you now and call John Evans. He's got the contacts up there. He'll take care of it."

"Hey, not so fast," Joe said. "These are U.S. Senators we're talking about. You can't push guys like that around. If they wanna see me, they'll see me."

"Fine. *After* the trial. After the trial, you can testify all you want. After the trial, you can dance naked on the White House lawn for all I care, but for right now, you're not talking to *anybody.*"

Joe did not go to Washington. John Evans called MacNamara; Deputy Attorney General Civiletti called Senator Kennedy, and the only reference to the ILA at the sub-committee's public hearings came from Gary Bowdach, a convicted loanshark from South Florida. Bowdach testified that he had seen Anthony Scotto give $40,000 to a courier for Meyer Lansky. Next day, Scotto, through his attorney, called Bowdach a liar.

The trial now seemed set to begin on January 29, 1979, before U.S.

District Court Judge William M. Hoeveler, who had already made it known that he would entertain no motions for continuance beyond that date. To Ann, this meant that Joe had only until then to get the letter of commitment she wanted from the government, for once he testified, whatever bargaining power he had would disappear. As far as she was concerned, every day that passed without progress toward an agreement was a day wasted, and Joe had to bring Mel Kessler in to help him out.

"Did you tell him what happened?" she said. "About the wedding invitation?"

"Yeah, I heard," Kessler said. "You've got to expect that."

"For the rest of my life?"

"Well, it's good to know who your friends really are, isn't it?"

She was not listening.

"We were just sitting here," she said. "Like we are now. And he calls and says, 'About the wedding next week. I know we invited you to come,' he says, 'and you accepted,' and all this, 'but would you mind not coming.' I mean, can you believe that? We've known them for years. As long as we've known you, Mel. But now it's like we've got a disease."

"She's right," said Joe. "It's like we got the plague. 'You're gonna get killed,' he says to me. 'Or you're gonna get hurt. And quite frankly,' he says, 'we don't wanna get hurt from being around you. It could even happen at our daughter's wedding,' he says, 'so if you don't mind, we don't want you to come.' "

"And I know that girl like I know Marilyn," Ann said brightly.

Kessler put his arm around her shoulders.

"Honey, I wish I could tell you it's going to get better," he said. "But I don't think it will until after the trial. You know what people are."

"I'm learning," she said. "And why will it be different after? If he doesn't have the marshals with him, it'll be worse, won't it?"

"They'll be there," Joe said. "Don't worry about it. Mel and me, we'll work something out with them."

"Well, if they're still there, then people will know to stay away from us, won't they? It won't be any different. How can it be different?"

"What do you want me to do?" Joe had been this route several times before. "Go out in the yard and shoot myself? Take poison? I mean, what do you *want?*"

"I want you to get a letter," she said, her voice rising. "I want you to tell these people you won't testify unless they promise to protect you. You're so good at making deals. Make one for *me.*"

"We're trying, Ann," said Kessler, soothingly. "I've talked to Levin, and he knows what he has to do. But it's up to Washington to make the decision, and we all know how fast they work up there."

"Well, fuck 'em," Joe said stoutly. "If that's all my wife and kids want out of this, then they're entitled. I owe 'em that at least. I mean, they didn't ask for this. It's like Ann says. If I don't get it, I don't testify."

Kessler sighed. "You'll testify."

"They can't make him," said Ann. "Not if he doesn't want to."

"Yes, they *can* make him. He knows that."

"But he's got a bad heart."

"If he says he's sick, the court will get its own doctor to examine him. So forget it. He'll testify."

"Then the court's against him, too? Is that what you're saying, Mel? My God, he doesn't stand a chance."

"I didn't say that. I'm just trying to tell you he can't go that route."

"Look, will you both stop talking about me as if I wasn't here?" said Joe. "If the court's against me, I'm finished, right?"

"Joe, the court's *not* against you, for Chrissake. In fact, the court's the best chance you got."

"Mel, how can you say that?" Ann demanded. "If the court can *make* him testify, the government knows that, too. It doesn't have to do *anything.*"

"Don't worry about it," said Joe. "I don't care. They can send me to jail. Doesn't matter. I'll stand mute. Levin knows that."

"Will you both shut up a minute?" said Kessler. "You're driving me crazy here. If the government won't do the right thing, then we'll petition the court to *order* protection for you."

Joe blinked at him. "You think it'll work?"

"I don't know. Maybe. *If* we can show you went ahead with this on the understanding the government would take care of you afterwards."

"Well, they will," said Ann. "In the witness program."

"That's the problem," Kessler agreed. "They're going to say *they're* not cutting you loose. You're cutting yourself loose."

"That's right," said Joe. "I heard that a hundred times already. So *that's* no good. I just gotta make Levin understand I mean business, that's all. No deal, no spiel. That's all there is to it."

"No, that's *not* all. That's not even part of it. Levin understands all right, Joe. You're the one who doesn't understand. You defy a court order to testify, and you'll leave the judge no choice. He'll have to send you to jail."

"Then I'm dead, right?"

"Well, the marshals won't go with you, that's for sure."

"Okay. So it's up to Levin to see I don't get put in that position, right? If he wants me to testify?"

"No, it's up to Washington."

"I don't even care about that," said Ann. "I'm not worried about *before* the trial. I'm worried about *after*. If Joe doesn't get something in writing, all they have to do is say, 'Okay, we'll take care of you,' and then just drop him afterwards if he doesn't do like they say. He's got to get a written commitment. From Washington."

"Ann, that's exactly what we're trying for," said Kessler. "Levin, too.

With the case going to trial, he doesn't need this kind of aggravation, believe me."

She shook her head. "Those are maybes. I just want you to know if Joe testifies without getting a letter first, I'm leaving this house. We might as well have that understanding. The day the marshals go, that's the day *I* go."

Joe avoided Kessler's eye, and sat in silence for a moment.

"Look," he said. "I'll do my best. I'll get this for you if I can. But I can only give you what I have. And that's done. Mel will tell you. It's all yours. The money we have. The houses, the cars. I wrote a new will. Opened trust accounts for you and the kids. Everything's taken care of."

"Joe . . ."

"No, just listen," he said. "Because there's only one more thing I can do for you. If I hurt you this bad, if I ruined your life like you say, then I don't want to hurt you anymore. If you want to leave, if you want a legal separation or something, then I'll give you that as well. And Mel is my witness."

Ann was trying hard not to cry.

"Oh, for Chrissake," said Kessler. "You know what *I* think? I think you'd both feel better if you let it all out, if you had a real, old-fashioned, knockdown family fight, with no holds barred. If you get rid of some of that anger, maybe you can sit down like two sensible people and work this thing out. Only let me out of here first before you get started."

Ann went to pour herself another glass of wine.

"There's nothing to fight about," Joe said. "Anything she wants is all right with me."

"Well, maybe she doesn't want you to be such a fucking saint," said Kessler, suddenly furious with both of them. "First you're a hero, now you're a saint. You any idea how boring that is? Maybe she'd settle for plain old Joe Teitelbaum, ever think of that? You're both getting totally screwed up just when you ought to be closest. We'll work something out with these people, don't worry about it."

"Mel, you don't understand," Joe said. "We're not even talking about that. Underneath all this bullshit, she knows I'm not gonna beat this thing."

"Oh, for Chrissake."

"No, Mel. Do me a favor. Let's face it just once, so we know where we are. They're not gonna let me walk away from this. Marshals or no marshals, before the trial, after the trial . . . they don't care. I hurt 'em. I hurt their business. Some of their people are gonna go down because of me, and they gotta get me for that. If I walk away from this, other people may think they can do the same. I don't know when or how it's gonna happen, and they don't either, but I made my bed. And that's all I'm saying. If Ann wants to leave now, before anything worse happens, she's free to go. And I wouldn't blame her. It's all I got left to give. And this is plain old Joe Teitelbaum speaking."

"Oh, bullshit," said Kessler. "Everything's got to be a drama with you."

Everything was a drama anyway.

Gus Teitelbaum died early in December. He had grown very frail in two years, but he had promised Joe he would live to see him put the thieves in jail, and Joe had counted on it. He had also counted on his father to keep a place for him in the family. When Joe went to his funeral with four armed men at his back, his relatives seemed like strangers. Even his mother and sisters.

A few days later, he came close to death himself. At about 6:30 in the evening on December 19, when it was almost dark, the two marshals who were with him at the terminal spotted "a white man of average build" trying to hide behind a car that had just been loaded onto a barge.

They identified themselves as federal officers, and ordered the intruder to halt. When he ignored the challenge, and then a second warning, they opened fire with their handguns. After six shots, three of which struck the car, the man dived, or fell, off the barge into the oily blackness of the river 20 feet below, and disappeared.

"All right," said Joe, breaking the unnatural stillness. "Target practice is over. We got a ship to load, and I'd like to get home tonight."

When the Metro Police and Marine Patrol arrived, his longshoremen were back at work as though nothing had happened. For almost two hours, police divers crisscrossed the river bottom, while squads of uniformed men and detectives searched the barge, the ship, the dock apron, the terminal buildings, and both banks of the river for some distance up and down stream, looking for bombs, weapons or some other sign of the intruder. They found nothing.

Then the reporters arrived.

"Teitelbaum . . . paced nervously in front of the Caribbean Lines freighter *Mereghan V,*" wrote John Arnold, in the *Miami Herald* next morning. "He was nervous that his wife would find out about the shooting.

"He denied that anybody had shot at anybody. 'My wife has already had a nervous breakdown,' he said. 'She reads something about this in the paper, and it's going to put her in the hospital.'"

The trial was due to begin in little more than a month, and no decision had yet been made on his future protection, but he need not have worried about Ann. If anything, the shooting helped, for the government was now very clearly dragging its feet in the hope of wearing him down, and her natural loyalties came strongly to the fore.

A week later, still without word from Washington, they met John Arnold of the *Herald* in a downtown restaurant. Joe was still not prepared to discuss the case, but saw no reason to keep his views about the government's behavior a secret. On December 28, Arnold shared them with all of Miami.

"The Teitelbaums sometimes wonder whose side the government is really on," he wrote. "They have been subjected to intense and disquieting pressure to go on the run, to give up their lives with family and friends for a hide-and-seek existence to avoid the cross hairs of assassins' guns.

"And they dislike the glare of publicity intensely. They blame the FBI for breaking a promise to keep their names out of the newspapers eighteen months ago, when news of the investigation first broke."

Asked how she saw the future, with the government apparently anxious to save the $4,000 a day the marshals were said to be costing, Ann replied: "My husband is not a man who can be pushed. I believe that God looks out for drunks and babies and Joey Teitelbaum."

Detecting a note of pride in her exasperation, Joe felt they had turned a corner. It was the nicest thing she had said about him in two years.

Their evening out, if not exactly a celebration, marked the beginning of the final phase of Joe's embattled progress to the witness stand, Earlier that day, the outwardly united front presented by the defendants since their indictment for conspiracy had begun to collapse. Following the lead of Hector Calderon, president of CCT, who would have made their number 23 had he not already pleaded guilty to bribing William Boyle, the two principal officers of Chester, Blackburn & Roder agreed to cop a plea, and testify for the government if required.

Alvin Chester, board chairman, and Jeremy Chester, president, appeared before Judge Hoeveler and admitted paying more than $80,000 to George Barone "to insure labor peace and other benefits." According to attorney Irwin J. Block, they were pleading guilty, not because they *were* guilty, but to avoid a long trial and its likely effects on their business. The Chesters were victims of extortion, he said, not criminals. They were fined totals of $30,000 and $17,500 respectively, and placed on probation for one year.

That was encouraging, even though the terms of the plea bargain seemed overgenerous, but Joe had to wait a little longer for the final vindication of his efforts.

On January 17, 1979, a federal grand jury in Manhattan indicted Anthony M. Scotto on 56 counts of racketeering and racketeering conspiracy, involving $300,000 in illegal payoffs, mail fraud, and income tax evasion. Indicted with him were Anthony Anastasio, Joseph A. Lacqua, and Vincent E. Marino.

Most of the illegal payments were said to have been made to Scotto by the John W. McGrath Corporation, and its Brooklyn subsidiary, Quin Marine Services, between 1975 and 1978. According to Alan Levine, the federal prosecutor, the money was intended to reduce the number of fraudulent accident claims filed by longshoremen working for these firms, and to obtain new business. Lacqua and Marino were accused of making payoffs for the same reasons on behalf of CC Lumber Inc., Marine Repair Services, and the American Navigation Corporation.

(Scotto and Anastasio were also charged with participating in a scheme to defraud Prudential Lines with a questionable lease on a warehouse in Brooklyn. This count was later dropped because it relied on the testimony of John Morano, a former Prudential executive, who miraculously survived one murder attempt after the indictment was published, and whom the government hesitated to expose to another by bringing him into court.)

"Indict Scotto in 300G Shakedowns," ran the headline in New York's *Daily News* on January 18. "The indictment . . . climaxes an effort of almost three years by Federal authorities against the leader of Local 1814. At one point, more than 30 FBI agents here were thrown into the investigation—the case includes widespread bugging of Scotto's offices and of restaurants he frequented—but the big break did not come until late December, the *Daily News* learned.

"It was then that William (Sonny) Montella, described as head of Quin Marine Services Inc., was put under protective custody and spilled information to the sitting Manhattan grand jury on alleged payments."

In fact, Montella had been in protective custody since August 1978, when he had pleaded guilty to conspiracy and agreed to testify against Scotto. But there was an even more damaging witness against him who had managed to escape the paper's attention. On January 16, the day before Scotto's indictment, Walter D. O'Hearn, Jr., chief executive officer of McGrath, secretly pleaded guilty to conspiracy, and testified that he had paid Scotto $60,000 a year to reduce accident claims on the docks. O'Hearn was willing to appear for the government to describe how these claims had risen during 1973 and 1974 "to a point where it involved the survival of our company." He and his partners had feared for their safety if they went to the FBI, and "we felt we had no choice."

The New York Times reviewed Scotto's career and affiliations at length on an inside page.

"To his admirers," wrote Robert D. McFadden, "he is a dedicated, progressive, articulate leader of the longshoremen's union, an up-from-the-docks scrapper with street savvy, a college education and a social conscience . . . To his detractors, he is a hoodlum who has never been caught, a shrewd, tough opportunist who parlayed his marriage to a waterfront boss's daughter into a position of union trust, then forged lucrative political friendships and enriched himself with a variety of shadowy deals . . . It is as though Anthony M. Scotto is two people."

In sharp contrast with the press coverage of the Miami indictments six months earlier, there were no pictures of Scotto in handcuffs, not even in the *New York Post,* which instead showed him shoulder to shoulder with President Jimmy Carter and Mayor John V. Lindsay. Left with little to add after the morning papers had finished with the story, the *Post* invited Governor Hugh Carey to comment.

"I have been informed of the indictment," he said cautiously, "but I have no knowledge of the circumstances involved . . . My knowledge of Anthony Scotto is as a long-time friend, constituent, and respected resident of the district I represented in Congress . . ."

Evidently feeling that this understated the nature of their relationship, the *Post* reminded its readers that, among the other offices held by Scotto, was his membership on the New York State Economic Development Board, and his chairmanship of the EDB's Transportation Committee. It also cited Bertram Perkel's appointment to the Waterfront Commission, since quietly dropped, as further evidence of "Scotto's power with Carey."

In all the uproar, the *Post*, and the *Washington Post*, were among the few newspapers to make the point that the New York indictments represented the latest stage of an investigation that had started in Miami and would probably unseat the entire hierarchy of the American shipping industry before running its course. But Joe Teitelbaum by now was past caring about who got the credit for it. *He* knew.

Scotto was down. Anastasio was down. Field, Barone, Boyle, and Vanderwyde were down. And everybody else who would one day answer to a jury for their actions on the waterfront, they would all come down because of what he had started in Miami. He knew, and the government knew, who had kicked out the props, and why the whole crooked edifice had started to topple. If he went down himself for it, he would have taken the worst of them with him.

Next day, Laura and Francesca Cotrone caved in, each pleading guilty to a single felony charge of conspiring to pay off George Barone at the rate of $1,500 a month on behalf of United Container. They admitted placing "phantom" employees on the firm's payroll ledgers, and "shorting" the number of man-hours reported to ILA welfare and pension funds to cover the cash disbursements, and agreed to testify against their co-defendants if called. In return, the government dropped four other felony charges against them, and recommended leniency, which the court certainly showed. Facing a maximum penalty of five years' imprisonment and a $10,000 fine, the Cotrone sisters were each fined $1,500.

The trial was only 10 days off, and there was still no decision from Washington. Joe had reviewed his testimony, grudgingly, with Levin and Maria, for he knew it was not their fault, but his disillusionment was complete. He could see little to choose between the methods of the government and those of the ILA. The Justice Department seemed no more concerned with his rights, with humanity, or with justice even, than the bosses of Local 1922. Neither side cared if he lived or died. They had both squeezed him to suit their own ends.

On Monday, January 29, 1979, the trial of *U.S.* v. *George Barone* et al. began before District Judge Hoeveler in a small, overcrowded courtroom on the second floor of Miami's federal courthouse.

The culmination of a three-year investigation, costing taxpayers millions of dollars, into an area of business corruption costing them billions of dollars, the first day was all anticlimax. Most of it was taken up with the disposal of routine defense motions and procedural matters, preceding the still more tedious business of selecting a jury.

Day Two was somewhat more eventful. Relieving the congestion considerably, Benny and Joseph Cotrone, Vincent James Fiore, Jr., and Robert Bateman each pleaded guilty to one or more felony counts and bowed out of the trial as defendants, reducing the original 22 to 13. (Max Forman, the Cotrones' former accountant, had already been severed from the case and was to be tried separately.) The Cotrones' defection was particularly damaging to the defense, for they now admitted, and were ready to testify, that they had paid substantial bribes to Fred Field, George Barone, William Boyle, Landon Williams, and James Vanderwyde.

"I *am* naive," said Joe, still waiting even now for word from Washington. "Really. You know who runs this country? Apart from guys like Scotto and Barone? Accountants. That's who we got on our side . . . accountants. And fucking attorneys who think like accountants. They don't even *need* me anymore."

"Yes, they do," Kessler said. "They need you to connect these people to prove conspiracy. They need you to validate the tapes. Don't worry. You're still the only witness they've got who can lay the whole case out for them."

"Then why are they fucking me around?"

"Why? Because they don't like little Jew sons of bitches who won't knuckle under and do as they're told. I don't know. But they're going to take you right down to the wire on this."

He shook his head. "Mel, they're not gonna move. I'm telling you, they're gonna have the court make me testify, and then they're gonna say, 'All right. Thanks a lot. This is it. The witness program. Take it or leave it.' "

"I don't think so," said Kessler. "I wouldn't *like* to think so. It's a big case. With all the publicity and all the politics, why would they want to risk screwing up their star witness for the sake of a few bucks? These guys are under pressure, too. They're going to leave it till the last minute, but they'll deal. So hang in there, kid."

"I don't know, Mel," he said reluctantly. "It's changed. A few months back, I was the whole case. But not now. With all these new witnesses? Plus the agents? Okay, I'm still important. But now they can win without me."

"Why would they want to take that chance?"

"They don't care. And anyway, we ran out of time."

"No, we didn't. The way they're going, it'll take a couple of weeks to pick a jury. And with better than two hundred witnesses, we're talking about a six-month trial at least. Just sit tight. There's plenty of time."

"No, there isn't. Levin says I could be on the stand next week."

Kessler thought about that. "He's going to call you first?"

"That's what he said. But maybe he's in for a big disappointment."

"Joe . . ."

"I know, I know. I'll be there. But how good a witness am I gonna be with *this* on my mind?"

"Now you be careful, Joe." Kessler looked at him seriously. "Never mind about them. You do *yourself* justice."

"Hey, I didn't come all this way just to let 'em go." Then he laughed. "Isn't it something? This was my big moment, right? This was gonna make it all worthwhile? Shit. Can *you* tell me what I did it for?"

"Sure. You did it for you, Joe. The rest of us just got lucky."

On Tuesday, February 13, Joe put on his best blue suit, and was delivered to the courthouse by a squad of eight marshals. As he got out of the car, they formed a wall around him with their bodies. Solemn as pallbearers, they escorted him up the steps, preceded by photographers and television cameramen walking backwards, and watched over by police riflemen stationed on the rooftops.

Epilogue

It was April 4, 1979—seven weeks later—before Joe Teitelbaum completed his testimony in the case of *U.S.* v. *Barone* et al. and stepped down from the witness stand.

The matter of his protection was still unsettled, although on March 7, the Justice Department had at last made a written offer. If he refused to relocate under the Witness Program, the government was prepared to keep the marshals in place for six months after the trial or to pay half the cost of a private bodyguard for two years.

Joe rejected the proposal out of hand. Six months was not long enough to cover even the appeals; the defendants would still be at large when the marshals withdrew. Secondly, as a taxpayer, he saw no reason why he should have to pay twice before the government performed its clear duty to protect a citizen going about his lawful business.

With the trial in its sixth month, Neal Harrington was severed from his co-defendants on July 12 in order to stand trial separately, and on August 3, the Reverend Elizah Jackson, of Local 1414, Savannah, secured a directed verdict of not guilty on the grounds of insufficient evidence. Only 10 of the original 22 defendants were still before the court, and the government's case against them finally went to the jury on August 11, some 27 weeks after it had started.

But the drama was far from over. The transcript of the proceedings already ran to 22,000 pages, and the inventory of evidence to 32 pages, each with 150 items, many of them composite entries representing anything from 10 to 100 documents. It was just too much for one of the jurors, who broke down on August 20 with "emotional problems" and brought deliberations to a halt.

Understandably reluctant to declare a mistrial and begin all over again, Judge William M. Hoeveler failed to uncover a federal precedent for replacing a member of a jury after it had retired, but did so anyway, citing a somewhat similar case in California state law. With the consent of the other 11 jurors, he seated an alternate whom he had kept standing by, and on August 22, sent them back to start considering the evidence afresh.

Ten days later, on Saturday afternoon, September 1, the jury at last delivered a verdict on nine of the ten defendants, failing to agree only on the guilt or innocence of Isom Clemon, whom Judge Hoeveler ordered to be retried. The others—Barone, Field, Boyle, Vanderwyde, Turner, Williams, the Kopituks, and Morales—were each found guilty more or less as charged, but remained free on bond pending sentence.

In New York, meanwhile, the investigation had brought down 11 more waterfront racketeers, union leaders, and businessmen on charges of conspiracy and corruption. Among those indicted on March 6, were Michael Clemente, Field's now aging sponsor in the rackets and a capo in the Genovese crime family; Tino Fiumara, another Genovese captain, and boss of the New Jersey piers; Thomas Buzzanca, stand-in for Barone as president of Manhattan Locals 1804 and 1804-1; Vincent Colucci, president of Newark Locals 1236 and 1478-2, and Carol Gardner, president of Newark Local 1233.

By late summer, no fewer than 110 people had been indicted as a result of Joe's Operation Unirac—61 of whom had already pleaded guilty or been convicted. But all these various proceedings were now overshadowed by the pending trial of Anthony Scotto and Anthony Anastasio. Profiting from its experience in Miami, the government simplified the indictment on September 10 by dropping the charges involving Vincent Marino and Joseph Lacqua, so that when the trial began next day, the case rested on just three key witnesses—Sonny Montella, Walter O'Hearn, Jr., and Nicholas Seregos (who testified against Anastasio)—and 37 tape recordings, made either by the witnesses or by a listening device in Scotto's office.

Unable to deny taking money from Montella and O'Hearn, Scotto tried to show that the payments (illegal in any case) were "political contributions" to the campaign funds of Governor Hugh Carey and Lieutenant-Governor Mario Cuomo of New York, thereby embarrassing both of them considerably. Even so, Governor Carey testified for him as a character witness, as did former New York Mayors John V. Lindsay and Robert F. Wagner, Justice William C. Thompson of the New York State Supreme Court, and Lane Kirkland, George Meany's successor as president of the AFL–CIO.

But neither this imposing parade of political debtors nor yet the ingenious defense mounted for Scotto by criminal attorney James LaRossa could offset the damning effect of the tapes. When the jury returned to the courtroom on November 15, after five days of deliberation, it found both Scotto and Anastasio guilty of most of the charges in the revised sixty-count indictment.

In Miami, the detail of U.S. Deputy Marshals guarding Joe Teitelbaum went on full alert.

In New York, Ethel Kennedy sent Scotto a personal note inviting him to a fund-raising dinner for Senator Edward M. Kennedy.

Many lesser figures were also going down. Tony Morelli, another key associate of Barone's in New York, had meanwhile pleaded guilty to paying $50,000 to Michael Colletti, former general manager of Ford Export Corporation, for the contract to prepare cars for shipment between 1974 and 1976. He also admitted paying a further $50,000 to three officials of Zim line, each of whom had returned to Israel within hours of the investigation going public.

Joseph Lacqua and Vincent Marino, however, were allowed a walk. The government presented "insufficient evidence," in the opinion of at least one juror, to convict Lacqua at his trial in January 1980, while Marino has not yet been tried at all, presumably as part of some undisclosed deal with the U.S. Attorney's office.

As for everybody's friend, John Caputo, he is thought to be in the Federal Witness Program, like Sonny Montella, although he has yet to surface as a witness against any of the FBI's targets.

On Friday, January 11, 1980, the Miami defendants made their final appearance before Judge Hoeveler. George Barone was sentenced to 15 years' imprisonment; William Boyle to 12 years; James Vanderwyde to 10 years; Fred R. Field, Jr. to six years; Cleveland Turner to six years; and Landon Williams to five years. Raymond and Dorothy Kopituk received sentences of three years and three years' probation respectively, and Oscar Morales, four years.

Eleven days later, in New York, it was Scotto's turn. Observing mildly that he had abused his position of trust, Judge Charles E. Stewart sentenced him to a moderate five-year term of imprisonment and a fine of $75,000. The following day, January 23, Anthony Anastasio received an almost nominal two-year sentence with a fine of $5,000. Both remain free on bail while the noted Washington lawyer, Edward Bennett Williams, prepares their appeals.

Joe Teitelbaum, meanwhile, remains under sentence of death. As public opinion is his only court of appeal, his best hope seems to rest with the U.S. Senate. There is again talk of having him testify before one or more committees on the need for federal regulation of the waterfront. Given the chance, he will also argue the case for a witness program that will *encourage* businessmen to work with law-enforcement agencies, rather than reward them with the choice of murder or expropriation. Without it, corruption may well become the American way of doing business.

The prospect of a Washington appearance has kept the marshals in attendance, but in the end, Joe Teitelbaum's future, if he has one, depends on which comes first: some sort of recognition from his fellow citizens for what he has done, or the mob's retribution for it.

Donald Goddard
May 1, 1980

Index

A & G, 148ff., 167, 174, 212ff.
Abbott, Jim, 152ff.
Aber, Dick, 210, 213ff., 221, 227, 235ff., 242, 243, 260
Abernathy, Ralph, 24
Ackalitis, Albert, 36, 66
Adams, James B., 282
Adelstein, Zeno, 31–2
Adonis, Joe, 67
Africa trade, 199, 203ff., 231, 260
Alabama (*see also* Mobile; names), 193ff., 220
Albery, 19, 34
Aluotto, Nuncio, 37
Amarnic, 87
American Export Lines, 80, 132
AFL, 35–6, 68
American Hemisphere Marine Agencies, 21, 32
American Marine Industries, 262
American Navigation, 153, 298
American Star Line, 33
Anastasia, Albert, 36, 37, 67, 68
Anastasio, Anthony, 40, 67–8; Caputo, 167–8, 175, 184, 190, 195; Gleason, 68; indicted, 297, 298; Scotto, 39, 40; Savannah, 167–8; trial, 303, 304
"Anti-Communism," 37
Applegate, Jack, 95, 100–3, 105
Arabian trade, 45, 214, 236
Army truck shipments, 216–17
Arnold, John, 296–7
Arsenal Mob, 36, 66
Artin, Richard (*see also* Aber, Dick), 260, 263–4
Astorino, Benny, 8–13, 24, 34

Bahamas trade, 41ff.
Barone, George, 23, 64ff., 79, 99ff., 113, 125, 166, 171–2, 188, 262; Boyle, 61–2, 76, 88–9, 99–100, 188, 193, 222, 239–41, 249ff.; checkers, 10ff., 24ff., 29, 34, 44, 59–60; Cotrones, 59–60, 84ff., 227–9, 250, 252, 254; Field, 75, 85, 188; Garcia on, 261; Harrington, 127, 128, 184–5; Ilan, 223ff.; indicted, 285–7; Jacksonville, 139; Mamenic, 84; Miami (*see also* subjects), 10ff., 64ff., 139, 128ff. 143, 166, 222, 284; Mobile, 214–15; New York, 37ff., 128, 152, 163–4, 167–8, 172–3, 174, 226; payoffs to admitted, 297, 299, 300; payoff attempt in New York, 247–53; PTO, 255–6; repair racket, 84ff., 131–2; Savannah and Zim, 130ff., 139, 141ff., 151ff., 166–7, 172ff., 177, 196, 211, 222ff., 245–6; Scotto, 75, 152, 163–4, 173, 174, 226, 238–41; *Siboney,* 76–7; suspicions of Teitelbaum, 192; Sykes, 179–82, 186ff., 225–6; taped, 126ff., 136, 138, 142–4, 148, 149; territory, 173, 183; trial, 300ff.; Vanderwyde, 43; as witness, 264, 279–80; witness intimidation, 263–5, 268–9
Bateman, Robert L., 235, 263, 285, 300
Baton Rouge, 183
Baumgard, Herbert, 129–30, 148, 256
Baxley, Bill, 199
Bay Container Repair, 262
BCIE, 48–9

305

Koch, Edward, 71, 73
Kopituk, Raymond and Dorothy, 261, 285–6, 303, 304
Kratish, Bobby, 61–2, 113–15, 121, 133, 135, 172, 173, 210–11, 243
Kratish, Morris, 14–16, 19
Kratish, Mutzie, 14, 29, 30, 48, 92, 121, 123, 133, 251; agent assigned to, 210–11; Bahamas, 43; checkers, 33; company control, 171–2; finances, 113–14; Georgia Containers Agencies, 227, 233; Jacksonville, 44; James Stevedores, 242ff.; payoffs, 24, 61–2, 123, 124, 164, 171–2; Teitelbaum as witness, 266, 267; Zim, and Savannah, 133, 135
Kratish, Sam, 24, 48

LaBrecque, Ron, 287, 290
Lacqua, Joseph A., 69–70, 73, 74, 132, 153ff., 213; indicted, 297–8, 303; Savannah, 132, 135, 137, 139, 149ff., 154, 166–7, 173, 174; territory, 173; trial, 304
Lacqua, Leo, 69–70, 73, 74, 132, 135, 137
Lacqua, Phil, 132, 135, 139, 166, 213, 280; Savannah, 149ff., 166–7
Lansky, Meyer, 292
LaRossa, James, 303
Lashing (L.C.) Co., 262
Laur, Wilbur, 274
Lazzeri, J., 120
Lee, Nathan, 20
Levin, Mike, 162, 170, 218, 229, 235, 237–8, 279, 283; grand jury witnesses, 264, 268–9, 279, 280, 285; Witness Protection Program and Teitelbaum, 256ff., 274, 277–8, 288, 291ff., 299
Levy, Manny, 50, 58, 60–1, 78, 81, 82, 96, 98, 113, 195, 281; Conasa Line, and Honduras, 107–11
Lindsay, John V., 71, 298, 303
Lloyd-Brasileiro, 47, 131
Lombardozzi, Carmine, 67
Lopez, Oswaldo, 93
Lopez, Sra. Oswaldo, 81
Lorillard, 217, 222, 242, 243

MacMillan, Doug, 65
MacNamara, Robert, Jr., 292
Maddox, Frank, 199, 202–9, 235–6
Mafia, 71ff.
Maisin, Michael, 264
Mamenic, 21–2, 33, 83–5, 87

Manor, Avner, 176
Marcello, Carlos, 279
Mardi Gras, 63–4
Maria, Raymond, 126–8, 135–49 *passim,* 153ff., 161–73 *passim,* 210, 211, 217, 218, 221, 235, 241–2, 247, 254, 299; Army trucks, 216; taping setups, 138, 144, 149, 178, 218, 219, 229, 251ff.; witness intimidation, 263, 271; Witness Protection Program and Teitelbaum, 256ff., 265, 271, 272, 278–9, 288, 292
Maria Rosa, Sister, and orphanage, 81–2, 92–4, 108, 110
Marine Repair Services, 153, 213, 280
Marine Terminals, 60–1, 76, 186, 241, 262
Marino, Vincent, 213, 262, 280, 297–8, 303, 304
Maritime Administration, 208, 215–16
Maritime Cartage, 87, 89, 134–5, 137, 166, 176, 181, 228
Marro, Anthony, 282–3, 286
Martinez, Oscar, 49, 81, 90–1
McClellan, John L., 70
McCormack, William J., 36
McFadden, Robert D., 298
McGrath (John W.) Corp., 213, 297–8
McGrath, Eddie, 36, 66, 128, 148, 153, 213
McVey, Robert, 261
Meany, George, 35
Metropolitan Marine Maintenance Contractors' Assn., 250, 262
Miami (*see also* Dade County; names), 5ff., 76ff., 132ff., 176, 188, 210ff., 222ff., 229, 242, 287ff., 300; federal grand jury, 256, 259, 263–5, 279–80, 285–6; police, 218
Miami Herald, 21, 23, 120, 262, 286–7, 290, 296–7
Miami News, 120, 269–70, 284, 287
Mobile (*see also* names), 193ff., 212ff., 222–3, 229, 235, 242–3, 283
Money, marked, use of, 197, 236
Montella, William, 153, 154, 167, 173, 174, 213, 298, 303, 304
Morales, Oscar, 261, 285–6, 304
Morano, John, 298
Morazan, 49–50, 80ff., 87, 92–4, 96ff., 245
Morelli, Tony, 153, 155, 156, 157, 162–3, 172, 176–7, 193, 303
Murder, Inc., 36, 67
Murga, Nicholas, 83–4, 87
Murphy, Francis, 8ff., 23, 37, 38